potential **MISC.** reader?
Take this handy quiz.

Want to improve your golf game?
Want to lose weight and feel great?
Want to successfully juggle marriage, family, and career?

...THE BIG BOOK OF **MISC.** can't help you.

Seeking the latest celebrity dirt?
Seeking the biggest looks for this fall?
Seeking the inside story about today's biggest stars?

...THE BIG BOOK OF **MISC.** hasn't got it.

Need the secrets of America's leading companies?
Need to learn how to invest in no-load mutual funds?
Need to know the top career choices for the next decade?

...THE BIG BOOK OF **MISC.** isn't the place.

BUT...

If you can live without easy answers,
If you want to laugh and cry and think,
If you like to read about a once-remote port city,
If you enjoy politics, aesthetics, and cereal equally,
If you're prepared for a frenetic, zig-zagging journey
across the fissures and connections of today's world,
Or if you'd like something funny to flip thru in the can,

...THE BIG BOOK OF **MISC.** welcomes you.
Enter this way...

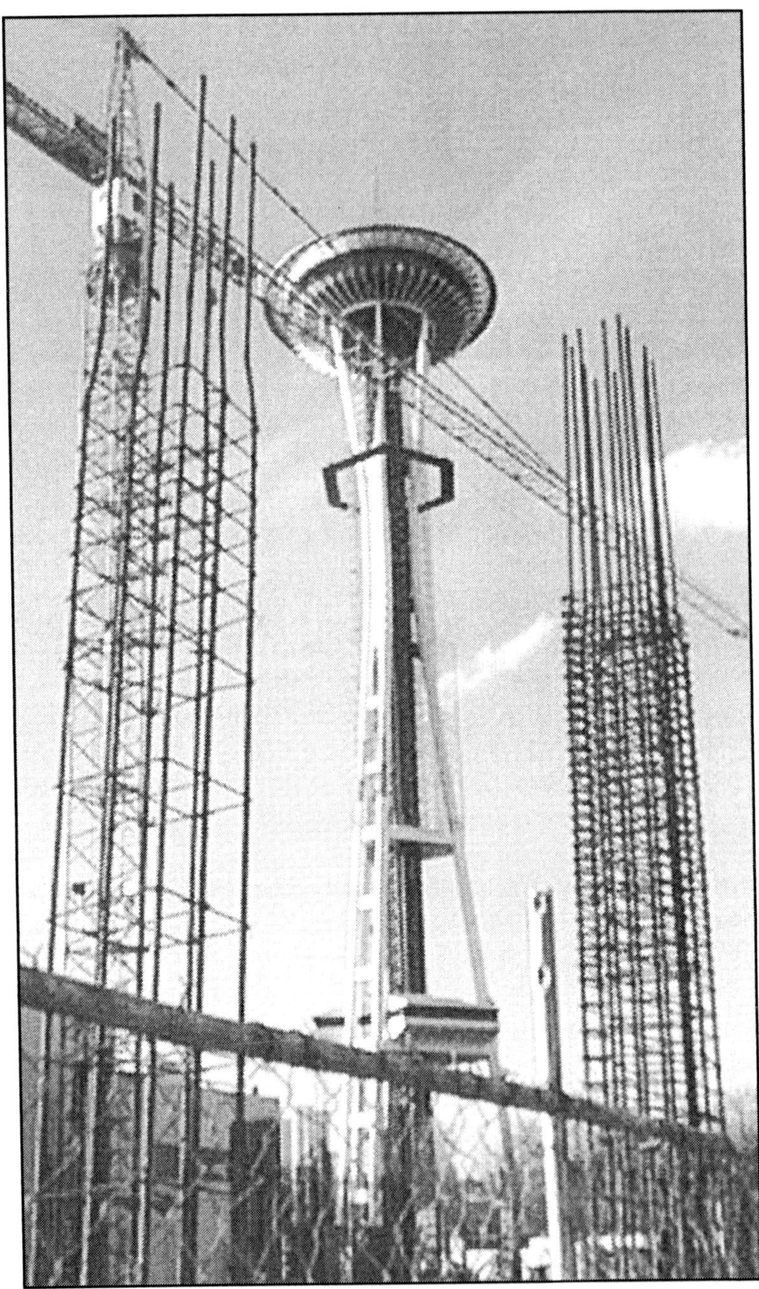

the big book of MISC.

Pseudo-Random Remarks on Popular Culture in Seattle and Beyond 1986-1999

by CLARK HUMPHREY

Clark Humphrey also wrote

LOSER: The Real Seattle Music Story

(Feral House, 1995; second edition by MISC. Media, 1999)

and

THE PERFECT COUPLE: A Story in 178 Scenes

(Eastgate Systems, 1991)

and contributed to Rob Wittig's

INVISIBLE RENDEZVOUS

(Wesleyan University Press, 1994)

ISBN 1-929069-23-5

MISC. MEDIA
2608 Second Avenue, P.M.B. #217
SEATTLE, WA 98121-1276 USA
www.miscmedia.com

Printed in USA.

First edition: June 1999.

Thie is copy 17 *of a limited first edition of 500.*

CONTENTS

INDEX OF MARGINALIA

PREFACE

MISC.

A Column By Clark Humphrey

Unfortunately, Horsey's contempt for his characters is too heavy-handed, his gags more bludgeoning than humorous. Every strip ends with an unfunny punchline lettered in boldface italic with an exclamation point. While Horsey's in Britain, he should get some lessons from Andy Capp cartoonist Reg Smythe in making unsympathetic characters appealing.

recruiting brochures to high schools with a cover photo of the Phinney Ridge traffic sign pointing in opposite directions for Zoo and **Seattle Pacific University.** The comparison was intended, not just with big universities, but also with other little religious schools.)

You certainly wouldn't have seen any Free Methodists among the

1986.

What This Book Is: It's a compilation of some 650 items taken from a column called **Misc.** These are items of their time, only lightly revised for book form, with only a few latter-day notations and introductions added.

The items cover a variety of vaguely interrelated topics, as arranged here into some three dozen chapters; with even shorter or more random quips scattered along the margins. The various items within each chapter are usually arranged in chronological order, except when they more logically fit otherwise.

You may find some of what you read here contradictory. You may find some of it redundant. You may not understand all the passing references to politicians and personalities of the time. But that's all part of the game with periodical journalism. It's also all part of the game with North American society at the dawn of Century 21.

I don't claim to make sense of my city or of my world. Rather, I'm cajoling you to come to terms with the chaos of contemporary life and society. It's just gonna keep getting more chaotic, so you might as well start getting used to a society of umpteen subcultures, religions, ethnic subgroups, sexualities, and aesthetic-taste systems; a few of which are written about in this book.

What Misc. Is: An at-large compendium of notes and comment on public life and culture, from the viewpoint of a specific place (Seattle) at a specific time (the successive ages of Grunge, Gates, and Gentrification). It has appeared in various formats and forums since June 1986, as follows:

June 1986-July 1989: Monthly in ArtsFocus, *a small tabloid published originally by the Lincoln Arts Association and later independently by Alice Savage and Cydney Gillis.*

September 1989-January 1995: Monthly, self-contained newsletter.

November 1991-October 1998: Weekly in The Stranger, *an arts-and-news tabloid.*

June 1995-present: Weekly online at Misc. World *(http://www.miscmedia.com).*

Who I Am: I was born in Washington's capital city, Olympia (before The Evergreen State College or the Olympia Music Scene existed) and raised in Marysville, a town known to most Washingtonians as a cluster of gas stations and a pie restaurant along Interstate 5, just across the Snohomish River delta from Everett. I've personally known the only semi-celebrities from Marysville, ex-Phillies pitcher Larry Christiensen and ex-Hole drummer Patty Schemel. Aside from a couple of years I spent in Corvallis (home of the Oregon State Beavers), the only place I've lived in as an adult has been Seattle.

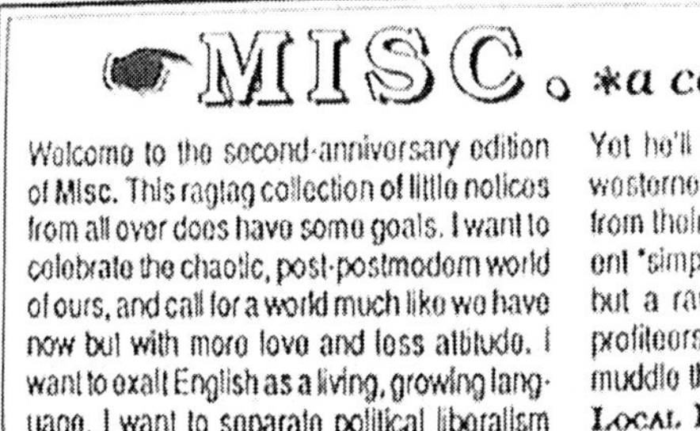

MISC. *a c

Welcome to the second-anniversary edition of Misc. This raging collection of little notices from all over does have some goals. I want to celebrate the chaotic, post-postmodern world of ours, and call for a world much like we have now but with more love and less attitude. I want to exalt English as a living, growing language. I want to separate political liberalism from the cultural conservatism that led so

1988.

It's where I served as editor of the University of Washington *Daily;* where I was one of the first new-music DJs on the now prominent UW radio station KCMU; where I co-edited *The Comics Journal* for two years; and where I wrote what's still the most achingly-detailed book about the so-called "grunge revolution," *Loser: The Real Seattle Music Story.*

My Memories of Seattle: My earliest memory of Seattle, aside from riding through it in cars, involved the day I got to go to the 1962 Seattle World's Fair (officially known as the Century 21 Exposition) with its promises of a bright, wonderful world awaiting us in the next century.

The city has indeed changed greatly since 1962, but not in anything close to the images of mass progress advertised at the fair. Instead of the world according to the Century 21 Exposition, we got the world according to Century 21 Real Estate. Instead of fast streamined mass transit, we got America's worst commuter traffic. Instead of equality and prosperity for everybody, we got a city where only upscale baby boomers were made to feel welcome. Instead of shiny domed cities, we got condo projects on those few square miles of city land not reserved for the upscale boomers' "restored" bungalows. Instead of a Forward Thrust (a '60s civic-building-project slogan) toward a better community for all, we got schemes like the Seattle Commons, which would've had citizens subsidize a narrow strip of playground space in an industrial zone condo developers wanted to take over.

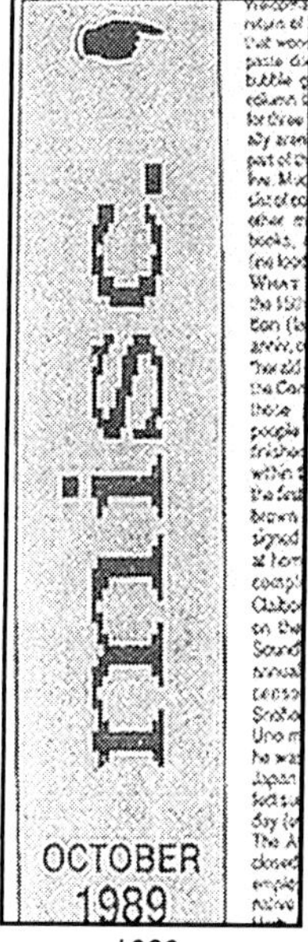

1989.

In spite of (or rather, in reaction to) these trends, several counter-trends also developed. Many people who longed for (or were old enough to remember) a slightly less "success" oriented, slightly more populist, slightly more fun and easy-going Seattle rallied around whatever scenes or causes they could. Some of these causes could seem "progressive" to an outside observer (preserving industrial areas from gentrification, fighting official crackdowns against the music scene). Some of these causes could seem "regressive" to the same observers (keeping residential neighborhoods zoned for only low-density housing, making "jokes" fantasizing about border checkpoints to keep Californians from moving in). And a few of these causes could even seem quaintly Quixotic (trying to save old restaurants, stores, or breweries whose wares had fallen out of popular fashion).

Which leads to the column's second big, overarching meta-topic...

My Memories of Popular Culture: I'm hardly the only North American writer who's sent a few trees and some ink-producing soybeans to their demise in order to pontificate about popular culture. There's dozens of those guys-'n'-gals out there, including at least a score of tenured professors who've made whole careers out of deconstructing Madonna videos.

But you'll soon see I'm a little different from most pop-cult commentators.

I actually like the stuff.

In general, at least.

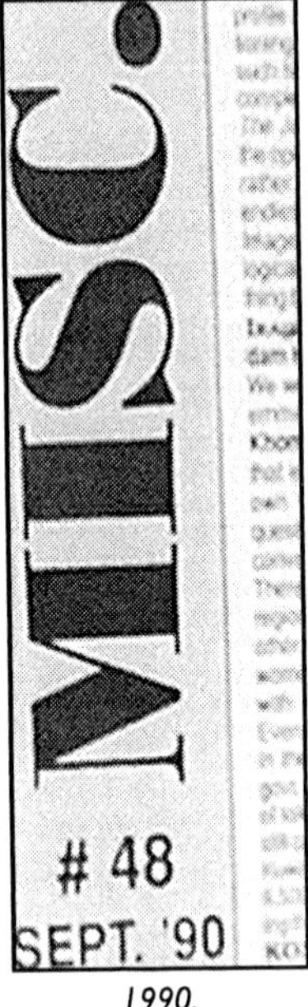

1990.

You can't really love a loved one without expressing your disapproval when said loved one does something that really distresses or annoys you. The American scene has certainly given me plenty to go "tsk-tsk" about, from dumb conglomerate-produced "mainstream" culture works to tired, hackneyed "alternative" culture works, from radical "conservatives" to conservative "radicals." (I happen to think that politics is a subset of culture and not the reverse, at least in this country.) But on the whole, I love pop-cult (which I define broadly as all the stuff that non-highbrow, Anglophone North Americans read, see, hear, wear, eat, and drink). And I like it even better now that it appears to be getting even more mongrel than it used to be.

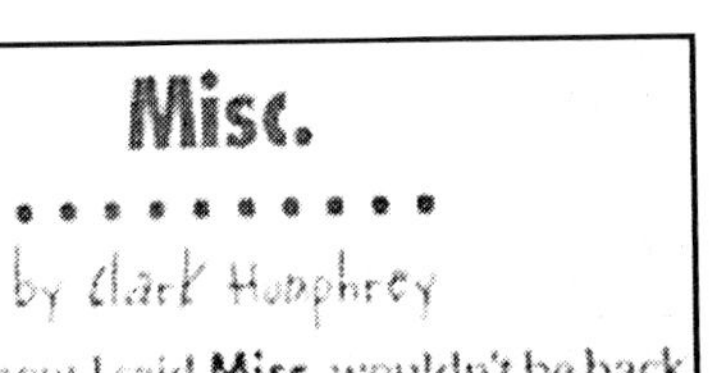

Misc.

by Clark Humphrey

I know, I know, I said **Misc.** wouldn't be back 'til next year. I was wrong, thankfully, so I can now bring you a last-minute **Xmas gift guide.** Again this year the **Hasbro** cartel

1992.

In his 1995 book *Jihad vs. McWorld,* social critic Benjamin Barber claimed world society was simultaneously becoming more global (with corporations and financiers setting up outposts anywhere and everywhere) and more tribal (with ethnic, religious, and other subgroups challenging postwar notions of nationhood everywhere from Canada to the Baltics). Similar, seemingly opposite, trends have long been underway within the U.S.

As the movie studios get more obsessed with huge, loud blockbuster movies, indie filmmaking has grown exponentially (thanks partly to cheaper equipment and the rise of film schools as places for middle-class young adults to waste some of their best years). Of course, that's lead to a glut of semipro-quality, formula B movies full of "hip" inanity and violence, some of which get picked up for distribution by the "indie" divisions of the major studios. But that just leads other indie filmmakers to proclaim their own works "the real independents," as shown on those alternative-to-the-alternative-to-the-alternative film festival circuits.

MISC.
CLARK HUMPHREY
My Definition

1995.

But even in commercial dross there's usually something of worth, waiting to be sifted out. Sometime in the 2010s, someone like me will surely come along, sort through the best/worst of the whole mess, and offer up some rigorous debate over the period's neglected masterworks. ("No way was *Body of Evidence 2* the best direct-to-video ripoff of *Fatal Attraction*. Any film lovers smart enough to have held onto their DVD players after the industry-wide shift to copper-ROM playback cartridges knows it was *Poison Ivy 3: The New Seduction*!")

A big part of a popcult critic's role is to find the best popcult works out there, or at least the most worthy of criticism. That involves making one's own critical standards (unlike the situation in highbrow-arts criticism, where the standards and criteria for judging something are pretty much already set).

My own standards, as you'll surmise from what's in this volume, can sometimes seem contradictory. But popcult itself can be contradictory; and that's one of the things I love about it. North American pop culture (which is to say, North American culture) is brash and timid, populist and elitist, inviting and exclusionary, and, yes, global and tribal.

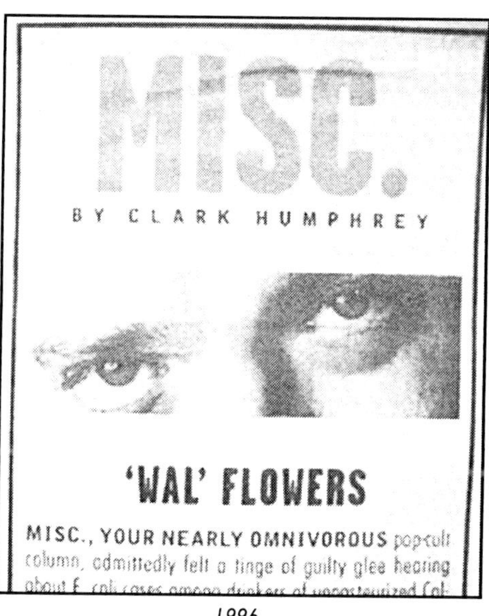
MISC.
BY CLARK HUMPHREY
'WAL' FLOWERS
MISC., YOUR NEARLY OMNIVOROUS popcult column, admittedly felt a tinge of guilty glee hearing

1996.

But at its best, American popular culture expresses an energy, a vigor for real life and real work. That's what Jack Kerouac, in his essay *Origins of the Beat Generation*, loved about both hot-jazz 78s and Three Stooges movies. It's what I love about both a searing rockabilly guitar lick and an over-the-top soft drink ad. It's what I find sorely missing in the *uber*-bland music that used to be called "soft rock" and now's more likely to be called "smooth jazz."

My Memories of the Column: The first **Misc.** was written in one June afternoon at the Lincoln Arts office, on an old 8-bit NEC computer with a clunky daisy-wheel printer. Over the years, the technology's evolved, and so has the content. Longer essay-like pieces began to sneak in among the short celebratory items. In the years the column was in *The Stranger,* I was asked to avoid topics that stepped onto the beats of other writers at the paper, to the point that eventually its editors decided the paper no longer had room for a little-bit-of-everything column.

Some weeks, writing the thing was a struggle, a battle of wits against oneself. Other weeks, the thing practically wrote itself. More often than not, the column installments which took the least effort, or which were strewn with gimmicks and throwaway gags, got the most positive reader responses. At one point in 1996 or so, I found myself writing the difficult segments as space-fillers, until another good topic for a cheap-gag segment came along.

The excerpts in this book, which roughly comprise about 8 to 9 percent of the column's total verbiage to date, preserve the mix of really-thought-out ruminations and quickie laffs.

If you're after funny bathroom reading, there's a little more of that in the marginalia to the side of the main texts.

1998.

Acknowledgments: Thanx and a hat tip to all my loyal readers, sources, and informants over the years, to my website servers at the Speakeasy Network, and to the *Stranger* staffers who for seven years helped to keep it accurate, pretty, and properly-spelled. A special nod goes to Matt Cook and James Sturm, who first helped get the column into *The Stranger* back in 1991, and to Alice Savage, who commissioned its original incarnation at *ArtsFocus.*

For this collection, gracious acknowledgement goes to Hank Trotter, who helped immensely on the cover design, and to the various proof-edition readers who let me know about all the mistakes they found. No, really, I needed it.

How To Read This Book: You can flip through the pages, landing on what interests you most, or follow the chapters as they lead into one another, starting with a little more background info about the column.

66 Bell, the column's first home base.

1: INTRODUCTIONS

or, the value of breadth

I've regularly stated and restated the column's premises, starting with the first item in the first column for ArtsFocus. *I found I had to. From the start,* **Misc.** *generated misinterpretations. Some readers thought it was just a parody column with made-up info and/or insincere opinions, along the lines of the* Weekly World News *or Merle Kessler's character "Ian Shoales".*

As if the real news wasn't funny enough.

This "At Large" column will mainly discuss things that don't fit into the other *ArtsFocus* departments, but which are still a part of the culture in which we live. All opinions are my own, not necessarily those of the Lincoln Arts Association or its affiliated artists, supporters or advertisers. This column does not settle wagers. *(June 1986)*

Unlike that national "arbiter of popular culture" Ian Shoales, I'm not a fictional character created by a comedian. To the best of my knowledge, I really exist. *(July 1986)*

This ragtag collection of little notices from all over does have some goals. I want to celebrate the chaotic, post-postmodern world of ours, and call for a world much like we have now but with more love and less attitude. I want to exalt English as a living, growing language. I want to separate political liberalism from the cultural conservatism that led so many post-'60s youth to view liberals as old fuddyduddies. I want to proclaim that you can be intellectually aware and still like TV. *(June 1988)*

I'm not "just kidding folks." When I say something here in **Misc.**, I MEAN IT. (OK, the call for a crackdown on violent opera music was a bluff, but nothing else.)

The louder I state that these are my sincere opinions, the more some people brush me off with a smug wink. If I were the uncaring, insincere cynic I've been cracked up to be, I'd be a Republican, or at least the [KING-TV daytime talk show] *Good Company* producer who put a Gamblers Anonymous show on election day. *(December 1988)*

Popular culture is a far more accurate portrayal of a society than highbrow culture. You won't find the real character of England, for instance, on

The Misc. FAQ

Far from imminentizing the "Death of Writing," the new electronic media are replenishing our language with new words, phrases and genres. Among these is the "FAQ List" (for "Frequently Asked Questions"), a handy format to bring new users of bulletin boards and newsgroups up to speed. In our quest to be first to steal a good idea, here's our very own **Misc. FAQ**.

How do you pronounce **Misc.**?

Just like it's spelled.

How do you spell your name, Humphreys or Humphries?

It is, and always has been, Humphrey — no "s."

Why do people think Dave Barry's funny?

Wish I knew. Probably it has something to do with the ingrained reflex of the ethnic joke, adapted for a baby-boomer audience. Instead of treating people of other races as subhumans, Barry gives the treatment to non-boomers, allowing his readers to still think of themselves as The Superior Generation.

Masterpiece Theatre. You'll find it in room-temperture beer, cucumber sandwiches, fish and chips wrapped in newspaper, and the horrid things they make out of the variety meats. On the other hand, popular culture isn't an exact replica of popular beliefs. The millions of women who buy sleazy crime books don't necessarily want anything in the books to happen to them. *(Nov. 18, 1991)*

Several readers complained about the shorthand used in the report's segments. I don't always explain the local news events I'm commenting about, out of the presumption that you're already aware of the underlying issues. Many of you told me that **Misc.** is your only local news source. Whoa — way too much responsibility for me, man. To paraphrase the Residents, ignorance of your community is not considered cool. If you only read the *New York Times* or only watch *McNeil-Lehrer*, you'll never know what's really going on.

In the meantime, here's a brief guide to **Misc.** terminology: When I say "Portland," I mean Oregon, not Maine. "The *Times*" means the *Seattle Times*. "Rice" refers to our mayor, unless it appears in the "Junk Food of the Month" department. And "Bellevue" means a vast low-rise suburb, not the New York psychiatric hospital (and no jeers from the balcony about how do you tell the difference). *(April 1992)*

The real value of a three-dot column isn't depth but breadth. At a time when knowledge and careers are increasingly specialized, there's a need for generalists who can explore the contexts, juxtapositions, and connections among seemingly unrelated phenomena, from something as general as global socioeconomic trends to something as specific as a candy bar.

This column's treated fashion, food, politics, music, architecture, medicine, painting, porn, magzines, talk radio, etc. etc. as equally important disciplines, each with something to reveal about the larger world.

It's treated its readers as intelligent humans, not as some target-marketing stereotype. It hasn't told you what bands, movies, or shows to see; it hasn't promised to make you wealthier or slimmer or more sociable or more orgasmic; just to inform and entertain. It's taken a personal point of view, yet hasn't tried to promote the author as its own biggest topic. It's been opinionated, but without any in-your-face "Attitude."

The column's also tried to reflect and respond to today's ever factioning, increasingly complex society.

Canadians used to say the U.S. was a "melting pot" but Canada was a "mosaic," where different ethnic and cultural groups got to maintain more of their own identities with less pressure to conform to a "mainstream" norm. Nowadays, the U.S. is getting more mosaic-y than ever (while Canada's searching for some kind of social grout that'll keep its tiles from flying apart).

It takes a generalist to detect the patterns among the tiles, the developing harmonies and disharmonies and color schemes — without excessively oversimplifying the patterns, without invoking obsolete stereotypes of one "dominant culture" vs. one "counterculture."

While having fun with the convoluting minutae of modern urban life, the column's tried to advocate the idea that this unmelting of the melting pot's an overall good thing. Much as I enjoy the documentation and ephemera of our cultural past (movies, magazines, postcards, records), I've no wish to return to any "good old days" when racism was official national policy, or when book publishing was firmly controlled by a few tweed-suited men in Manhattan.

We need more tribes, more virtual communities, more ways for individuals to find their own voices and form their own affinity groups. But along with that we need ways for these communities to learn about, and from, one another. *(Oct. 8, 1998; the last* Stranger *column)*

Doesn't it seem weird that the politicians and the news media claim everybody's a flaming right-winger these days, but MTV and the fashion magazines are full of punk and alternative attitudes?

Absolutely not. Corporate "alternative" music, fashion, et al. is a calculated attempt to short-circuit people's innate cravings for a culture more "real" than that associated with corporate entertainment, while still keeping these people as consumers feeding the business trough. Right-wing "empowerment" rhetoric operates exactly the same way. It persuades people they're "rebelling" against The Establishment (bureaucrats) when it's really getting them to suck up to the real power elite (corporations and their PACs). Disgust at politics-as-usual and at entertainment-as-usual are related and both valid. A left that worked would reach out to both frustrations.

Over the years I've discussed many things, loosely tied to the concept of "popular culture in Seattle and beyond." I've shared a few laughs and a few tears. But through it all I've had one overriding subject — the city with which I have an ongoing lover's quarrel. Seattle's always had more than its share of vibrant, creative people. But they've long struggled against a social order opposed to anything too unclean, unrich, or unquiet.

The Seattle Commons people never understood why so many have grown tired of a city government exclusively By The Upscale, Of The Upscale, and For The Upscale. The "Parks Are For Everybody" slogan was clearly a desperation move by campaigners uncomfortable with the existence of non-yuppies and the need to appeal to such proles.

In much of the U.S., politics is controlled by money-stooges pretending to be "conservatives." In Seattle, it's controlled by money-stooges pretending to be "liberals." Other politicians pay lip service to abortion foes and censors; ours pay lip service to gay-rights advocates and environmentalists. Both sets of politicians do these to

But wasn't there a headline in *Fortune*, "Today's GOP to Big Business: Drop Dead"?

Yeah, but the meat of that story was that Republican leaders care more about certain businesses (western land and resource exploiters, financial speculators) than others (the Northeast industrial infrastructure). Neither side is appreciably on "our side."

The story also claims what's really best for business is long-term economic and social stability, not the Newtzis' scorched-earth policy. That's a point worthy of more serious debate than I can offer here.

But you don't really like ____ (football/beef/regular supermarkets/ cold cereal/TV/ heterosexuality), do you? Don't you have to be a redneck fascist to like that?

(a) Yes. (b) No.

(continued)

buy votes while holding to their real cause, the worship of Sacred Business.

But I also believe politics is a subset of culture. Seattle's politics tie directly into a culture that merely pretends to value "diversity." A culture so thoroughly whitebread, it remembers the '60s only as a playtime for college boys. A culture descended from Anglo Protestant "progressives" who championed an elitism of educated, understated "good taste;" of moderation to extremes.

When **Misc.** started, Seattle's arts had been for seemingly ever (at least since 1973) under the thumb of an extremely conservative "liberalism" I've called Mandatory Mellowness. You know, the standard of "good taste" that wouldn't merely discourage but forbid any art more challenging than Dale Chihuly, any music more contemporary than Kenny G, any theater more immediate than doo-wop versions of Shakespeare, any literature more urbane than whale poems, any apparel more daring than "Casual Friday" suits, or any lifestyle more "decadent" than drinking whole milk instead of two-percent.

While this aggressively bland anti-aesthetic still rules the city's official culture, something else arose from the underground. Punk rock remained a relevant stance in Seattle throughout the '80s precisely because it was the best available means of rebellion against the hypocrisy of mellowness. What the media called "grunge" was and is an aesthetic of darkness, but also one of honest discourse, passionate expression, and real pleasures. It values thrift and ingenuity, not the dictates of fashion. It sees Seattle as a city for Tugboat Annie, not for Niles Crane. It loves the south Lake Union neighborhood as it is. It would rather be "unhappy" yet truly alive than succumb to the Stepford-Wifedom of "The Northwest Lifestyle."

What the media call the "cocktail nation" is the expression of these values through other means, to relive the best of pre-hippie pop culture and even to make jazz a populist genre again. Indeed, the staccato, disjointed Misc. format has always been a (perhaps feeble) effort to preserve the jazz-age three-dot column of Walter Winchell, Irv Kupcinet, and the *P-I* era Emmett Watson — perhaps America's greatest literary invention.

If I've played any tiny part in popularizing these values, the values that made Seattle and real progressivism great, then I've succeeded at my goal — the *Highlights for Children* slogan, "Fun With a Purpose." *(June 6, 1996)*

SUVs on a "mountain" sales display outside downtown.

2: URBANITY DENIED

or, Seattle IS a big city, damn it!

Despite the population, the skyscrapers, the industry, and the traffic jams, many Seattleites continue to insist in the shared delusion that they're not in a city but merely a big "small town."

Local opinion-makers and influence-peddlers have for decades spread the notion that "big cities" represent everything wrong with America. Leftish locals would associate cities with the financiers and tycoons whose control of the railroads and the banking system left the Northwest's economic destiny in flux. Rightish locals would associate cities with various Wrong Kinds of People (blacks, Chinese, Catholics, socialists, labor unionists).

Seattle was supposed to be different — a place where everybody was "nice" or at least polite. Where an educated Leadership Class would rationally decide what would be best for everyone. Where the wholesome pursuits of mountain-climbing and gardening would outdraw the temptations of nightlife. This dream was particularly popular in the 1970s and early 1980s, as successive waves of aging baby boomers sought to escape the messes Ronald Reagan's minions had made of California. (Of course, their vision of "getting away from it all" only resulted in bringing a lot of "it all" with them.)

This dream of a big "small town" has always been at odds with another western dream, that of builders and boosters who'd settle for nothing less than A World Class City. Neither fantasy, of course, has a lot to do with reality, but denying reality's also a western tradition.

One attempted compromise between these visions was to preserve the city's low-density residential blocks (especially those where the affluent lived) while encouraging big projects on the remaining plots of land (especially those where the less-affluent lived). The Seattle Commons was one such scheme; another was "Urban Villages," which would've rezoned several of Seattle's less-wealthy neighborhoods for higher-density construction. Reaction was harsh and widespread; neighborhood activist Charlie Chong took homeowner rebellion against the rezoning to a successful City Council run and an unsuccessful candidacy for mayor.

Seattle is a major American city, damn it, and ought to start acting like one. We need people who are willing to make it a better city — people willing to work in the arts and community service. We don't need any more people who just want to go to the mountains for the weekend or buy a million-dollar waterfront "cabin." *(Nov. 18, 1991)*

Clothes Hoarse: A fashion trade magazine noted the increasing prominence of Seattle menswear designers, but the *Times* tried to stick a nonexistent spin onto the story by claiming these designers "show no Seattle influence" — they

The Misc. FAQ
(continued)

Isn't the Seattle scene "over"?

If you mean a hegemonous gaggle of bands all playing the exact same "sound," that never existed. If you mean people gathering to explore art and make statements, that's just getting started. What made Seattle bands wasn't a sound, but a non-Hollywood (sometimes even anti-Hollywood) attitude toward cultural production and consumption.

I hate Seattle bands because I hate ____ (long hair, flannel, backward baseball caps, distortion pedals, heroin, teen angst). How can you possibly like them?

The media "grunge" stereotype became so precise that no local band came close to completely fitting it. The only thing all Seattle bands have in common is that they all now boast that they're "Notgrunge."

don't have prints of outdoorsy scenes, but instead show a variety of influences from around the world.

What rubbish! Seattle is, if you haven't noticed (and a lot of reporters haven't), a real city, an international trade center and home of the machines that made the Jet Set possible. A fashion that mixes the best of America, Canada, Europe and urban Asia could be as distinctly Seattle as you're likely to get. *(July 1991)*

Yes, But Is It Alive?: Belltown Inside Out was billed as a celebration of the "artistic neighborhood;" it turned out more like a wake. The big exhibit was highlighted by people who used to live and/or work downtown, before the arrival of the real-estate speculators.

The new and "restored" apartments and condos on display were shoddy-to-average pieces of construction, gussied up with thick rugs, goofy light fixtures and weight rooms. The image of an art community is considered important by the developers who are driving out all the artists (one brochure touts "Sidewalk cafes, galleries, pubs, the market and the most vibrant downtown north of San Francisco"), so expect more such events.

The area was swarming with cops that Friday night, like the tower-dwellers' political lobby has wanted for some time; only they didn't seem to be going after any dealers providing pharmaceuticals for the fratboy-disco clientele, but just stood near the gallery spaces looking reassuring. It was also the first weekend of the Donald Young Gallery (nothing from here; nothing anybody here not named Gates can afford) and the last weekend of the Belltown Film Festival at the Rendezvous (a program and space virtually made for one another).

The promotion seems to have worked overall; as of the first week of the UW fall quarter, the First Avenue bars were overflowing with the fresh faces that make old hippies squirm in disgust/jealousy. Seattle's various hipster scenes over the decades never fully capitalized on the largest student population west of Austin. It's happened now, for good or ill. *(November 1991)*

I used to scoff at outsiders. But the people coming here now are making real contributions to our community. They're moving here to be part of something. People used to come here to avoid involvement. That horrible "Emerald City" slogan, adopted by the Convention and Visitors Bureau in 1982, typified a post-hippie generation wanting to get away to a dreamland where nothing ever happens. So many people wanted their own nature oasis that they destroyed a lot of nature so they could have their big ugly estate houses. We don't need that. We do need all the people we can get to make great cultural stuff, to make a better community. *(June 1992)*

This has always been a town whose dreams far exceeded its pocket contents. For over 30 years we've planned or built an array of "world class" structures on the limited wealth of a regional shipping and resources economy, plus Boeing. The result: A handful of refitted older buildings, another handful of decaying newer buildings, and one truly world-class structure (the Space Needle, built with all private money).

These days, we're besieged with ideas for a new stadium or two, a square mile of condos and token green space, a concert hall, a big library, an addition to the convention center, a new airport nobody except bureaucrats wants, a new city hall and/or police HQ, and three or four potential transit systems.

Just 'cuz there's some Microsoft millionaires buying Benzos on the Eastside, it doesn't mean Seattle's become a town of unlimited resources. Of course, the politicians (most of whom never met a construction project they didn't like) will support as many of these schemes as they can get away with, rather than bother with comparatively mundane initiatives like health care and low-income housing that don't lead to campaign contributions from contractors and construction unions. *(November 1994)*

Demographics On Parade: Austin, one of the towns billed a few years ago as a potential "Next Seattle," has achieved that dubious goal, sorta. According to Census Bureau estimates, the Texas state capital (and "alternative country" music center) surpassed Seattle as the 22nd most-populous city in America. They're up to 541,278 folk; we've just gotten up to 524,704. (We had over 550,000 in the 1960 census, back when households were having more kids; we declined in the '70s and started climbing again in the '80s.)

Of course, they're benefitting from immigration more than we are, and they're in a position to annex much of their outlying sprawl.

Other towns you might not know are bigger than Seattle: San Antonio, El Paso, Memphis, Milwaukee, San Jose, Indianapolis, Columbus, and Jacksonville. Some other towns you might not know Seattle's bigger than: Nashville, Cleveland, New Orleans, Kansas City, Atlanta, Minneapolis, Pittsburgh, Cincinnati. *(Dec. 4, 1997)*

How much do you really like the Northwest?

Mostly I think of my region like the big sister I never had, the kind of gal all the guys in school are in love with. I adore her dearly but I still feel the need to shout out, "She's not the goddess already! She used to throw spitwads at me!"

You must have loved growing up out in the country. You want to move back there, right?

Absolutely not. I was bored to tears as a kid; the place has a few more things to do now, but it's also turned into big ugly houses as far as the eye can see. The "Back to Eden" fantasy is one of the chief things wrong with America.

Why do college professors still obsess about Madonna, years after everyone else has stopped?

Shh. Let's not tell them there's been other music in the past 10 years, or that these days "a woman in charge of her music" means one who can write songs andr play an instrument.

Now that the dream of economic empowerment thru entrepreneurism is available to more and more Americans, aren't liberals obsolete?

Absolutely not. A forest that's been clearcut by 20 small companies is just as dead as one that's been clearcut by one big company; small business can shaft employees and customers just like big ones — heck, those old slave plantations would now be classified as "family farms."

The basic tenet of liberalism, as I see it, is that the business of America isn't just business. We need to care for our people and our land, not just our bottom lines. Indeed, in an evolving economy we have to pay extra attention to non-material values.

Still, a decentralized, small-biz economy is the best hope for urban neighborhoods (make your own opportunities, don't depend on big employers or big government), minority rights, free speech, and renewed creativity (though boho types will need another philosophical basis when there's no more "Mainstream" to rebel against).

Dough Boys: A few weeks back, *Times* columnist Jean Godden claimed 59,000 millionaires now reside in western Washington. (She attributed the figure to unidentified speakers at a CityClub luncheon.)

Thought #1: Now we know how these chichi restaurants with the menu items marked "Market Price" can stay open.

Thought #2: With all that spare cash floating around, howcum we still can't get decent funding for (insert your choice of non-sports-related causes)?

Thought #3 (and a hunch about #2): Seattle's old, reclusive upper class might not have staged a lot of dress balls or high teas, but they made an occasional semblance of acknowledging their role in, and duty to, the larger community. But there's a new breed of becashed ones, here and across the country, some of whom revel in "lone wolf" images. One of these, Ted Turner, called last year for his tax-bracket brethren (naming Bill Gates as an example) to donate more for bettering the world instead of just buying more goods.

A nice sentiment, but there are problems with today's wealth concentration that alms alone won't solve. Can America afford to keep turning over larger portions of its material resources to a small population segment, increasingly made of "self-made" wheeler-dealers who see social institutions (from environmental rules to progressive tax codes) as personal threats?

Perhaps the mark of a materially rich community isn't the number of residents who've got more than they know what to do with, but the degree to which its other residents can at least semi-comfortably get by. *(Jan. 8, 1998)*

Bubble Bursting?: Many of Seattle's art-world and "alternative" denizens like to think they're not part of the planes-and-software boom economy.

But we're all affected. There are also plenty of writers, actors, cartoonists, photographers, illustrators, videographers, graphic designers, and audio engineers toiling away at assorted high-tech outfits on both sides of the lake, and at these companies' subcontractors and spinoff firms. With the ripple effect of these bucks passing among retailers, landlords, etc., the commercial underpinnings of local alt-culture haven't been higher.

So are its potential underminings. There's a housing crisis threatening the fiscal well-being of most anybody who's not rich. When housing prices go up, they seldom go back down. So if the Asian slump ravages Boeing and agribusiness exports, and if fears of a market saturation in the computer biz come true, more of us will be scrambling for the remaining affordable abodes. *(April 9, 1998)*

Coming Home To Roost: Seattle's housing crisis can be compared to the International Monetary Fund's prescription for third-world economies: Enforce "austerity measures" on the masses, so financiers and speculators can have unfettered opportunities. As IMF shock-treatments are justified as being for everybody's trickle-down benefit, Mayor Paul Schell's proposed tax-and-zoning breaks for condo developers are touted as help for the thousands being priced out by the developments Schell wants to encourage.

Another intrepretation: When Schell became mayor, he inherited a municipal establishment that had tried to prevent Seattle from becoming one of those islands of urban poverty surrounded by suburban affluence. We've had a government/business elite devoted almost exclusively toward making Seattle's population as upscale as possible — not by improving the lot of those already here, but by encouraging the upscale to move and stay here (and by almost criminalizing the underclass, when and where that was deemed necessary).

You could see it in ex-mayor Norm Rice's caving in to Nordstrom's every demand; in the school district's use of busing to prop up enrollment in affluent-neighborhood schools; in the developer-friendly Urban Village and Seattle Commons schemes; and in city attorney Mark Sidran's crackdowns against anyone too publicly black, young, or unmellow. If the pursuit of demographic purity meant other populations were discouraged (actively or passively), even when it made a joke of our professed love of "diversity," it was considered a necessary cost.

But now, it's gone far enough to price middle- and upper-middle-class folk out of Seattle — the core voter base of Seattle's political machine. So the insiders are reconsidering their policy of demographic cleansing, at least on the PR level. They're talking about providing special incentives to make homes affordable to the merely well-off instead of just the really-really rich.

It's way too little, and for the politicians it might be too late. If the "single-family neighborhood" populists who stopped the Commons and the Urban Villages spread the idea that Schell's scheme will help only developers by encouraging more replacement of existing affordable housing by new "market rate" units, we could witness a movement that could eventually topple the municipal regime like a house of cards. *(Sept. 17, 1998)*

However, change can work for people or against them. We've seen change done wrong in the ex-socialist countries, as pensioners and working families get the shaft to make their countries more inviting to global financiers. Can we do better? Only if we treat this transitional time with truly moral concern, not with the pious faux-morality of the right.

What were Yogi and Boo-Boo doing in the same bed all winter?

You'll have to ask Dan Savage that one.

(March 22 and April 5, 1995)

3: GENTRIFICATION

or, the first dreaded G-word

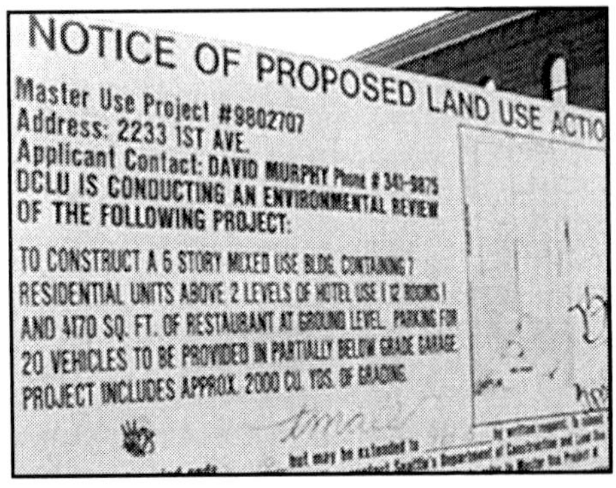

NOTICE OF PROPOSED LAND USE ACTIO
Master Use Project #9802707
Address: 2233 1ST AVE.
Applicant Contact: DAVID MURPHY
DCLU IS CONDUCTING AN ENVIRONMENTAL REVIEW
OF THE FOLLOWING PROJECT:
TO CONSTRUCT A 6 STORY MIXED USE BLDG. CONTAINING 7
RESIDENTIAL UNITS ABOVE 2 LEVELS OF HOTEL USE (12 ROOMS)
AND 4170 SQ. FT. OF RESTAURANT AT GROUND LEVEL. PARKING FOR
20 VEHICLES TO BE PROVIDED IN PARTIALLY BELOW GRADE GARAGE.
PROJECT INCLUDES APPROX. 2000 CU. YDS. OF GRADING

The great cities of the American west were made and remade many times. Seattle started in one location, moved to another, was rebuilt after an 1889 fire, and has grown and morphed constantly since.

So why should I get so upset about the 1990s rash of demolitions and reconstructions? Maybe because they so often involve key pieces of the city I've grown to love (such as the Frederick & Nelson department store or working-stiff eateries like Steve's Broiler), replaced by things gaudier, slicker, and blander. Maybe because each such replacement means Seattle's less and less the old city of tasteful modesty, more and more a brave new city of brash-yet-smug ostentation.

Yet, the column loved those certain developments which promised a more urban city, such as the massively-disruptive project that led to a 1.3-mile tunnel beneath the heart of downtown Seattle – even though the tunnel wasn't initially built to carry trains but mere buses.

This has been a summer of torn streets, noisy construction, disappearing bus stops and other hassles, many of which will be with us for the next four years. The good news is by that time, the only people left downtown will be those of us who demand urban life.

Life may soon become a lot less overcrowded for those who refuse to go to Bellevue. Sadly, we're losing Chapter 2 Books in the University District to that Nowhereland to the east, and are in danger of even losing the Pacific Science Center. This threat to Seattle's cultural life must be stopped. You wanna have to tell your kids someday that they can't pitch pennies into the fountains or get their hair raised in the static-electricity exhibit without spending an hour on the bridges? The only arches that belong in Bellevue are golden.

(September 1986)

It's summer, and Seattle is like a bombed-out ruin as the tunnel goes down and all the towers go up. It's great! Central downtown has finally become a place of excitement and activity. The Westlake Mall controversy has brought public activism back into city planning (the '70s live again!). And the best part is Pine Street at the Roosevelt Hotel, reopened just in time to give a great view of the biggest current street hole.

For future scholars, the old mid-downtown wasn't a great place. A few islands of human energy (the 211 Club, the Turf Restaurant) were isolated among block after block of dull five-to-ten-story brick buildings, whose only character came as they were allowed to deteriorate before they were torn down. The cheap new buildings will age much faster. Since they're so "contemporary" in design, they'll also look really odd to future generations. *(July 1987)*

Underground News: The postmodern, engineered-by-committee bus tunnel turns out to be a visual masterpiece, comprising five waiting areas that any corporation would be proud to have as its office-tower lobby. It's a blast to visit and to ride through. It's a monument to the pretentions of today's Seattle, one of those self-conscious boasts of "becoming a world class city."

It's more successful as a meeting place and art project than as a transportation solution. Amenities sorely lack (subway stations with no newsstands? Unthinkable!). The lack of restrooms was a deliberate decision, by officials who prefer that the homeless relieve themselves in streets and alleys. The whole expensive thing tore up downtown traffic for four years and clearly was meant to appease bus-hating affluent commuters.

Most buses running through it (starting next year) will be suburban routes (the reason for the specially built coaches that run on electricity in the tunnel but on diesel on highways and bridges). The layout of the tunnel (just slightly longer than the Monorail) was designed to move buses quickly onto I-5, I-90 and SR 520, not to get them around the city. What we oughta have is a light rail system like the cities to our north and south. *(October 1990)*

Kudos to *The Weekly* for its recent follow-the-money expose of the downtown building boom. Turns out all those glass boxes haven't been built because anybody needed the office space, but because the old tax law and deregulation of banks and pension funds made real estate speculation a lucrative proposition whether or not the buildings themselves made any money. Therefore, expecting the free market to regulate tower growth without public intervention is useless.

This cancerous growth has been going on in most U.S. cities. In Manhattan they call it "gentrification;" in San Francisco they call it "Manhattanization;" in Seattle they call it "becoming more like San Francisco." In Houston they call the new, unleaseable glass boxes "see-thru buildings." *(January 1987)*

The Pike Place Market authorities are all a-flutter over what they claim are semi-secret plans by the N.Y.C. spec-

Aphorisms & Gags,

or, Even Misc.-er

News Item of the Month (Shelby Gilje, Times, *2/12): "Playskool has Dolly Surprise, whose hair grows when you raise her right arm." I knew the Sisterhood-is-Powerful look would come back. (March 1988)*

Which Came First: University Way now has restaurants called China First and New China First. They could've called the new space China Second, but that'd be a throwback to the old Two-China Policy. (November 1988)

Yuban Coffee is sponsoring this year's performances of The Nutcracker. *If the girl had had the coffee, she wouldn't have slept and there'd be no show. (December 1988)*

Here at ***Misc.****, the slickest column around, we think Exxon ought to go back to one of its former names, Humble Oil (though a name with a double cross in the middle is also somewhat appropriate). (April 1989; circa Exxon Valdez spill)*

*Welcome one and all to the never-say-die return of **Misc.,** the only column in town that wonders why "original flavor" toothpaste doesn't taste like "original flavor" bubble gum. (October 1989)*

Put your official Berlin Wall souvenir on the bookshelf, next to your jar of Mt. St. Helens ash as '80s bookmarks. (January 1990)

Russia's getting a multi-party system! (Wish we had one.) (March 1990)

Lithuania, Latvia, now Quebec. Who says the divorce rate's down? (July 1990)

Appreciate the appropriateness of the big Marilyn Monroe mural inside the Broadway Pay n' Save (shouldn't all drugstores bear the images of people who died from prescription overdoses?). (December 1990)

Ennui is finding Zippy the Pinhead's "Are We Having Fun Yet" on a Garfield Post-it Note. (April 1991)

Good thing Danny Partridge has a big sister who's a lawyer now. (May 1991)

ulators who may or may not own the buildings to turn the Market into a high-priced, chain-stored parody of itself. What they're not saying is that this would only accelerate a process the Market leaders had already instigated, starting with sweatshirt stores and tourist-oriented parking projects.

The promotion of the Market as a sight rather than a marketplace has already affected the remaining farmers, who see Saturday after Saturday of crowded walkways full of sightseers but bereft of actual food purchasers. *(March 1990)*

Why the Commons Is a Dumb Idea: South Lake Union is Seattle's version of the "cheap merchandise district" depicted in Ben Katchor's great comic, *Julius Knipel, Real Estate Photographer.* Every thriving city needs a low-rise, low-rent district adjacent to downtown, for all the commercial activities that need to be near the center but can't afford tower rents. We need the suppliers, distributors, and photo studios that are there now.

The problem is that to civic planners, there are no old low-rise buildings — just redevelopments that haven't happened yet. The visionaries don't see the needs of the real city, just the fantasy of an "Emerald City."

They can't see the beauty of the Washington Natural Gas and Pacific Lincoln-Mercury neon. They demand their "piece of the country in the heart of the city." They can't see the beauty that's already there. They can't see that urban landscapes can have their own beauty. They can't see the city for the trees. *(February 1993)*

Street Stories: The daily papers launched a campaign for more government aid to their business friends, by trumping up an "instant crisis" about the downtown retail "atmosphere." The papers, wholly recycling the Downtown Seattle Association line, apparently want downtown to be as sterile and monocultural as the malls, hinting that cops should remove the homeless (to where??) so the sidewalks can look nicer.

The anticlimax came with a full-page *Times* story full of crime-scare tactics, while reluctantly admitting in a sidebar item that most downtown crime categories are down this year (after peaking in 1985).

Downtown retail's real problems are *(1)* a continuing national downturn in consumer spending, partly due to the long-term consolidation of personal wealth towards the wealthiest; *(2)* the decline of the dept. store biz, of which Frederick's and I. Magnin were the weakest local players; and (3) layoffs at banks and other offices, bringing fewer commuters downtown.

Locking up the panhandlers and chasing out the skate teens won't solve any of that. I've lived down here nearly two years; sure, I'd like to see fewer suffering people on the sidewalks, but the real way to do that is to try and alleviate their suffering, not to corral them into some other neighborhood. We need a war on poverty, not one more war against the poor. And skateboarders don't hurt anyone, they just speed up the ol' wear-'n'-tear on Westlake Park facilities.

I say let 'em skate. Rebuild the park platforms and pottery to withstand skate wheels, and turn the kids into a tourist attraction. *(June 1993)*

Throwin' the Book At 'Em: The city has forced me to choose between aspects of my belief system: Do I encourage you to support libraries or to oppose yuppification? The bureaucrats, who truly never met a construction project they didn't like, are using the promise of a spiffy huge new library as an excuse to raze what's left of the glorious temple of hard knocks that once was First and Pike — including Fantasy (un)Ltd., Time Travelers, Street Outreach Services, and the former second-floor-walkup space of punk palace Danceland USA. (At least one place I like, M. Coy Books, is in one of the two buildings on the block that'd be left).

Once again, the political/media establishment is out to remake Seattle into a plastic yuppietown, where if you're not an upscale boomer you're not supposed to exist.

I believe in libraries as the original Info Hi-Ways, as resources for growth and empowerment and weird discoveries. I also believe that cities need to be real places for real people. That's the same belief held by the activists who "saved" the Pike Place Market, only to see it teeter closer every year toward becoming a tourist simulacrum of a market.

Some of the blocks just outside the Market have retained their enlivening mix of high, middle and lowlife; I'd be the first to admit that some personally destructive or unsightly activities can take place there.

But to pretend to deal with poverty or crime by removing places where lower-caste people gather is worse than corrupt. It's an act of stupidity, something libraries are supposed to fight against. *(October 1994)*

Deja Vu lost its lease on the First and Pike strip club where countless businessmen and longshoremen paid

Remember when we all used to scoff at the USSR's idea of fun — tanks and missiles on parade, "honoring" those who obeyed orders fighting to prop up dictatorial puppet regimes? (July 1991)

Guns n' Roses: First white band to make headlines for NOT starting a riot. (August 1991)

In the Robert Venturi design with its vertical relief stripes, the name SEATTLE ART MUSEUM appears to be spelled with dollar signs. (September 1991)

Why are most jazz festivals held in all-white towns? (September 1991)

NOTE TO OUR OUT OF TOWN READERS: 90 percent of Seattle's bands don't sound a thing like Soundgarden. (October 1991)

George Bush is like those small-town lawyers on Scooby-Doo after their ghost masks are taken off. The difference is those characters were businessmen pretending to be monsters. With George, the reverse is true. (Nov. 18, 1991)

Bush campaign head Will Petus (in USA Today*, 1/12), insisting his campaign was not hopeless: "George Bush has been declared dead more times than Elvis Presley." The thing is, Elvis was declared dead just once, accurately. It's the folks who declare him undead who are insistant and wrong. Which is the better metaphor for Bush's chances? (February 1992)*

If you still believe you must move to a country town, look for the three most prominent main-street storefronts. If they're all real estate offices, drive back. The place is already lost to suburban sprawl. (May 1992)

Make Your Own Joke Here: In the unauthorized bio Hard Drive, *an ex-girlfriend of Bill Gates describes him as "a combination of Einstein, Woody Allen, and John Cougar Mellencamp." (June 1992)*

What's a family value? To Woody's and Mia's lawyers, a few hundred grand in legal fees.... (September 1992)

out big bucks to momentarily feel slightly less lonely. The daily papers were aglow about the possibility that entrepreneurs might turn the ex-Deja Vu space into an 1890s-retro "general store."

A general store was a place that sold most of the basic needs of frontier life. Downtown could certainly use a basic-needs retail outlet today.

But, of course, this wouldn't be anything like that. The would-be storekeepers want to sell T-shirts, gourmet jams, lattes, "fine art" (that stuff that's not as good as just-plain art), and "unique gifts" that'd undoubtedly be just the same as all the other "unique gifts" sold in and around the Pike Place Market. For at least a year, the Samis Foundation landlords had openly expressed their wish to be rid of Deja Vu as a tenant as soon as they could legally kick it out. On my scale, of course, the human physique is totally wholesome and yupscale trinket stands are a little closer to obscene. *(Nov. 13, 1997)*

Making the Square Squarer: From a pproximately 1971 to 1991, the official live music genre of Seattle was white-boomer "blooze," as played at Pioneer Square bars. The "blooze" bars of 1st Avenue South play on today, virtually unchanged.

Yet *Seattle Post-Intelligencer* writer Roberta Penn recently claimed Seattle didn't have a blues club. Her *P-I* lament probably meant we lacked a club that treated blues as a serious art form, instead of formulaic "party" tuneage. It's worth noting that the only national star to emerge from this scene, Robert Cray, split for California as soon as he hit big (and bad-mouthed the Pioneer Square bars promptly after he left).

Now, the forces of development want to rechristen the Square as luxury-condo territory. Some developers say they'd like to rid it of such elements as nightly noisemakers (even if they're sport-utility-drivin' caucasisn noisemakers). I wouldn't personally miss the "blooze" bars (though there's something quaint about standing outside the First and Yesler bus stop on a Saturday night, hearing three bands from three bars playing three cacophanous variations on the same theme). But I wouldn't want the clubs to be forced out by demographic cleansing, especially since the area's handful of prog-rock and electronic-dance clubs would likely get the boot at the same time, if not first. *(May 28, 1998)*

Historic Preservation In Our Time: Despite what it seems, not every old, low-rise building in greater downtown Seattle's being razed for cheap office buildings and glitzy condos. At least a dozen have been meticulously saved from the wrecking ball, so they can house the offices of the architects designing the cheap office buildings and glitzy condos.

I'm reminded of a slide lecture I once saw by some noted architectural critic. Among his examples of bad modern architecture was a mid-size city in central Europe with narrow, winding streets faced by quaint, homey, romantically worn-down buildings. When the socialists came into power, they hated the place. They had a new city built across the river, designed on all the efficient, rational, no-frills principles of Soviet-inspired central planning. The only government workers permitted to still live and work in the old city? You guessed it — the architects who designed the new city. *(Nov. 30, 1998)*

There's no organized conspiracy of all men to oppress all women. (If there is, I sure haven't been invited to its meetings.) Men tend not to see themselves in solidarity with all other men. What's why men have these little things called wars. (September 1992)

(continued)

4:
SEATTLE PLACES
(many of which aren't here anymore)

Coffee Messiah: Good to the last supper.

One of the ironies behind popular nostalgia for the businesses and places of the circa-1976-1988 Seattle is that many of my old punk-rock and glam-rock acquaintances largely hated the city at the time. The town was "genteel" in an exclusionary way; defensively and aggressively middlebrow. It had no place for punks, and punks had no place for it. We wanted more of that East Coast panache and pizzazz. We wanted to be more closely connected to the worlds of fashion design, contemporary art, and media production.

These wishes were finally granted, but in ways that still didn't quite seem right. Maybe because we'd become so used to a romanticized fantasy of N.Y.C. glamour that the reality of the glamour industries, as they developed here, couldn't hold up in comparison; more probably because the version of glamour-biz that took root here seemed to be a mutant strain, less obsessed with the things we loved (such as urbane youth and beauty) than with the garish wealth-displays of the newly middle-aged.

These changes are part of a national trend away from the mid-century, middle-class dream behind the New Deal and the Great Society, toward an America where wealth more rapidly flowed toward the already wealthy; where both main streets and postwar malls were eclipsed by posh shops for the upscale and strip-mall chains for the rest. A climate where even coffee shops turned from simple student hangouts to places-to-be-seen, where corner gas stations gave way to franchised convenience stores. Where the office buildings housing lawyers and financiers kept getting taller (in town) or wider (in the suburbs); while the institutions of basic industry were increasingly considered superfluous.

What's Your Sign?: The North Broadway 76 station was demolished, ending an era when the street began and ended with turning 76 balls. I'll never get to live in the second-floor apartment on 10th Avenue East that directly overlooked that sign, its bright orange globe turning outside like a postmodern successor to the blinking neon signs outside every seedy *film noir* hotel room. *(May 1991)*

Columbia Center sounds as strange as it looks. The climate-control hum and rushing air from elevator shafts give the Fifth Avenue entrance cool noises (they'd be great for a sci-fi movie). Even weirder is the Seafirst Corridor, a passageway under Fifth and Columbia from Columbia Center (where the bank execs work) to Seafirst Fifth Avenue Plaza (where the back-office staff works). It's the most surreal walkway since the United terminal at O'Hare. On the walls, plastic-covered pastel lights flash in a slow sequence of colors, while New Age music and ocean sounds enhance the creamy dreamscape.

At the end, two elevators take you one flight up to the harsh utilitarian corridors of the Fifth Avenue Plaza, where a security guard waits to let you back into a numbing temp job. *(April 1993)*

The Last Exit on Brooklyn, Seattle's oldest extant coffeehouse (est. 1967), is closing any week now, thanks to UW development plans. Another restaurant with the same name, staff and menu will open on the north stretch of University Way, by the University Sportsbar, but it won't be the same without the cigarette-smoke-aged wallpaper, the big round tables, the convenient location at the campus's edge where profs (not always male) wooed students (not always female), where grad students played all-night sessions of the Japanese board game Go, where pre-PC-era programmers from the nearby UW Academic Computing Center pored over their FORTRAN code, where umpteen bad folk singers attempted umpteen open mikes, where countless starving students had countless pots of coffee and cheap peanut-butter-and-banana sandwiches. *(December 1993)*

The Marginal Way: There's been a big media blitz over the county's plan to revive the beautifully rusty Industrial District between the Kingdome and Tukwila. The stories quoted officials claiming that unless We Act Now, the zone could become a "rust belt" a la the abandoned factories of Michigan and Ohio. The top paragraphs of the stories mentioned all-well-'n'-good stuff like fixing roads and cleaning up toxic waste.

But if you read further you find there really aren't many vacant sites in the area, that it's well-occupied by small and medium businesses. Most of the horror stories cited in the articles about companies leaving the district turn out to be about firms that wanted bigger tracts than they could get. It doesn't take much between-line reading to wonder whether the politicians are really seeking an excuse to condemn and consolidate tracts down there, evict some of the little guys, and turn the area over to bigger operations by bigger companies — the sort of companies that employ proportionately fewer people, but make bigger campaign contributions. *(May 1994)*

What's Really Wrong With the Ave: No merchant-sponsored rent-a-thugs harassing the street kids will improve

Aphorisms & Gags

(continued)

Allure *cover blurb: "Sophia Loren, The Goddess Next Door."* Vogue *cover blurb, same month: "Geena Davis, The Goddess Next Door." For an upstart little mag,* Allure *seems to have landed in a ritzier neighborhood. (November 1992)*

Great New Game: Since the Times *now publishes wedding pictures only once a month, you can look through all the faces and exchange guesses about which couples have already broken up. (November 1992)*

Misc.*'s Loopy Lexicon defines "Teen Slang" in ads as how old white people think young white people think young black people talk. (March 1993)*

Correction of the Month (UW Daily, 2/3): "...an erroneous and insulting headline ran above yesterday's page one article about Microsoft executive Bill Gates's lecture on campus. The headline should have read, 'Microsoft's Gates foresees conversion to "digital world."'" The original headline on 2/2: "Bill Gates admits he's a homely geek." (March 1993)

Ah, modern commercials, that take 30 minutes to describe a car wax and 30 seconds to describe a car. (May 1993)

The real message of "educational" cartoons: You can get away with really shoddy work as long as it meets the bureaucratic requirements. (September 1993)

***Misc.**'s Index: Number of local bands profiled or reviewed in* The Rocket *since June 1992 that are described as "not a typical Seattle band": All of them. (October 1993)*

the currently sorry state of U District retail. The District's problems go back a decade, to when Ave landlords decided to jack up rents in one big hike. Longtime indie businesses were replaced by chains. Some of those, like Crown Books and Godfather's Pizza, then bugged out of their leases at first opportunity). Other stores spent so much on rent, they cut back on interior improvements, merchandise, personnel, etc. Meanwhile, the long-slumbering University Village mall on the other side of the UW campus blossomed into a shopping theme park for the Volvo set.

The Ave has risen and fallen several times before. It can rise again. But strong-arm tactics won't do it; indeed, they'd just make the street's young-adult target market feel unwelcome. *(Dec. 5, 1996)*

My Cup Runneth Over.: The religious-kitsch camp collecting fad has been bubbling under the radar of media attention for a few years. It's now gone above ground with the opening of Coffee Messiah (neon window-sign slogan: "Caffeine Saves"), the latest espresso concept on Capitol Hill's East Olive Way. The joint looks terrific, with more cool prayer candles and crucifixes and Mary statues and religious paintings than you'd ever find in any Italian-American grandma's house.

So what if some might call it sacreligious. I see it more as sincerely celebrating the human expressions of faith and devotion, neither insistant nor perjorative about the ideological content of any particular belief. It's like a small-business version of the Unity Church: all the reassuring ritual and artistry of worship, without any potentially troublesome theology. *(July 10, 1997)*

Steve's Broiler has lost its lease and closed. The 37-year-old downtown restaurant/lounge was beloved by old folks, sailors, and punks for dishing out ample portions of good unpretentious grub and drinks, in a classic paneling-and-chrome-railing setting. (It was also the setting for Susan Catherine's '80s comic *Overheard at America's Lunch Counters.*) The owners might restart if they can find another spot. It was the last tenant in the former Osborn & Ulland building, which will now be refitted for the typical "exciting new retail" blah blah blah...
(Feb. 26, 1998)

Squarely Gay: ARO.Space, the new mostly-gay dance club in the old Moe building, is as clean looking a night spot as any I've seen. With its muted pastels and recessed lighting, and retro-modern furnishings, it could easily pass for a set in a '60s sci-fi film or in the future world fantasized at the Seattle World's Fair. It might also be seen as a desperate attempt to be fake-London, or as something too damn institutional looking to be really fun, or as an expression of gay designers too enraptured by Ralph Lauren colors or by that new interiors magazine *Wallpaper.* Under this theory, the space evokes gay men trying to prove they're just as respectable as anybody else by being bland in a Zurich airport terminal kind of way. But I prefer to see it as a "neutral" gallery-type space, only with the dancers and clientele as the "art" on display. It enhances its clientele's outrageousness by not competing with it. *(April 16, 1998)*

The Destruction Continues: Among the old buildings demolished in recent weeks for yet more homely office/retail/condo collossi was the old church just east of downtown known from 1979 to 1985 as The Monastery, an all-ages, primarily-gay disco.

Its operators had Universal Life Church mail-order ordinations and called its DJ events "church services." As a place where underage males publicly came out, it would've attracted negative scrutiny even without the rumored use of common disco and/or teen drugs. Rumors at the time (unconfirmed then and unconfirmable now) claim a dad with major city-government connections blamed the Monestary for his son's emergence as an openly gay user of some substance or another; the dad then persuaded his politico pals that all-ages nightlife was A Menace To Be Stopped.

The result: The infamous Teen Dance Ordinance, widely blamed for helping make (live or recorded) music shows for under-21s nearly impossible to profitably mount in this town. Only today, with a slightly less reactionary faction on the council authorizing a Music and Youth Task Force, is anything being done to correct this past over-reaction. By now, though, it might be too late. The cost of real estate's getting so damned high in town, even if larger booze-free clubs were legalized (small ones like the Velvet Elvis have been exempt from the ordinance), there might be no place available in which one might feasibly be operated. *(Jan. 18, 1999)*

Malled Down: Northgate management, admitting the "Mall That Started It All" (the first modern U.S. suburban shopping center, built in 1950) has looked a bit dowdy of late, announced expansion plans. The central corridor

Misc.*'s Loopy Lexicon defines "classic rock" as the work of radio station managers wistfully looking back to a more innocent age, before the radio was controlled by people like them. (April 1994)*

Misc.*'s Loopy Lexicon defines "race-blind casting" as the courageous risk of daring theatrical directors to award all major roles, no matter what ethnicity the characters may be, to white actors. (May 1994)*

We can't wait for the longtime local label K Records to start a joint venture with the new local label Y Records. The connection between the two would undoubtedly go very smoothly. (May 1994)

Welcome back to ***Misc.,*** *your friendly roadside diner along the Info Hi-Way, the kind with the big neon sign facing the road that just says EAT. (June 1994)*

Old semioticians never die; they just deconstruct. (October 1994)

As remote-happy fools, we couldn't help but notice at the time Mick Jagger was on the MTV awards, A&E's Biography *was profiling John D. Rockefeller. On one channel you got a wrinkly old rich monopoly-capitalist famous for putting his assets in trusts and tax shelters, and on the other you got an oilman. (October 1994)*

The cover of the 11/7 New Republic *has this huge banner, THE REPUBLICANS COMETH, followed by the smaller blurb line INSIDE. Gee, I was wondering why we hadn't heard anything from Packwood lately… (November 1994)*

(continued)

and the exteriors would be spiffed up, but more important (and more problematic, zoning-approval-wise) are the new buildings to be added in the vast parking moats and across the street.

Here's why: There's a nationwide decline of sales in mall stores, in favor of freestanding "big box" chains.

To see the near-future of suburban shopping, look at the vast industrial-park expanses surrounding Southcenter. Where warehouses had replaced farmland, now Target and Circuit City and Borders and PetSmart have replaced the warehouses. Malls are trying to fight back with everything from frequent-shopper incentive programs to mini-boutiques like "Piercing Pagoda." But the one thing that keeps folks from avoiding Southcenter's interior is the food court, which feeds big-box-store customers as well as mallrats. As department stores have served as traffic-drawing anchors for malls, now malls themselves are repositioning themselves as anchors for big-box clusters.

Malls, for all the limitations caused by their restrictive management, remain the closest things to "gathering places" in a lot of sprawling suburbs and exurbs. If they continue to decline, will these communities become even less communitarian, even more isolated? Or will a revived fascination with urban living (as seen in "restored" downtowns and the upscaling of places like Fremont) lead suburbanites to crave more real gathering places of their own? (Already, some Lynnwood residents are talking about wishing to build a "downtown" in that stretch of sprawl that never really had one.) *(June 4, 1998)*

5: BUSINESS, SEATTLE-STYLE

or, some stars and their bucks

While locally-based businesses have declined in many parts of the country, the Seattle area has experienced a blossoming of mighty corporate concerns, many of which are among their fields' national and world leaders, and which at least partly achieved their leadership status via hardball tactics not previously associated with our supposedly-fair city.

This shouldn't have been as shocking as some other observers thought. As one of the last white-settled parts of the 48 contiguous states, the Northwest was a place that valued pioneer courage and obsession. Early events in Seattle's history (the fights with all-powerful railroad bosses, the fight to become the main port to Alaska) further entrenched Seattle's business acumen. When modern transportation and communication networks helped erase the geographic barriers that had kept some national companies from expanding here, our old-boys' network tightened ranks behind our local beermakers and department stores and drugstore chains. Some of these institutions eventually did fall away to the forces of consolidation. But others found the resources to become consolidators.

One great thing from the '70s we're losing is the classic Starbucks Coffee mermaid. The chain's new logo, previewed in flyers for its first out-of-state store (in Chicago), not only covers up the mermaid's bust but makes her look like the "international-style" symbol of some Swiss bank or Danish tractor company. *(November 1987)*

Giving Workers the Rack: I was set to write about the closure of Nordstrom's U-District branch, but more important news came in the state's $30-million decision in favor of employees stuck working extra hours for free. It took the pro-business but out-of-town *Wall Street Journal* to print the workers' side of the labor dispute (kudos to reporter Susan C. Faludi, who uncovered not just mandatory volunteer overtime but a corporate culture of bullying, treachery, bigotry, and forced "happiness").

The local media have been as one-sided as they could, taking the angle of "Bad News for Nordstrom" (*Times* headline, Feb. 16), never "good news for Nordstrom employees." I can believe the worst stories and still understand the pro-management employees leafleting outside the stores.

Some sincerely believe in the total-hustle policy; others just might be into the "defender" role familiar to analysts of dysfunctional families. What the cracks behind the mandatory Nordic smile mean to Nordstrom's "service" reputation remains to be seen (computer magazines regularly publish columns suggesting it as a customer-relations role model to computer companies).

Even more importantly, many facets of the scandal relate back to the laid back/mellow reputation of the Northwest, whose consumers made the Big N what it is today. Nordstrom is one of a handful of institutions that mean the Northwest to the rest of the world (along with the Nordstrom-founded Seahawks, Boeing, *The Far Side,* Heart, and Ramtha).

What does it say when so many of us prefer to buy from a place that hires people on the basis of their conformity to the corporate "look" (a nebulous criterion that could be used against those with too-kinky hair or too-dark skin), and apparently treats them like well-dressed little Oliver and Olivia Twists? *(March 1990)*

Pine Cleaners: The holidays are when merchants put on their friendliest seasonal spirit. Not so for Jim "Ebenezer" Nordstrom. With all the civic-blackmail skills his family learned as ex-NFL team owners, he's promising (after months of hedging) to move his store into the old Frederick's building as part of Mayor Rice's pet development scheme, but only if the city re-bisects the tiny Westlake Park and lets commuters careen down Fifth and Pine again. Granted, the street isn't used much, except as a parking strip for cop cars and a walkway between the park's two little plazas (themselves poorly planned and expensively built).

The city's done so many things to aid private developers downtown, and so few have worked. Westlake at least partly works, so a lot of people are understandably upset at its threatened desecration. It doesn't take an urban-planning degree to see what really works in downtowns: Lively streets and sidewalks with something intriguing every step of the way.

Vancouver's got lively street retail along Robson (which has car traffic) and Granville (which doesn't). What will save downtown Seattle are *(1)* more stores for all tastes and income levels, not just the upscale, and *(2)* an adventurous day-and-night street life. *(January 1995)*

The Bon may be bought by a Canadian company. If it happens, don't expect the name to ever revert to The Bon Marche. The original (1890-1975) name, borrowed from a Paris store, originally means "good buy," but in colloqui-

Aphorisms & Gags
(continued)

***Misc.** is pleased as punch that Hale's Ales is building a new facility on Leary Way, but slightly saddened that it's going to take over the site now occupied by one of my all-time favorite Seattle building names, the House of Hose. (May 10, 1995)*

The thing about those new X-rated videos on CD-ROM is that the images are so small and lo-res, the old adage about risking blindness via overuse might in this case actually be true. (May 10, 1995)

Headline of the Week (Times, 6/4): "Boating Accidents Swell." I happen to think they're rather tragic, myself… (June 21, 1995)

Someone from L.A.'s been dropping flyers around town selling $19.95 mail-order booklets on how to build your own time machine. I don't know if she invented these plans herself or if somebody just came back in time and told her. (June 21, 1995)

al French has come to mean "cheap" in the demeaning sense — not the best image to promote to the French-literate Canadians who drive to Seattle to shop... *(November 1986)*

What's In Store: The downtown Bon has been running this big "Return to Elegance" ad campaign. Seattle's newcomers might be fooled into thinking this was some grand dame of merchandising that had lost its focus before recovering its past glory. But we know better. We know this is the same place that used to have flannel fabrics and a great homely budget floor and acres of Qiana and stretch pants and a quintessentially 1977 boutique called "Annie's Hall." *(December 1991)*

Frederick & Nelson, 1890-1992: Department stores were the retail flagships of mid-century America. They set the aesthetic/cultural tone for their towns, both in the styles they promoted and in the newspapers their ads supported. Seattle had the middlebrow Bon Marché, the lowbrow Penney's and Sears, and the also-rans Rhodes, Best's, and MacDougall-Southwick.

But Frederick's was the queen, the setter of style. Its distinction wasn't just Frangos or a doorman. In our rough-hewn port city it was a bastion for the traditionally feminine arts of fashion, decorating, interior design, food, and society. It was headquarters for a clientele of women with upbringing and money but not jobs. It was considered such a female institution that it set up a special Men's Grill where gentlemen could take a respite from shopping among all the ladies.

Its decline was predicated on a series of tightfisted owners (starting when longtime owner Marshall Field's wouldn't let it build a Northgate store). But its dominance really passed in the '60s when Nordstrom expanded from shoes into clothes, selling flashy career outfits to women who had more to do during the day than sit in Frederick's tearoom. Frederick's reacted by turning inward, taking pride in its refusal to change with the times. (It only admitted blue jeans in an obscure corner under a plain "Today Casuals" sign.) The store was weakened, prime for a series of raiders to bleed it dry. Now, maybe too late, people are looking back fondly at a store that had real standards of quality and service, without the designer-trash styles and motivational sales-zombies found across the street. No matter what happens to the buildings, the impending loss of Frederick's is a major turning point in our history. *(March 1992)*

The Bride Wore Black: I'm fully supportive of the Gothic Singles Network, a new for-profit enterprise aiming to bring pale-skinned types together for mutual moping and potential groping. I just don't wanna be around when they exchange rings... (Aug. 9, 1995)

Prepaid phone-sex cards, now sold in the back pages of some alternative publications, are like buying a single bed. They're both acts of admitting you'll be alone and desperate for the foreseeable future... (Aug. 23, 1995)

*Welcome back to **Misc.**, the pop-culture column that gets slightly disoriented when given a "Welcome to Fred Meyer" bag upon leaving the store. (March 6, 1996)*

*Welcome back to **Misc.**, the column that tried to follow its bliss, until its bliss filed a restraining order against it. (April 10, 1996)*

McDonald's now offers official Babe *Happy Meal toys with purchase of a hamburger, cheeseburger, or Chicken McNuggets. No, you can't substitute a Sausage McMuffin (I tried). (July 11, 1996)*

The rest of the local media were more than a bit mistaken about the hyped-up overimportance of a certain out-of-state chain restaurant [Planet Hollywood] opening up shop in Seattle. Now if White Castle had moved into town, that would've meant something.
(July 18, 1996)

Auto-Erotica: A home video called How A Car Is Made, *currently plugged on TV ads, is sold in separate adult and children's versions. Does the adult version show more explicit rivet scenes? Or maybe nice slow shots of a car's steel frame descending into a paint bath, emerging moments later all dripping-damp and pink?*
(Aug. 29, 1996)

We've figured out the easy way to decide whom to vote for next month. Vote for all the candidates who appear in TV ads in color, and against all the guys who appear in black-and-white.
(Oct. 10, 1996)

The Nowogroski Insurance Agency closed its old office across from Safeco Tower in the University District, and moved out somewhere by Northgate. It wouldn't concern us, except the storefront office (an ex-A&P store) still bore the name of one of the operations that had been merged into it: the James M. Cain Insurance Agency. I always wanted to take out a life policy there, just so I could ask if they had a double indemnity clause. *(July 1993)*

Thanks to all the Aldus people who E-mailed words of reassurance after the piece here about the software giant last time. One guy said not to worry about Aldus's future, that the firm's forthcoming merger with Adobe Systems would be more like a "marriage" than a corporate takeover. (I think we've all seen marriages that were like corporate takeovers, but that's beside the point…) *(May 1994)*

There are four major national retail institutions from Seattle: Nordstrom, REI, Starbucks and Costco. The latter chain is the closest to the "Seattle scene" aesthetic. At first, punk rock and Costco might not seem to have much in common. Punk is an urban thang; most warehouse stores are located way out there. Punk is built around independent retailers filling highly specialized desires of cult audiences. A warehouse store offers only a few popular items in each department; Costco's puny CD department doesn't sell any alterna-rock more obscure than the censored-cover version of Nirvana's *In Utero.*

But look further: We're not a scene of debutantes spending Daddy's money buying designer duds and snorting nose candy in discos. We're a scene based on thrift, no-nonsense graphics, and the glorious excesses of the common capitalist American. We thrive on low-budget spectacles of glorious lowbrow pleasure. We believe in empowering small business (something Costco claims to also believe in), and in subcultural communal experiences (which Costco shopping certainly is). We like to gather at obscure sites away from the glare of malls. And we much prefer to shop among Laotian immigrant families and self-employed cab drivers than among the Bellevue Squares. And Costco's got great beer and coffee prices. *(August 1994)*

The May *Esquire* had an article about Seattle's "baby boom slackers," whitebread liberal-arts grads of the magazine's target demographic who used to have time-consumin' bigtime careers but now hang out at the Honey

Bear Bakery, having chosen "voluntary simplicity" instead of the work-hard-spend-hard ideology long advocated by the magazine. I certainly hope the mag's readers will realize the selectivity it used.

The story notes that only 70 percent of U.S. adult males now work full-time year-round at one job; but from personal knowledge I can assure you a lot of those guys walking around in the daytime with desktop-published "consultant" business cards aren't there fully by choice. Not to mention the millions who haven't had the chance to quit a well-paying job. *(May 10, 1995)*

Dunno 'bout you, but ***Misc.*** *is a bit leery about this week's touring performances of* The Wizard of Oz On Ice. *When the witch melts, do they freeze over her remains before they resume skating? If they don't, how do they finish the show? (Nov. 21, 1996)*

Drop That Metaphor (Bastyr Naturopathic Univ.ersity trustee Merrily Manthey, quoted in a big Jan. 3 *N.Y. Times* story on the King County Council's project to start a subsidized alternative-health center): "This clinic we're trying to set up here will be the Starbucks of the health care world." Will it offer red-and-black designer colostomy bags, or Holiday Blend prescriptions? Will it dispense spitcups in regular and grande sizes? (I know it won't serve lattes; the standard naturopathic diet forbids dairy products, along with meat and wheat.) More seriously, will it become a brand name known for adequate but unexceptional work within standardized bland surroundings?

Could be worse, metaphorwise. I recall the unfortunate street-poster slogan used in the mid-'80s by Capitol Hill's otherwise admirable Aradia Women's Health Center: "Are you tired of the sterile environment of a doctor's office?" *(Jan. 17, 1996)*

Just can't think of any good jokes about the Eastside having its own area code. When the outer reaches of western Washington became "360," at least one could joke about "going full circle" or "matters of degrees." But there's nothing worth saying about a nothing number like "425." It's the Bellevue of three-digit numbers. (May 29, 1997)

The Sonics' recent successes reminded me how one of the joys of televised sports has always been the excuse to loiter among a department store's TV displays, sharing the moments of triumph/despair with instant friends without having to buy (or drink) anything. But that's another of those disappearing urban pleasures.

The Bon Marché's new management, having disposed of the Budget Floor, the Cascade Room restaurant, and the downtown pharmacy, is now closing the electronics departments. Besides leaving Radio Shack (and pawn shops) as the only source for home electronics in the central downtown, the loss (effective August) leaves but a few public TV walls in the greater urban core (Sears, Fred Meyer, Video Only). *(July 4, 1996)*

This installment of Misc. is being written on a gorgeous, sturdy office table obtained dirt cheap at the old REI

*Off the Rack: The Spice Girls, that singing group (Sporty Spice, Sexy Spice, Strong Spice, Scary Spice, Posh Spice) that claims in interviews to not be the shallow studio-manufactured image machine it really is, has proven so popular it's spawned knockoff quintets throughout Britain. Here's my idea for my own "**Misc.** Spice Melange":*

Asthmatic Spice: *Can only perform during the 30 minutes between the time her prescription antihistamines take effect and the time they knock her asleep.*

Obsessive-Compulsive Spice: *Always holds up the tour bus by insisting on chewing her food exactly 32 times.*

Fiscal Spice: *Business-dress-clad; dances with the efficient long steps of a FedEx courier. Always begging the other members for the authority to invest the group's record royalties in dubious offshore mining stocks.*

store's after-closing fixture sale. While many of us working in the Pike/Pine corridor are thankful to no longer compete for parking with Suburbans from the suburbs, there's still a certain feeling of loss over what was a solid, utilitarian place selling solid, utilitarian goods.

REI began as an outgrowth of the '30s Mountaineer movement, a quasi-bohemian subculture that believed communing with Nature could bring empowerment and even spiritual growth. These folks wanted a consumer-run resource for practical tools. That's a ways from the mass-merchandising behemoth that is today's REI, with its huge new Retail Theater Experience on Denny Way.

Another survivor of the pre-WWII co-op craze, Group Health Cooperative, admits to being in merger negotiations with Kaiser Permanente, a huge HMO with operations in 18 states. Some news accounts questioned whether such a scheme could preserve Group Health's "cooperative spirit."

I say without the actual practice of cooperative governance, such a "spirit" is little more than an image; and at organizations the size of today's REI or Group Health, real hands-on co-op management might not even be possible. *(Oct. 3, 1996)*

Best Products is closing its last 13 Washington stores. These include the final remnants of the former locally-owned Jafco chain and catalog, which supplied moderately-priced jewelry, sporting goods, home furnishings (including foam sofa-beds), and stereo gear to two generations of Northwesterners.

I can still remember the day one of my high-school teachers showed off her brand new engagement ring (from a fellow teacher) in class. Just weeks later, I happened to find that exact ring in the Jafco catalog; giving me direct evidence that education was perhaps not the most lucrative of professions. *(Oct. 24, 1996)*

Pay Less Drugs, R.I.P.: The Pay n' Save stores, once the flagship of the local Bean family's retail empire, were sold to N.Y.C. speculators, who then sold them to K mart, which merged them with the Oregon-based Pay Less, then spun off the combined chain to private investors, who merged it with California's Thrifty Drug. Along the way, House of Values, G.O. Guy, and Gov-Mart stores also joined the circuit. Now, these 1,007 outlets will be part of the East Coast-based Rite Aid circuit. It's a good thing drug stores don't have the same combination-warning labels drugs have. *(Oct. 31, 1996)*

Lilia's Boutique, the fancy women's-clothing store in the condo tower next to the Vogue, started to hold a going-out-of-business sale. Soon after the SALE signs appeared in the windows, representatives of the real-estate company handling the building's retail leases taped a "Notice to Comply or Vacate" paper to the store's front door overnight. The notice told Lilia's essentially to stop going out of business or be forced out of business. Apparently, there were terms in Lilia's lease forbidding "distress sales" or any public acknowledgement that business conditions in the building were less than perfect. Anyhow, the dispute got quietly resolved, and Lilia's got to continue going the way of 80 percent of new U.S. businesses.
(March 20, 1997)

In the Bag: By the time this comes out, QFC should've opened its big new store on Capitol Hill and finished branding its own identity on Wallingford's once-feisty Food Giant. The new Capitol Hill store was originally to have been a Larry's Market, but QFC outbid Larry's at the last minute. (If the retail development had gone as originally planned, we would've had Larry just a block away from Moe!)

Meanwhile, a strip-mall QFC's under construction in the formerly rural Snohomish County environs of my childhood, bringing 24-hour, full shopping convenience to a place where a kid used to have to go two miles just to reach a gas station that sold candy bars on the side.

These openings represent small steps in a chain that's gone in 40 years from a single store on Roosevelt in '58 (still open) to 15 stores in the mid-'70s (including five taken over when A&P retreated from its last Pacific stores) to 142 stores in Washington and California today. It's rapidly expanded in the past decade, even as many larger chains retreated from neighborhoods and whole regions. (The once-mighty A&P name now stands over only 675 stores, down from 5,000 in the early '60s.)

While the new store isn't QFC's biggest (that's the Kmart-sized University Village behemoth), it's still a useful 45,000-square-foot object lesson in the economics of the foodbiz. The first real supermarkets, in the '30s, were as small as the First Hill Shop-Rite. New supermarkets kept getting built bigger and bigger ever since, in stages. QFC was relatively late at building 'em huge; in the early '80s, it proudly advertised how convenient and easy-to-navigate its 15,000-square-foot stores were compared to the big 'uns Safeway and Albertsons were then building in the suburbs.

Curious Spice:
Nancy Drew wannabe, forever skipping rehearsals to investigate strange mysteries, like the mysterious connections between music-industry people and (gasp!) the sale and use of illicit drugs. Regularly getting herself caught in sticky situations, needing to be rescued by...

Heroic Spice:
Has no super powers, but that doesn't stop her from athletically rescuing concertgoers from purse-snatchers, ticket-scalpers, and T-shirt price-gougers.
(Sept. 4, 1997)

Welcome back to **Misc.,** *the pop-cult column that thinks it's finally figured the reasoning behind the Spice Girls' second CD cover, which looks almost exactly like their first one except the letters SPICE are tall instead of wide. It's probably a subtle claim that these women can cause anything to become elongated.*
(Jan. 22, 1998)

Misc. *still remembers overhearing two men at a 1991 party recommending the most profitable way to sell a Seattle house — advertise it only in the* L.A.Times. *Such subterfuge is probably no longer necessary; now most Angelenos can't afford a house here either. (Aug. 6, 1998)*

Seafirst Bank now has "Celebrate Diversity" checks, in a sort-of rainbow design — only this "diverse" colorscape is all mellow and pale. A lot like Seattle in general... (Sept. 10, 1998)

Would you even want to live in the same building with all the maniacally-grinning GQ *models depicted in all those condo ads? (Sept. 10, 1998)*

Grocery retailing's a notoriously small-profit-margin business. The profits come from volume, from higher-margin side businesses (wine, deli, in-store bakery), and from gaining the resources to muscle in on wholesaling and processing. QFC started as a Thriftway franchise, part of the Associated Grocers consortium. AG's one reason indie supermarkets can survive in Washington; it gives individual-store owners and small chains a share in the wholesaler's piece of the grocery dollar. What QFC pioneered, and others like Larry's and the Queen Anne Thriftway have since further exploited, is a "quality" store image. The idea's that if your store's known for "better" items and service, you can retreat a little from cutthroat price competition (i.e., charge more). From the Husky-color signs to the old Q-head cartoon mascot (designed by ex-KING weatherman Bob Cram) to the "QFC-Thru" plastic meat trays, every visible aspect of the store's designed to say, "Hey, this ain't no everyday corn-flake emporium."

Of course, now with everybody in the biz trying to similarly fancy themselves, QFC still has to keep prices in line with the other guys, at least on the advertised staple goods. But it remains a leader in the game of wholesome-yet-upscale brand identity, a shtick most of the now-famous chain retailers from Seattle have adopted; indeed, an image the city itself has tried to impose upon us all. *(May 8, 1997)*

Big Storewide Sale: Why, you ask, would Fred Meyer (the regional everything-for-everybody chain) want to buy up QFC (the fancy-pants grocery specialists)? Besides the normal drives for consolidation in today's chew-'em-up, spit-'em-out corporate world, QFC was threatening to infiltrate Freddy's Oregon stronghold, and QFC's role in the Pike & Broadway urban-strip-mall complex (with its food-drug-variety-banking combo) is too close to Freddy's under-one-roof hypermarket concept for Freddy's to afford to ignore.

Media coverage, natch, emphasized the merger's potential impact on the Q's upscale core clientele. The Q responded to this press-generated nonissue by running full page ads promising the Q will remain the Q. Tellingly, there've been no ads promising Freddy's would remain Freddy's; just a brief reassuring statement from Meyer management. But with seemingly everything else getting gentrified these days, I know I'd be afraid of such possible consequences as Ralph Lauren goods taking over the Pant Kingdom department, Smith & Hawken on the hardware shelves, Aveda at the cosmetics racks, Bang & Olufson replacing the Panasonic boom boxes in the Photo & Sound section, or even a wine shelf with F. G. Meyer's Choice Beaujolais Nouveau. *(Nov. 27, 1997)*

Delivering Influence: A recent *Wall Street Journal* told how United Parcel Service tried to pay the University of Washington to lend its institutional credibility onto pro-corporate research. The formerly-locally-owned UPS offered $2.5 million to the UW med school in 1995. But instead of directing its gift toward general areas of study, UPS insisted the money go toward the work of UW orthopedic surgeon Stanley J. Bigos. The *Journal* claimed UPS liked Bigos because "his research has suggested that workers' back-injury claims may relate more to poor attitudes than ergonomic factors on the job." The company's fighting proposed tougher worker-safety laws, and wanted to support its claims with "independent" studies from a bigtime university that happenned to need the money. Negotiations with UW brass dragged on for two years, then collapsed.

Bigos insists he wouldn't have let UPS influence his work if he'd gotten its cash. But if companies can pick and choose profs already disposed to tell 'em what they wanna hear, "academic independence" becomes a bigger joke than it already is. *(Feb. 26, 1998)*

Class-Action Racism Suit Hits Boeing: Some of you theoretically might ask, "But aren't pocket-protector-clad Boeing engineers the virtual epitome of squaresville fair play and quiet devotion to duty?" Maybe, in myth; but any huge organization with an almost all whitebread leadership (even an officially "nice" whitebread leadership) can be prone to insult "jokes," promotion preferences and other discriminations, even anonymous threats and attacks.

It's happened in the past decade (according to suits and pubilshed accusations) at Nordstrom, City Light, the fire department, the ferry system. And with affirmative action under attack and with every boor and bigot using the all-justifying label of "political incorrectness" as an excuse to actually take pride in their own obnoxious inhumanity, we might see more ugliness ahead.
(April 2, 1998)

Our eternal search for unusual grocery stores has led to a true find. Jack's Payless Auto Parts and Discount Foods is a large yet homey dual-purpose emporium just beyond

The Fine Print

From a Mr. Coffee coffee filter box: "Additional Uses: Use as a cover when microwaving. Line the bottom of your cake pans. Create snowflakes and Christmas decorations." (May 1990)

Sign on a cigarette machine at an International House of Pancakes: "No refunds. Use at your own risk." (July 1990)

From the Wild Orchid *video box: "This unrated version contains explicit 'footage' not included in the R-rated version released theatrically in the United States. Discretionary viewing by minors is strongly advised." (March 1991)*

The entire official disclaimer at the start of Bret Easton Ellis's American Psycho*: "This is a work of fiction. All of the characters, incidents, and dialogue, except for incidental references to public figures, products, or services, are imaginary and are not intended to refer to any living persons or to disparage any company's products or services." (April 1991)*

From Cakes Men Like, *Benjamin Darling's book of photostatted pages from old food-company recipe brochures: "The recipes in this book are the product of an earlier era, and the publisher cannot guarantee their reproducability or palatability for contemporary readers."* *(June 1992)*

On a bag of Fritos: "You may have won $10,000. No purchase necessary. Details inside." *(December 1992)*

On the outer wrapper of Deja Vu Centerfold *trading cards: "Models' stage names are used. Neither photos nor words used to describe them are meant to depict the actual conduct or personality of the models."* *(January 1993)*

At the bottom of a billboard on a Snohomish County Community Transit commuter bus, selling houses in my ol' hometown of Marysville by showing a whitebread yuppie nuclear family picnicking in all-white clothes: "Models do not represent any race or family formation preference." *(Feb. 7, 1995)*

the south end of Beacon Hill at 9423 Matrin Luther King Way S. The south wing's all spark plugs and tires and replacement gaskets. The north wing's got staple and convenience foods (cereal, canned goods, pop, snacks, wine, beer) at amazing prices. (Last week they had full cases of Miller for $3.99.) If you're there at the right time, you might be serviced at the checkout by the manager's nine-year-old son (who makes change fast and accurately, and without benefit of a computerized cash register). *(July 16, 1998)*

Just What's A Brass Plum, Anyway?: To me, the new Nordstrom store's opening will be the final true end of Frederick & Nelson; I've been able to half-pretend the grande dame of Seattle retailing was still around, I just hadn't shopped in it for six years.

It's also (as of yesterday) the end for the old downtown Nordstrom. I'll miss that awkward amalgam of three buildings, with the front-and-back-doored elevators, the unpretentiously-pretentious all-lower-case signage, the cramped awkward floor spaces (which suited Nordy's then-novel "collection of boutiques" concept better than any open-plan mall space could) — a place where, no matter what year's fashions were on the hangers, the style year was always 1974.

I've previously criticized Nordy's sweetheart deals with the city over the new store, its parking garage, and its reopening of Pine. But let's remember what else this company's wrought, for good as well as for ill. The downtown Nordy's as we've known it opened when lots of downtown office towers were going up. Instead of the affluent-yet-careerless women F&N targeted, Nordy's targeted office people (particularly women) who'd begun seeing themselves not as sedate corporate drones but energetic corporate warriors. (Not exactly a feminist ideologue's vision of empowerment, but still a change.)

It also told the country our far corner indeed had a fashion sense (an early *Forbes* article mockingly called the store "Bloomie's in the Boonies") — and an entrepreneurial sense. Nordy's helped perfect the workforce-as-cult model of employee relations now associated with the likes of Microsoft.

Like its dressing-for-success clientele, its staffers were encouraged (or hounded or pressured) to give their all to the company and then some. Even as its catalogs and its out-of-state stores spread an image of the Northwest as a land of carefree outdoor leisure, its practices instilled a vigorous (or obsessive or oppressive) work ethic now common at "growth oriented companies" here and elsewhere.

A piece on Microsoft's online zine *Slate* last year suggested companies like MS and Starbucks had to have copied N.Y. or L.A. styles of institutional aggression; such drive couldn't possibly be indigenous to our countrified region. Nordy's proved it could be and is. *(Aug. 20, 1998)*

At the bottom of a "No Food/Drink" sign outside a video arcade on University Way: "Thank You For Your Coordination." (Jan. 4, 1996)

From the Internet service provideer Xensei: "The requested URL was not found on this server. No further information is available. I'm sorry it didn't work out. And it looked so promising for a while there too." (Jan. 11, 1999)

Too Clothes For Comfort: After a couple of weeks, I think the new Nordstrom store looks a LOT like the Forum Shops mall at Caesar's Palace in Vegas, the kind of place that doesn't even pretend to be sublime or understated.

It was made clear from the start that nothing recognizable from Frederick's, except for the exterior facade and the thick supporting posts, would be preserved. (Even the elevator and escalator shafts were moved.) But I don't think many expected the new store's total in-your-face experience of New Money, all proud and boastful and coldly showoffy yet trying conspicuously to be proper. If Bloomie's or Saks had installed such a store, everybody'd complain how indiscreetly un-Seattle it was. *(Sept. 10, 1998)*

The Pacific Place General Cinema elevenplex means, even with the permanent closure of the UA 70/150 (the "200 penny opera house") and the temporary closure of the Cinerama, there are now a whopping 39 commercial movie screens in greater downtown Seattle (including Capitol Hill and lower Queen Anne), plus the Omnidome, IMAX, and 911 Media Arts. No more the days when high-profile new films would premiere no closer to town than the Lake City, Ridgemont, or Northgate (still open!) theaters...

Lessee, what would have been the movie for me to see in this giant multiplex, on the top two floors of a massive, climate-controlled environment totally dedicated to commercialism and with no visible exits? Hmm, maybe — *The Truman Show*?

As for the mall itself, a tourist overheard on opening day of Pacific Place said, "It reminded me of Dallas." I can imagine the likes of J.R. Ewing and Cliff Barnes hanging amid the huge, costly, gaudy, yet still unsophisticated shrine to smugness. This penultimate major addition to downtown retail (the last phase of downtown's makeover will occur when the old Nordstrom gets permanent new occupants) constitutes one more shovelful of virtual dirt on the old, modest, tasteful Seattle. The PP management even kicked out a branch of the Kay-Bee Toys chain the day before it was to open, solely because Kay-Bee's

Barbies and Hot Wheels weren't upscale enough for the tony atmosphere the mall wants everything in it to have!

At least one good thing you can say about PP is it makes the 10-year-old Westlake Center (also built with partial public subsidy) look comparably far more egalitarian, with its cafeteria-style food court and its Beanie Baby stand and its "As Seen on TV" cart selling your favorite infomercial goodies: Ginsu knives! A "Rap Dancer" duck doll! Railroad clocks that whistle on the hour! Magna Duster! Citrus Express! EuroSealer! Gyro Kite! Bacon Wave! EpilStop Ultra! And Maxize, $39.95 Chinese-made foam falsies ("Avoid risky, expensive, ineffective surgery")! *(Nov. 5, 1998)*

Nailed: Eagle Hardware, the Washington-based home-superstore circuit, is selling out to Lowe's, a national home-center chain with no prior presence up here.

Flash back, you fans of '70s-style '50s nostalgia, to the *Happy Days* rerun where Mr. Cunningham lamented the threat to his Milwaukee hardware boutique by an incoming chain from out of town called Hardware City: "They've got 142 different kinds of nails. I've only got two: Rusty and un-rusty."

Now, flash ahead to the mid-'90s, when *P-I* editorial cartoonist Steve Greenberg ran a fish-eating-fish drawing to illustrate mom-and-pop hardware stores being eaten by regional chains like Ernst and Pay n' Pak, who are then eaten by big-box superstores. Greenberg neglected to include the final fish, the national retail Goliath eating up the superstore operators. *(Nov. 23, 1998)*

Times of the Signs

Best sight in today's Vancouver is a stencil-painted graffito downtown, "Jesus Saves," modified by the spray-painted addition, "Gretzky scores on the rebound." (October 1989)

At University Hair Design: "Someday we will live in a world free of shallow people who make judgments based on physical appearance. Until then, make your perm and color appointment today." (June 1991)

Taped to the inside of a Magazine City window: "Please don't support the belief that panhandling supports drug abuse. The fact is, most 'homeless' people don't have the mental capacities to get on government legal panhandling programs like welfare and food stamps. Besides, it's your money and your decision right?? O.K. Pal... Thanx, 'a homeless person.'" (November 1991)

(continued)

Flyer posted on Capitol Hill, circa 1998.

6: CYBER-SEATTLE

or, MS: the great cripper of young adults

In some other ex-frontier regions of North America (including the less-urbanized parts of Washington state), local economies have sputtered as the Global Economy's machinations battered old resource-based industries such as forestry and farming. But Seattle and environs have thrived. The Asian trade, the Alaska trade, and Boeing have all enriched the area.

But the biggest new rush of cash up here has been from individual and business computer users throughout the world, into a new caste of cyber-moguls. Their companies have ranged from one-person website shops to such big names as Aldus (which merged into Adobe), RealAudio, Amazon.com, Attachmate, and the U.S. division of Nintendo. But the most powerful of them all was the creation of the son of one of Seattle's most pivotal old-boy-network lawyers, a boy who grew up knowing the values of backstage dealmaking and onstage PR.

All You'll Hear Me Say About Windows 95: Jay Leno was the perfect choice to emcee the Windows hypefest in Darkest Redmond (the talk-show host who's almost as good as Letterman but not really, shilling for the operating software that's almost as good as the Mac OS but not really).

Still, I understand why Windows 95 could be considered a significant introduction in some quarters. So many people have been suckered into using Windows, and have been so frustrated by it over the past five years or so, that the promise of a Windows version that sucks even a little less is cause for celebration among 'em. *(Sept. 6, 1995)*

The Macintosh platform's demise has been predicted almost every year since it came out. This time, the nay-sayers are citing everything from intensified price competition to over- or under-production to the hype machine over Windows 95 (Bill Gates's version of the old Ritz cracker recipe for "Mock Apple Pie").

Some want the Mac to die, and not just Gates loyalists. Umberto Eco once wrote that the Mac and MS-DOS worlds were like Catholics and Protestants — the former visual, sensory, and collectivistic; the latter verbal, coldly rational, and individualistic. (Windows, Eco wrote, is like Episcopalian spectacle atop a base of Calvinistic doctrine.) Others say the Mac's intuitive approach and seamless hardware/software integration are more attuned to right-brain creative folks; Windows keeps its users stuck in left-brain logic mode. Today's

Times of the Signs
(continued)

At the Varsity concession stand: "Special Award for an act of distinction: Scott White, 'a man of congeniality,' for explaining that 'Exclusive Engagement' is not the title of a film."
(October 1991)

On a city Landscape Department truck: "A city without trees isn't fit for a dog."
(December 1991)

At the Christopher Paul Bollen print gallery on 3rd: "Hi. Popcorn, candy, children and pets are most WELCOME in this gallery. If you break it, no big deal. No shoes, no shirt? Goodness, it must be sunny. COME ON IN."
(June 1992)

At Front Street Specialty Nutrition in Issaquah: "Always lowest prices! Well, usually — O.K., O.K., at least sometimes!"
(August 1992)

A meticulously painted sign on the facade of Sam's Super Burger, 26th & Union: "No trespassing. No loitering. I don't come to your place and sell my burgers, so don't you come to my place and sell your drugs."
(June 1994)

centers of economic and political power, including Wall Street and the business press, are as left-brain-centric as any institutions in history. Many in these subcultures see Macs as artsy-fartsy playthings or as annoying symbols of Windham Hill/NPR propriety, definitely not as acouterments for the Lean-'n'-Mean mentality of Global Business.

Yes, I'm a Mac loyalist. But more, I'm an advocate of creative thinking and of Stuff That Works. To millions like me, the Mac's an extension of the mind, not just another overgrown calculator. It could be improved on, but there's no real substitute in sight. *(Jan. 31, 1996)*

Fast Money: Somebody tried to tell me once how computer technology was like *Jeopardy!*, an answer in search of a question. I replied if that was the case, then Microsoft was more like *Family Feud,* where the most popular answer is decreed to be correct. Whether this means Gates will be compared by posterity to the eternally glad-handing Richard Dawson (or even to the more tragic figure of Ray Combs) remains to be seen. *(Feb. 27, 1997)*

Error Messages: Hardly a day goes by without somebody saying something nasty about Microsoft. The Department of Justice disses the way MS tries to strong-arm PC makers. Nader warns about MS trying to monopolize "electronic commerce," wanting a piece of every buck that'll change hands online. Sun and Netscape claim MS wants to quash their "cross-platform" software, which threatens the MS-dictated computer universe. *Mother Jones* charges an MS-funded antipiracy group promised not to prosecute offices for using unpaid-for software if they promised to buy all-MS software. And MS's temps and perma-temps complain about their second-class treatment within the firm (including, thanks to new state legislation, no more overtime pay).

In most of these cases, the company claims it's being unfairly targeted due to its "success" at creating products that just happen to be "popular among consumers." That's not quite the way it is. Just about anybody who's not working for the company (or its media joint-venture partners) will acknowledge MS writes better contracts than code.

Instead of innovation and competition, it operates by buying friends and crusing enemies. While its staff ideologues publicly pontificate about a cyber-future of decentralized societies and limitless opportunity, it behaves like an old-fashioned oil or railroad monopoly.

In the past, MS's enemies wanted the feds to split the company in two, spinning the DOS/Windows side into a separate company. That move by itself wouldn't solve anything now, since the DOJ's main argument is against MS turning Internet application software into a piece of Windows, making it tough for others to sell separate browser programs. It's not just using its operating-system dominance to sell application software, but to give away software other companies want to sell. In other industries, it'd be called anti-competive "dumping."

Our fair region is the born-'n'-bred home of perhaps the most widely hated American company outside the oil or media businesses. Gates and Allen come from what passes for "old money" in this relatively new corner of western civilization. What does it mean to the longstanding image of this place as, for better or worse, "The City of the Nice" (as proclaimed by Tom Robbins in 1981)?

That, of course, always was an exaggeration. We weren't "nice" so much as polite and businesslike, eager to please when in our interest. (Author Roger Sale wrote in 1975 that Seattle was "bourgeois from the start.")

Despite the popularity of drunks, scoundrels, labor radicals, and whoremongers as local historical icons, most of the real settlement of the city was led by would-be timber, transportation, and real-estate barons. The ones who made it didn't just have what the new agers call "prosperity consciousness;" they maneuvered themselves into the right places, befriended the right people, made the right deals.

Behind today's Boeing boom lies a heritage of sales execs who forged long-term friendships with airlines, sealing deals Lockheed and Douglas couldn't match. Rainier and Olympia beers stayed prominent as long as they did because regional Teamster boss Dave Beck used his influence to make sure local beer sellers preferred local beers. The burgeoning Seattle biotech industry's due to Sen. Warren Magnuson's pipeline of federal bucks into the UW medical school.

Microsoft started by signing deals with early hobbyist-computer maker Altair, and became a giant by signing deals with IBM. Much of the Seattle/Olympia "indie rock" philosophy has to do not just with alternative kinds of music but with forging alternatives to the music industry's contractural practices. Seattle's a town of dealmakers as much as it's a town of engineers. MS took this craft to a hyper-aggressive level. The extent to which this aggression succeeds or backfires will affect the company, the region, and the world. *(Jan. 15, 1998)*

"Clues That You're In the Wrong Age Group: You walk into the party and everyone hides their beer. Your bell bottoms and platform shoes are originals. No one knows who Marlo Thomas is. Rad is not a unit of radiation. They talk Star Trek and you drop the name William Shatner. All your friends are taking Retin A and Alpha Hydrox (isn't that a cookie?). You were around when martinis and Tony Bennett were cool the first time." — Sign outside Megan Mary Olander Flowers on 1st Ave. S. (August 1994)

From a flyer for a concert at the Velvet Elvis Arts Lounge Theater: "No alcohol. No nihilists." Gee, nihilists never get to have any fun! (February 1994)

Marquee at the Varsity Theater: "1-900, Seven, To Die For." If you call 1-900-7-TODIE-4, by the way, you get the psychic hotline run by Sly Stallone's mom. (Dec. 20, 1995)

On the readerboard at the Eastlake flower shop: "Pro-Environment Bumper Stickers — Joke of the Century." (Aug. 29, 1996)

One of the "Rules of Conduct" at the Wizards of the Coast Game Center: "#6. We want our guests to feel at home in the Game Center, so please practice daily hygeine and tidy up after yourself." (June 5, 1997)

Sign at Larry's Deli on 4th Avenue: "'Food' Stamps Accepted Here!" Perchance a comment on the actual-food status of convenience store staples? (Jan. 22, 1998)

With the opening of the Third Avenue Deli in the former Bon Tire Center, downtown has its own mobile, curb-based readerboard sign with arrow-pattern chase lights. Strip-mall flavor in the heart of the city! (Aug. 27, 1998)

Sodden: Damn! The webzine *Salon* already did what I wanted — to request your own phony Microsoft support letters. The *L.A. Times* had revealed a scheme wherein MS's PR firms would concoct a gush of letters and newspaper opinion pieces, begging state and federal governments to back off from antitrust actions against the software giant. (Commentator Jim Hightower calls these fake-grassroots campaigns "AstroTurf politics.") MS denied the allegations; the paper stood by its story.

It does read like something MS could conceivably try. Except the trickery would've been all-too-obvious if these supposed ordinary civilians all spouted the same line — that the company's dominance wasn't the result of deal-wringing and strong-arm tactics, but of releasing "popular" products within an open marketplace. It's the kind of reality-distortion construct that too easily collapses when you try to translate it from spin-doctor lingo into plain prose.

That's where *Salon*'s invite comes in. They're asking for original, equally preposterous, leave-MS-alone arguments. (Their example: "Since I upgraded to Windows 95, my pancreatic cancer has gone into remission, my daughter was accepted to law school, and I won $50 in the Lotto Quick Pick.") *(April 30, 1998)*

Window Pains: We'll keep coming back to the Microsoft legal flap over the next months. But for now, consider the notion advanced by some MS supporters (including *Fortune* writer Stewart Alsop) that a software monopoly's a good thing. The company's address, "One Microsoft Way," expresses the dream of Gates and his allies in associated industries to impose a structured, top-down order involving not just a single operating system and Internet browser but a single global culture controlled by a handful of corporations.

They claim it's for a higher purpose of "standardization," a unified technology for a unified planet. It's an old rationalization of monopolists. AT&T used to use the slogan "One Policy, One System." Rockefeller invoked similar images with the name "Standard Oil."

Yet at this same time, the Net is abetting advocates of a different set of ideals — decentralized computing, cross-platform and open-architecture software, D.I.Y. entertainment and art. Not to mention thousands of religious sub-sects, sex fetishes, political factions, fan clubs, fashion trends, etc. The MS case won't alone decide the fate of this diversity-vs.-control clash, but could become a turning point in it. *(June 18, 1998)*

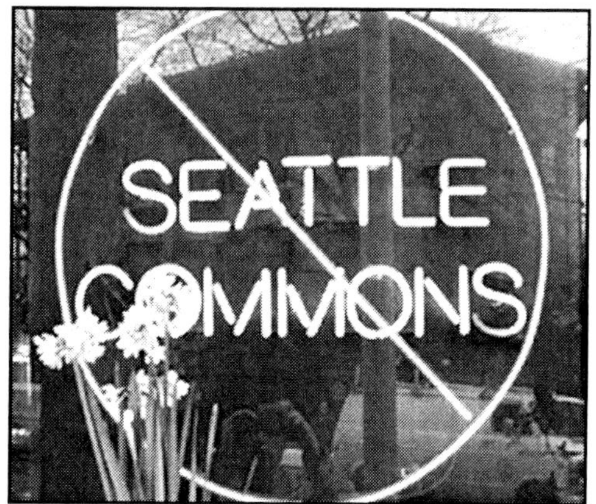

Still protesting the Commons plan: Sign at the 5 Point Cafe.

7: NORTHWEST POLITICS

or, pro-business Democrats and anti-city Republicans

The local old-boy network Bill Gates grew up in belonged to an era of relative political stability. After commie-bashers and labor radicals were both shut out of power in the early '50s, and until Gov. Dixy Lee Ray brought the anti-environmentalist backlash into vogue in 1976, governance in Washington state was about as middle-of-the-road as you could get. Democrats represented the cities; Republicans represented rural areas and some of the wealthier suburbs; everybody promised social progress and economic growth, and tried their hardest to steer business developments toward their own constituencies.

It's a little different nowadays. The region's Republicans, once among the nation's most progressive, now march more or less in lockstep with the Christian Coalition/National Rifle Association ideological line — anti-gay, anti-wilderness, anti-abortion, anti-feminist, anti-immigrant, and anti-urban. That leaves Seattle to be run by a pro-business-Democrat municipal machine, with the polite-old-boy network of Gates's dad's friends in firm control.

Seattle politics is run by square-liberal boomers, by a Democratic machine in cahoots with high-powered attorneys and construction magnates.

This machine's progressive reputation is now cracking, as its obsessive-compulsive ideal of "A Clean City" (all-affluent, all-boomer, almost all-white) becomes more irreconcilable with reality and also with basic ideals of social decency. We're witnessing an end to the premise that whitebread 1968 liberal arts graduates know what's best for everybody and have everybody's best interests at heart.

With the poster law, the sitting law, the Commons plan, and the concerted drive to subsidize a bigger Nordstrom without bothering to replace Woolworth's, it's clear that the square-liberal boomers, and the politicians who strive for boomer appeal, aren't always on the side of what's best for the whole city. *(July 1994)*

The Real NW: One guy who'd just gotten off the plane from northern California two months ago was talking about how Washington voters "turned conservative" in the last election.

I tried to explain how we keep turning down progressive tax plans and bottle bills, how the near-loss of the women's-choice initiative was due more to

Airing It Out

After years of seeing favorite radio stations die from low ratings, what should happen but I get my very own one-week Arbitron diary. For $2 cash, I was to faithfully record every station I heard, whether at home, in a car, at work, or blaring out the neighbors' apartment at 2 a.m.

To carefully choose which stations deserved my temporarily-important endorsement, I kept the dial moving all week. Herewith, selected results:

KXPA-AM (1540): *The first big find of my search: Spanish-language music all day! (Except in some early-evening and weekend hours, when they've got programming in other languages.) It's on the onetime "Rock of the '80s" frequency where I first heard (among countless other 1979-81 alterna-greats) Wall of Voodoo's "(I'm On A) Mexican Radio."*

opponents' well-funded lies than any deep anti-choice sentiment, how we kept sending the build-more-bombs Scoop Jackson to the Senate, how we're no more or less conservative than ever. It's just getting harder to live up to this fantasy of Laidbackland, invented in the early '70s by the hippie diaspora who redefined every place they moved to according to late-hippie priorities.

The reality of pre-1970 Seattle (and its kids) is that our "tolerance" was more like apathy. We're not mellow; we're cold and sullen. The real spirit of the Northwest isn't in a Poulsbo bed-'n'-breakfast, it's in the acerbic Dog House waitresses and the bland Boeing corporate culture. *(January 1992)*

The spotted owl is just a symbol of a whole eco-scape in danger. It's not "environmental elitists" reducing timber-country jobs, it's companies with their "efficient" automated clearcuts and log exports. If the forest lands now used were used in a more sustainable manner (as opposed to the short-term cash amortization of "high yield forestry"), we wouldn't need to destroy the last of the old growth. *(May 1990)*

The Owl and the Pussycat: In endorsing the destruction of most spotted owl habitat in Washington, George Bush gave final proof of his total submission to big bucks. The owl is an indicator species whose disappearance signals the decline of an ecosystem. To move a few birds away as an excuse to level that ecosystem is the most cynical action that could be taken.

Few jobs will be saved by clearcutting at an already too-high level. Timber workers are out of work because of log exports, mill automation, corporate consolidation, and excess cutting from past years that's left too little old growth left and not enough tree-farm stands to replace them. *(June 1992)*

Behind the Pine Curtain: Oregon's Proposition 9, which would have officially dehumanized gays and lesbians, lost — but by a dangerously small margin. Its sponsor, the Oregon Citizens Alliance, plans to keep resubmitting the measure, to gain administrative control of the state Republican Party (onetime home to progressives like the late Gov. Tom McCall and Sen. Wayne Morse), and to start a Washington branch.

The OCA and the Idaho Nazis are not aberrations to the recent mystique of the "laid back" Northwest. Their presence reflects the logical extreme of the myth of "getting away from it all" to a refuge populated only by "people like us." This was one of the last parts of the continent that whites conquered. After that, we had race riots against Chinese laborers; after that, we sent our citizens of Japanese ancestry off to wartime internment camps. The "Northwest Lifestyle" ideology promotes turning one's back on "urban problems" (such as nonwhite people) and putting down roots in "God's country" where everybody's identically "nice" and wholesome.

We don't need any more of that. We need to attract people into the region who are willing to live among other people. *(December 1992)*

Karma Corn: If the new-age people are right when they claim that your fate in life is primarily determined by how positive or negative your attitude is, then perhaps the state's latest welfare reform craze is doomed from the get-go.

The current public-assistance system is a network of embarrassment, frustrating procedures and cumbersome eligibility requirements, a surefire way to get people to feel dejected and hopeless about their futures.

So of course, some of our legislators want to make the requirements even more picayune, the bureaucracy even harsher, to deliberately turn the system into a kind of psychic punishment for the sin of being poor. By the theory of karma, that's no way to turn depressed, hounded paupers into confident, assertive citizens.

Of course, conspiracy theorists might claim that's just what politicians want — to keep poor people feeling helpless, so they won't think about rising up to challenge the status quo. The same arguers might claim the current cry for a "War on Crime" throws money into an ever-bigger prison system expressly to turn amateur criminals into professional criminals, thus keeping the crime rate up, thus maintaining the perceived need for a police state that would gnaw away against personal rights.

I wouldn't go that far. I've been around long enough to see social systems (legal, bureaucratic, corporate, et al.) get sidetracked by traditional procedures and end up working against their ostensible original goals. It should be clear by now that we need an assistance system that encourages self-respect and initiative, and a justice system that teaches and encourages non-violent behavior. That is, it might be clear if we weren't living under government-by-talk-radio.

The real goal of our welfare system is to let politicians and affluent voters feel like they're getting tough on those

KGY-FM (96.9): *The second find: From Olympia, it's Real Country! The classics, plus those few recent Nashville hits that don't sound too wimpy alongside the classics.*

KMPS-FM (94.1): *"Hot Country" is formerly-country music for people who live in the former countryside, drivin' SUVs from the new subdivision to the new strip mall and imagining they've gotten back to the land. It's also less popular than it was last year.* A Media Inc. *article claims it's due to a glut of mediocre new acts, and also claims "country listeners don't want to hear failed rock 'n' roll garage bands that have turned to playing 'hot' country." The normally-astute* Media Inc.*'s wrong: Those garage-rockers all want to be the next Hank Snow, not the next Billy Ray Cyrus.*

KKDZ-AM (1250): *The former KidStar, now Radio Disney and airing in 24 U.S. cities, still plays a mix of novelty oldies, children's-CD tracks, contests, and phoned-in jokes. The main differences: More Disney-movie songs, and the Disney marketing muscle.*

KIRO-AM (710): *The grande dame of Northwest news-talk plows along at or near the top of the Arbitrons year after year. To indigenous Seattleites, the voices of Dave Ross and Bill Yeend are as familiar as Dave Niehaus's "Fly away!" News listeners like a voice of stability telling them about global chaos.*

KIXI-AM (880): *The Little Nostalgia Station That Could is now Seattle's #3 AM station (ahead of the higher-budgeted KJR, KOMO, and KNWX). Proof that there's occasionally justice in the world, even in the Arbitron world.*

KBKS-FM (106.1): *"The Kiss 106 Music Mix" is essentially the MTV playlist with fewer black acts, or the KNDD playlist without all the Pearl Jam copy bands. An adequate office choice if your cubicle-mates are too square to appreciate KIXI.*

KUBE-FM (93.3): *Black music played for (and by) white people; currently Seattle's #1 station. Its success means tuff luck for those who've pleaded for it to play some local hip-hop.*

bad ol' good-for-nothings. In this sense, we're already spending our tax money to make people feel good about themselves, but we're doing it in the wrong way for the wrong beneficiaries. *(April 1994)*

No Place Like Dome: The local TV stations, especially KOMO, still persist in their tirades against so-called "government waste," usually involving state or county buildings that were constructed for more money than they absolutely had to have been. Apparently, KOMO would prefer that all public works be built as cost-efficiently as the Kingdome originally was… *(September 1994)*

Dictatorship of the Upscale: This column and *The Stranger* have talked more about the Commons than the other money issue on next Tuesday's ballot, the new baseball stadium. The stadium measure, like similar measures across North America, is a simple matter of asking taxpayers to subsidize businesses. That's a story as old as the west, as old as railroads, agribusiness price supports, and unneeded weapons systems. (In western Canada they use slogans like "Partners in Progress" to promote subsidies for worthless oil scams.)

But the Commons represents a twist on public pay for private gain, a twist with implications for our future.

Around 1969-70 there was a revolution in City Hall: A slate of progressives ousted a machine of tired, inbred business interests. That new regime has calcified into a replica of the regime it replaced. Politics in Seattle is now essentially the same as in D.C.; i.e., money, power, privilege and to hell with anyone who can't offer any of them.

Seattle's political machine doesn't even claim anymore to speak for "The Little Guy." Seattle, steadily over the past 20 years but now accelerating rapidly, is becoming a city by, of, and for only one class. The upscale control the politicians, even the "progressive" politicians. The Upscale control the media (cf. KIRO-TV's hype-laden puff piece on the Nordstrom family, promoted as "The faces behind the brand name everyone loves!").

The upscale loathe real cultural diversity; they accept a culture of all races and nationalities who believe and behave exactly alike, like Disneyland's "It's A Small World" robots. Anybody who neither belongs to the upscale nor can be dismissed by it as "quaint local color" is beyond the pale. (Belltown condo dwellers circulated petitions some months back demanding the Vogue's closure.) Certain non-upscale subcultures have returned this loathing, though by and large the upscales don't know they're hated. (Corporate "designer grunge" fashion was such a joke because the "Seattle scene" aesthetic was anti-fashion, specifically anti-Nordstrom.)

The Seattle Commons is essentially a scheme to create an upscale haven *a la* Vancouver's West End, anchored by a mini-Stanley Park. It's an upscale wet dream; it removes blocks of non-Upscale businesses for upscale condos, stores, and dineries. And it'd remove some of those disgusting punk clubs too! The upscale insist on making Seattle a World Class City, even if it's ruined as a place for the rest of us to live. *(Sept. 13, 1995)*

Steamed Or Fried?: TV commentators on Primary Night claimed to be mildly astounded by the size of Norm Rice's loss in his run for governor. They attributed the defeat to his failure to get out the vote among his supposed core constituency of "urban liberals." Nobody mentioned how Rice wrote off that vote before his second mayoral term started.

From his status as a wholly-owned subsidiary of Nordstrom to his (or rather, the city's) continued attempt to remake Seattle into a city where only upscale baby boomers are welcome, Rice had nothing to offer progressives and little to offer voters elsewhere in the state. He made no viable promises that he wouldn't sell out the rural environment to agribusiness and Weyerhaeuser the way he's tried to sell out the urban environment to the condo developers and Paul Allen.

(Then there's the way his development program as Seattle mayor played against the rest of the state, by vying for housing stock and nonindustrial jobs that might otherwise go to other jurisdictions.)

I knew several Rice campaign staffers; while they're articulate, outgoing folks, they couldn't tell me what Rice's candidacy had to offer non-affluent and non-boomer voters. He might have had a chance running as a Dan Evans-style, mainstream, pro-business Republican, if that party were still run by sane people. Indeed, Demo primary victor Gary Locke is now running against GOP nominee Ellen Craswell as just that voice-O-moderation the GOP once claimed to be. *(Oct. 3, 1996)*

The Political Spectacle: I'd long wondered when the three not-all-that-compatible branches of Republican ideology (unfettered capitalism; moral prudery; anti-governmental ranting) would stumble apart on an issue. It might be happening in the newly-incorporated suburb of Shoreline, directly north of Seattle.

KYIZ-AM (1620): *Not much local hip-hop on the black-owned "Z Twins" stations either. But at least they've got DJs who insert some heart into their soul.*

KVI-AM (570): Times *columnist Michele Malkin, noting KVI's steady ratings drop in recent years, said it needed a dose of Viagra. I'd say its problems weren't due to medical deficiencies (or, alas, to shifting political tastes) but simply to the laws of entertainment.*

Rush Limbaugh's "unguested confrontation" schtick has about run its course; as he goes, so go the scores of Limbaugh-clone hosts around the country. Stations built around Limbaugh wannabes will stay in their ratings funk 'til the next talker fad (Dr. Laura clones? Financial advice?) heats up. Until then, expect hosts to keep spending ten minutes reading one news item, acting angry about it, and goading listeners to call in.

It's also an opportunity for those who've been yearning for a real progressive community station. There's several low-rated, probably unprofitable conserva-talk stations in the 1200-1600 AM neighborhood (plus new frequencies being allocated in the 1600-1700 range). The progs should get together, hit up friendly moneybags in the music and tech bizzes, and buy one of these.

(July 9, 1998)

There, managers and staff of the Sugar's strip club are circulating petitions on an initiative that, if it makes the ballot and passes, would change the new town's set-up to add an additional layer of bureaucracy. Sugar's management openly says it's doing this because it wants a government less capable of restricting operations at the club.

Anyhow, the initiative's chances of success are questionable. The Sugar's people (most of whom, along with most of the club's clientele, live outside Shoreline) have done a good job of publicizing their effort, but have done a poor job of communicating how their proposed governmental change would benefit the suburb's 5,000 residents.

Still, it's interesting to see the sex industry reaching out for public support, instead of just lobbying politicians and suing in courts to defend its right to exist. Club managers are betting that commercial pseudo-sex has become mainstream enough that Shoreline voters will agree to help the club stay in business. After all, it's not like they're a sports team demanding a subsidized arena or a department store demanding a pedestrian park be sliced in two.

[The initiative to change Shoreline's governmental system made it to the ballot but was voted down. Now, Sugar's is trying to avoid being over-regulated out of business by claiming it's not a business but a private club, dunning its patrons for "membership fees" instead of cover charges.] *(Oct. 23, 1997)*

Crass? Well...: Ex-GOP gubernatorial candidate Ellen Craswell has quit the Republican Party to start her own political movement, one where the purity of her authoritarian right-wing ideology wouldn't be compromised by those success-obsessed corporate Republicans. She plans to call her movement the American Heritage Party.

She apparently hadn't realized the name "American Heritage" is already trademarked, by a magazine and book line owned by that quintessential corporate Republican Steve Forbes, who's currently on a personal crusade to keep Religious Right followers within the Republican fold.

Will Steve object, or even care? Time will tell, or rather Forbes will. *(April 16, 1998)*

Our first major-league baseball team; it lasted one year.

8: SPORTS

and a few bad sports

Some Seattle development schemes, such as the Seattle Commons and the Urban Villages, were canned after agitators raised ruckuses over subsidizing private ventures. But other public-spending-for-private-gain measures have gone through. Citizens were dunned to support a new Nordstrom store in the former Frederick & Nelson building, and the ritzy Pacific Place mall next to it. And taxpayers here, as in other localities, have been persuaded to support fancy new sports palaces.

Seattle's teams (except University of Washington football) haven't furnished as many love fests as sympathy fests. Fans escaped their frustrating lives by entering the frustrating lives of their teams. The Sonics won an NBA championship in '79, and got as far in the mid-'90s as any Jordanless team could. The Mariners have recently approached baseball's top ranks. But on the whole, our teams have been loveable losers.

That hasn't stopped fans and politicians from trying to keep them around during the industry's years of fiscal turmoil — even while many younger fans turn away from old-line sports in favor of such trendier spectacles as women's basketball, snowboarding, and TV wrestling.

Thus, the dank yet homey Kingdome will be replaced by a new football palace; thanks to a tax package assembled by new Seahawks owner Paul Allen after the previous owner threatened to move to Anaheim, Calif. The Coliseum from the Seattle World's Fair was demolished for a new basketball house; and a baseball field rises next to the Kingdome site, on land originally assembled for a basketball house before that project moved to the Coliseum block.

Sonic Doom?: It's quite appropriate that Barry Ackerley's proposed basketball arena, for which city taxpayers would directly and indirectly bribe him not to move the Sonics, is on the site of a former railroad yard, near the old terminus of the Great Northern and Northern Pacific. These and other lines received massive tracts of free land by the U.S. government and decades of virtual land-transportation monopoly in their operating regions, in return for "opening" the American west to white settlement. *(June 1990)*

What's Your Sign?: The *P-I*'s Art Thiel wants the city to rename a street near the Kingdome in honor of the late Seahawks radio announcer Pete Gross. There's already Royal Brougham Way, a short side street south of the Dome named for a *P-I* sportswriter who died (in the press box!) in 1977 after 60 years on the job. I think the city also oughta turn one of the streets on the Dome's Fourth

Avenue South side into "South Long Street," so the Hawks could have an official street address at Fourth and Long. *(January 1993)*

I asked you a few weeks back to suggest Disneyland character mascots for what might become the Anaheim Ex-Seahawks. Your choices included Scrooge McDuck (natch), Jafar, and Cruella DeVil. My favorite was from the reader who, commenting on recent Seahawk seasons, recommended Sleepy. *(March 13, 1996)*

Whither the Kingdome?: It's not the echoing fan noise that made it such a good home for our teams. It's the way its homeliness, its blatant architectural mediocrity, complemented the lovable-loser status of the Seahawks and pre-Griffey Mariners. Its concrete cheapness symbolized an ex-frontier town wanting to become a Big League City but unwilling or unable to do it right. Paul Allen sez he won't buy the Hawks if they're stuck in an aging, luxury-boxless Dome. The new Ms owners said the same. Besides the economic considerations, I think both parties were uncomfortable with an overcast-grey box whose un-gussy-uppable look of thrift contradicted today's mania for yupscale pretension. Dunno 'bout you, but I'll miss the humble giant hamburger bun if Allen gets the county to tear it down. *(Dec. 19, 1996)*

I know it's impossible, but here's my fantasy: We move the now-surplused Kingdome to the Interbay landfill, then turn it into a community of tomorrow.

In the stands: moderately priced housing, artists' studios, offices, and light-industrial work spaces. In the corridors: tasty brewpubs and burger stands, charter schools, and convenient shops.

On the playing field: a combo park, playfield, bazaar, and art/performance space.

At least let's dismantle and rebuild the Dome's prefab pavilion annex for a year-round street fair, complete with food and merchandise booths, exhibits, and an all-ages music club. The gracefully-curved pavilion looks too neat (like an inner hallway in some giant space station) to just trash. *(July 3, 1997)*

Big Stadium Fall Down and Go Boom: It's more or less official. The homely yet homey home of Griffey and the Big Unit, of the Sonics' 1979 championship, of Promise Keeper rallies and U2 shows and monster trucks and Boeing strike votes, will go away, almost certainly in one

Other Voices
or Wish I'd Said That — Oh Wait, Now I Just Did

(Note: Dates below refer to when **Misc.** *first quoted these people,* **not** *when they originally said what was quoted.)*

"Great spirits have always encountered violent opposition from mediocre minds."
— Albert Einstein
"The mediocre mind you encounter may be your own."
— Gilbert Hernandez
(June 1986)

"A first-rate soup is more creative than a second-rate painting."
— A.M. Maslow
(April 1987)

From Shaka Zulu *(the live-action nudity-violence miniseries from the producers of* Robotech*):*
"Don't just stand there like a pack of old women, kill me!"
(June 1987)

Some of Team Chalk's work at Bumbershoot: "Outwit the great thief despair — an exercise in radical trust... It's always tornado season in someone's heart."
(October 1987)

"I have no relish for the country; it is a kind of healthy grave."
— Sydney Smith
(April 1988)

spectacular implosion. But when? If our area politicians had succeeded in attracting the 2000 Democratic National Convention, the Kingdome would probably have had to stay up until that August. But now that the Dems have removed Seattle from their list of convention hopefuls, the Dome can go boom whenever the exhibition facility in the south lot, between the Dome and the new baseball field, is done. Work on the exhibition hall can't really start until the adjacent new baseball stadium's complete, sometime around July 1999. Likely, that won't allow for an implosion party on the big Millennial New Year's, alas. *(May 21, 1998)*

Insurance Runs: Those ESPN *SportsCenter* punsters have lotsa fun with corporate-arena names. Vancouver's GM Place, they call "The Garage." Washington, D.C.'s MCI Arena: "The Phone Booth." Phoenix's BankOne Ballpark: "The BOB."

But what could be made from "Safeco Field" (paid-for moniker to the new Mariner stadium)? "The Claims Office" doesn't fall trippingly off the tongue.

'Though you could call the stadium's scoreboard "The Actuarial Table." Two games in a day could be a "Double Indemnity Header." Home and visitors' dugouts: "Assets" and "Liabilities." The retractable roof will be "the adjustable rate;" when the roof's enclosed it'll provide "blanket coverage." Fielding errors would be called "deductibles." Umpires would be "claims adjustors." A starting pitcher on a pitch-count limit would have "a term life policy," and would be pulled from the game when that policy "reached maturity." TicketMaster surcharages: "Co-Payments." *(June 18 and July 16, 1998)*

Good Buy, Baseball!: The Mariners' woes have a lot to do with a flaw in the social culture of Seattle. In the pioneer days, people (particularly women) came here to build a city, to create a society. In the recent past, Seattle attracted people who wanted to escape to "lifestyles" close to nature but far from people. It's a powerful fantasy that gives would-be baseball investors (or arts patrons) an excuse not to get involved. The sports that work here are those with tradition here (football) or league salary caps (basketball) or low costs (junior hockey).

Baseball, with 81 stadium-capacity home games, farm teams, and salaries essentially decided by the N.Y./L.A. teams, requires more (and more loyal) fans, more broadcast money, more ad money, and more long-term investment. Can we raise those things for good? *(October 1991)*

"There are many in this old world of ours who hold that things break about even for all of us. I have observed, for example, that we all get about the same amount of ice. The rich get it in the summertime and the poor get it in winter."
— Gambler-lawman Bat Masterson (June 1988)

"America is a continent composed completely of mongrels, and the only way someone can prove that they are pure is by pointing out someone else who's a mongrel."
— Playwright George C. Wolfe, at the Group Theatre (August 1988)

Ponder whether Shelley was predicting oldies radio when he wrote, "The world is weary of the past/ Oh, might it die or rest at last." (January 1989)

Appropriate-for-Valentine's line from local writer Theodore Roethke: "I think the dead are tender. Shall we kiss?" (February 1989)

"Everything that needs to be found out has been found out. The hard part is finding it again."
— Goethe
(November 1989)

"Two people who love the dream above all else would soon vanish altogether. One of them must be on earth to hold the other down. And the pain of being held down by the earth, that is what our love of others shall be."
— Anias Nin, in The All-Seeing
(December 1989)

"Try again. Fail again. Fail better."
— Samuel Beckett, in Worstward Ho
(January 1990)

"More people fail at becoming successful businessmen than fail at becoming artists."
— Author/educator John Gardner
(February 1990)

Bowing Down: For years, the Huskies struggled in the L.A. powerhouses' shadows, even though the UW was far bigger than any single California campus. But in the '80s the team grew toward three straight Rose Bowls and one of those "mythical national championships." We now know these achievements partly came by cheating on the vague regulations that let college ball pretend to be an amateur sport. Husky players had pathetic graduation rates, despite simplified classes and elaborate tutoring. There were allegations of drug dealing in the team dorm. Some players got cushy jobs and cushier cash, arranged by rich boosters.

Now, the Pac-10 Conference has saddled the team with recruiting restrictions, a two-year ban from bowl games, and other penalties. Coach Don James (who wasn't implicated in the charges) quit.

The violations had to have been known by authorities. How could they excuse the overzealousness? I think it's 'cuz the UW itself has become a big-money grant factory that relegated teaching to a very low priority. The campus got obsessed with being "a world class research institution," regardless of how well it serviced the state's kids.

We've discussed the yuppification of KCMU in the context of the UW corporate culture. The administration thought the station could raise more donations [and "underwriting"] with tamer programming; they'd funnel that into enough salaried staff positions to qualify the station for public-broadcasting grants. The men who turned KCMU into the New Coke of radio weren't malicious; they just behaved like good UW administrators. They saw no purpose higher than organizational growth.

Similarly, the football program was allowed or encouraged to grow by any means available. While tuitions skyrocketed and academic budgets stagnated, the team generated big cash surpluses. But little football money went up to the main campus. If rich alums want to pay for football, let 'em, within limits. But funnel part of that income, and a portion of Husky merchandising money, into academic scholarships. And go further with a professed priority of new athletic director Barbara Hedges: getting the players an education. They're risking permanent injury for the slim chance of a brief NFL career. If they can't get under-the-table cash, they oughta get a degree that might help 'em earn some bucks in the future. *(October 1993)*

Foul Tip: The Mariners opened another season amidst new hype about the team actually maybe winning a division this year (a new mini-Western Division shorn of the powerhouse White Sox). And as usual, a new season brings out the usual media hype of "Whither Baseball?" Here's what I think's wrong with the game: *(1)* a new TV contract worse than hockey's, with half the national cable games, no network games until July, and regional-only playoff telecasts — a setup that won't help promote the game to new fans; and *(2)* its reputation as the sport of writers and other dullards, who blather on about such esoterica as the dimensions of the field (I've never seen ponderous essays on how a basketball court's 96 feet long, a multiple of the sacred numbers 8 and 12). When they're not doing that, writers use baseball to conjure up images of that Bygone Innocent America, that nice all-white-middle-class wonderland that never was.

A game marketed to exploit grandpa's selective memories isn't gonna attract enough kids to maintain a decent supply of players, let alone a decent supply of fans.

(May 1994)

Snowed Under: I'd hoped that springtime would bring a seasonal end to articles about snowboarding, full of the requisite *MTV Sports*-style hyperbole, neon-drenched graphics, "unfocused" typefaces, and Prince-esque spellings ("D Place 4 U 2 B"). But instead there are now at least six year-round snowboard magazines, all more or less drenched in "grafique XS."

The art aside, there's a bigger issue at work: the case of a countryside athletic activity attracting an urbane-hip mystique. I'm meeting intelligent, club-going, artistically-minded young adults who play the sport, who either don't mind the hype about it or like it. To many old-line punkers and wavers such as myself, athleticism was the suspect domain of the Evil Jock Mentality, or of anti-intellectual adults (cf. "Get High On Sports Not Drugs" programs in school, which posited that the only alternative to being a mindless junkie was to be a hopeless jock).

Artistically-aware people weren't into sports; they were more likely to be beaten up by the guys who were into sports. But in recent years, some free-thinking youths have begun to accept that the human body might be useful for activities besides dancing, fighting, fucking, and dressing (cf. Eddie Vedder's surfer-dude acrobatics).

(May 1994)

It's the annual high week for commercials, culminating on Sooper Bowl Sunday. Recent years have seen far more excitement for the freshly-premiered ads during the big

"And after doing everything they do, they get up, they bathe, they powder themselves, they perfume themselves, they comb their hair, they get dressed, and so, progressively, they go about going back to being what they aren't."
— Julio Cortazar, in the "Love 77" chapter of A Certain Lucas
(February 1990)

"Guilt involves a sense of importance in the drama. To say that one is not guilty is also to acknowledge that one is in fact quite powerless."
— Philosopher Elaine Pagels, interviewed in Bill Moyers's A World of Ideas
(March 1990)

One of the less-controversial lines in Salman Rushdie's The Satanic Verses*: "Should the inflight movie be thought of as a particularly vile, random mutation of the form, one that would eventually be extinguished by natural selection, or were they the future of the cinema? A future of screwball caper movies eternally starring Shelley Long and Chevy Chase was too hideous to contemplate; it was a vision of Hell."*
(May 1990)

Tracey Ullman on her role in I Love You to Death: *"Because the accent is Northwestern, it was tough to stay in character all the time. Southern accents are easy and so are New York accents, but the Northwest accent is the most pure of all the accents. You can't just put one accent on top of another. You have to lose your accent completely." (May 1990)*

"I left my exercise session after I'd only done one leg. I risked asymmetry." — Author-social critic Barbara Ehrenreich (Fear of Falling) *in* New York *magazine (June 1990)*

"Novels, except as aids to masturbation, play no part in contemporary life." — Gore Vidal, quoted in the underground newspaper East Village Other *(10/68) (July 1990)*

Words in Moby Dick *that don't make it into most adaptations: "Better to sleep with a sober cannibal than with a drunken Christian." (August 1990)*

game than for the game itself, which is usually either a rout or a dogged defensive battle. I know it's fashionable in "hip" circles to denounce football and those who watch it.

I also know why. Virtually every sensitive young intellectual in America had to survive adolescent harassment from crude jocks or bitchy cheerleaders, in schools that often gave more honor to touchdowns than to learning. But part of growing up is getting beyond old pains.

Besides, you can't understand this culture without understanding how American football encapsulating the essential myths and images of America. It's a vast real estate on which violence and raw ambition are held in place by persnickity bureaucratic rules. It's gross caricatures of masculinity, tempered on the sidelines by gross caricatures of femininity. It's the dream, fulfilled only occasionally enough to remain tempting, of flying and running free. *(Jan. 24, 1995)*

'Xtreme' Prejudice: Matt Groening's comic *Life in Hell* used to run an annual list of "Forbidden Words" for the new year. If he were still doing it, I'd nominate "extreme" and its recent variation "Xtreme." Marketers everywhere are out to exploit that "extreme sports" fad. Afri-Cola's consumer-hype number is 800-GO-XTREME. And Pacific Northwest Bank offers an "Xtreme CD."

Easy why companies want to identify with snowboarding, Rollerblading, bungee and even the socially-maligned skateboarding. They bear a vener of "alternative" or even "punk" street-cred, but can be interpreted to celebrate today's "lean and mean" corporate aesthetic — especially the way ads downplay the camaraderie of group noncompetitive adventure and emphasizing the solitary white-boy athlete triumphing over gravity and other squares' laws.

One can imagine your Benzo-drivin,' cell-phone-yappin' New Right hustler imagining himself as a sailboarder of business, riding waves of Power and Money while conquering the turbulence of do-gooder environmentalists and regulators. *(Oct. 11, 1995)*

The Seahawks' recent attendance woes coincide with the slow decline of the NFL. American football was "The College Game" for the first half of the century. The pro game was a novelty sport, far less popular than baseball, before TV showed how to market it. The networks and NFL Films took what was structurally a game of coaching, of the execution and interruption of pre-planned plays, and turned it into a spectacle of heroes and villains, of noble warriors and ignoble bullies.

But now, the league's owners have come to believe themselves to be the invicible warriors lionized by NFL Films. Despite sagging attendance and TV ratings here and in other areas, the owners are playing stadium blackmail with cities on such a scale that I'd need to use a Telestrator on a map of North America to explain it. They're going all-out for subsidized luxury-box arenas now, because they've seen the Telestrating on the wall. With the long-term decline of network TV, so will go the first real made-for-TV sport. Why watch a bunch of guys whose faces you can't see knocking each other down when there's women's college basketball on Prime Sports? *(Nov. 29, 1995)*

Junior's Mint: So we'll keep Ken Griffey Jr. after all, for only the highest salary in baseball history. Sure, we all have to pay a piece of it thanks to the complexities of the Ms/Kingdome lease. But for that, we get a genuine star athlete, a living mascot for the new stadium deal (a role he can keep playing even if he gets another half-year injury), and an affable spokesperson for Nintendo and whoever else can pay him.

Griffey also said he wanted to be on a team that doesn't sell off some of its best players, like the Ms keep doing so they can afford to keep him. The Ms' problems as a "small market franchise," trying to keep one megastar plus an adequate team behind him, are well known. What isn't known is how to keep big players in small cities in an age of luxury boxes, owner-city blackmail, and splintering TV audiences.

Baseball was historically a hierarchical business. Minor leagues fed players to the majors, which had an established pecking order with the Yankees and old N.Y. Giants always around the top, the Washington Senators and St. Louis Browns around the bottom. Lesser teams sold any promising players to the Yankees just to pay their hotel bills. (Remember the early years of Thunderbirds hockey, when they traded a player for a team bus?)

In today's baseball, under the right circumstances, a Cleveland or maybe even a Seattle can win a pennant. Is this situation a trend or just an anomaly? Wait 'til this year. *(Feb. 7, 1996)*

In-Bounds Pass: Many of you remember Bob Blackburn Jr. as the sometime statistician and broadcast assistant to his dad, the SuperSonics' original radio announcer. Bob

"It's important that human life not be reduced to stereotypes of production and consumption, but that it be open to all possibilities; it's important that people not be a herd, manipulated and standardized by the choice of consumer goods and consumer television culture… It is important that the superficial variety of one system, or the repulsive grayness of the other, not hide the same deep emptiness of life devoid of meaning."
— Vaclav Havel, in Disturbing the Peace *(August 1990)*

"Our view of reality is conditioned by our position in space and time, not by our personalities as we would like to think. Thus, every interpretation of reality is based upon a unique position. Two paces east or west and the position is changed."
— Lawrence Durrell, in The Alexandria Quartet *(October 1990)*

Graphic novelist Moebius, in the afterword to one of his tastefully-drawn stories of spaceships, pyramids and breasts: "I never give the keys to my stories. My stories are not like a box of spaghetti, they don't come with the instructions on them on how long you must put them in boiling water before you eat." *(November 1990)*

It's a shame the local black community weekly The Facts *has such ugly design and typography, because some truly eloquent African-American voices may be found there. For example, hear the bitter "Life Among the Thorns" edition of F. Justina Nubay's column "Say It With Flowers": "I wholeheartedly believe that Thanksgiving should continue to be the only day when public spirited people ply the hungry with turkeys, pies, and other filling foods, enough to last them the entire year. Like the howling hyena, the hungry and the homeless, for the time remaining, should continue to gorge themselves on carrion and roam their jungles in wild anguish."* *(December 1990)*

Jr. also played in assorted Seattle bands (including the Colorplates) before moving to L.A. in '89. He now works for the Westwood One satellite-radio empire, conducting celebrity interviews and organizing promotions. Last month his job led to the fulfillment of a longtime dream, the chance to meet '50s bondage model Betty Page.

Blackburn chatted with her for an hour and got her to autograph a picture for his friends in the Seattle sleaze-punk outfit Sick & Wrong. He says Page "still looks really good" at 73, but won't let herself be photographed. I think Blackburn should invite her to come work with his ex-employers. The Sonics (especially Shawn Kemp) could use someone to teach some discipline! *(May 15, 1996)*

Sonics postmortem: For four glorious days, the whole city (save a few droller-than-thou alternative conformists) believed. Imagine — a team of great players could beat a team of spokesmodels! Like the Seattle music scene (to which the Sonics have consistently made closer overtures than any other local sports team), the Sonic victories celebrated talent, diligence, and cooperation instead of celebrity, arrogance, and corporate hype. How appropriate that it happen two weeks before the opening of Planet Hollywood, that chain restaurant expressly devoted to corporate celebrity hype, and which staged a PR stunt with professional hypemeister Cindy Crawford telling us if we were smart we'd root against our own team. Can you say, "Not quite the way to make new friends for your business"? *(June 27, 1996)*

For as long as I could remember, Seattle was a sometimes-lovable loser of a city, whose "leaders" (mainly engineers, land developers, and steakhouse owners) wanted to become "world class" but usually muffed it. The Mariners, who played unspectacularly for so many years in that homely cement pit, matched this civic image perfectly. The same time Seattle became known as an assertive seller of software and coffee and sportswear, the Ms started becoming winners. This year, they not only won their division but had been widely expected to do so.

Microsoft and Starbucks have become so dominant, they've generated ire within their respective industries as hyper-aggressive organizations bent on total domination. The Ms are a ways from that kind of rep, but how many consecutive seasons at or near the top would it take before they became as nationally reviled as the old-time Yankees? Just wondering. *(Oct. 2, 1997)*

A Lovely Mat Finish: The Monday after Newt Gingrich resigned and Jesse Ventura became governor of Minnesota, I tried to watch the competing pro wrestling shows on cable. No longer the pseudo-sport for dummies, wrestling's now a pair of complex soap-opera plot threads that no first-time viewer can even hope to sort out. These threads play out all year long on the basic-cable shows (one of which, WWF's *Raw Is War,* will hold a cablecast from the Tacoma Dome on Dec. 14); leading to climaxes not during Neilsen ratings sweeps weeks but on separate pay-per-view events.

On some shows (the World Wrestling Federation has four hours a week on USA; the Time Warner-owned World Championship Wrestling has seven weekly hours split between Time Warner's TNT and TBS channels), the shouting and the theatrics drag on far longer than the action.

The theatrics, the action, and the characterizations are all far more "X-treme" than during rasslin's last heyday when Ventura pretended to hate Hulk Hogan. The matches themselves now bear only a miniscule resemblance to real (high school, college, and Olympic) wrestling, and have more in common with that banned-in-every-state gorefest known as "ultimate fighting" (tactics include kickboxing, bare-knuckles boxing, and explicit crotch-grabbing).

The combatants' grandiose personas and rhetorical bombast certainly have a lot in common with Newt's now-disgraced system of governance by blowhardedness — except wrestlers, unlike Republicans (and particularly Republican talk-radio hosts) are always ready to directly confront their foes, instead of staying safely within one-sided environments. In this regard, Ventura (as the first candidate from Ross Perot's Reform Party to make it to a high office) may actually prove more effective than Perot himself would have.

And then there's the strange case of WWF proprietor Vincent McMahon. A few years ago he presented himself to the world as the underdog of faux-sports titans, a third-generation family businessman (with a son he was grooming to eventually take over from him) struggling to compete against the conglomerate-backed WCW. These days, he's taken on the TV persona of a corrupt corporate overlord, taking personal sides in the matches he telecasts to favor the baddest of the bad guys. (He even designates his favorites as "corporate champions"!)

At one time, rasslin' villains bore colors of Russians and Iranians. Now, they've captured changes in the popular

"Maybe the American Dream is like the Civil War chess set: Once you've bought the board you're committed to buying the rest of the pieces."
— Spin *magazine founder Bob Guccione Jr., in a 1986 editorial (February 1991)*

From **Misc.** *subscriber Steve Shaviro's book on social theory,* Passion and Excess: *"Power itself never notices, but the one thing it cannot regulate or pacify is its own violent arbitrariness, its own quality as an event." (March 1991)*

The only memorable lines in Manoel De Oliveira's obscure 1983 Portugese film Francisca *(about a beautiful woman dying of consumption): "Men have hearts like dry bread;" "I love you like God loves sinners." (March 1991)*

"There is no clear borderline between the past, which grows and feeds on the present, and the future, which, it would seem, is neither inexhaustible nor incessant, so that in some places it is reduced or comes in spurts."
— Milorad Pavic, in Landscape Painted With Tea *(April 1991)*

"I have a little story to tell and I end neither with a death nor a marriage. Death ends all things and so is the comprehensive conclusion of a story, but marriage finishes it very properly too and the sophisticated are ill-advised to sneer at what is by convention termed a happy ending. It is a sound instinct of the common people which persuades them that with this all that needs to be said is said. When male and female, after whatever vicissitudes you like, are at last brought together they have fulfilled their biological function and interest passes to the generation that is to come."
— W. Somerset Maugham, in the introduction to The Razor's Edge *(May 1991)*

imagination and re-emerged as the toadies of Big Business. McMahon, who's perfectly willing to be hated by his audiences as long as they keep watching, has caught onto a shift in the public zeitgeist, before WCW's sister company *Time* magazine discovered corporate welfare. He could've taught ol' Newt about this, if either had cared. (Does Ventura know about this shift? Most likely.) *(Nov. 19, 1998)*

You Gotta Love Them, Or It, Or...: The Seattle Reign's a great B-ball squad, but that darned name just doesn't fall trippingly off the tongue.

These awkward singular-named sports teams just could be the one and only lasting legacy of the 1974-75 World Football League (whose teams included the Chicago Fire, Southern California Sun, and Portland Storm). What, exactly, do you call one member of the Reign (or the Miami Heat or Orlando Magic or Utah Jazz, for that matter)? *(Dec. 21, 1998)*

Misc. was amused by the double standards and double dribbles in that front-page *P-I* headline on Dec. 22: "Reign star Ennis judges basketball, parenthood." Y'ever see a headline like that about, say, Shawn Kemp?

Alas, that *P-I* story was one of the last written in the local dailies about the Seattle Reign before the team's parent American Basketball League announced its sudden, permanent shutdown, leaving fans as bereft of pro women's b-ball as it is of the men's game. One could lay the blame for the ABL's demise on the rival WNBA, with its megabucks backing, its marketable-superstar orientation, and its stranglehold on sponsors and TV outlets.

But a less-discussed factor was the league's management structure. While it claimed to be a grassroots, fan-level outfit, it was really a centralized company which owned all its teams, hired and assigned all its players, and otherwise tightly ran all operations and marketing — just like the Roller Derby, Arena Football, and other assorted marginal team-sports ventures of the past three decades.

The graveyard of new team-sports organizations in North America is full of four decades' worth of great and less-great visions, from the American Basketball Association the World Football League, and the U.S. Football League, to World Team Tennis and several attempts at indoor soccer.

Aside from the American Football League (which got all its teams merged into the NFL in the late '60s), none were long-term successes. (The only current such ventures with a chance at making it big are Major League Soccer and the aforementioned WNBA.) None of those attempts found the formula for nationwide popularity and profits; though some tried to find such a formula through centralized management.

A single-ownership league structure (like that of the ABL) can present a unified public image and prevent a single well-heeled team owner from attaining an uncompetitive dynasty situation (like that which ruined the old North American Soccer League). But it also means local team managers can't build their own squads, around personalities or playing styles popular in their own towns. And when league HQ runs out of cash or ideas, there aren't local team owners (or buyers) to come up with individual solutions other teams can copy.

But for now, the WNBA (with its emphasis on megabucks and celebrity-driven advertising, and its neglect (or worse) of any lesbian fan base) is the remaining structure for women's pro hoops, at least until the parent NBA can no longer afford to subsidize it (which, if there's not even a mini-NBA season, might be more likely). Wish I had more encouraging news for stranded Reign fans, but a pro league of any sort, especially one with teams scattered across the continent, is an undertaking requiring immense logistics, savvy, and long-term backing. The ABL way didn't work, and neither has just about any other way. *(Dec. 28, 1998)*

Loss of Down: Another Super Bowl Sunday's on the way, and with it the usual pseudo-intellectual garbage about pro football as an institution of violence and stupidity and that perennial fall guy testosterone — even though football puts more kid through college than any other sport, even though it's really a game of coaching and choreography as much as one of hitting and tackling, and even though it's got enough female fans for QVC to have once offered NFL-logo costume jewelry trinkets.

Time staff essayist Lance Morrow recently claimed, "Football, still in bad odor among thinkers, needs a fancier mystique;" then proceeded to offer up a "deconstructionist theory" of the sport — which, natch, turned out to be less a defense of the gridiron game than a send-up of PoMo egghead jargon. ("Football enacts the Foucaultian paradigm wherein all actions, even involuntary motions or 'fakes' or failures (quarterback sacked), coalesce in meaning, and everything that the game organizes in the way of objects, rites, customs (the superstitious butt slapping, the narcissistically erotic Bob Fosse touchdown

David Landis in USA Today, *5/20, on the Miss Universe pageant: "As usual, the universal competition included a large contingent — 73 — from Earth, but no contestants from any other planet or solar system." (June 1991)*

From Aristophanes' play Lysistrata, *a love poem of a Spartan warrior to his lady: "How shines thy beauty, O my sweetest friend! How fair thy color, how full of life thy frame! Why, thou couldst choke a bull!" (June 1991)*

"Love, well made, can lead to wisdom." — From Peter Brooks's film version of The Mahabharata *(October 1991)*

"Our next age is the first in human history that will have all prior ages to gaze upon at will." — Walter Kendrick, in The Thrill of Fear: 250 Years of Scary Entertainment *(November 1991)*

"When a man tells you he got rich through hard work, ask him whose?" — archy and mehitabel *creator Don Marquis (December 1991)*

"Intellect alone has never changed anyone. All change comes from the heart." — *Child-development expert Joseph Chilton Pearce, in the Canadian journal* Edges *(February 1992)*

Swedish author Par Lagerkvist imagining the sayings of a Delphi oracle in The Sibyl *(1956): "We gather knowledge which we call truth from those in whom we least believe, and unconsciously let ourselves be led by what we most heartily detest." (March 1992)*

Role-playing-game creator Steve Jackson's policy on not depicting fantasy swordsmen/women in G-strings: "Battle is not the place for recreational nudity." (March 1992)

"Nostalgia is the eighth deadly sin. It shows conempt for the present and betrays the future." — *Stephen Bayley, in* Taste: The Secret Meaning of Things *(April 1992)*

dances) constitutes a coherent whole — the game *lui-meme.*")

I, however, am not afraid to stake whatever remaining highbrow street-cred I might have on the line by actually and sincerely stating my praise for the game. I've (largely) grown out of my sensitive-post-adolescent jock-hating phase (my above remarks about snowboarding hype notwithstanding), and have come to an honest appreciation of the Big Game played by Big Dudes, their bodies (and usually their faces) hidden beneath the group-identity of the uniform, their individual heroics interdependent upon the coordinated effort of the entire team. A game with separate offensive and defensive players, in which fully half the participants can usually achieve nothing but "loss prevention." (Hmm — maybe Safeco should've bought the naming rights to the new football stadium instead of the new baseball stadium.)

Here, then, is my partial list of what makes the perfect Super Bowl experience (please feel free to print this out and keep score at home):

- At least four hours of increasingly shrill yet picayune pregame "coverage."
- The National Anthem sung by somebody who can't hit the high notes or forgets the words.
- At least one safety.
- A missed point-after-touchdown.
- A successful really-long field goal.
- First and third quarters ending within the 10 yard line (if the teams are going to change sides at the quarter breaks, it should be as overt as possible).
- A homemade sign in the stands listing a Bible verse other than John 3:16. (My fantasy: To hold up signs displaying the verse numbers for the passages about Onan spilling his seed, or King David spying on the bathing Bathsheba, or the sequence of "And Judas went into the potter's field and hanged himself," "Go thou and do likewise," and "Whatsoever ye do, do so quickly.")
- At least 20 increasingly shrill promos for the premiere of a new hit series, or the special episode of an established hit series, to air "immediately following the game."
- A marching-band rendition of a contemporary hit song not originally meant for horns. ("Mmm Bop," or maybe "Cop Killer.")
- A scoreless third quarter (so you can get to the convenience store for restocking without missing the halftime extravaganza).
- A really ridiculous touchdown-celebration dance. (Perhaps involving pirouettes.)

• A pair of wasted time outs early in the fourth quarter.

• A penalty assessed against one team for having 12 men on the field, negated by a penalty for the other team having 13 men on the field.

• A true blooper-reel moment (a player running in the wrong direction, or the inadvertant tackle of a sidelines microphone operator).

• A good Master Lock commercial.

• A dumb Pepsi commercial.

• The whole thing coming down to one last come-from-behind miracle play that either somehow succeeds or at least comes very close.

• At least an hour of anticlimactic postgame rehashing.

• A premiere premiere of a new hit series, or the special episode of an established hit series, eventually following the postgame denouments and turning out to really suck. *(Jan. 25, 1999)*

"People who look for trouble never fail to find it. Other people never look for misfortune, pain, or woe, but it finds them just the same." — Miami crime reporter Edna Buchanan in Never Let Them See You Cry *(April 1992)*

(continued)

9: SEATTLE PEOPLE

or, stars in a place supposedly without stars

Canned-music company's Hendrix statue.

Besides sports stars, every big city needs a quotient of "local celebrities" to co-host telethons and benefit dinners, pose for lifestyle magazine covers, provide fodder for newspaper feature stories, endorse restaurants and politicians, and fill time on radio talk shows. Seattle didn't used to have a lot of national celebs, but we've had a goodly supply of homegrown stars and semistars; plus a few folks who left here for true fame or infamy. Then came the rock scene and performance artists and glass artists and software czars and coffee moguls.

In the new Heart video, all shots of Ann Wilson are filmed in wide-screen, then "squeezed" to disguise her real width. It's a sad piece of denial, far more disfiguring than an honest portrayal of her true self would be. *(January 1988)*

A Classic Tragedy: Cable's American Movie Classics channel seldom lives up to its name; but on Jan. 14 it ran one of the weirdest pieces of video ever shot: the Frances Farmer episode of *This Is Your Life.* The 1958 live telecast, made at the start of Farmer's return to public life after her years in and out of psychiatric hospitals, shows the Seattle-born actress staring into space while greasy-haired host Ralph Edwards (who also created *Truth or Consequences*) rattled off a summary of her sad life story. During her turns to speak, she looked offstage (possibly to a prompter). In an elegant but slurred voice, she slowly explained that "I did not believe and still do not believe that I was truly ill." At the end, she was rewarded for her bravery with a new Edsel. *(February 1990)*

We're bemused by the recent flap that Chief Sealth (the Milli Vanilli of the 1850s) never spoke about buffalo and railroads (which he never saw) and may not have said all attributed to him in the famous 1887-published translation of an 1854 speech. Hate to disillusion you, but folks often get famous for things they never actually said (Jesus never spoke in King James English, Bogart never said "Play It Again Sam"). Sealth has become a figure around which a body of ideas has coalesced — the best way for anyone to become immortal. *(August 1991)*

Robert E. Lee Hardwick, 1931-1992: Before what we now call "talk radio" took off here, he ran a chat show with a few records. He was adamant that non-rock radio need not mean "middle of the road." He ruled Seattle radio (adult division) from the late '50s to 1980, when new KVI management decided his postwar-jazz sensibility was an anachronism.

He spent a decade wandering from station to station, supported in some years only by commercial endorsements. Sponsors loved his straightforward, no-nonsense persona; station managers hated it, because it contradicted the hype and hustle of modern radio. He was a Scotch-on-the-rocks guy in a wine-cooler world.

Two months after losing his last gig (on KING-AM), he drove into the Cascades and blew his brains out. The KING-TV newscast that announced his death had one of his commercials (for Honda dealers). *(July 1992)*

Recluse Disregard (*Times*, Oct. 24): "Paul Allen is the shyest multibillionaire you'll never meet."

Fact is, almost all our rich people are private souls. Throughout the town's history, and especially since the foiled kidnapping plot against nine-year-old George Weyerhaeuser in 1936, our "prominent" families have been among the most reticent of any local elites in the country. While other towns' tycoons hosted charity balls and funded symphonies and museums, our rich kids went home every night to their suburban estates and their car collections. It's always been a bitch trying to get high-culture or nightlife things started here, 'cuz too many of our "civic leaders" wanted no part of social activity. Even now, attempts to start entertainment concepts for rich kids usually fail, 'cuz even young Microsoft stock millionaires will drive from Woodinville to Seattle only when they absolutely must. *(December 1993)*

Church Windows: Some members of St. Mark's Cathedral want glass artist Dale Chihuly to design the Episcopal landmark's still-unfinished interior. I'd always thought of the Episcopalians/Anglicans as a religion of grandeur and spectacle. Chihuly, who sells prosaic decorative bowls to Microsoft millionaires, would be all wrong for that (though I like his idea to freeze neon lights inside the Tacoma Dome hockey surface). His passionless work would be more appropriate to my alma mater denomination, the Methodists. *(July 1993)*

Mouths-O-Babes (overheard gleeful shriek of an 8-year-old girl on a bus, passing the Bon's Chihuly window promoting ArtFair '94): "See mom, I told you! Big cereal bowls!" *(March 1994)*

Other Voices
(continued)

*"So let us love and eat and mulch, there isn't any other obvious reason to be here."
— from Gregory Hischak's zine* Farm Pulp *(May 1992)*

*"The trouble with us Americans is we always want a tragedy with a happy ending."
— from Hal Hartley's TV movie* Surviving Desire *(May 1992)*

*"Anything worth doing is worth doing badly, at least for a little while."
— local artist Joanne Branch, in her recent show at Art/Not Terminal (June 1992)*

John Kricfalusi, the cartoonist-director-actor who made Ren & Stimpy *into the cult sensation of the year (and just got fired for his trouble by Viacom bureaucrats), quoted in* Film Threat *before his dismissal: "Everybody's ugly in real life. You just have to look close. Look inside anybody's nose. Look in — who's the big actress today? Look inside her nose and then think about porkin' her." (October 1992)*

"I've heard it said, the more simple people are, the more complex they seem to other people, because those people are so complex that they don't understand simplicity."
— Charita Bauer, near the start of her 35-year acting stint on Guiding Light *(November 1992)*

Cyberpunk author John Shirley, quoted in the Mondo 2000 *compilation book: "It's a big world. t's a swollen world. It's a tumescent world. It's an overburdened, overflowing, data-loaded, high-content, low-clarity world, soaked in media and opinion and, above all, lies. What's important in all this input? Who decides? Which filters have you chosen? Have you mistaken the filters for the truth?" (January 1993)*

AutoWeek *publisher Leon Mandel, quoted on the sales surge in big pickup trucks: "Something in the American spirit likes great size and a lack of subtlety." (February 1993)*

Dixy Lee Ray, 1914-1994: Dr. Ray was a quintessential Northwest Strong Woman: individualistic and headstrong, refusing the rules society prescribed for her yet very willing to impose social rules on others, turning reactionary when confronted with ideas newer than hers. Her gruff schoolmarmish charm made her one of KCTS's first stars, leading to her appointment to run the science exhibits at the 1962 World's Fair. She championed the fair's predictions of a soon-to-come utopia, to be fueled by cheap, safe atomic power (part of a giant federal hype campaign to bring civilian investment into Cold War technology).

A year after the fair closed she became director of the exhibit's permanent successor, the Pacific Science Center. There, she shooed hippies away from the reflecting pools with her self-described "bullhorn" voice, keeping the messy present from interfering with her pristine atomic future. In 1972 Nixon put her in charge of the Atomic Energy Commission, where she shilled for the nuke industry while snubbing the bureaucrats she worked beside. She registered as a Democrat as a flag of convenience in the post-Watergate 1976 election, when her "outsider" image and insider connections helped her get elected governor. Like the Republicans in 1980, she ran as a valiant populist but became a suck-up to big business. During and after her single term (irate liberals blocked her re-nomination), she bashed environmentalists as know-nothing obstructionists meddling against the righteous path of growth.

Even in her final week, she scoffed at scandals over old U.S. radiation tests on unknowing human subjects. She used her mastery of scientific jargon not toward "scientific method" but to advocate blind trust in authority. She was a true pioneer, stubbornly holding to the frontier mentality of relentless exploitation. *(February 1994)*

Mia Zapata, 1965-1993: In the past three years I've said goodbye in print to six members of the local music/arts scenes. They all died needlessly and too soon. This may be the most senseless death of them all. Zapata, a poet, painter and singer-lyricist for the Gits, was found strangled in an alley near 25th and South Washington, an hour and a half after she left a small get-together at the Comet Tavern, honoring the one-year anniversary of her friend Stefanie Sargent's fatal overdose. Zapata died a week before she was to have finished the Gits' second CD. I knew her only as a presence on a stage, a dynamic presence delivering some powerful and fun tunes, a voice rooted in the early notion of punk rock as a statement of positive defiance, not just a lowbrow lifestyle.

Some people ask me how Seattle bands can be so strident and negative, contradicting the official image of Seattle as heaven on earth. I tell those people to look around themselves: There's a madness here, subtlely different from the madness in the nation at large. Due partly to our western boomtown heritage and surviving Greed Decade attitudes, far too many people here believe they have the right to do anything they want, to whomever they want. Seattle's "nice" image is at best a cover-up, at worst an emotional repression. Beneath the enforced attitude of passivity, you'll find a barely-contained force of sheer terror. There's no running away from it; you'll still find that terror in the white-flight suburbs and the hippie-flight countryside. Don't move out, stay and reclaim the public space. Do that and we can help fulfill the pledge shouted by the people at her wake, "Viva Zapata!" *(August 1993)*

Kholerik Korner: Bruce Chapman, whom I'd always thought to have been one of that increasingly-rare breed of respectable, thoughtful conservatives, wrote in a *P-I* op-ed column a few weeks back, "Is the conservative revolution running out of steam? No — not to hear John Carlson tell it on his KVI talk show. Indeed, the jovial Carlson, who infuriates liberals, is even more gleeful than usual these days"... "I have enjoyed John's company ever since he was a delightfully irreverent college student at the University of Washington, assaulting the choleric dogmas of the *UW Daily*."

(1) As I've said before, if KVI said it was raining outside I'd still want it confirmed by a credible source.

(2) Carlson's not so much "jovial" as snide, his snickers more like the sneers of a comic-book-movie villain or a schoolyard bully.

(3) "Infuriating liberals" is a mark of laziness at the art of offense. It's almost as easy as offending Christians.

(4) Carlson's really quite reverent toward the three things in which he's publicly demonstrated sincere beliefs — power, money, and ego.

(5) I was editor of the *Daily* when Carlson, then a member of the Board of Student Publications, tried to censure me for editing down a "humor" piece by a friend of his about Ted Kennedy, similar to modern O.J. "jokes." If Chapman wants to call me "easily angered; bad tempered" (the *American Heritage Dictionary* definition of "choleric"), I can take it. If somebody called Carlson

"I like men who have a future and women who have a past."
— Elbert Hubbard, in the June 1911 edition of his self-published tract (the old term for zine) The Philistine *(March 1993)*

"The confusion is not my invention... It is all around us and our only chance is to let it in. The only chance of renovation is to open our eyes and see the mess."
— Samuel Beckett, quoted in 1988 by Lawrence Shainberg (March 1993)

"Beliefs are ideas going bald."
— Surrealist Francis Picabia (April 1993)

James Darren in a pseudo-profound moment in Venus in Furs *(1970): "When you don't know where you're at, man I tell you time is like the ocean. You can't hold onto it." (May 1993)*

Updates: Last time, we commented on the fad for every business to have a "mission statement." The cool new Xerox art/literary zine Hel's Kitchen *has one of its own: "Mission Statement: Missions were built in California to obliterate the native customs and spread colonization... We hate them." (June 1993)*

"The west does not need to explore its myths much further; it has already relied on them too long. The west is politically reactionary and exploitive: admit it. The west as a whole is guilty of inexplicable crimes against the land: admit that, too. The west is rootless, culturally half-baked. So be it." — Wallace Stegner (June 1993)

something like that, the rich pretty boy would probably whine about the Big Bad PC Thought Police trying to stifle his daring voice of rebellion. People who can raise out-of-state capital to start newspapers and think tanks are not helpless silenced voices. And people who suck up to the real centers of power in this society are not rebels, no matter how big their Harleys are. *(Dec. 13, 1995)*

You'd expect MTV to go all hyped-out over Madonna's baby. Sure enough, the day the birth was announced, the channel went to all Madonna videos, with congratulations by MTV Online users crawled across the bottom of the screen, interspersed with predictions by infomercial psychics about the kid's future life.

What at least I didn't expect was an MTV promo ad featuring drag queens dressed up as aged versions of Madonna and Courtney Love, re-enacting a scene from the cult-film classic *What Ever Happened to Baby Jane?*, complete with barbed dialogue like "Why don't you go reinvent yourself?" Given Love's former taste for baby-doll dressing and Madonna's former Joan Crawford fixation, it's a wonder nobody thought of it before. *(Oct. 31, 1996)*

By the time this comes out, we'll have seen if the local media that got aghast over Annie Dillard's remarks about the area's intellectuals (or lack of them) will be equally incensed over the more deliberately nasty barbs of Nanci Donnellen, KJR-AM's former Fabulous Sports Babe.

In her new book, predictably titled *The Babe in Boyland,* the now-syndicated gabber calls her ex-stomping ground "a hopeless zero" and "a fucked-up backwater town... filled with the dumbest people in the world." Her KJR colleagues? "Small-time nobodies who thought that because they lived in Seattle they were some big deal and that the rest of the world should come kiss their asses." Further, she writes how when she moved here from Tampa she pledged to work to get the Mariners moved there. Her introduction thanks Jeff Smulyan, the ex-Ms owner who tried to facilitate such a move, whom she calls one of her "true friends." Yawn. *(Nov. 28, 1996)*

I'm still thinking about the pathetic spectacle that was the Jimi Hendrix statue dedication in front of Audio Environments Inc.'s Broadway offices. It's an extremely hideous artifact, with less artistry than seen on a Franklin Mint collector's plate. Some saw irony in the statue being commissioned and funded by AEI, a background-music company. I didn't see that as much as another instance of white boomers fetishizing the guy as an icon for their notions of the black man as sexy savage. I'm positive Hendrix, an intelligent and innovative artist who seemed to be slumming in rock for the money, would've spurned that image and settled into a prog-jazz career (maybe finding a jazz-rock melange that would've prevented the development of fusion). He also left Seattle at 18 and only performed here again as a touring act. From all accounts, he found Seattle a town with neither the racial nor artistic opportunities he needed. For boomers to enshrine him as the city's pride 'n' joy is something he'd probably have had a time getting comfortable with. *(Feb. 6, 1997)*

Pilot Light Extinguished: We neglected to previously report the passing of Dewey Soriano, the tugboat pilot who took control of the Pacific Coast League in the mid-'60s, and was rewarded by the baseball establishment by getting Seattle's first MLB franchise, the 1969 Pilots. He held a name-the-team contest as a PR stunt, but had already chosen to name it after his own profession; that's why its logo had a nautical, rather than an aviation, theme. His thin pockets could only take one year of losses at a creaky old AAA ballpark; by April 1970 (the same season Boeing laid off half its staff) the Pilots became the Milwaukee Brewers (now threatening to move again). The City of Seattle sued the American League, and got the Mariners seven years later. While local obits praised Soriano for bringing the majors to Seattle, I still wished the Pilots had owners who could've kept the team alive until the Kingdome got done. And it was touching to see the 1998 Mariners remember Soriano by serving up Pilots-quality relief pitching in recent weeks. *(April 30, 1998)*

Freak Out: A second book about the Jim Rose Circus Sideshow is coming out, and this one's unauthorized. *Circus of the Scars,* from writer Jan Gregor and illustrator Ashleigh "Triangle Slash" Talbot, is a lavish hardcover account of the troupe's early years (from the viewpoint of ex-troupe roadie Gregor and ex-member Tim "Torture King" Cridland). I haven't seen it, but its creators hint Rose might not like its portrayal of him. Like he gives a darn about his reputation (except to make sure it's nasty)? I could only imagine one way you could damage Rose's image: Claim he's a mild-mannered teetotaler who plays gentlemanly golf, never cusses offstage, cried at multiple viewings of *Titanic,* and loves to mellow out to the Smooth Jazz station. *(Aug. 6, 1998)*

From "Queen of the Black Coast," one of the original Conan the Barbarian stories by the suicide-at-30 Robert E. Howard:
"Let me live
deep while I live:
let me know
the rich juices
of red meat
and stinging wine
on my palate,
the hot embrace
of white arms,
and the mad
exultation of battle...
I burn with life,
I love, I slay,
and I am content."
(June 1993)

Louis M. Haber, in a Washington Post *Op-Ed essay, defending* Barney the Dinosaur: *"Is this incredible hostility toward Barney just a reflection of societal prejudice against idealistic and cheerful people who are often discounted as simpletons? Against males who are not afraid to reveal a delicate and sensitive persona and to display gentle mannerisms?... Are you so hard-boiled as to be unable to accept anyone who accepts everyone? So cynical as to think of those who are undauntingly optimistic as obsequious?"*
(July 1993)

(continued)

10: SEATTLE SCENES

or, displays of reflection

With Bill Gates and Courtney Love as prominent exceptions, most of Seattle's "local celebrities" have tried to appear as regular folks. And while Portland displayed far more interest in ladies' societies and beauty pageants, most of Seattle's big public scenes have been decidedly middle-class and middlebrow. Or they were, until the upscale baby boomers arose to patronize chi-chi restaurants and more class-conscious forms of public display. But the boomers and the nouveau riche aren't everybody (as much as they think they are). Seattle's still got plenty of gatherings and gathering places for the big mongrel rest of us.

The Pacific Northwest is not, nor has it ever been, Paradise. It did not suddenly come into existence when you moved here, nor even when the first white people moved here. I'm from here, so I have no illusions about the so-called "Northwest Lifestyle" invented in the mid-'70s. *(Nov. 18, 1991)*

Passionately urban life does seem to be catching on in Seattle as a permanent thing. Broadway this summer has been a wonderland of all different kinds of people making all different kinds of scenes. At Dick's alone you can find some 200 people being sociable at 1:30 a.m. Whenever anybody in Seattle has this much fun, somebody tries to outlaw it. Already business interests are demanding something be "done" about this "problem" — really the best thing for Seattle since the saving of the Market.

Any real city has spontaneous street scenes — gatherings of ordinary people who may not have a destination in mind when they take to the streets, but have an invigorating time getting there. Not everybody who stands on a sidewalk is a criminal; we should be glad the attempts to make Broadway a district for yuppies only has gloriously failed. Now if they can only tear up those nauseatingly-cute footsteps… *(September 1986)*

One of Seattle's best dinner-floor show combos was at the Broadway Jack-in-the-Box one recent Friday night. Patrons were treated to watching an endless stream of teens barging in, walking past the counter to the restroom doors, discovering that they're now locked to non-customers, and barging right out again without buying anything or speaking to anyone. *(October 1987)*

The most telling moment at *The Transit Project* [a performance-art production which took place while the actor/dancers and audience were all aboard a moving Metro bus] came at the end. I stayed at the start-finish bus stop, waiting for a real bus to take me home. The rest of the audience all left by car. For all I know, perhaps nobody at any of the performances had ever ridden a Metro bus before. They're missing a lot of real-life drama, much more interesting than the Yuppie angst of *The Transit Project,* though not as well choreographed.
(November 1987)

Astral Plane: Twice a year, enlightenment comes to a warehouse-like space in a lonely Kent industrial park, next to the Domino's Pizza plant. It's the Boeing Activity Center, home of the Boeing Employees' Parapsychology Club Psychic Fair. A bazaar of merchants offered tarot decks, crystals, astrological charts, and motivational tapes on everything from attracting a soul-mate to improving your vocabulary (sample affirmation: "The dictionary is my friend"). Local company Loving Spoonful (not the '60s band) sold a kids' success tape with cartoon squirrels promoting the fun of obeying your parents. A guy who channels information from dolphins cancelled a scheduled appearance, but over 60 psychics and palm readers gave 10-minute consultations. The big room was crowded with eager true believers — the opposite of the stuffed-shirt image outsiders have of Boeing.
(April 1989)

Concrete Poetry: The literary quality of local graffiti has risen dramatically. Since April, a romantic monologue (or possibly dialogue) has been written with wide-tip markers on walls and electrical units within a five-block radius of Frederick's. Some salient entries: "You love me. I know. I love you too, as if you were/are the world and the truth for me. That's our tragedy"... "Yes, it's your one and only babe; I have chosen you as my #1 wall lover"... "Join me for a coffee? We'll talk about art and poetry, as we prepare to run away." *(July 1989)*

Who the Hell Are You?: The Kids Fair at the Seattle Center Exhibition Hall was an ex-substitute teacher's nightmare. A whole hall full of screaming kids, frenzied parents, and merchant booths grabbing for the parents' wallets. Everything from Looney Tunes frozen dinners to back yard jungle gyms, professionally installed. The high/low-light was when they brought out guys in seven-foot Bart

Other Voices
(continued)

"People are operating on many levels of insanity only clear to themselves."
— Night of the Living Dead *master George A. Romero*
(August 1993)

"In an accelerating, fast-evolving universe, whoever does not change moves backward relatively. Did you ever notice that takes only 20 years for a liberal to become a conservative, without changing a single idea?"
— Robert Anton Wilson, in Reality Is What You Can Get Away With
(September 1993)

Bonnie Morino on the Vicki Lawrence show, telling how excited she was to be hired as a Playboy *model: "It's a once-in-a-lifetime opportunity that doesn't happen very often in one's life."*
(October 1993)

Raymond Carver, now the most popular dead sage since Jim Morrison, with some advice for life I've tried to follow all my career (as quoted in Jon Winokur's Friendly Advice*): "Eat cereal for breakfast and write good prose." (December 1993)*

"The planet is an unstable being. Little earthquakes rumble up and down our coast. The earth has a lot of bottled up stress... pent up aggression. The earth really needs to get out more. Spend more time in the woods. Feed the ducks. The planet needs to stop operating on that second shift mentality."
— Gregory Hischack, in Farm Pulp
(March 1994)

and Homer Simpson felt body costumes, hugging adoring little fans who lined up for photos. If the real Bart were there, he'd have pelted the oversize imposter with a pile of *Ninja Turtles* coloring books. *(May 1990)*

Fun for the Whole Dysfunctional Family: What I love/hate about Seafair is what I love/hate about this town in general. I love its unabashed hokiness. I hate its coldness, its Protestant stoicism concealing a face of sheer terror. It started in the early postwar years, when our raucous post-frontier city was trying too hard to prove it had grown up. A civic-development group, Greater Seattle Inc., devised a series of rough-and-tumble events with a veneer of good clean fun. The core events reveal two facets of Seattle: An obsessive blandness on the surface (influenced by the Boeing corporate culture) and repressed frustrations underneath.

Newcomers hate it. It contradicts the laid-back stereotype of the modern Northwest. It's a throwback to the clumsy, pre-pretension Seattle. It's also an example of what feminists call "imbalanced male energy." Officials try to downplay the rowdy parts, especially the Seafair Pirates, costumed mischief-makers, originally recruited from Elks lodges. (In the '50s the Pirates used to "kidnap" a young woman at their annual landing ceremony, "releasing" her at the end of the afternoon with a big badge that said, "I was raped by the Seafair Pirates.") But there's still the hydros (250,000 people getting drunk and waiting for a boat to burn). There's the Blue Angels, loud fast planes that terrify dogs and neighborhoods for Navy recruiting. There are shiploads of sailors on the streets, courtesy of the same Navy that brought you Tailhook. There's a Friday-night parade before 300,000 spectators who are eager to release their ids but are instead shown marching bands, motorcycle drill teams, corporate floats, and sideshow clowns. Take that many people (many with Thermoses of booze), bore them to tears, and some are bound to end up fighting.

The chief female energy comes from a beauty pageant that was already innocuous, and is now toned down further to avoid charges of sexism. Turning it into an amateur talent show reduces its ability to add any yin to the yang-heavy activities.

Compare Seafair to Portland's more civilized Rose Festival. On the Saturday of the (daytime) main parade, the *Oregonian* devotes its full front page to a color photo of the Rose Queen and her court, in a healthy respect for traditional feminine power. Or compare it to Mardi Gras, where Catholic passions and Creole sensuality are gleefully celebrated.

Still, I do like the hydros. There's something noble about big, fat machines of wood and fiberglass, run on obsolete surplus airplane engines, maintained by mechanical geniuses who spend the year scrounging for enough parts to challenge Budweiser's big bucks. These great manic-depressive machines either bounce above the water at a roaring 150 mph or conk out and die. There's a lesson for us all in there. *(September 1992)*

Bring On the Warm Jets: In past years, I used to annually print my arguments in defense of Seafair. I skipped it last year, but with the Blue Angels' noisy spectacle returning to the lineup this weekend I figure it's time. With Bumbershoot admission getting pricier every year, the Seafair parade and hydro races comprise two of the city's three most populist gatherings; the first is the Bite of Seattle.

This annual triumverate of events reject both the "quiet good taste" of Seattle's yuppified official culture and the too-cool-to-have-fun taboo that constricts much of our "alternative" community. Sure these are "family" events, as advertised; but they're for real families: Bratty kids, horny teens, dysfunctional parents, grumpy oldsters. They promise pleasant times out-of-doors with food, drink, and unpretentious entertainment (plus a lot of noise). They deliver humanity in all its gross-out, homely, cantankerous, troublesome, pathetic, amazing, loveable variety (plus a lot of noise).

Nature poets (like the poets who used to hold anti-Seafair reading events every year) love to move to communities connected to The Land and The Water, but have a hard time cohabiting with the castes of people who live off of said resources. Seafair honors the people who work in and on the water (sailors, fishers, shipbuilders, stevedores) and those who feel affinity with them (regular working stiffs) — not the people with million-buck "cabins" on the islands.

Similarly, the Bite (particularly the *Times*-sponsored portion) purports to honor the town's yupscale restaurant segment, but really celebrates the all-American deadly sin of gluttony as thoroughly as Mardi Gras revels in lust and modern Christmas honors greed. Unlike Folklife's moderate hammer-dulcimer lovers, the Bite's a true celebration of the common person.

The streets of downtown, increasingly unhospitable to the non-affluent, became on Aug. 1 a temporary invasion

Stanford "industrial psychologist" Dr. James Keenan, in a 1967 speech to Muzak executives quoted in Joseph Lanza's book Elevator Music*: "Muzak helps human communities because it is a non-verbal symbolism for the common stuff of everyday living in the global village... Muzak promotes the sharing of meaning because it massifies symbolism in which not few, but all, can participate." (April 1994)*

Words of love from the animated 2 Stupid Dogs*: "The world is our pancake house, and you're my flapjack stack with a scoop of butter and maple syrup and a side of hash browns and some toast and a large orange juice." (May 1994)*

"I hear noises which others don't hear and which disturb for me the music of the spheres, which other people don't hear either." — "Self published aphorist" (zine publisher) of '20s Vienna, Karl Kraus (June 1994)

Prophetic words from a 1970 Esquire *fashion spread about the "Pepsi Proletariat" look: "It consists of overalls, flannel shirt, and heavy work boots, the traditional accoutrements of the working class... To adopt the Pepsi Proletariat guise is to express one of the more euphoriant pipe dreams of the counterculture: the hope that a coalition may someday be fashioned out of workers and freaks." (July 1994)*

An anonymous Searle pharmacologist, quoted in that spiritual guide for our times, Listening to Prozac: *"If the brain were simple enough for us to understand, we'd be too simple to understand it." (July 1994)*

site for the forgotten Seattleites. This weekend, the brahmins of Lake Washington are bracing for the onslaught of gauche sex-joke T-shirts, decidedly non-REI rubber rafts, and people at least officially not drinking alcohol in a public park. Plus a lot of noise. Even noisier with the Blue Angels back. I can't wait. *(Aug. 7, 1997)*

'Round this time in previous years, the Kingdome used to host the annual Manufactured Housing Expo. It's now held at Cheney Stadium in Tacoma. Last year's Kingdome closure had something to do with the move, but it's wiser for what used to be the "mobile home" industry to have its showcase closer to the path of new suburban development.

Here in town, only a few small areas are zoned for factory-built housing, and they're threatened by redevelopment. One of Seattle's last big mobile home parks on Aurora was razed this past summer for a Home Depot, that shrine to the stick-built house.

Still, the Kingdome was a great site for the show. They used to build a mini-neighborhood on the AstroTurf, with walkways lined with plastic landscaping. 'Twas a fantasy world reminiscent of the domed cities in which, according to the 1962 Seattle World's Fair, we'd all be living by now. *(Oct. 18, 1995)*

I enjoy the arrival of autumnal weather. I claim to be not really a weather person, but I can't help but feel more comfortable when the outside changes from garishly bright 70mm Technicolor back to muted 16mm Eastmancolor. *(Oct. 2, 1997)*

The Big White-Out: The news media love few things more than a huge, region-encompassing Act of God story. In the winter around here, that means either flooding (which tends to actually show up at the predicted times and places) or snow (which doesn't).

All the boomers I know hate snow ("How on earth will we get to that bed-and-breakfast we already made reservations for?"). All the squares I know fear snow ("How the hell do you expect me to commute to and from Woodinville in this goddamned weather?").

I, however, love snow. And I don't mean but-only-in-the-mountains. Snow in Seattle is a rare and wonderful thing. It puts everyday life, and everyday reality, on hold for a day or two of diffused light, an eerie yet inviting silence, and the sharp contrast between grumbling grownups and ecstatic kids and kids-at-heart.

It's been a few years since we had a really good snow in town, so when the radio stations start up their stern warnings of a Big White Peril today-or-maybe-tomorrow I can't help but get excited.

But invariably, like parents who keep promising that trip to the Grand Canyon but who take you to see the cousins in Topeka every summer instead, the snow-threatening announcers leave me with little else but brief moments of joy and hopes for the next winter. So to me, for a few flurrying moments before the big football telecast, it really was Super Sunday. *(Jan. 31, 1996)*

Fat, Not Sassy: As a civic booster, I've always been a bit embarrassed by Fat Tuesday, the Mardi Gras for people who are just too boomer wimpy or too laid back to do a real Mardi Gras.

Mind you, it's a screwy notion for a stuck-up Protestant city to attempt a Mardi Gras in the first place (even the northern towns that pull off successful Winter Carnivals tend to be in Catholic-dominated places like Quebec and southern Germany), but the way the idea's been executed usually hurts.

I was at the 1978 Fat Tuesday, the last big nighttime-outdoor one, and it almost became for real (i.e., people getting shitfaced and fucking in public, or dressing up like all get out). Since then, it's been tamed into a promo tool for the boomer-blues-bar circuit, and it's been an experience not unlike a boomer blues bar on a bad night: predictable, unoriginal, yet annoying.

Every place needs a real letting-go time, a healthy respectful vacation from inhibitions; many of us could use a real Lent too, but self-denial isn't part of the consumer society's agenda. *(March 8, 1995)*

Spin and Mardi: Sit & Spin's little *Mardi Gras Burlesque Revue* was everything one could reasonably expect from a Carnival celebration among the infamous reservedness here in City Light. It expressed a more sophisticated debauchery, and a more spirited approach to sexuality, than "alternative" subcultures usually endulge in.

Among the most pleasant surprises at the show was the presence of a large deaf contingent (serviced by a sign-language interpreter) at such a relatively non-saintly affair.

Blind people, in media representations, get to have the full range of human qualities (Ray Charles, *Scent of a Woman,* that Air Touch Cellular spokesdude), but deaf people are stereotyped as benchmarks of PC propriety

"We have now reached the point where every goon with a grievance, every bitter bigot, merely has to place the prefix, 'I know this is not politically correct, but...' in order to be not just safe from criticism, but actually a card, a lad, even a hero. Conversely, to talk about poverty and inequality, to draw attention to the reality that discrimination and injustice are still facts of life, is to commit the new sin of political correctness... Anti-PC has become the latest cover for creeps. It is a godsend for every curmudgeon and crank, from the fascists to the merely smug."
— Fintan O'Toole in The Irish Times *(August 1994)*

"Power corrupts; obsolete power corrupts obsoletely."
— Computer visionary Ted Nelson *(inventor of the term "hypertext"), in* New Media *magazine (November 1994)*

"Never offend people with style if you can offend them with substance."
— Tony Brown
(December 1994)

"Preserve Farmland. Live In Town."
— Found on a bumper sticker on a Honda
(January 1995)

"Always live in the ugliest house on the street. Then you don't have to look at it."
— David Hockney
(January 1995)

"Copyright infringement is your best entertainment value."
— Slogan of the Minneapolis music zine Cake
(April 12, 1995)

"Those who restrain desire, do so because theirs is weak enough to be restrained."
— William Blake in The Marriage of Heaven and Hell
(Oct. 18, 1995)

"Trying to find morals in politicians and bankers is like trying to find morals in cockroaches."
— Citizen-activist Makoto Sataka at a meeting about Japan's bank-loan crisis, as quoted on CNN
(Feb. 7, 1996)

(the closest thing to an exception was Ed Begley Jr.'s womanizing poet character on *Mary Hartman, Mary Hartman*). Even Edison and Beethoven are usually depicted as saintlier figures than they really were.

Until TV closed-captioning and opera "supertitles" became widespread, the only culture thangs the hearing-impaired were welcomed into tended to be either evangelical church services or concerts by self-congratulatory folk singers. I'd always figured that putting up with such unrelenting sanctimonies could be a tougher thing to live with than deafness itself. *(Feb. 27, 1997)*

Let's discuss the annually-weirder spectacle that is grownup Halloween, now America's #2 shopping holiday. Is it me, or have grownup Halloween parties gotten simultaneously more elaborate and blasé?

The art of costuming, of adopting temporary personas for celebration or for awakening, is among humanity's oldest traits. But the way middle Americans (even young, urbane middle Americans) do it is like the way middle Americans do a lot of things, half-hearted and aloof.

"Square" middle Americans often keep their inner passions inhibited because they're afraid; "hip" middle Americans often keep their passions inhibited because they're afraid, but pretend they're doing it because they're too cool. The mainstreaming of fetish dance parties might have helped change that, but (at least in this town) that trend seems to have peaked.

I don't think the answer is to replace today's Halloween festivities with World Beat-style "tribal" role playing events. The gods, demigods, devils, and myths of pre-industrial societies are those people's property — in many cases, the only things colonists didn't take from them.We have plenty of our own gods, demigods, devils, and myths to explore; including the myths propagated via popular entertainment and media. So keep going to parties as Audrey Hepburn or Captain Janeway or Ross Perot — but don't stop at the clothes. Become Hepburn or Janeway or Perot for one night. Explore the presence of Hepburnness, Janewayism, or Perotosity within your soul. *(Nov. 7, 1996)*

Because last week's Misc. was a "theme" column, this post-Bastille Day edition's our first chance to say there's something about a great Fourth of July fireworks show, particularly when accompanied by stray car alarms in one ear and the show's official soundtrack in the other (though at least one observer complained that the Lake

Union show's choice of music by Queen — a British band — and music from *Titanic* — a film about a British ship — seemed odd).

Anyhow, those bigtime fireworks really are the perfect expression of (at least some aspects of) the modern-day American Way. That is to say, they're big, loud, flashy, smoky, and made by cheap labor in China. *(July 16, 1998)*

More imaginative play equipment might be found at Seattle Surgical Repair, 10726 Aurora Ave. N. The location (right next to the cemetery) might not be the most tasteful site for a dealer in used medical equipment, but the tiny building's crammed full of goodies. Examination tables! Speculums! Knee-reflex hammers! Stethoscopes! Gurneys! (Old car and motorcycle parts, too.) Just play safe when you're playing doctor, and don't perform any actual procedures that should be left to qualified personnel. *(March 26, 1998)*

Apology, sort of: Some music clubs are sensitive that I referred to their clientele with the adjective "fratboy" some months back. I'm sorry. Few businesses want to be associated with guys who think "Handicapped Parking" signs are really "BMW Parking" signs, who scream sexist jokes at bartenders from their tables via cellular phones, who insult anybody on the street whose looks they don't like. Now if fewer universities felt the same. *(September 1992)*

Club Etiquette: Remember, anytime you go to see a band at a bar that's supposed to be cool, there will be uncouth ruffians to watch out for. These people will prey on anyone they perceive as weak — harassing women, fag-bashing men, "accidentally" shoving against people in order to spill their drinks. Fortunately, these goons are easy to spot. They travel in male pairs or trios (very rarely in co-ed couples). They're always the most clean-cut looking guys in the bar, with the biggest jawbones, the costliest "ordinary" haircuts, the widest game-show-host smiles. You're safe with the people who look like freaks; it's the suburban slummers you must never speak to. *(February 1993)*

The opening of the Capitol Club, the new Blank Generation cocktail bar and fusion eatery on East Pine Street, is a sea-change event for several reasons. First, it signifies the "Cocktail Nation" phenomenon as not just a slumming fad but as a bankable long-term trend. Second, its smart but non-aggressive style calls out for an

"People are inherently good. Bad people are created by other bad people; their survival is guaranteed because of their safety in numbers."
— British-Israeli-American social critic Eli Khamarov, in Surviving on Planet Reebok *(Feb. 28, 1996)*

"We are all worms, but I do believe I am a glowworm."
— Credited to Winston Churchhill (April 17, 1996)

"Know the difference between success and fame. Success is Mother Teresa. Fame is Madonna."
— Erma Bombeck (May 1, 1996)

"Work is worship. Play is a waste of time. Night clubs, parties, and socializing saps your energy and gets you nothing, but unwanted notices from snoopy gossip journalists. Avoid the night spots and dark circles. It's even helpful in avoiding pimples."
— Indian movie star Madhuri Dixit, in the magazine Cineblitz *(June 13, 1996)*

"Personally, I'm sick and tired of old-world media, and I'm also a little bit tired of old-world values... This is an opportunity not only to do something new, but also an opportunity not to surrender to the powers that be. And in creating this new commercial place and this new commercial paradigm, our generation has the opportunity to maintain control over something we're implementing." — Hikaru Phillips, telling the mag Go Digital *about his online gambling enterprise, Virtual Vegas. (Sept. 12, 1996)*

end to generation gaps. Tasteful and comfy but still non-pretentiously elegant, it's meant to appeal to everyone from neo-swingers to grand dames. It's a force for community unity amid an increasingly fragmented society.

The aspect of the place that initially disturbed me was the lower-level dining area. Call me a traditionalist, but when I think of the restaurant half of a real Cocktail Culture restaurant-lounge, I think of either classic American fare (burgers, chicken), standard American expense-account fare (steaks, seafood), or that pseudo-Euro stuff dissed by author Calvin Trillin as "Maison de la Casa del House, Continental Dining." Instead, the Capitol Club offers fancy-schmancy entrees (grilled egg-plant, Saffron Seafood Rosetto) and appetizers (Grilled Chorizo, Sauteed Spinach). "What're they trying to be," I initially thought to myself, "another stuffy Cuisine-with-a-capital-C site for condo boomers?"

I've since been reassured by management and early customers that that wasn't the intention.

I'd forgotten how many young-adult artists and musicians have spent years in restaurant work, much of it at joints with more exotic fare. I'd also forgotten how many of these folks, when they do come into money, prefer to dine on the fare of places like Il Bistro and Marco's Supper Club. *(Feb. 13, 1997)*

Swankosity: The Pampas Club opening was like a scene out of the 1990 debutante movie *Metropolitan*, with exquisitely-dressed rich kids of a type I'd not previously known to exist here, all in the former site of the raucous My Suzie's and Hawaiian-kitsch Trade Winds.

It reminds me of a scene in the memoir of a Depression-era U.K. labor activist. After living through nearly three decades of mass deprivation due to the depression, the war, and Europe's lengthy postwar slump, he was shocked and astonished to find teenagers running around the streets of late-'50s London with the cash to spend on clothes and music and partyin'.

One side effect: The new Belltown wine-'n'-dine clientele is, on the whole, much better-behaved in public than the Bud Light-chugging fratbar crowd more common in the neighborhood two or three years ago.

Another side effect: The ex-Sailors Union building where Pampas, El Goucho, and the (separately owned) Casbah Cinema are is right across from Operation Nightwatch, where homeless folk line up for shelter-bed tickets. What used to be called "limo liberals" climb out of pug-ugly Mercedes SUVs, only to witness the less-than-formally dressed standing and arguing and cussing in line. While few affluent persons feel personally responsible for an economy that creates a few "winners" and a lot of others, maybe the sight will at least give some "winners" a sense of there-but-for-the-grace-of-God humility. *(April 9, 1998)*

Scary Coincidence #1: In this space last week, I promised this week I'd list things I was thankful for. Little did I know I'd be grateful to the fates for some relatively lucky timing. I was on the southbound Metro #359 bus at 3:15 p.m. Thursday, heading back from the ol' family dinner — exactly 24 hours prior to the incident in which a presumably deranged passenger shot the driver on a southbound #359 on the northern reaches of the Aurora Bridge, just above the Fremont Troll. (The bus crashed through the guard rail and plunged to the ground below. The driver fell out and died.)

Scary coincidence #2: A KIRO-TV reporter, mentioning cops scouring the wreckage site for evidence, noted how investigators spent months combing the seas off Long Island, N.Y. after the TWA Flight 800 crash several years ago. A friend of mine had been on that plane from Paris to N.Y.C. that day; the fatal flight was to have been the plane's return trip.

Scary coincidence #3: As part of the part-time duties I'm still handling for *The Stranger,* I'd scheduled to turn in a website review this week about *www.busplunge.org,* a site collecting every English-language news story containing the words "bus plunge."

Scary coincidence #4: The driver, Mark McLaughlin, was shot in the arm. Mudhoney singer Mark Arm's real surname: McLaughlin.

Back in the late '80s, Metro Transit's ads tried to discourage citizens from thinking of bus riders as underclass losers and winos, by serving up images of well-scrubbed, pale-skinned models and the slogan, "Metro. Who rides it? People just like you."

Then in the '90s, as headlines blared of "road rage" and roads became clogged with "out-of-my-way-asshole" SUVs, bus riders got plastered with the PR image of social do-gooders who did their part to reduce traffic congestion and encourage social mingling, people whose efforts deserved to be furthered by the regional light-rail referendum.

Will this tragedy re-ignite the old stereotype of bus people, or be perceived as the wheeled equivalent of a drive-by? *(Nov. 30, 1998)*

"Any girl can be glamorous. All you have to do is stand still and look stupid."
— Hedy Lamarr
(Oct. 10, 1996)

Improbably risqué remarks attributed to Phyllis Schafly: "Marriage is like pantyhose. It all depends on what you put into it."
(Nov. 28, 1996)

"Never eat in a restaurant where the menu is larger than the table, the pepper mill larger than your date, and the baked potato larger than your steak."
— Philadelphia restaurant critic Jim Quinn
(Dec. 5, 1996)

(continued)

11: GETTING AROUND

or, planes, trains, and SUVs

The Monorail, in more hopeful days.

For the world capital of airplanes, Seattle's a laggard in regard to ground-level public transportation. Our bus system likes to issue press releases about how great it is, but it's still just a bus system, and in many parts of the county a quite inefficient and infrequent one. Our traffic jams are among America's worst, and they get worse every year.

Finally, two competing mass-transit concepts came to voters in the mid-'90s: The Regional Transit Authority, a.k.a. Sound Transit (a regional light rail/heavy rail/bus system, designed over many years by professional planners and bureaucrats) and the Monorail Initiative (a city-only plan drawn up by a cab driver and volunteer assistants, and put on the ballot by an initiative petition). Sound Transit took two votes to get passed, and even then faced opposition from minority residents in South Seattle (where light-rail trains were slated to run at street level).

When Sound Transit's second referendum vote passed, the Monorail Initiative had already gotten enough petition signatures to make the next election. Despite official opposition by the upper-crust, the initiative passed. It became the city's job to start monorail planning (and, if certain officials have their way, to bury it within the bureaucratic purgatory euphemistically known in the local press as "The Seattle Process").

Exhaust: The Presidential candidates are all talking about where all our next cars will be made. Few of them consider that maybe we don't need more cars. We've got too many autos, used too inefficiently. They give us the suburban sprawl that destroys true community along with the landscape. You know the dangers of pollution and of military alliances with emirates. Eastern-hemisphere governments subsidize rail transit, as a reasonable price to reduce those maladies. Only Tom Harkin understood that we'd have a smoother-running, cleaner-burning economy if we redirected some of the money spent making, selling, feeding, and servicing the metal monsters. If we had decent mass transit within and between metro areas, we could have closer-in and more affordable housing. We'd have a renaissance of street-corner retail, the drop-in shops strip malls just can't match. We'd have more people meeting by chance, interacting and (if we're lucky) learning to get along. *(April 1992)*

We're always mesmerized by the Horizon Shuttle billboards with the digital clocks flashing in half-hour increments every second, bearing the slogan "Nonstop Non-stops to Portland." As I recall, Delta was the first to run billboards proclaiming, "Fly Non-Stop to Portland." Every flight from Sea-Tac to Portland is non-stop. There's no place for a commercial-class plane to stop, except an emergency landing at McChord Air Force Base. *(June 1992)*

Boeing Bust III: It's happened before, in the early '70s with the cancellation of the federal SST project (the unbuilt plane the SuperSonics were named after) and in the early '80s (after the post-Vietnam defense slump, but before Reagan's defense hikes sunk in). In the mid-'80s, airline deregulation and the defense boom led to many more planes and war goods than anyone had a practical use for; so now 18-28,000 laid off workers are paying for that overexpansion. The country never needed all those missiles and bombers. And while civilian airline over-building led to cheap air fares, it's no bargain if nobody's making money. Like many industries, aviation's in an upheaval due to bloat and outmoded concepts.

We oughta (but probably won't) take advantage of this restructuring opportunity to rethink our domestic transportation system. High-speed rail could move people more efficiently and cheaply, especially on routes that don't cross the vast inland west. At today's levels of freeway and airport congestion, intercity trips up to 300 miles could even be faster by rail than by car-to-airport-to-airport-to-car. It'd be a great investment opportunity, with just a directing push by the feds needed.

We could've already had this, but the feds pushed aerospace (like nuclear power) to bring civilian investment into Cold War military technology. Even the Interstates were first promoted as a defense investment (because the movement of war goods wouldn't be threatened by railroad strikes). Our real national security's to be found in building a secure economy. *(March 1993)*

Keep On You-Know-What Dept.: This year, it's Seattle's turn to get acknowledged on a nameplate with the Olds Aurora. Next year, according to automotive trade mags, there'll be a light-duty pickup called the Toyota Tacoma! Besides falling trippingly off the tongue, the name implies a tuff, no-nonsense truck for a tuff, no-nonsense town. My suggested options: Super Big Gulp-size cupholders, Tasmanian Devil mudflaps, half-disconnected mufflers. My suggested color: Rust. *(November 1994)*

After all these years, I finally got to the famous Boeing surplus store. It's well worth the trip to the daytime nightmare that is Darkest Kent's vast miles of faceless, win-

Other Voices
(continued)

"We must have respect for both our plumbers and our philosophers, or neither our pipes nor our theories will hold water."
— John W. Gardner (Jan. 30, 1997)

"Love's greatest enemy is cynicism. (Cynicism's) power lies in the fact that it makes sense. The optimism that love requires does not make sense... Cynicism is based on the absolute facts of the world. Optimism requires one to accept a supposition difficult to affirm — that the facts are not always the truth."
— Stanford chaplain Floyd Thompkins, in Enemies of the Ebony Warriors of Love *(Feb. 13, 1997)*

"Having been unpopular in high school is not just cause for book publication."
— Fran Lebowitz (Feb. 20, 1997)

"If I had to give young writers advice, I'd say don't listen to writers talking about writing."
— Lillian Hellman (May 1, 1997)

"We live under continual threat of two equally fearful, but seemingly opposed destinies: unremitting banality and inconceivable terror. It is fantasy, served out in large rations by the popular arts, which allows most people to cope with these twin specters."
— Susan Sontag
(May 29, 1997)

"Music may not save your soul, but it will cause your soul to be worth saving."
— Incredibly Strange Music organist Korla Pandit
(Oct. 9, 1997)

"Hell is anything which continues long enough."
— William T. Vollman, in The Atlas
(Nov. 13, 1997)

dowless warehousery and wide, sidewalkless arterials. Best to get there just before its 10 a.m. opening, to mingle with the mechanics and home-improvement crowd waiting for first chance at the bargains.

The day I was there, alas, no airplane seats or beverage carts or 10-foot-tall landing-wheel tires could be had. But many other things were there, all dirt cheap: Sheets of aluminum. Office furniture, including drafting tables. Computers (and their parts and accessories) of varying vintages and operating systems. Drill bits. Welders' heat-shield masks, a la *Flashdance.* Safety goggles. Cash registers. Huge rolls of upholstery fabrics, in those reassuring dark blue colors psychologically tested to make passengers less restless. Platforms and podiums. A bicycle with no handlebars or pedals. A huge old photo-typesetter, the kind of machine that made words like these in the pre-desktop-publishing era. Fifteen- and twenty-minute VHS tapes from the company's in-house production studio, now erased but bearing labels announcing such former contents as *Confined Space Awareness, Commitment to Integrity: The Boeing Values,* and even *Accident Investigation: It's About Prevention.* *(March 13, 1997)*

One event nearly ignored by the media this equinoxal season was the 50th birthday of Sea-Tac Airport. Airport management held a relatively low-key reception inside the main terminal recently: cake, mini-sausages, a kiddie choir, displays of '40s-'50s flying memorabilia.

The highlight was stilt walker Janet Raynor, dolled up in a ten-foot-tall version of a vintage-1967 Alaska Airlines flight-attendant's dress. Raynor strode, pranced, and even danced in the long dress (which gave her the look of a mid-'70s Bon Marché fashion-ad illustration) while deftly fielding jokes from passers-by about which airline has the most legroom in business class. She also passed out reproductions of an old publicity photo with the dress's original wearer standing beside the airline's president. The guy in the photo's just tall enough to provide the model with a degree of personal service not even Alaska Airlines is known for. *(Oct. 2, 1997)*

You can tell it's election season 'cause the TV and newspaper ads, normally full of appeals to be a "rebel" by buying consumer products, are instead saturated with images of authority figures exhorting citizens to do as they're told and just say nope to those crackpot initiativest. There's cops against (mild) handgun control, and nurses against (very mild) health care reform. Another case in point: the Monorail Initiative, denounced by the increasingly rabid-right propagandists at the Greater Seattle Chamber of Commerce. Instead of opposing the initiative as the work of "crackpots" (i.e., of people outside the government/business elite), our business leaders should welcome the chance to add more in-city mileage to a light-rail scheme initially intended for suburban commuters, and to add them in the form of a hi-profile, futuristic-looking elevated train system people would want to ride on.

We ought to pass the Monorail Initiative this election. Then we'll let the city and the Regional Transit Authority (established in last year's transit referendum) work out how best to incorporate the initiative's mandate with the in-progress RTA planning and the future RTA operation. RTA was and is about reducing smog, easing freeway congestion, and making life easier for motorists by getting a few other motorists off the road.

The Monorail Initiative is about those things, but it's also about something more. It's about dreams for the future, and about wresting control of these dreams from the suits, from the consultants and focus-group researchers and the politicians who never met a condo project they didn't like.

Historically, urban transit projects in the U.S. have been proposed from on high by political inner-circle members who would never deign to use public transit themselves, but who love the opportunity to award construction contracts to potential campaign contributors. This is something dreamed up by ordinary citizens, without years of bureaucratic "process." And it appeals to everyone who's ever loved the short Seattle Center Monorail and ever wanted to believe it really was the transportation system of the future. Here's a chance to realize at least a piece of the fair's promised "World of Tomorrow," to be finished just a few years into Century 21. *(Oct. 30, 1997)*

Instead of spending Election Night at the Municipal League's annual media gathering or one of the big candidate bashes, **Misc.** watched the returns on a tiny portable TV in Linda's Tavern with a dozen or so members of the Monorail Initiative campaign. (One campaign leader was named Grant Cogswell — same last name as a *Jetsons* character!) As the tiny-type updates beneath *Mad About You* and *NYPD Blue* kept displaying a solid lead for the measure, the bar's ambience of conversation and DJ music kept getting punctuated by cheers and loud kisses.

"Like life itself, my stories have no point and get absolutly nowhere. And, like life, they are a little mad and purposeless. They resemble those people who watch with placid concentration a steam shovel digging a large hole in the ground. They are almost as purposeless as a dignified commuter shaking an impotent fist after a train he has just missed. They are like the man who dashes madly through traffic only to linger aimlessly on the opposite corner watching a fountain pen being demonatrated in a shop window."
— Topper author Thorne Smith (Nov. 20, 1997)

The closing words from the last broadcast by ex-Seattleite and pioneer network newscaster Chet Huntley: "Keep the faith; there will be better and happier news, one day, if we work at it." (Oct. 8, 1998)

"Vice is a monster so frightful to mein, that but to be seen is to despise; yet seen too oft familiar with her face, we first endure, then pity, then embrace."
— Alexander Pope (Oct. 29, 1998)

"Americans are caught up in this American Dream, yet at the same time, in order to service that dream, they have to constantly deny what people are really like, what they really want... You really like to do something but you don't tell anybody because you hate yourself so much for doing it so you have to persecute everybody for doing what you are doing."
— German director Ulli Lommel, in Ian Grey's Hollywood-exposé book Sex, Stupidity, and Greed *(May 7, 1998)*

"At this stage in its evolution the Web resembles a typical Australian goldfield, with vast mountains of low-grade ore."
— Denis Dutton, webmaster of Arts and Letters Daily (Dec. 14, 1998)

"Man is the only animal that can remain on friendly terms with the victims he intends to eat until he eats them."
— Samuel Butler (Jan. 11, 1999)

The rest of the election went pretty much as polls predicted, with Paul Schell's slightly-narrower-than-expected victory for mayor reassuring a municipal political machine that believes government's highest and best purpose is construction, what Canadian politicos call "megaprojects." But this night, at this place, belonged to a civic project the machine hated and the people liked.

Now it'll be up to the people, and to the new neo-progressive wing on the City Council, to shepherd this unusual city-transit vision into reality without letting the machine and its planning corps literally "derail" it. The Seattle machine's been rather effective at taking popular concerns and re-interpreting them into problems best solved by more business-as-usual. *(Nov. 13, 1997)*

Wheelin' and Dealin': Call me retro, call me picky, but I know I'm not the only one to believe there hasn't been anything really good in U.S. automotive design since the fall of American Motors. From the awkward K Car, to the once-innovative but now-tiresome Taurus teardrop, to today's bland minivans and macho-gross sport utilities, mediocrity rules showrooms across the land. The new VW Beetle represents a small forward step, though it doesn't look enough like the old Beetle and costs too much. Things are a little brighter overseas, especially in Japan. Nissan's got a number of way-rad cars it sells only in Asia (including a slug-shaped miniwagon called the "S-Cargo"), while continuing to saddle its U.S. division with the same poor-selling Altimas.

Now I have a new object of desire. The Smart Car, made by the unlikely joint venture of Mercedes and Swatch, was supposed to hit Euro streets this month (production-startup problems have now held back the launch 'til fall). Think of it as a scooter with a roof. It seats two people snugly inside its eight-foot-long plastic body (surrounding a steel safety cage). It looks like the perfect super-fuel-efficient tool for urban errands, leisurely country drives, or any other transport use that doesn't involve mucho cargo or wintertime pass-climbing. Naturally, there are no plans to bring the Smart to North America. They don't think enough people here would want a human-scale vehicle to be worth developing a U.S.-street-legal version and setting up dealers to sell and service it. Sadly, they may be right. *(Feb. 19, 1998)*

The Merge Lane: So Chrysler's gonna let itself be bought out by Daimler-Benz, makers of Mercedes snobmobiles (and of the infinitely cooler Freightliner trucks). This means the Germans will now own the Jeep trademark, originally coined to describe the U.S. Army's "general purpose" vehicles in WWII.

However, we ought to think of this as an opportunity to wring some favors out of the company during the antitrust and SEC approval hearings. Let 'em merge, I say, if they promise to *(1)* bring that ultracool tiny Mercedes-Swatch Smart Car to America; *(2)* fire that Dodge commercial spokesdork and bring back Ricardo Montalban; *(3)* re-introduce some Chrysler Chlassics like the Dart Swinger and the Plymouth Duster (not to mention some of those old American Motors cars Chrysler now owns the rights to, like the AMX and the Pacer!); and *(4)* pay to track down, buy up, and melt down all K Cars still on the road. *(May 21, 1998)*

Misc. wonders if Vancouver essayist Brian Fawcett was right when he said malls and subdivisions are typically named after the real places they replaced, whether a corollary might be made about car commercials promoting further traffic-jamming steel tonnage with images of the wide open road, or (even better) SUV ads using nature footage to sell landscape-ruining gas-guzzlers. *(June 11, 1998)*

A current anti-drunk-driving public service ad and a current motor-oil commercial both use ultrasound fetus imagery. The former spot shows what the titles claim are in vitro images of a baby who was "killed by a drunk driver on her way to being born." The latter shows an animated baby who repositions himself from the classic fetal position to a stance approximating the driver's seat of a race car, and who then pretends to grab a steering wheel and roar away (tagline: "You can always tell the guys who are going to use Valvoline"). Wonder if the second baby will grow up into someone who'll run over someone like the first baby. *(Nov. 12, 1998)*

After years of ignoring non-crime stories in south Seattle, local media now highly publicize opposition efforts to Sound Transit surface light-rail in the Rainier Valley. Are the papers and TV stations really listening to the neighborhood advocates who'd rather have a subway tunnel in the south end (and under Roosevelt Way in the north end)? If I were a conspiracy theorist, which I'm not, I'd consider whether emphasizing public opposition to surface-level transit tracks was part of a larger strategy to re-discredit Monorail Initiative supporters. *(Dec. 14, 1998)*

Insville & Outski

At the start of each year, ***Misc.*** *publishes what it humbly claims is the most accurate In/Out list published anywhere. Here are some past examples.*

Joe Isuzu/
Spuds McKenzie
Residents/
Developers
Lavender/
Pink and gray
Magazine stores/
Balloon stores
Charm bracelets/
Diamonds
Chicago/
Los Angeles
Brigitte Bardot/
Marilyn Monroe
Frostbite Falls/
Lake Wobegon
Neo-folk/
Skinny English boys trying to sound black
Graphic novels/
Action-figure dolls
Compassion/Power
Safe Sex/No Sex
Semiotics/
In-Out lists
(January 1988)

(continued)

12: JUST BEYOND SEATTLE

or, telling a sprawl story

If some Seattleites spend too much energy looking up to the two or three big-media cities, some residents in the rest of Washington look up to Seattle. "Up," of course, doesn't always mean "admiringly."

While the Eastside suburbs gathered more wealth and political clout over the years, Seattle always had the lawyers, the corporate offices, the art galleries, the live theaters, the University of Washington, the sports teams, the prestige and the power. The strip-mall suburbs north and south of town, and the rural communities beyond, got to be what the rest of America used to think of the Northwest (or Americans used to think of Canada): Hewers of wood and gatherers of water.

That includes the town where I spent my own formative years.

Ever So Humble: I've talked in the past about my hometown of Marysville, a place that once meant sawmill workers in dark taverns, clutching beer mugs with all seven remaining fingers. It has since become a Boeing suburb. But the Tulalip Reservation across I-5, home of several tribes "united" by Federal edict (and of the former Boeing test site where live chickens were once blasted from cannons onto windshields) is nearing approval to expand its bingo parlor into full casino gambling. While there won't be any Vegas nightlife, it'll still be the most exciting thing there since the Thunderbird Drive-In used to show soft-core sex flicks, fully visible from the freeway. *(March 1991)*

Surreal Estate: *For Rent* magazine has a front-page ad inviting people to come live at Walden Pond, "A home that the heart never leaves... Sense the peace of living by the pond... In this fast-paced world of hustle and bustle, it's nice to know that there is someplace where you can enjoy the peace and comfort of easy living." It turns out to be a south Everett condo on a man-made lake. The "luxurious 1, 2, & 3 bedroom homes" offer designer fireplaces, covered parking, free aerobics classes, an exercise room, tanning salon, pool, sauna, video lounge, and gym. "And it's only minutes from work, school, Boeing, Everett Mall, and all major conveniences." *(May 1992)*

'Don't Walk' This Way: Bellevue officials are promising to make their town "more pedestrian friendly" — by beefing up citations against people walking against the "Don't Walk" lights. If they really wanted to help walkers, they'd change the lights on some intersections that allow walking for only three seconds every three minutes, so you have to jaywalk to get anywhere on time. *(October 1992)*

Brave New World Dept.: A few weeks ago, KING-TV reported that the state's highest youth suicide rate was on the Eastside.

I could believe it, after having gone for a job interview in the heart of Darkest Redmond. Once-lovely farmland, ploughed under and paved over with winding roads to nowhere, abutted by finished and unfinished cheap poured-concrete low-rise office park buildings, some with gaudy entrances tacked onto their otherwise hyperbland facades, all recessed from the road by moats of parking and/or dirt where grass will eventually be. No "public space," no pedestrians, just people working in isolated cubicles writing software that presumes that we'll all someday be working in isolated cubicles. A sterile landscape of silent dread that only author J.G. Ballard or filmmaker Atom Egoyan could properly fictionalize. *(March 1994)*

Nomenclature Dept.: While recently heading back to the safety of town from Darkest Redmond, feeling the sensations of comfort I always feel when I make it to the west side of the bridge, I tried to devise an alternative to Tricia Romano's description of suburban dance-club goers in a recent *Stranger* as "tunnel people." That's a term used by Manhattanites to insult those who live in other N.Y.C. boroughs or Jersey. If we have to use an N.Y.C. term to describe Eastsiders, it oughta be one based on the N.Y.C. meaning of the name "Bellevue."

I suggest "floaters." It symbolizes not only the floating bridges and certain airheaded attitudes, but also compares the suburban everywhere/nowhere experience to the old Japanese floating world, the culture of aristocrats and courtesans who traveled around in leisure, unconnected to the land surrounding them. *(July 26, 1995)*

Was amused by the minor brouhaha when a Seattle urban-advocacy group issued a report a few weeks back claiming you're physically safer living in town than in suburbs, 'cause we might have a few more violent crimes but they've got a lot more car wrecks.

The suburb-lovin' *Seattle Times* found a UW traffic-engineering prof to call the study flawed. He claimed the report's methodology was insufficiently documented, and questioned its choice of neighborhoods to compare

Insville & Outski
(continued)

Video phones/ Car phones
Elizabeth Perkins/ Sigourney Weaver
Hockey/Football
Spain/Australia
Roseanne Barr/ Sam Kinison
Tacoma/ Port Townsend
Emo Phillips/ Pee-wee Herman
CD-ROM/CD-3
I Dream of Jeannie/ Leave It to Beaver
Seduction/ "Married to your work"
Crystals/Gold
Toast/Croissants
Grant's Ale/ Dry beer
Light rail/I-90
Lemon yellow/Beige
Indoors/Outdoors
Plays/Movies
Post-futurism/ Nostalgia
Waffles/Oat bran
Estonia/ Afghanistan
Glasses/Contacts
Social workers/ Lawyers
Atom Egoyan/ Woody Allen
Women singers/ Supermodels
(January 1989)

Soviet writers/ New England writers
Busby Berkeley/ Frank Capra
Anne Rice/ Stephen King
Hasselblad/Vivitar
Plaid/Pinstripes
The Simpsons/Disney
Nose rings/earrings
Living Colour/ "Metal love songs"
Sake/ Sweetened "juice cocktails"
Storytelling/ Stand-up comedy
Camper Van Beethoven/ Weird Al Yancovic
Winona Ryder/ Lisa Bonet
Spokane/ Gig Harbor
Volleyball/Tennis
Daniel Day-Lewis/ William Hurt
Anthony Braxton/ Philip Glass
The Wonder Stuff/ The Wonder Years
Cheese steaks/ Cajun food
War on poverty/ "War on drugs"
Glitter/Neon
(December 1989)

— the gentrifying upper Queen Anne Hill vs. the sprawling, insufficiently-roaded outskirts of the formerly-rural Issaquah.

While I can buy the validity of the prof's hesitations, I also think the report's premise is definitely worth further study 'n' thought. For too long, we've allowed "personal safety" to be defined by interests with a decided bias against cities and walking, for suburbs and driving. I know I personally feel more secure in almost any part of Seattle than in almost any part of Bellevue. *(May 1, 1996)*

Up Against the 'Wal': Like a storm system finally enveloping over the nation's furthest reaches, Wal-Mart arrived in the Seattle metro area. It's on Renton's Rainier Avenue, one of those near-soulless strip-mall hells grown parasitically around the remnants of what was once a real town. Unlike the towns where Wal-Mart became the infamous Great Sprawlmaker, Renton was lost to chain stores and parking moats long ago.

I got to the store its first weekend; it was expectedly swamped. The thing's huge and imposing, even by hypermarket standards. While Kmart and Fred Meyer at least try for inviting atmospheres despite their size, Wal-Mart simply overwhelms. The fluorescent lights are somehow harsher; the shelves are taller and deeper; the ceilings are higher; the colors are colder; the signage is starker. And everywhere, posters and banners shout out what a dynamic, energetic, powerful outfit Wal-Mart is.

It's easy to see how this formula worked in the south and midwest towns where Clinton's late pal Sam Walton started the chain. To residents used to small-town humdrum, Wal-Mart barged in with the biggest retail-theater experience they'd seen, one with the spirit not of nostalgia or homeyness but of a company (and a nation) on the go-go-go. But in a community that already has big-time retail, the Wal-Mart formula seems just plain shrill. Even the (nearly deserted) Kmart up the highway felt like a cozy neighborhood boutique in comparison.

And as for prices and selection, Wal-Mart's endlessly-touted "buying power" might work against the indie stores in the small towns, but it can't significantly undersell other hypermarket chains and can't match the selection of specialty stores.

I finished my afternoon at the nearby Lazy Bee, a highly independent restaurant and Boeing workers' hangout. With model planes hanging from the ceiling and booths made from surplus 727 seats, it's a place no chain operator could conceive of. (Even my chalkboard-special meal was priced to come out, with tax, at $7.07!) I was reminded of zine editor Randolph Garbin's *Recipe for an American Renaissance*: "Eat in diners, ride trains, shop on Main Street, put a porch on your house, live in a walkable community." *(Nov. 14, 1996)*

Goin' South?: The Portland tabloid *Willamette Week* ran an essay package on the topic "Seattle Envy." For those whose only notion about either Portland or Seattle is they're not New York, the essays provide a valuable intro to the real differences between the two towns, only 185 miles away and nearly identical in size (though Seattle's greater metro area has almost a million more folks than Portland's).

All six writers (four Seattleites, two Portlanders) agree Portland's older, smugger, and more civic-minded, while Seattle's brasher, louder, and more globally aware. That leaves them to disagree on which they prefer.

Intro-story writer Kris Hargis claims, "for all its charms, Portland has always seemed a bit burdened by what you could call a Napoleon complex. 'So we're little, so what?' we say. 'We can still kick your town's butt on social services, city planning and parks' — all the things Seattle forgot about in its quest to become a Goliath of global commerce."

Now if you ask me, the differences are more blatant and more subtle than *Willamette Week* suggests. The subtle ones come from Portland's stronger sense of "society," the kind of community-spirit that means both public-transit systems and beauty pageants get taken a lot more seriously there than here.

The blatant ones come from one prime source, Boeing. Without Boeing, Portland was free to build its economic base on timber, shipping, and insurance. With Boeing, Seattle came to see itself as a player on the world stage.

Also with Boeing, Seattle gained a civic hierarchy built around the dual elites of gladhanding deal-makers and obsessive-compulsive engineers, hierarchies which would eventually find their ultimate meeting point at Microsoft. (Though Nike proves Portlanders can easily match Seattleites in the ruthless pursuit of profits and market share at any cost.) *(Nov. 19, 1998)*

*Johnny Depp/
Charlie Sheen
Bowling/Hiking
Survivors/Winners
Working to live/
Living to work
Tattoos/
Cosmetic surgery
Quilts/Tie-dye
Target/Kmart
Alexander Cockburn/
P.J. O'Rourke
Nile Spice Cous-Cous/
Cup Noodle
World music by
its creators/
P. Simon & D. Byrne*
Pacifica News/
All Things
Considered
*Sky blue/Brown
Cheesecake/
Pudding cups
Crying on the inside/
Laughing on the
outside
Impetuous
romanticism/
Righteous alienation
Joyce Carol Oates/
Hall and Oates
Fractal geometry/
Supercolliders
Eating/Dining
Dystopias/
Novels with "Elf"
or "Dragon" as
prefixes in the titles
(January 1991)*

(continued)

13: THE OUTSIDE WORLD

or, lands of contrast and brightness

As a big Pacific Rim seaport town, a near-border town, a big settling point for immigrants, and one of America's top foreign-export regions, Seattleites like to fancy themselves as hip to the ways of the world. We're really just about as ignorant as other Americans about life in other lands, but at least we like to think we try to learn.

As for the rest of America, even places within Seattle's greater economic zone like Alaska and Idaho, we're often more honest (even proud) about our ignorance. We like to think we're an isthmus of civilization that doesn't really belong in the same milieu with those uncouth loggers and miners and ranchers out in the big western expanse.

No, we like to think we're "world class" (as in the frequent funding requests to support a world class university, a world class zoo, a world class baseball park, etc.) — but still "nicer" and more human-scale than those bigger Pacific Time Zone towns, the snobby San Francisco and the unlivable Los Angeles.

I'm a recipient of these received ideas, and at times have also been their carrier.

Eat Your Heart Out, Updike: The Brasil restaurant on First Avenue showed scenes from the latest Rio samba parades as part of its Sunday-night film series. Among the 18 "schools" (each with at least 3,000 amateur performers) were several save-the-rainforest parades and one in honor of Brazilian author Jorge Amado (*Dona Flor and Her Two Husbands*, et al.). Can you imagine giant floats, musicians, singers, children, feather-headdressed men, and topless women parading for a living American writer? Brazil has a few serious problems, but at least it has people who actively participate in their own culture. *(May 1989)*

The Discovery Channel's quest for cheap, informative programming makes for some astounding time-wasters. On Christmas morning they offered a years-old Alaska travel video.

The late Lorne Greene narrated, calling it (as all regions in travel videos, films and articles are always called) "truly a land of contrasts." As part of the tourist biz, every town Greene mentioned had a stage show or museum honoring frontier-era prostitution ("but at this saloon, only the beer's for sale"). Alaska's tourism division publicizes actresses who dress up as old-time floozies, while its police arrest anyone in the profession for real. *(January 1990)*

Did You Saw What I Saw?: The British Columbia provincial government, finally becoming concerned about public-image effects of its industry-at-any-cost philosophy, is spraying grass seed from helicopters over massive clear-cut areas near the coasts of Vancouver Island, so they'll not look ravaged from tourist boats.

This sort of environmental make-believe is not likely to fool many, and can at best postpone a full backlash against the province's rapid growth. *(August 1990)*

Just Say 'Non'?: You realize if Quebec ever does leave Canada, it'd mean no more bilingualism in the rest of Canada? What would we do without bilingual Canadian food packaging, such as Diet Coke with "NutraSuc"? Without CBUF-FM and the great way its announcers pronounce words like Chilliwack and Okanagon? Maybe Vancouver could go bilingual English/Mandarin, but it wouldn't be the same.

On the other hand, a *Christian Science Monitor* commentary by Washington, D.C. corporate lawyer Mark Schwartz called the Parti Quebecois one of the world's last "hard-line leftist" movements. Schwartz's piece feared an independent Quebec might attempt "a new social order" that'd neglect the proper coddling of foreign investors and instead pursue "full employment, a more equitable society for all citizens, and a lessened role for the marketplace in people's lives." He was agog that the separatists' "64-page vision of an independent Quebec fails to mention a single word about the private sector's role in creating jobs." A place where 49.4% of voters declared humanitarian and cultural values more important than business? *Alors! (Nov. 8, 1995)*

North of the Border: The fanning out of Hollywood bigshots across the western states continues. I'm told the most recently "discovered" homesite for frequent-flier showbiz commuters is the outer exurbs of Boise.

As you've seen from the Little Hollywoods in New Mexico, Montana, Colorado and the San Juans, when the L.A. types show up three things tend to happen:

(1) Real estate prices soar so locals can't afford to live there anymore.

(2) These millionaires who proudly live half a gas tank from the closest supermarket and 100 gallons of jet fuel from their jobs start preaching to the locals about eco-consciousness.

(3) They bring in their favorite L.A. chefs to invent a "traditional regional cuisine" for the area. It'll be fun to

Insville & Outski

(continued)

Black rock bands/ White blues bands
Reality/ Virtual reality
Ocean Shores/ Bainbridge
A seductive whisper/ Screaming
Teachers/ Entrepreneurs
Photography/ Big sculpture
Molly Ivins/ Dave Barry
Parks/Office parks
Adrienne Shelly (Trust)/ Julia Roberts
"Venus in Furs"/ Vegetarians in leather jackets
Ph.D's/MBAs
Buffalo Bills/ LA Raiders
"Made in USSR" products/ Baseball cards
Little black dresses/ Bustiers
Martinis/ Margaritas
Box sets by one-hit bands/ Books on tape
Making your town better/ Moving to the country
Pet turtles/ Pot-bellied pigs
United Europe/ The "new world order"
(January 1992)

Short-short fiction/ Techno thrillers
The year 2000/ The year 1968
Dandyism for men/ Menswear for women
Maroon/Purple
Contraceptive implants (or cosmetic imitations)/ Fertility drugs
Lesbian cowgirl kitsch/ Ralph Lauren
Alberta/Montana
Internet/Prodigy
Looking well-fed/ Looking emaciated
Martin Heidegger/ Robert Fulghum
Women doctors/ Anchorwomen
Dark Horse Comics/ Marvel
Art from rusted iron/ Pilchuck Glass
Drinking/Smoking
Hard news/Analysis
The power of beauty/ The beauty of power
Release/Submission
What you know/ Who you know
Pajamas/Sweats
Edith Piaf/ Jim Morrison
Smart people/ Smart drugs
Judy Tenuta/ Jerry Seinfeld
Hockey/Basketball
Trolls/Teddy bears
Saving jobs/ Cutting costs
Dancing/Jogging
Snapple/ Crystal Pepsi
Letterman on CBS/ Arsenio Hall
The Afrocentric look/ The Seattle look
(January 1993)

find out what the "traditional regional cuisine" becomes for a state whose very license plates promote "Famous Potatoes," whose only movie-based association with dining came from Steve Martin's cameo in *The Muppet Movie,* as a waiter offering "Sparkling Muscatel by Fine Wines of Idaho." *(Feb. 14, 1995)*

L.A. Riots II: The Sequel failed to make its scheduled premiere, gravely inconveniencing the original producers (police) and distributors (news media). Back when *Repo Man* came out, one of my gothic-punk acquaintances described for me what was so different about it. His first sentence: "It was made in L.A." He meant that this film used the parts of L.A. that other L.A. films didn't (and mostly still don't).

A few weeks ago, I found myself in the company of a semi-retired Hollywood bigshot. He talked about how he's looking to move here, how "everybody (in the business) wants to get out of L.A." The L.A. people scattering across the western states are just re-creating the La La Land mentality in an exile made possible by faxes and FedEx.

The airheads are leaving Hollywood so they can keep their worthless Hollywood culture alive, so they can stay unbothered by the issues of people other than themselves. They symbolize America's withdrawal from social community into private hedonism. Beverly Hills is the reason South Central exists.

The "Northwest Lifestyle" described in newspaper "Living" sections is usually defined according to misplaced L.A. priorities, as a narcissistic life of private pleasures. The yuppie dream of "Moving to the Country" (without depending on a rural economy) is just an upscale version of the suburban dream/nightmare. It reflects the abandonment of neighborhoods, cities, social services, education, health, infrastructure, etc.; all as guided by a politics that purported to celebrate the Rugged Individual but really just gave more power to the already-powerful.

Reagan was the Spielberg president — and not just because both shared a nostalgia for a nonexistent past. Just as Spielberg turned the genres of sleazy fringe movies into the foundation of the modern film biz, so Reagan turned the hatemongering and quick-buck tactics of the west's right-fringe political circles into the foundation of national government policy. Both camps trafficked in contrived sentimentality, not in real social intimacy.

It's way past time for this to end. Don't move to the country. Stop running from your problems, America! Stay in town! Fight to make it better! *(May 1993)*

Bean There: They hate Starbucks in Frisco. Every snide Bay Arean zine, columnist and cartoonist I've read has ranted against the non-funky, high-rent-paying green coffee stands increasingly dotting the City That Thinks It's God. You never saw any of these people complaining when Frisco-based BankAmerica absorbed Seattle's two biggest banks.

I say it's the least they should accept in return for Northern California's past domination of Northwest arts and its present domination of Northwest finance. Besides, experience here has shown Starbucks hardly drives independent coffeehouses under, as the Frisco writers warn. It increases interest in specialty coffee, which leads some of its new customers to graduate beyond its own chain-store atmosphere toward independents. *(Jan. 31, 1995)*

One More Reason to Hate San Francisco: The December *Wired* (now owned by N.Y.C. magazine magnate S.I. Newhouse Jr. but still based in Frisco) has this cover story listing "83 Reasons Why Bill Gates's Reign Is Over." I actually got into it, until I got to entry #31: "All Microsoft's market power aside, building World HQ near Seattle has not shifted Earth's axis or altered gravitational fields. The Evergreen State is still the sticks..." A sidebar piece recommends Gates "get connected — move software headquarters to Silicon Valley."

Look: You can badmouth the big little man all you like (I've done so, and will likely do so again). But when you disparge the whole Jet City and environs, them's fightin' words. *(Nov. 23, 1998)*

Straight folks faking gayness/
White folks faking blackness
Lovers/Rebels
Rechargeable batteries/
Disposable diapers
Community involvement/
Cocooning
Finding cool people everywhere/
Looking for the Next Seattle
Cocoa/
Instant cappuccino
The Economist/
Fortune
2 Stupid Dogs/
The toned-down Ren & Stimpy
Crossroads/
Bellevue Square
Independent political movements/
Two-party system
Cabarets/Moshpits
Crying at movies/
Laughing at tabloids
'50s doo-wop revival/
'70s guitar-rock revival
Czech Republic/
England
Women's bowling/
Beach volleyball
Transnational labor organizing/
"Free" trade
Cheap motels/
Bed & Breaakfasts
Yearning/Denial
Prozac/Crack
Old gas-station uniforms/
The REI Look
1/4-ton pickups/
Upscale 4 x 4s
Campy Catholic art/
Neo-paganism
Flop/Gin Blossoms
Face painting/Pierces
Bill Nye/
Carmen Sandiego
(January 1994)

(continued)

14: NATIONAL AFFAIRS

or, the gilded right and the gelded left

Billboard from the days when the GOP was the Rural Party.

As previously mentioned, the political balance-O-power's still a bit different here than in the nation as a whole, but much less different than it used to be.

And we're just as affected by the machinations of national power as regions geographically closer to "the other Washington," from brief military escapades abroad to interminable "culture wars" at home; from Republican strategies to marry the money of Big Business and the shock troops of Big Religion, to Democratic counter-strategies to make them split up.

"In a world where victory is the only thing that matters, the only way to win is by risking it all." —This Paramount ad for the video release of *Days of Thunder* would have only sounded as stupid as any other commercial had it not premiered during the second week of January. It could be said that a decade of pro-violence culture has led to the war's start on Jan. 16, from joy-of-slaughter movies (approved for juvenile consumption by the make-war-not-love attitude of the Ratings Board) to the stuffing of the Pentagon budget and starvation of schools, keeping people hungry and manipulable for recruiting and propaganda purposes. *(February 1991)*

I'm still baffled by a term consistently used in letters-to-the-editor to stereotype anti-war protesters. Just what is an "ultraliberal"? I know liberals, and I know radicals, but I've never heard anybody describe themselves as an "ultraliberal." Is that somebody who wants to smash the state but keep the Weather Service? Or somebody who wants to demolish multinational corporations but only if he can still get Kenyan coffee and keep his Walkman? *(April 1991)*

In Living Color, normally the most astute sketch show on TV, ran an "Iraqi fashion show" segment with women totally draped in black, including their faces. The catch is that Iraq had been one of the secular Arab states, eager to round up all political opposition but ambivalent towards modern clothes. It's our friends in Saudi Arabia and our once-and-future friends in Iran who jail women for showing their faces.... *(May 1991)*

Bulldozers of the Spirit: The real political history of Washington state, and the western U.S. in general, is a few crackpots, a few innovators, and a lot of fiends. The ugliness of much of today's American landscape matches the ugliness of American politics, for a reason. The GOP is now controlled by the western land and resource industries, who made strip mines and strip malls and and tract houses and shrillily demand the right to destroy the few "real" spaces left.

They built the S&L biz to pump money into subdivisions and then, with Reagan's deregulation, into all forms of swindles. George (in oil) and Neil (S&L's) Bush are insiders in this gang.

The Religious Right is a mere tool, callously used by the moneybags to barter for votes and promote an authoritarian culture. Charles Keating, who financed anti-porn drives with loot from S&L frauds, was a pivot man in the scheme. The guys who made southern California what it is today have no qualms about what their hirelings Nixon and Reagan did to the nation's social terrain. *(January 1992)*

That 'N.W.O.' Phrase Won't Go Away: Leftists still utter those three words in every second sentence, a year after Bush said it just once as a throwaway line.

Stuck-in-the-sixties left-wingers, as much as demagogic right-wingers, yearn for the good old days of American imperialism. Neither wants to believe that we're in relative socioeconomic decline. Instead of seeking today's answers, they'd rather pretend we still had yesterday's problems.

Kuwait was not Vietnam. We weren't colonizing anybody; we weren't claiming to bring them "democracy" or even "free enterprise". We sent an army-for-hire to restore a 70-year-old mercantilist monarchy on whom the western economy had become dependent.

If there really is a new world order (that's questionable, considering how disorderly the world is getting), its nexus isn't in Washington, D.C. but in Tokyo and Berlin. This doesn't mean the end of America. It could be our renewal. For moral-righteousness types, there are advantages to a country off the cutting edge of world dominance. It's easier to make your ideals into your country's national policy when you're in a backwater to the currents of conquest (cf. Sweden). *(March 1992)*

'Family' Feud: If patriotism is the last refuge of scoundrels, family values are their next-to-last refuge. Or, as GOP loyalist George Will says, "morality is the last refuge of the politically desperate."

Almost any destructive policy can be trumped up as a pean to "The Family" (as if there were only one kind anymore, and as if all families were good for the people in them). Bush/Quayle, in their total lack of contact with the real world, haven't noticed the spectacular rise of

Insville & Outski
(continued)

Pocket watches/ Swatch
Blue drinks/ Clear drinks
Determination/ Defeatism
Brooklyn/Berkeley
Count Chocula/ Pop Tarts Crunch
Mini satellite dishes/ Cable
Video dialtone/ Pay-per-view movies
Hi-8 camcorders/ "Kill Your TV" bumper stickers
Old Country/ Young Country
Voodoo/ Faith healing
EastEnders/ Days of Our Lives
Hinduism/ Baseball as religion
Lives/Lifestyles
Scotland/Spain
Democracy/ Demographics
Horse shampoo/ Spray-on hair
DIY culture/ Global entertainment empires
Whiskey/Vodka
Jazz/Funk
Curling/ Snowboarding
Old Dart Swingers/ Mercedes
Sampling/ Intellectual property
Men who wish they were lesbians/ Whites who wish they were Indians
(Jan. 3, 1995)

Sun-Netscape/ Intel-Microsoft
Gentlemen/Guys
Pinky & the Brain/ X-Men
Community syndicalism/ Global capitalism
Condo-izing office towers/ Exurbs
Albuquerque/ New Orleans
Rotterdam/Prague
Avant-Pop fiction/ Cyberpunk
Steak houses/ Coffee houses
Puppetry/ Computer animation
Fedoras/Baseball caps
H.L. Mencken/ Hunter Thompson
Shoe Pavilion/ Payless ShoeSource
Indian musicals/ Special-effects thrillers
Poker/ Magic: The Gathering
Union jackets/ Gas-station jackets
Mandalas/Fractals
Skepticism/Cynicism
Braided pubic hair/ Genital piercings
Garcia sightings/ Elvis sightings
Black Jack/Bubble Yum
Free Quebec/NAFTA
Percogesic/Melatonin
Ang Lee/Paul Verhoven
Aldous Huxley/ Terence McKenna
Hypertexts (finally)/ In-Out lists
(Dec. 27, 1995)

"dysfunctional family" 12-step groups and other forces that are pointing out the basic structural faults of the nuclear-family system. "The Family" is, to millions, an image of stifling cruelty and authoritarianism — just what the Right loves. *(August 1992)*

Strategy for Defeat #3: The Republican convention was like an ad for an impulse product (beer, cigarettes, candy) that offers no claims about the product, only images of its ideal consumers. If you're not an evangelical, country music-loving, hetero nuclear family (white or white-wannabe), they don't want to see your face.

Not long ago, the Republicans promised to become the new majority party for the next century. Last month's convention abandoned this ambition, along with any coherent political or economic policy.

The only remaining GOP agenda is cultural: The promotion of a British-style class system, with financiers and influence peddlers on top and passive-aggressive fundamentalists beneath. If you don't belong to those categories, the Repos want nothing to do with you. Like the '80s Left, the '90s Right is obsessed with purifying its own ranks, not with building a sufficient base of support. *(September 1992)*

Election Aftermath: The electorate issued a big dose of reality. A positive reality, as in waking up dazed yet refreshed, to find Patrick Duffy telling you the past 12 years were just a bad dream.

For too long, our government and its business backers lived in a fantasy, in which the declaration of one's innate "morality" excused all immoral actions, in which the stagnating defense of old socioeconomic privilege could be sold as a "growth policy."

The denizens of this delusory Pleasure Island, long since having turned into asses, expected that with enough money (ours) and lies (theirs), they could maintain the fantasy forever. But the lies ran out quicker than the money.

The sleaze machine will finally be out of the Executive Branch. No more gag rules, no more Council on Competitiveness, no more friendly dictators, no more executive orders to appease Pat Robertson. No more race-baiting or gender-baiting as official policy. Now for the boring part: establishing a long-term, active constituency for getting done what needs doing.

The two drug cartels (illicit and prescription) are still bleeding the nation dry. The pro-unemployment and anti-environment lobbyists maintain their unelective offices; they and their pundit pals still brand anyone who dares oppose them as "special interests." Think it's OK to go back to hip apathy? Get real. *(December 1992)*

The Buzz of the Nation: Note that Pepsi was a sponsor of the Clinton pre-inagural TV special. Traditionally, Coke was the Democratic pop (owned by Atlanta Dixiecrats) and Pepsi was the Republican pop (owned by Wall Street investors). During WWII, FDR pushed sweetheart deals to give Coke extra sugar rations and to let it build plants wherever our troops landed. In the '50s, Nixon deliberately staged his "kitchen debate" with Kruschev in front of a Pepsi display at a Moscow trade fair.

In the '80s, Pepsi's rise in the "cola wars" (under a management full of ex-military officials) mirrored the GOP's power surge; as the Democrats compromised and struggled, Coke lost its way with New Coke and ill-advised Hollywood investments. Now, it's Pepsi that's going weird at one end (with dumb ideas like Crystal Pepsi) and digging in at the other (buying fast-food chains to insure a captive market for its drinks). Clinton himself claims to be a Coke loyalist. *(February 1993)*

Brave Old World Revisited: The election debacle confirmed several trends I've often cud-chewed about in this space. Chiefly, the right-wing sleaze machine's got a grip on the late-modern (not yet postmodern) political economy, efficiently funneling cash and influence from both eastern Old Money and western New Money into smear campaigns, stealth campaigns, one-sided religious TV and talk radio operations, etc. They're good at convincing voters that they're Taking Charge when they're really getting them to suck up to the forces that control most of the real power and money in this country.

The middle-of-the-road Democrats, having shed most populist pretenses in the futile dream of winning corporate cash away from the GOP, is trapped in limboland; while too many left-wingers still think it's a statement of defiance to stay out of the electoral process and let the Right win. The GOP effectively controlled Congress the last two years anyway, but now it's gonna create Gridlock City, getting nothing done in a big way and blaming the "liberals" for everything. At least it might, just might, force Clinton into the spin doctor's office for an emergency backbone transplant.

How to change this around? Like I said at the end of 1992 and again this past April, we've gotta rebuild a pop-

Forest green/Teal
Reno/The Vegas Strip
Gwyneth Patrow/ Demi Moore
Absinthe/Ecstasy
Dick's Deluxe/ Arch Deluxe
Writing/Literature
Tacos/Wraps
Women with nipple rings sneering at women with implants/ People in leather sneering at people in fur
Georgetown/Fremont
Hype! *soundtrack/* Pulp Fiction *soundtrack*
BSA/Harley-Davidson
ADSL/Cable modems
Chubby and Tubby/ Niketown
Phone cards/ Baseball cards
Wallace Stevens/ Charles Bukowski
Morris Minor/ Range Rover
Plymouth Prowler/ Lexus
Mensa tests/Drug tests
Orgies/Raves
Slot-car racing/ Snowboarding
"Dee-lish"/"X-treme"
DIY Internet radio/ NPR
Home sweatshops/ Overseas sweatshops
Donuts/Bagels
Drew Carey/ Robin Williams
'30s revival/ '70s revival
Toques/Baseball caps
Straight-edgers drinking/ Vegans smoking
Shuffleboard/Doom
Sorbonne/Evergreen
Rebuilding cities/ Deconstructing texts
Chanel #5/Patchouli
Flaxseed/Hemp
(Dec. 26, 1996)

St. John's Wort/Prozac
Working for Amazon.com/
Working for Microsoft
Meredith Brooks/
Sarah McLachlan
Old-hotel wallpaper/
"Faux" wall finishes
See-thru/Wonderbra
Superstore/Megamalls
NY Times *in color/*
Commercials in B&W
Wapato/La Conner
International Channel/
Fox News Channel
Payday loans/
Home-equity loans
RVs/Houseboats
New symphony hall/
New Nordstrom
R.D. Laing/
Deepak Chopra
Homemade CDs/
Fake indie labels
Sleep capsules/Futons
Men's make-up/
Women's suits
Beacon Hill/
Upper Queen Anne
Pectoral implants/
Penile implants
Wormwood/
Crystal meth
Bad Badz-Maru/Elmo
Rowan Atkinson/
David Schwimmer
Imps/Angels
Peasants/
"Peasant food"
Seattle housing crisis/
Potholes
"Super duper"/"Rad"
Cool/Hot
Old magazine art/
Photomosaics
Empowerment/
Self-victimization
Chocolate-covered graham cookies/
Mazurkas
Pepper pot/Lentil soup
Silk shirts/
Silk jackets
Do-gooders/
Go-getters
(Dec. 31, 1997)

ulist Left from the ground up. "Progressive" movements that refuse to venture more than a mile from the nearest college English department aren't worth a damn.

We've gotta persuade working-class people, rural people, parents, and ethnic minorities that corporate ass-kissing is not people power. The Right's effectively played on voters' justified resentment at centralized power structures, only to rewire that energy back into those structures.

We've got to reroute that wiring, to lead people away from the Right's faux-empowerment into real empowerment. We'll have to do it against deliberate apathy from corporate-centrist media and hostility from right-wing media.

And we shouldn't depend on help from mainstream Dems, who might revert to their Reagan-era coddling (the equivalent of S&M's "consensual bottom role").

Eventually, the Right's hypocrisies should collapse as an emerging decentralized culture supersedes today's centralized culture — if we stay on guard against those who would short-circuit the postmodern promise into the same old hierarchical system. *(November 1994)*

After the Smoke Clears: It's not the liberal wing of the Democratic Party that failed this past November, it's the conservative wing. The wimpy, submissive Lite Right tactics, the tactics of Dems from Scoop Jackson through Jimmy Carter and beyond, utterly collapsed.

Now that there's no further purpose in preserving the careers of "moderate" Democratic officials, liberals should take over the party machinery and offer up a strong, no-compromise, no-apologies alternative to the Right. To do that, the Democrats will have to stop playing by the Republicans' rules. This isn't a matter of simply infiltrating precienct committees and party organizations, in order to force a set of policies onto party platforms. I'm talking the whole big boring job. We've gotta rethink everything from constituency groups to organizing to fund-raising to advertising. We've gotta flush away the stinking turd of the idea that liberalism can't become really popular.

There's another way out there, a way that favors small business over big, close communities over sprawling suburbs, new decentralized media over old centralized ones, thinking over obedience, passion over zombiedom.

This is the way that could build a coalition among punks, intellectuals, immigrants, minorities, feminists, the downwardly-mobile working class, people who like a healthy environment, people who prefer real economic progress instead of pork-fed defense industries.

It won't be easy; it'll be hard to keep all these disparate elements together. But it's the only real way toward a post-conservative future. *(January 1995)*

Falling Flat: The most inadvertantly fascinating part of last month's PBS *Fight Over Citizen Kane* documentary was William Randolph Hearst's creaky newsreel sermon against FDR's increases to upper-bracket income taxes. It reminded me a lot of Steve Forbes's flat tax nonsense. Both publishers' tactics use populist rhetoric to promote the self-interests of the wealthy, particularly those with significant inherited wealth such as themselves.

The comparisons go beyond there. Forbes and Hearst are/were party-lovin' men-about-town known to hobnob with movie stars. Hearst's papers provided a self-contained information system, in which no voice too far from his own worldview got heard or respected.

Forbes's magazines haven't gone that far, but the right-media universe of talk radio, televangelists and opinion magazines (whose support the GOP candidates are courting) fulfill Hearst's formula better than the old man could have imagined. *(Feb. 21, 1996)*

Pat-aphysics: Buchanan's proving to be more than just another lifetime D.C. political/media insider pretending to be an "outsider." His momentary campaign success signals the first significant crack in the GOP's 16-year ruling coalition of fundamentalists and corporations (something I've been predicting or at least desiring for some time).

About a quarter of the things he says (the parts about the plight of the downsized and the ripoff that is "free" trade) make more sense than what the other Republicans say. It's just the other three quarters of the things he says are so freakish (the tirades against gays, feminists, immigrants, pro-choice advocates, and other humans guilty only of not belonging to his target demographic).

If there's hope, it's that Buchanan's polls rose after he started downplaying the hatefest talk and emphasizing the anti-corporate talk. Why's the only candidate to challenge the sanctity of big money also the biggest bigot and bully? Why don't any national Democrats speak against the corporate power-grab like Pat does? *(March 13, 1996)*

Ennui Go Again: November 5's just around the metaphorical corner, and acquaintances of mine say they can

Pipes/Cigars
"Got __?"/ "Yo Quiero __"
The WB/Fox
Elan/Panache
Linux/Windows 2000
Cracked Divx videos/ MP3 music files
Saving the Kalakala/ Stopping the Makah whale hunt
Lions Gate Films/ DreamWorks
Perfect 10/ Barely Legal
Mode/Vogue
Bento/Pan-Asian
Less Than Jake/ Better Than Ezra
Westwood Village/ University Village
Pachinko/Megatouch
Toupees/Propecia
Bars subsidized by pulltab sales/ Bars subsidized by cigarette ads
Black/"The new black"
Pinot noir/Merlot
Mutts/Dilbert
Mystic pseudo-science/ Fundamentalist pseudo-science
Pokémon/Rugrats
South Park (the Seattle neighborhood)/ South Park *(the TV show)*
Hungarian operettas/ New Star Wars
Plane-crash videos/ Animal-attack videos
Creators/Celebrities
Outlandish heteros/ "Mainstream" gays
Streaming net video/ Cable access
Partying naked/ Wearing "Party Naked" T-shirts
"I love everyone and you're next"/ "Do I look like I give a damn?"
Doing your own thing/ Following advice on web sites
(Dec. 28, 1998)

hardly wait. They're psyched n' primed to head out, wait patiently in line, and be the first to buy the CD *Presidents of the United States of America II*, which cleverly goes on sale Election Day.

As for the election itself, has any major election in my lifetime been so near and yet so not-there? I'm not talking about voter apathy or ineffectual complaints about the electoral status quo; those have always been with us. I'm talking the total slouching-through-the-motions aspect of the exercise.

I've struggled for a metaphor for this anti-spectacle: An end-of-season football game between two going-nowhere teams? The last, fitful, sex act of a couple about to split up? The rote "excitement" of Elvis- and Marilyn-dressed waiters at some silly theme restaurant, or a cover band at a high-school prom?

Sure, in 1984 everyone recognized and dismissed Walter Mondale for being what Bob Dole is now — a seasoned insider who got nominated thanks to connections and fundraising prowess, but whom nobody had great fondness for as a potential Prez. But then there were other things going on (like the Booth Gardner/John Spellman gubernatorial race).

Now we've got uninspiring sideshows like Ellen Craswell looking all lost and confused when speaking to anyone outside her ideological clique. I was sorta hopin' for a final public-discourse confrontation with the Religious Right's central tenet (how Jesus Christ Himself wants you to cede all authority and power to Big Business). Instead, Clinton and Locke did an end-run and positioned themselves as the sane choice in pro-business politicians. They're just as receptive to the desires of big campaign contributors as the Republicans are — but without the annoying baggage of a social agenda, without dependencen on followers who just might someday get around to reading that Bible verse about not serving God and Mammon. *(Oct. 31, 1996)*

While I'm glad this electoral season's done, I already miss the near-subliminal background music used in political "attack ads." I know these relentlessly menacing synth tones come from professional stock-music libraries; some enterprising entrepreneur should license these 30-second alarms for use by ambient DJs looking to darken the evening's mood. *(Nov. 14, 1996)*

Misc. proudly offers the simple, elegant solution to the ideological quandry that's gripped the American dis-

Good & Scary

Researchers at the University of Amsterdam are embarking on a study to see whether virtual-reality technology can treat people's phobias. Their idea is to immerse patients in 3-D video-game-like scenarios to help people confront, and ultimately overcome, their deepest fears, all within the safe real-world confines of a clinic. It's good news because, if it works, it could help a lot of people. It's scary news because, if it works, I might one day feel the urge to use it myself. Here, for examples, are some of the situations I might ask to be programmed into a VR headset for me to face:

I must persuade a gaggle of stoned-out neohippies and ravers to leave a burning building.

I must get somewhere. But all along the street, I'm hounded by adamant people demanding things from me. "You! Three blocks away! Tell me the time, NOW!" "Where's Third Avenue from here?" "Hold it, kid! You're not going anywhere until you tell me the capital of Nebraska!"

course for the past month: Both sides in it are right. Larry Flynt is a defiant First Amendment crusader AND a shameless money-grubbing sleazebag!

(He's also an epitome of the late-century business libertarian, who promoted an even purer religion of unfettered capitalism than the GOP hypocrites who hounded him. His relentlessly anti-niceness approach toward lust, religion, and other base desires in the '70s just might have indirectly helped influence the Trump/Murdoch aesthetic of unapologetic avarice and the subsequent Limbaugh/Gingrich aesthetic of unapologetic bullydom.) *(Jan. 30, 1997)*

Why are followers of Lyndon LaRouche manning card-table protest stations downtown, pleading with passers-by to support Clinton against the GOP goon squad? Maybe because the Repo men could quite easily be seen as trying to accomplish what LaRouche (before he was imprisoned on credit-card fraud charges) used to accuse liberals and Jewish bankers of conspiring to establish — a quasi-theocratic "New Dark Ages" where demagougery and raw power would overtake all remainiing semblances of representative democracy.

Another potential interpretation of the whole mess: Clinton's lite-right political stances were engineered from the start to tear asunder the most important bond of the Reagan-era coalition, the bond between the corporate Republicans and the religious-authoritarian Republicans — not necessarily to improve the political lot of those more liberal than Clinton himself, but more likely to simply improve the playing-field chances of corporate Dems like himself.

With the impeachment frenzy being whipped up ever more noisily by the authoritarians (to increasing public disinterest), Clinton may be almost deliberately setting himself up as a potential self-sacrifice to this Quixotic quest, to finally disrupt the Religious Right's ties not only to its big-biz power brokers but its pseudo-populist voter base.

Of course, an institution at the heart of U.S. political maneuvering for some three decades or more (going back at least to Phyllis Schafly's major role in Barry Goldwater's 1964 Presidential bid and the concurrent drive to impeach Supreme Court Chief Justice Earl Warren) won't go away, and won't give up its hold on the system without a fight.

By driving the theocrats into increasingly shrill, dogmatic, and hypocritical positions, Clinton's setting up

I'm dying from a heart attack on the sidewalk, surrounded by dozens of people who just stand around laughing.

I'm dying of starvation, and meet a long series of people with plenty of food on hand who simply tell me I should be glad I'm not at risk for any of the long-term health problems related to obesity.

I'm in Hell, which turns out to be a really bad comedy club.

I'm in Hell, which turns out to be a video store with a thousand copies of each Meg Ryan movie and no copies of anything else.

I'm in Hell, which turns out to be a recording studio where a bearded engineer makes me eternally listen to the same Steely Dan song while he explains the technical brilliance behind its recording and mixing.

next year to be the year the theocrats either shrink into just another subculture or finally achieve their darkest dreams of quashing the democratic system of governance as we know it. Tuesday's midterm Congressional elections might or might not mean that much in the main scheme-O-things, but the months to follow will be a bumpy ride indeed. *(Oct. 29, 1998)*

There will surely be more to say about it in the weeks and months to come, but for now let's just say it's no exaggeration to call it a coup attempt, a kill-or-be-killed attempt by the Rabid Right to destroy the two-party system in favor of a quasi-Iranian theocracy. It's because the GOP Sleaze Machine's seen what Clinton and the Pro-Business Democrats have been up to (and largely succeeding at) — turning the Demos into the new "party of business," thereby marginalizing the Republicans into the party of demagogues and hatemongers. It's worked so well, all the Republicans can do anymore is to become even more extreme demagogues and hatemongers.

I don't believe Clinton will be forced out of office, but it'll be interesting (as in the old curse, "May you live in interesting times") to see just how much damage to the national discourse is made, and how many careers on both sides are destroyed, along the way. *(Dec. 21, 1998)*

All that can be said now is Clinton won what may have been a calculated risk, putting his own career and the institution of the Presidency on the line in an attempt to break the Religious Right's popularity base. After he spent his first term trying to woo big business away from the GOP, he's spent his second term engaged in bringing the Right's pious hypocrisies toward a kind of public referendum.

I'm not saying he tried to get caught cheatin' on his wife. I am saying he and his team artfully managed the crisis, to turn it away from being a judgement on him and into a judgement on his accusers. It's worked out about as well as he could've wanted it to. *(Feb. 15, 1999)*

I've been spending decades happily in the afterlife of my choice, until a descendant posthumously prays my way, against my will, into the Mormon Heaven.

I impatiently wait for my guru to tell me the ultimate meaning of life. But it turns out to be just like one of Richard Pryor's early appearances on Merv Griffin or Mike Douglas — a seemingly-endless, carefully detailed set up for a single punch line, that's completely bleeped out. Only instead of silence followed by howls of laughter, I hear silence followed by gasps of realization among all the other disciples in the audience.

(Feb. 22, 1999)

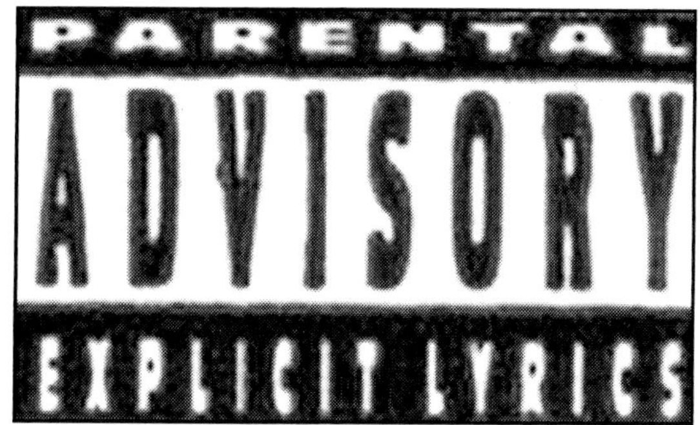

15: CUTTING REMARKS

or, in the realm of the censors

Republicans stage carefully-crafted media events in which they pontificate against the evils of the mass media. They crusade against public arts funding, while hob-nobbing with the wealthy whose formula entertainments are arts funding's chief beneficiaries.

Democrats, meanwhile, talk about building information superhighways to empower the commonfolk, while deregulating cable TV and letting a few huge companies take over all the major-market TV and radio stations.

But then again, if American culture weren't full of contradictions, it wouldn't be American culture.

Culture Club: With something of a budget finally passed and health-care reform a while away, the right-wing Gridlock Machine has been backtracking for targets. Among the "scandals" recently recycled on talk radio and in pundit magazines is that all-purpose nemesis, the National Endowment for the Arts. They're giving the same ol' blah-blah about Our Tax Dollars and flaky artist types who mock all that is pure and proper.

The real scandal about American arts funding isn't that taxpayers are supporting too much "controversial" art but too little.

A couple of people who say "fuck" on stage notwithstanding, most NEA money subsidizes formula entertainment for the rich. It's just as bad on the local level. Washington's reputation as an artistic center is overrated and based more on consumption than production.

Washington ranks well in the bottom half of states in terms of public arts support. And a lot of that money goes either to bland sculptures by out-of-state artists, to "major performing institutions," or to "support services" (buildings and bureaucrats); while the citizens who make images and films and texts, particularly of the non-touristy or non-upscale kind, scrape by as always.

The rich should pay for their own lifestyles, either directly or through corporate support. I don't wanna see any bassoonists lose their jobs in today's economy, but if the symphony and the Seattle Repertory Theater are gonna get public money, it should be for public stuff: free or discounted shows, in-school appearances, etc.

Since we're always gonna have inadequate arts funding, what we can spend should emphasize investment in new works, works that might or might not find a big audience, works that might or might not even be good (experiments must be allowed to fail). *(September 1993)*

New Cabinet Suggestions

Energy:
Who's got more than Robin Williams?

National Security Agency:
Leo Buscaglia makes everybody feel more secure.

Housing and Urban Development:
Nobody's created more housing for less money than the punk squatters.

Human Services:
Warren Beatty's serviced a lot of humans.

Naional. Endowment for the Arts:
Who knows more about art and endowment than the Men on Film guys on In Living Color*?*

Defense:
It'd take an army of millions to hold back Chuck D.

Central Intelligence:
Marilyn Vos Savant's the most intelligent person I know.

Treasury:
The computer phreakers of the Legion of Doom know deeply how "virtual" (imaginary) our money system is.

Ban, Roll On: Yes, the Washington legislature tried again to revive the Erotic Music Bill, a misguided attempt to shore up the morals of Those Kids Today by restricting selected rock records (Gov. Mike Lowry vetoed the "anti-porn" package of proposals that included the music bill). In the short term, control-freak schemes like this can be dangerous to free expression and personal privacy, and must be fought vigorously. But in the long term, the tide is starting to turn against the forces of cultural suppression, because it's bad for capitalism.

In the pre-industrial age, censorship was a tool of economic as well as social control. When only the upper classes were taught to read, the number of potential rivals for prestige positions was kept within means. The class system was kept in place by restricted information. In the industrial age, supporting censorship was a convenient way for big business interests to forge convenient political alliances with more populist right-wing elements (note Michael Milkin, Jesse Helms, et al.).

The Republicans of the rural west proved particularly adept at using the religious right to help elect politicians whose real loyalty wasn't to churches but to big ranchers, miners and real estate developers.

Censorship was also a convenient way for the corporate power structure to deny responsibility for some of the social upheavals its own machinations had caused. Corporate America could say: "We're losing our technological edge to Japan? Don't blame us; all we did was encourage slashes in education spending so the government could reduce business taxes. Blame the decadent liberals — Yeah, that's the ticket! Sexual permissiveness did it! That, and the devil's rock music, and those naughty TV shows!" Or: "Urban crime? We didn't cause it; all we did was move all our jobs to the suburbs! Blame the homosexuals, or the immigrants, or the lack of family values!" Or: "Child abuse? Don't look at us; we merely promoted a culture where selfish aggression was treated as a virtue. No, just get rid of those magazines with the pictures of those naughty women in them. That'll solve everything!"

But in the Information Age (which spread into the realm of politics about 18 to 24 months ago), censorship is a threat to what is becoming big business's most prized asset — intellectual property. Free expression is the new frontier of post-industrial capitalism. The Viacom-Paramounts and the Time Warners will begin to fight against the principle of censorship in the same way the timber industry has fought designated wilderness areas, or the way GM has fought pollution controls. A key connection of the old Reagan coalition has been severed, perhaps for keeps. The religious right, having outlived its usefulness to much of the business community, just might find itself sent back into the shadows due to a slow drying up of big-money support, destined to become just another of the many isolated subcultures in today's fragmented society.

But it won't go away quietly. There will be more kooky drives like the Erotic Music Bill and that initiative to legalize anti-gay discrimination. These campaigns will become blunter, shriller and more divisive, as their instigators strive to hold on to their own core support base. *(May 1994)*

While I still believe the upscale should be able to support their own leisure pursuits, I also oppose Newt Gingrich's crusade against arts funding — because it's really a crusade against what art ought to be. The Right is trying to silence all opposition, real or potential, to its societal vision of greed and obedience.

To fight this, art has to communicate a meaning to people, and not just to liberal-arts grads either. Part of the legacy of modernism is the way the upper classes used "sophisticated" art to define their differences from the masses. This alliance between modernism and elitism gave Stalin and Hitler their excuses to wage war against expressionistic, surrealistic, nonrepresentational, or oppositional artists, while mandating life-denying kitsch art (cf. *The Unbearable Lightness of Being*). Newt doesn't want to kill artists or destroy their works; he'll settle for isolating them into the margins of discourse. *(Feb. 7, 1995)*

The truth about 'Cyberporn': The totally ridiculous exploitation story in *Time* only proves the same lesson *Time*'s Pearl Jam cover proved: When you know the media are lying about a topic you know about, how can you trust them about other topics like politics?

Yes, there are pictures of female and male bodies on the web. Most are put up on amateur home pages, though a few such sites are commercially run (by such firms as adult-video distributors, magazines, phone sex purveyors, lingerie catalogs, and "glamour photographers"). The sites aren't easy to find unless you use search programs to find them. Most have introductory screens that ask you to type in your age before they'll let you in further.

But really, the whole gamut of sex-culture appears on the Web: Ads for "educational" CD-ROMs, exhibits of

Commerce:
Nobody in America knows anything about this anymore. Sell the dept. to Matsushita.

Internal Revenue:
We need someone with proven fundraising skills. Jerry Lewis could also work on increasing U.S.-European relations.

Interior:
The Mariners are great at keeping open spaces quiet and underpopulated.

Agriculture:
Orville Reddenbacher looks like he still gets up early to listen to the Farm Report.

Veterans Affairs:
The classic rock DJs know how to appeal to guys who're still obsessed with our last wartime era.

Labor:
Jane Pauley's been through it a few times.

Education:
Spike Lee's always ready to teach a thing or two.

Attorney General:
Anita Hill would be the obvious applause-getting choice, lest we forget her solid conservative stance. Otherwise, how 'bout someone who knows today's legal frontiers, like whoever's defending Negativland from U2's anti–sampling suit.

State:
Let's get someone who can bring people together and keep 'em smiling, like Studs *game-show host Mark De Carlo.*

Transportation:
Who shows more love for public transit than George Carlin, the new Conductor on Shining Time Station*?*

(December 1992)

neoclassical nude paintings, bondage stories, rambling essays about broken relationships, personal ads, listings of lesbian and gay community resources, pirated *Celebrity Skin* photos, video clips of topless pillow fights, and clips from women's-mag ads of supermodels selling clothes by not wearing them. Sex culture on the Web is (almost) as diverse as in life, which is what the advocates of a commercialized monoculture such as Time Warner probably really fear. *(July 12, 1995)*

Talk's Cheap, And I Like It That Way: First, that professional prissy-at-large William Bennett gets on the anti-gangsta-rap bandwagon. That was a surreptitiously almost-valid stance for a moralistic high-horser to take, since gangsta rap is essentially the product of Hollywood promoters selling white mall kids on a variation of the century-old showbiz stereotype of black men as stupid but sexy savages. But now, ex-Bush aide Bennett's taking his demagoguery further by attacking sleaze talk shows, claiming they "make the abnormal normal."

But Bill, the abnormal *is* normal, everywhere except in the minds of people like you. You've never been to a 12-step meeting? Never listened to old ladies' gossip? Never had a relative the elders only talk about when kids aren't around? The things on these shows are the stuff of real life, heretofore repressed from public consciousness. Yes, the shows are exploitive, but they're much less exploitive than Republican politicians. *(Nov. 15, 1995)*

Benaroya Hall.

16: THE ART WORLD

or, high culture as just another subculture

"Serious" art, "legitimate" theater, and classical music were cottage industries in Seattle before 1962, when the World's Fair left a "permanent legacy" of semi-functional theater buildings and companies to mount performances in them. The '70s national arts-funding boom followed, helping establish a creative-arts community that's struggled to keep going ever since.

This community, particularly in theater and performance art, became a subculture unto its own, with its own values and influences. As the '80s and '90s dragged on, it developed its own caste system.

At one end, there were the painters, sculptors and performers who blatantly worked for the patronage of people with money, offering nice, safe works like pastel-colored glass bowls and Wagner operas.

At the other end, there were those who blatantly worked for the patronage of people with a little less money, making street fair-style craft pieces and art that looks good next to a sofa.

Trapped between these infrared and ultraviolet extremes were the pro and semipro bohemians, the people who made plays that were fun to go see, dance pieces that ever-so-slightly challenged the way you see human forms, paintings and collages that combined the immediacy of cartooning with the depth of surrealism.

As public arts money dried up, and private arts money got gobbled by the art-for-people-with-money clique, the bohos dug in their heels and redoubled their efforts not to shock but to playfully entertain a new upper-middlebrow audience segment, made up of aging frustrated artists, young-adult scenesters, software people, and people who also go to rock clubs.

Musical Menace: At a performance of Seattle Opera's *Orpheus and Eurydice*, a man stood up from his seat, yelled "This is dogshit," and left. They're trying to identify him from his seat position, in hopes of revoking his season ticket. Earlier, a guy jumped to his death from the balcony at N.Y.'s Metropolitan Opera. I tell you, this Satanic opera music is causing demented behavior. Why aren't officials demanding warning labels on opera records? Why are opera companies allowed to serve wine at intermissions? Why aren't opera audiences strip-searched? You don't know what they could be hiding in those long gowns! *(March 1988)*

Yes, But Is It Crime?: By now you've heard the legend of Lawrence McCormick, the commercially unsuccessful artist who entered the Linda Farris Gallery on July 7 and poured red paint on four large glass works. You may not have seen

Book 'Em

This first ***Misc.*** *Midsummer Reading List is a totally random collection of titles, recommended for fun value and in some cases for insights into the writerly craft. Some of these aren't readily available in new-book stores; look for 'em.*

Infinite Jest, *David Foster Wallace. A half-million of the funniest, saddest words ever written about digital filmmaking, Quebec separatism, addictions (alcohol, media, sex), boarding schools, teen athletics, environmental catastrophe, and advertising. Maximalism at its finest.*

The Sadness of Sex, *Barry Yourgrau. Eighty-nine short-short stories of desire, longing, confusion, betrayal, more confusion, and more desire. Minimalism at its finest.*

The Last Days of Mankind, *Karl Kraus. The horrors of WWI, as written during the war (but published after it) by an antiwar Austrian intellectual, in the form of a* Ring Cycle*-length avant-garde play script. Minimalism to the max.*

his written statement, posted at Broadway's Espresso Roma: "I enacted my Art Action: Iranian Blood Deposited on American Art Commodities because of the cold abstract middle-class elitist art establishment mentality of American commercial art galleries and the Linda Farris Gallery as the Seattle 'avant garde' example of degenerative decoration." Farris, by the way, did not see the act, being in Moscow at the time.

I was there, and will remember the large, stern visage of McCormick, waiting outside to be arrested, while the petite gallery ladies stood in near-shellshock. [Latter-day note: McCormick committed suicide after this column was written but before it hit the streets.] *(August 1988)*

Body Language: Pat Graney's dance performance *Faith* eloquently succeeded in contrasting healthy, natural sensuality with the clumsy, contrived "sexiness" of modern life as exemplified in that symbol of everything ex-hippie women despise, high heel shoes, at one point compared by Graney dancer Tasha Cook to Chinese foot-binding. (That many younger women have found a source of power in black dresses and uncomfy shoes is dismissed in the course of the piece, with the dancers eventually shucking off their im-ped-iments of needless discipline.)

One must also mention the last of Graney's four segments, in which she and her six other female dancers crawled across the floor nude (mostly with spines arched out to the audience). That this was accompanied by Mideval-inspired music (by Rachel Warwick) did not seem the least bit sacrilegious.

Indeed (in a twist on liberal orthodoxy), Graney implied that old religious-based cultures held more respect for both body and spirit than current secular society. *(July 1991)*

The 'Hammering Man' Crash: I wasn't there at the time it fell, but got to see the massive wreckage. One can question whether the Seattle Art Museum should have spent $400,000 on a clone sculpture from L.A., the town whose business is imposing its culture onto the rest of the world.

One can question the smug condescension implied in a self-styled tribute to the Working Man at a development that represents the expulsion of working-class labor from downtown, overlooking the waterfront that now represents the expulsion of working-class labor from America. *(November 1991)*

'Twas something really peculiar about seeing the New City production of *Fever* (Wallace Shawn's monologue piece about the limits of rich-liberal guilt trips) performed at a substitute venue: First Christian Church, usually occupied by people who don't just go to upscale plays about poverty and suffering but actually try to do something about them. Shawn posited a world consisting only of the oppressed and the privileged (the latter including himself and, by implication, his audience). He conveniently concludes (or seems to, since he's conveniently equivocal) that there's little his class can do but feel sympathetic and give a little money to street people.

Sorry Wally, not good enough. Next time, try to see the rest of the world, not as an artist looking for source material but as a citizen looking for a task to be done. You could start at the church and its ongoing ministry to street people. *(December 1992)*

No Place Like Home: *The Etiquette of the Underclass* exhibit at Second and Pike was the sort of "social concern" experience my old Methodist youth group would have gone to. You walked past real street people (studiously kept outside) to enter a cleaned-up simulation of street life. You wandered thru a maze of tight corridors, small rooms, and plywood cutouts of muggers, drug dealers, johns, cops and bureaucrats; all to a Walkman soundtrack of interviews with street people (by a California art troupe), tightly edited to shock suburban innocents with near-romanticized images of urban squalor. It worked as a thrill ride, but didn't communicate how tedious and numbing that life can be. *(May 1993)*

I write lots about the aesthetic of community life, about how architecture, urban planning and the "everyday" arts affect life and health. These things have been thought about for a long time. One proof of this was the Northwest Arts & Crafts Expo, a collection of sales- and info-display booths earlier this month at the Scottish Rite Temple.

This wasn't street fair art, but work of the early-20th-century Arts & Crafts Movement. At its widest definition, this movement ranged from back-to-simplicity purists like Thoreau and U.K. philosopher William Morris to unabashed capitalists like author-entrepreneur Elbert Hubbard and furniture manufacturer Gustave Stickley. They believed an aesthetically pleasing environment enhanced life, and such an environment should be available to of all income brackets.

Chick-Lit 2: No Chick Vics, *Cris Mazza, Jeffrey DeShell, and Elizabeth Sheffield, eds.*
Feminist (or "post-feminist") stories with no victims, survivors, or avengers? It's not only possible, but the break from formula makes the contributors create proactive heroines and antiheroines who don't just take shit and react against it, they get up and do things — even bad things.

Let's Fall in Love, *Carol de Chellis Hill.* *Precursor to Chick-Lit, this 1973 tongue-in-cheek thriller about the sassy female leader of an international crime ring might have then been the most sexually explicit above-ground novel by an American woman at the time.*

The Great American Bathroom Book, Vols. 1-3, *Stevens Anderson, ed.* *Dozens of 2,000-word summaries of classic and contemporary lit, plus fun quotations, obscure-word lists, and valuable reference stuff mixed in.*

The movement's influenced peaked between 1900 and 1930 — the years of Seattle's chief residential development. It's no coincidence that the low-density "single family neighborhoods" Seattle patricians strive to defend are largely built around the low-rise bungalow, the A&C people's favorite housing style.

The movement died out with the postwar obsession for the cheap and the big — for the world of freeways, malls, office parks, domed stadia, subdivisions and condos. Our allegedly-feminist modern era disdained many traditionally feminine arts, including home design and furnishing. The beats and hippies knew the fabric of daily life had gone dreadfully wrong but couldn't implement enough wide-ranging solutions. You don't have to follow all the A&C movement's specific styles to appreciate its sensibility.

We haven't just been killing the natural environment but also the human-made environment. As shown by the Kingdome and our other collapsing new buildings (Seattle's real-life Einsturzende Neubauten), many of these sprawling brutalities aren't forever. The next generation of artistic people will have the task of replacing the sprawl with real abodes, real streets, real neighborhoods, and (yes) real ballparks. *(November 1994)*

Chasing Dirt: The American Pursuit of Cleanliness, *Suellen Hoy. The next time your out-of-town aunt remarks about how "clean" Seattle appears, read this and learn how looking clean wasn't always an American priority. We've come a long way from Huck Finn boasting of the benefits of drinking muddy river water to today's kitchens with Brita filters and antibacterial cutting boards.*

Wildmen, Wobblies, and Whistle Punks, *Stewart H. Holbrook. Northwest history the way we love it: Anarchists, labor agitators, frontier bordellos and saloons, religious cults, weird criminals, hoaxers, bombastic rail barons, and raging forest fires. In his later years, the prolific Holbrook (1893-1964) founded a tongue-in-cheek regional anti-development movement, the James G. Blaine Society (acknowledged inspiration for* Times *columnist Emmett Watson's "Lesser Seattle").*

A glowing *Times* story claimed there were approximately 1 million seats sold in each of the past two years to Seattle's top 12 nonprofit theater companies and the for-profit touring shows at the 5th Avenue Theater. Even then, more seats are sold each year to the major theater companies than to any local sports enterprise except (in a good year) the Mariners. If you add the smaller, often more creative drama and performance producers, the total might surpass the Mariners' more popular years.

Maybe Seattle really is the cultured community civic boosters sometimes claim it to be. Or maybe we're a town of passive receivers who like to have stories shown to us, whether in person or on a screen, instead of creating more of our own. *(November 1994)*

The Meyerson & Nowinski art gallery has instantly become the ritzy-upscale "contemporary art" emporium for Seattle. The splashy opening show gathers drawings and prints from artists of different nations and decades, collectively referred to by the gallery as "Picasso and Friends." It's really no worse than TNT sticking Tom & Jerry cartoons onto a show called *Bugs Bunny and Friends*. *(May 15, 1996)*

Pants Participles: Loved the notion of an all-female *Rosencrantz and Guildenstern Are Dead* (by the new troupe Heads Up Gorgeous at Book-it's stage). Shakespeare's plays were originally executed by all-male casts; it's only appropriate to have reverse-drag of sorts in Tom Stoppard's sideways take on *Hamlet.* It also gives a chance for actresses to appear in strong roles that have little or nothing to do with sex or romance, something classic and even modern-classic theater hasn't enough of. *(Dec. 11, 1997)*

Erika Langley's *Lusty Lady* coffee-table-book photos won't have their own Seattle Art Museum show (across from the peep-show emporium where Langley took her pix) after all. She'd been invited by one SAM official, then disinvited by highers-up (who've offered her a slot in a group exhibition next year instead).

The official line: The show would've been in a hallway, where kids on group tours might be exposed to the sight of beautiful women's physiques. (Langley had already agreed to leave sexually-suggestive shots out of the show.)

Yet Langley and her supporters noted that other nudes (female and male) have been on open display at SAM. I saw plenty of under-agers enjoy the drawn nudes at SAM's *Cone Collection* exhibit last year, including several young art students copying the drawings into sketchbooks. But art's gatekeepers have always preferred their nude images to be safely removed from the here-and-now. I believe as late as Monet's time, painters were expected to set nekkid people only in historic (ancient Greece), foreign (Mideast harems), or mythical (Biblical sinners) settings. But a modern-day gal willfully showin' off her bod *sans* shame? Never! *(April 23, 1998)*

The old multipurpose Opera House, with its acres of steak-house red wallpaper, symbolized a peripheral town trying (too hard?) to prove it had come of age. The new symphony hall, by contrast, symbolizes a civic establishment of Nordics and WASPs out to prove they're so already-there they don't need to shout their world-classness, just sit and bask in their own solemn collective presence; not unlike church ladies and gents.

Indeed, from the organ pipes at the back of the stage to the dark paneling on the main hall's relentlessly-angled walls to the seat-back brass plaques each honoring a different well-heeled donor (indeed, just about everything in the place except the toilets honors some rich person or

Dictionary of the Khazars, *Milorad Pavic. In 1988, this Serbian surrealist novel about fragmentations of religion, politics, history, and memory seemed an amusing fantasy. Now, it's more like prophecy.*

The Mechanical Bride: Folklore of Industrial Man, *Marshall McLuhan. His first (1950) pop-cult criticism collection, still imitated (knowingly or not) by all who've followed in the topic. Every exploitive sociocultural trait people now blame on TV, McLuhan found already entrenched in the media-ted environment of movies, radio, newspapers, and magazines.*

Hour of the Star, *Clarice Lispector. Forget your images of Samba Land: Young Brazilians, this novel asserts, can be as awkward, shy, and frustratedly virginal as young adults anywhere.*

Pale Fire, *Vladmir Nabokov. Seems everybody nowadays likes to snicker at the excesses of literary criticism, but the funniest Russian emigré novelist of all time did it best: A narrative poem, followed by a line-by-line "commentary" that tells an almost completely different narrative.*

(Aug. 14, 1997)

(continued)

company), the joint looks a lot like a tasteful mid-'60s Protestant church such as Plymouth Congregational or University Unitarian — only built to the scale of a suburban evangelical megachurch.

I was in the joint three times during its opening month. Two of those times, I stood in line in front of middle-aged boomers saying they hoped this prominent heart-of-downtown hall would help promote symphonic music to Those Kids Today. Both these overheard parties spoke under the unquestioned assumption that all Americans born after them were, virtually by definition, headbangin' ingorami desperately needing conversion to the secular religion of high culture.

As if these oldsters' parents hadn't said the exact same thing when the boomers were kids.

As if there weren't orchestral scores in every old movie and lots of recent movies (a few of which were recorded by the Seattle Symphony).

As if the new leading-edge music here in town weren't neo-improv and contemporary-composer stuff heavily based on hibrow and pre-rock traditions.

As if such a huge cut of our dwindling public arts funding weren't already going to arts-education programs (aside, that is, from the money going to auditorium-construction projects).

No, most kids' musical souls don't need saving. But it's nice to know some oldsters at least care. *(Oct. 1, 1998)*

Yesterday's rebels; today's plush dolls.

17: GENERATION GAPS

or, baby boomers are NOT the apex of humanity!

In the '80s, the boomers' ex-youth culture had become a culture of new old fogeys, who either ignored contemporary teens and youths or virulently despised them. Former top-40 stations switched to oldies formats and ran commercials belittling modern teens as subhuman idiots. Seattle Weekly, *the closest thing we had to an "alternative" paper then, ignored rock 'n' roll while giving cover stories to fashionable restaurants and romantic getaways. By decade's end, the media branded modern youth as the do-nothings of "Generation X."*

Not much later, a different image took hold. Young adults were seen as go-getter entrepreneurs and self-empowerers. It was an image inspired in no small part by the do-it-yourself credo of the Seattle music scene, and later by the publicized success stories of young cyber-moguls.

By the late '90s, the teen population had grown again and had reached the gunsights of corporate marketers, eager to sell it on studio-manufactured pop singers and "Xtreme" soda pops.

I'm not really part of any of those groups, having come of age in the late '70s, when the "baby bust" caused school enrollments to drop and when the most creative youth music was routinely blacklisted by boomer-run radio stations and clubs. To paraphrase punk pioneer Richard Hell, I belonged to the Blank Generation, and I could take it or leave it each time.

In MTV's most amazing promo yet, five young actors stand on a stage and chant, "How do you do, Mr. Ginsberg. I would like you to know that the best minds of my generation are rich and famous." Not quite true, of course; the best minds of my generation are really bankrupting themselves in self-publishing, paying off video camcorders, and fighting to get airplay. *(March 1988)*

Previews of *The Wonder Years,* the first show to treat people my age as the target of nostalgia, aren't encouraging: Horribly cute little boys and the same '60s soul classics you hear today in bad commercials. The 12-year-old kids I knew at the time thought those songs were OK but preferred the Monkees and the 1910 Fruitgum Co. — music for kids left behind by progressive rock. Just as we were becoming teens, suddenly it wasn't cool to be a teen anymore. We learned the media only cared about people 10 years older than us and always would… *(March 1988)*

Book 'Em
(continued)

For the second year, we've a pile of old and new bound verbiage (in no particular order) to recommend as mental companions while you sit in airports, on ferry docks, in the breakfast nooks of RVs, in rain-pelted tents, and wherever else you're spending your summer leisure hours.

The Ruins, *Trace Farrell. In the '80s I was involved in "Invisible Seattle," a group of writers who (among other exercises) fantasized about an alternate-universe Seatown with Old World traditions and grit. This is what local author Farrell's accomplished in her hilarous parable of working-class discipline vs. New Money hedonism; set in an Old World seaport town but based on a real Seattle supper club and on Seattle's current caste-and-culture wars.*

Is This a Cool World Or What?: *Times* columnist Don Williamson wrote on March 1 that modern teen standards of "coolness" promote delinquency; he partly blames the media for not depicting straight-A students and Meals on Wheels volunteers as sexy.

This argument goes back to the anti-rock-'n'-roll crusades of '50s parents and beyond. While hair and clothing styles change, the perennial definition of cool is to be that which your parents hate. Earlier in our century, kids found rebel styles in jazz and gangster movies. In the '70s, what we now think of as disco clothes were based on the flamboyant apparel of East Coast pimps. Selling squareness as a role model doesn't work.

You'll never get kids to stop smoking, snorting, or drinking if your only advertised examples of non-smokers, non-snorters, and non-drinkers are mama's boys, good little girls, and Jesus-jocks. Besides, it's hard to proclaim that smart is cool when Bill Gates still can't get a girlfriend... *(April 1992)*

The ex-"new morality" generation just doesn't understand the cultural implications of safe sex. They think that anybody having sex must be having it the way it was had in the '60s, either as strict monogamy or undisciplined licentiousness. They don't get that with today's much more assertive women, relations would naturally be more protection-conscious even without STDs to worry about. Contraception alone would be taken more seriously. Women taking more charge, even in short-term relationships, invariably means more discipline (I don't mean S&M but simply more thought and planning).

That attitude shows in the elaborate visions of club fashions, in dance music that's all about energy and control instead of "letting it all hang out." *(June 1992)*

The Bald Facts: The Hair Club for Men is now one of the top advertisers on MTV, showing middle-aged out-of-its enjoying second childhoods thanks to phony-looking hair transplants. Are 40-ish geezers really watching the channel, searching to stay young? Does that mean that imitation rap slang will soon be audible in lawyers' watering holes? Will we see Body Gloves in the Columbia Center Club? Worse things have happened (cf. every men's fashion ad in a 1971 *Playboy*). *(August 1992)*

The Young and the Clueless: To be young today is in itself an act of defiance. You're the target of both the whiskey-drinking old farts and the pot-smoking middle aged farts.

Some people will presume you're an idiot because you weren't around for WWII. Other people will presume you're an idiot because you weren't around for Woodstock.

Earlier this year, the conservative American Enterprise Institute held a pop culture symposium, dominated by a succession of old male Madonna-bashers. (Have any of them ever heard any other contemporary performing artist?) The panel purported to encompass a right-to-left spectrum: 50-year-old Republicans who whined that we've gone to hell since the golden age of movie censorship, and 40-year-old Democrats who whined that we've gone to hell since the golden age of Dylan.

More recently, Ken Kesey made very snide remarks about "the MTV generation" having no attention span, being somehow unable to digest a traditional narrative. If that's the case, howcum you see the bombastically long products of Sidney Sheldon and Jackie Collins in so many campus lunchrooms?

Then there's the charge made by self-styled "radicals" for 20 years now, that all college students since them are fascistic zombies. As if every college class forever must be compared to those three brief years of (mostly futile) Vietnam protests, that quickly wound down in '71 once the Army stopped trying to draft college boys.

I've seen plenty of campus political activity in the last 13 years, from big marches to backstage organizing, about everything from apartheid to nuclear power to the gulf war. These were mainly people who didn't have their own hides on the line, but who were disgusted enough to want to do something.

As opposed to being too disgusted to want to do anything. The opposite of activism isn't pacifism, it's defeatism. I find it in too many folks of all ages. Not voting is the exact same thing as voting for Bush. You can't change the system by leaving it as is. That's like stating that, as a protest against the injustice of the rain, you're not going to fix your roof.

Too many members of my own generation, the Pleasure Islanders of the early '80s, thought they were preserving their purity by being politically chaste. Instead, they (and we) wound up getting, well, you know... *(Oct. 19, 1992)*

Years-Reeling-In Dept.: Playwright Terrence McNally spoke at a big opera convention in town. He advised opera promoters to seek (what he thinks is) the youth market: "We have to find potential bel canto lovers at the

The Incomparable Atuk, *Mordecai Richler. From the Great Canadian Novelist, a 1963 fable still relevant among today's Paul Simonized nobel-savage stereotypes. Atuk's a supposedly innocent Inuit boy who's brought to Toronto as part of a mining company's publicity stunt, and who quickly falls right in with the city folk's hustling and corruption.*

Machine Beauty, *David Gelernter. One of these skinny essay-books everybody's putting out today; only this one's in hardcover. The premise is admirable (advocating simplicity and elegance in the design of industrial products and computer software), but it'd have been better if it were longer, with more examples and illustrations.*

Consilience, *Edward O. Wilson. Giant essay-book by biologist Wilson, who proposes all human behavior (and indeed all knowledge) can be ultimately traced to biology and physics. He puts up a solid defense, but I still disagree. To me, the world isn't a tree with a single trunk but a forest of interdependent influences. Life is complexity; deal with it.*

The Taste of a Man, *Slavenka Drakulic. For "erotic horror" fans, a novel of psychosexual madness by the Croatian author of* How We Survived Communism and Even Laughed. *Not much laughing here; just a heroine who takes the female sex-metaphors of absorption and consumption to their logical extreme.*

Self Help, *Lonnie Moore. Short stories by the author of* Who Will Run the Frog Hospital?, *reworking women's-magazine clichés into a far less "motivational" but more realistic worldview.*

next Steely Dan concert." Hate to tell ya, but Steely Dan broke up in 1980 and gave few live shows when they were together. *(February 1994)*

There's gotta be a way to stop mainstream media from proclaiming everything by or for young adults as "The Voice of Generation X" — a name Vancouver novelist Douglas Coupland stole from Billy Idol's old band, which broke up when today's 21-year-olds were nine. It's even dumber than "twentysomething," a name derived from a TV show about people who were in their thirties 10 years ago. Instead, MTV commentator Tabitha Soren (a *great* name — Kierkegaard meets the *Bewitched* baby!) wants us to call young adults "The Re-Generation." Finally, something appropriate — a generation where sci-fi nerds rule, named with a term from *Doctor Who*! *(February 1994)*

Thanks to artist-critic Charles Krafft, I've now gotten to see the original *Generation X* — the book Billy Idol's old band took its name from. It was written in 1964 by Charles Hamblett and Jane Deverson; the cover blurb on the U.S. paperback edition promised to expose "what's behind the rebellious anger of Britain's untamed youth." It's mostly about mods, rockers, teddies, all your *Quadrophenia* types. There's also two pages about playwright Joe Orton.

The title resulted from an ad the authors placed in a London paper, asking young people to send life stories. Responses included a poem titled *Generation X*, "written in the peace and tranquility of the trees and gardens of a psychiatric hospital" by "a female, age 20, suffering from depression and neurosis." Lines include, "Who am I? Who cares about me? I am me. I must suffer because I am me... Money, time, these are substitutes for real happiness. Where can I find happiness? I do not know. Perhaps I shall never know..." That original coiner of today's most overused media catch phrase, who'd now be 50, wasn't named. *(September 1994)*

Net-Working: In a *Harper's Bazaar* story about "Lolitas On-Line," writer David Bennahum claims there's a trend of teen females (including "Jill, a precocious 15-year-old from Seattle") acting out sexual fantasies in online chat rooms and newsgroups.

Bennahum proposes, that online sex talk isn't necessarily a Force of Evil but can, when used responsibly, be a tool of empowerment and self-discovery; letting users explore the confusing fascinations of sexual identity safely and pseudonymously.

In a recent *Wired* piece on "Kids' Cyber Rights," Jon Katz offered some similar notions. I'm particularly fond of his assertions that children "have the right to be respected," "should not be viewed as property or as helpless to participate in decisions affecting their lives," and "should not be branded ignorant or inadequate because their educational, cultural, or social agenda is different from that of previous generations."

Twenty years of punk rock should have proved kids can make their own culture and don't like being treated as idiots. Yet the Right still shamelessly uses "The Family" (always in the collective singular, as one monolithic entity) to justify all sorts of social-control mechanisms. Near-right Democrats try to muscle in on the far right's act, using "Our Kids' Future" to promote gentrification schemes that make family housing less affordable, while cracking down on any signs of independent youth culture (punks, skaters, cruisers) and going along with dubious "protection" schemes like V-chips and Internet censorship.

Yes, teens and preteens face a lot of problems. They always have. But they're more likely to get abused by daddy than by an e-mail correspondent. They'll hear more (and more creative) cuss words in the playground than on HBO. Let's stop stunting kids' growth by forcing them into subhuman roles they often can't stand. Instead, let's treat kids as human beings, who could use a little friendly advice now and then (as could we all) but who ultimately should, and can, take responsibility for their own lives. John Barth once wrote, "Innocence artificially preserved becomes mere crankhood." I'd add: Innocence excessively enforced becomes fetishization.
(July 18, 1996)

Pontiac's got this new ad with a computer-animated version of the Munch *Scream* man. A red sports car appears on his bridge. He gets in and immediately morphs into a shades-clad "dood," happily puttering down the road. By treating chronic depression or realistic world-weariness as a minor "attitude adjustment" problem, it ridicules the worldview of the young-adult generation it's trying to sell to. How typical. *(Jan. 23, 1997)*

Misc. is always bemused when mainstream media outlets suddenly discover the existence of "youth scenes" that are nearly 20 years old, like the *Times'* back-to-back

Coyote v. Acme,
Ian Frazier.
Light yet biting li'l funny stories like the old-old New Yorker *used to run. The cast includes a cartoon lawyer, a Satanist college president, Bob Hope, Stalin, Mary Tyler Moore, and "the bank with your money on its mind."*

Eastern Standard Time,
Jeff Yang, Dina Gan, and Terry Hong.
Asia's economies are on the ropes but Asia's pop cultures are going strong, as shown in this breezy coffee-table intro to everything from pachinko and sumo to Jackie Chan and Akira Kurosawa.

Sex, Stupidity, and Greed,
Ian Grey.
For all haters of expensive bad movies, essays and interviews depicting Hollywood as irrepairably corrupt and inane (and nominating the porn biz as a more honest alternative).

Behind Closed Doors, *Alina Reyes. An '80s teen-romance series,* 2 Sides of Love, *told its stories from the girl's point of view on one side of the book and the boy's on the other. Reyes applies this gimmick to more explicit sex-fantasies, putting her two protagonists through separate assorted sexcapades in assorted dreamlike settings with assorted opposite- and same-sex partners before they finally come together at the middle.*

Soap Opera, *Alecia Swasy. Intrigued by Richard Powers's corporate-greed novel* Gain *(presumably based on Procter & Gamble, and named for one of its detergents)? This real, unauthorized P&G history (named for the broadcast genre P&G helped invent) is even stranger.*

exposés of Goth and hip-hop (at least the latter series, by Cynthia Rose, was somewhat respectful of the genre and its participants). By this track, we're due for a two-page feature about, say, the ambient-dance scene sometime in 2011 (mark your calendars). *(Feb. 13, 1997)*

The Generation-Gap Gap: KMTT's promoting its "grownup rock n' roll" format with billboards proclaiming a mantra to "Turn On, Tune In, Drop the Kids Off at Soccer." The unspoken premise behind the slogan is the same premise that's ruled darn near all local mainstream media outlets for the past 15 years — that everybody (or at least everybody who demographically matters to advertisers) is an ex-Sixties radical, now domesticated with preteen kids.

The problems with this particular gross oversimplification: *(1)* Despite the eternal hype, a lot of folks who were around back in that still-overhyped decade weren't necessarily college radicals (in fact, more than half the people living in America during The Late Sixties weren't even college students at the time!); and *(2)* folks with preteen kids today are far more likely to have come of age in the late '70s and '80s.

That's why KMTT's sister station KNDD peppers its 9-to-5 hours with old U2 and Duran Duran tracks, to attract the commercially-desirable ex-waveoids now toiling away in dreary office parks. Of course, it'd be harder to make a flashy billboard slogan for grownup synth-popper parents. At the youngest end, there are now households with kids who know Jane Curtin only from *3rd Rock from the Sun* and parents who previously knew Curtin only from *Kate & Allie. (Nov. 6, 1997)*

A Word to the Wiseguys: A kindly reader suggested I stop using the term "yuppie," describing it as an '80s relic with no modern relevancy. To be exact about it, the small, monocultural caste for whom almost everything in today's Seattle is designed and marketed can no longer be called young urban professionals, no matter how many day-spa facial treatments and hair transplantations they endure. And many current young adults with careers don't necessarily share their elders' market-decreed preference for all things fetishistically bland. (Note the absence of James Taylor or Bonnie Raitt in that '70s revival youth fad.)

Still, the city's real-estate developers, politicians, fashion retailers, mainstream media outlets, big restaurateurs, et al. continue to direct their efforts at one and only one target market — the ever-venerated upscale baby boomer, with a liberal-arts degree, a lucrative career, and claims of former "'60s rebellion" participation contradicted by a relentlessly middlebrow aesthetic. Only a sliver of the region's population fit even close to this image, now or in the '80s. This fact doesn't stop the political and business leaders from proclaiming 'em the only people who deserve to live here.

So there is an urban-professional caste, powerful beyond its numbers, whether you call it by the Y-Word or not. If not, what would you? I've used such alternate terms as "the Demographically Correct" and "people who think giant glass bowls are art." *(March 12, 1998)*

Our item a couple weeks back, seeking a replacement term for the '80s relic "yuppie," engendered this email response from Bryan Alexander of Louisiana: "Liking your emphasis on their aging, how about 'boomer geezers'? Returning to the acronym, how about 'ayuppies' (aging young urban etc.) or 'dyuppies' (decrepit etc.), which raise both senesence and the victims' delusions of perpetual youth? The former is a more Southern pronounciation, the latter nearly Slavic."

Jesse Walker, meanwhile, takes umbrage at a throwaway line in the original column item which claimed the young adult bourgeoisie didn't share its elders' taste for bland pop songs. Walker felt I was wrong to "put Bonnie Raitt on the same level as James Taylor. And what about the revived popularity of the uber-bland Elton John?" John, of course, never really went away, at least not from Lite FM stations. A more serious challenge to my remark might involve the younger Lite FM stars (Fiona Apple, Sheryl Crow, et al.). *(April 9, 1998)*

I don't read the *Wall Street Journal* every day, so it took an attentive reader to let me know I'd missed its August 6 front-page story on the last of the slackers congregating in Seattle, where supposedly "Good Times Are Bad" for goateed Caucasians wishing to identify themselves as victims of a no-future society.

Writer Christina Duff took a rather snide attitude toward young-adult males who dared refuse to join in the *Journal*-proclaimed great boom economy: "Their ranks thinning everywhere, many aging slackers are congregating in Seattle, as if circling the grunge wagons... The slackers' last refuge here is the Capitol Hill area, where tattooed 20-somethings walk the streets giving hugs and high-fives... Faced with the depressing news that things

Underworld,
Don DeLillo.
Mega-novel spanning four decades and about many things, principally the U.S. power shift from the northeast (symbolized by N.Y.C.'s old baseball dominance) toward the inland west (symbolized by chain-owned landfills). But with the Yankees back in dynasty mode, and financiers now overwhelmingly more influential than industry (particularly resource-based western industry), DeLillo's march-of-history premise seems like reverse nostalgia.

The Frequency of Souls,
Mary Kay Zuravleff. The best short novel ever written about refrigerator designers with psychic powers.

(July 30, 1998)

Ad Verbs

Despite the posters, the local small-press book Young Men Can Sing *is not "the first novel with advertisements." Mass-market paperbacks have often had ads stuck in the middle. I remember one '50s paperback with an ad for* Time *magazine, promising to inform me all about "Pasternak, Voice of the World's Free Spirit... Einstein, Investigator Into the Unknown... Kruschev, Frank Lloyd Wright, Brigitte Bardot." And I'd always thought she was the Voice of the World's Free Spirit. (December 1986)*

The first arthritis ad with a rock song is now on the air. A portent of the decades to come, when my generation will have to pay for the much larger Big Chill *generation's Medicare... (February 1987)*

Using John Lennon music to sell sneakers is no worse than Gershwin for Toyota or Sondheim for stuffing mix. (July 1987)

(continued)

aren't as depressing anymore, some are shamed into shedding their angst."

Of particular scorn was one D.J. Thompson, belittled for choosing to only work part-time pouring coffee while his girlfriend pursued a Real Career. Duff's kinder to "ex-slacker Joanne Hernon," now "a computer consultant for law firms" with unkind words for her former fellow Linda's barflies: "They feel they need to be on the outskirts. Keep themselves in a poor position. Blame everyone but themselves. It's easy to make money these days."

Duff and Hernon don't say how it's easier for some (such as, admittedly, pale-skinned young-adult college grads) to make money than others; or how relative prosperity can more folks the option to choose not to devote their whole lives to material pursuits or the kissing of boss-butt. (Besides, Seattle's currently up-'n'-coming Boho-hood isn't the maturing Capitol Hill but the still-industrial Georgetown.) *(Sept. 3, 1998)*

Thoughts on the Beatles photo-print exhibit at the Animation USA gallery: Contrary to what dumb newspaper columnists like Tony Korsheiser still claim, Those Kids Today do not know the Beatles only as "the band Paul was in before Wings." Folks who've come of age in the late '80s and '90s have been inundated with Beatles nostalgia all their lives, but have never heard of Wings (except for poor Linda, who preached a healthy lifestyle and got cancer anyway). *(Nov. 12, 1998)*

The Big Chill is going to be re-released to theaters (in some parts of the country), giving late-'90s audiences a chance to relive the alleged good old days of early-'80s nostalgia for the late '60s. I say, forget the original movie (even though it was, and is, a depressingly-accurate depiction of the original *Seattle Weekly* target audience). Instead, why not remake it? The new *Big Chill-Out* could depict a circle of aging late-'80s punks who whiningly long for the good old days of simplistic heroes and villains, bond in the tribal solidarity of smug self-righteousness, and enjoy the timeless tuneage of Killing Joke (while sneering at those Hanson-listening Kids These Days). *(Nov. 19, 1998)*

Logos of two white-owned Seattle restaurants, the Coon Chicken Inn (1935) and ObaChine (1997).

18: THE RACE IS ON

or, a paler shade of white

At one point in the '80s, nobody liked to talk about minority affairs except minorities. Even many white radical leftists promoted an image of "The Oppressed" that reached little further than white women and white gays.

Then came the post-Rodney King riots (including, here, a small white copycat riot), followed by headlines about plummeting minority college enrollment, soaring minority imprisonment (often for minor drug possessions and other crimes whites often got off more easily from), and widening cross-racial communication gaps during the Reagan-Bush era.

By 1998, even "liberal" whites became so detached from minority interests that when right-wingers started an initiative to roll back affirmative action in Washington employment, the measure's opponents decided they needed to "whitewash" the whole issue.

The *Weekly* noted that the April 30 mixed-race window-busting spree downtown was smaller than fight scenes at two Rainier Valley dances last year that the white media ignored. As you know, the following night's mob scene was mostly white guys, led by U-District anarchists who wanted a riot of their own. They're the successors to the punks I'd known in the early '80s, whose idea of creativity was to imitate the latest L.A. fad. But like the second waves of most subcultures, today's circle-A guys are more orthodox and serious than their forbearers. They may think they were formenting revolution in solidarity with blacks, but (with the help of irresponsible media who exaggerated the threat) they just made white Seattle more afraid of African Americans, who will now be collectively blamed for the anarchists' work.

Most of the busted windows, except for the Bon and a 7-Eleven, were at youth- or hip-oriented stores, including a sneaker outlet, blue jean boutiques, the Broadway Jack-in-the-Box and Kinko's Copies. Most were independent businesses that could least afford the damage and the panic-driven loss of clientele; none had anything to do with the Rodney King verdict. The nightclubs that weekend were shut or mostly empty; the anarchists directly threatened a youth culture that's taken 10 tough years to build.

Back south, who's to blame for the conditions that sparked the rage? Every CEO who moves jobs to the suburbs, the Sunbelt or overseas. Every politician who ignores lower working class people or treats them as something to protect "decent people" against. Every baby-boomer who treats minorities as sexy savages, not as human beings. Every yuppie customer of drug dealers. Every bank that "invests" in funny-money schemes instead of in its own communi-

Ad Verbs
(continued)

The use of retro rock in TV ads gets ridiculous when Time *magazine uses the Byrds' "Turn, Turn, Turn," a song originally made in part to protest the Vietnam War — a war that* Time *supported.* *(September 1987)*

Weekly *classified, 7/25: "Frustrated? We need five people w/leadership and mgmt. ability. Must desire exceptional income. Unique oppty. with natl. company formed to help end world hunger."* *(August 1990)*

ty. A tax system that insures that only rich suburbs get the best schools.

I hope this is the end of La La Land, of the disgusting mythical SoCal of Fleetwood Mac and Tommy Lasorda, of limos and liposuction. Of celebrities who'd rather care for the rainforest than for their own city. Of violence movies celebrating "cops who break all the rules". Long before this, when people tried to turn me on to the latest "alternative scene" in L.A., I told them that L.A. is what everything else in the world is an alternative to. If L.A.'s so hip, how come it gave us Nixon and Reagan? California wasn't just home to those old student rebels, it was home to most of the things they were rebelling against.

Back then, few "relevant" white songwriters mentioned racism except as a pretext for peace-'n'-love sentiments. One that did was Frank Zappa's "Trouble Coming Every Day." In biting monotonic couplets that predate rap, Zappa describes watching the 1965 Watts riots through the then-new gimmick of live TV helicopters. At one point he shouts, "I'm not black but there are times when I wish I could say I'm not white." *(June 1992)*

The Nov. 23 *Times* says the number of self-designated Native Americans in Washington grew from 58,000 to 78,000 in the last census period, a figure far higher than that of officially recognized tribal members. I knew there were phony New Age shamen running around, but I didn't know there were so many. *(December 1992)*

Painful Realization for the New Millennium: By the time I'm 60, tourist towns will hold upscale rap festivals with mostly-white casts and all-white audiences sipping wine and basking in what they'll call the first art form of the 21st century. The music will sound like Gilbert & Sullivan patter songs backed by bad jazz. Already, a jazz combo has covered Grandmaster Flash's "The Message." *(December 1991)*

From Fly II Shai: Two years ago I predicted that by 2002 there'd be upscale rap festivals in tourist towns, where nouveau riche couples would listen to perky Vassar grads perform a cross between scat singing and Gilbert & Sullivan patter songs. Since then, new (arrested) developments made that obsolete. We've already seen the (PM) dawn of soft hip-hop, and it's different from my prediction (never trust sci-fi stories that think every present trend will keep going forever). You could see it at last month's KUBE Summer Jam: two dozen acts (most with recorded backing tracks), who had rap names but sounded like neo-Commodores or neo-Pointer Sisters. These groups celebrate the only recent black music hip white guys haven't muscled in on: "quiet storm" love songs of the '70s and early '80s. The new R&B eschews the white-hipster image of blacks as lust-crazed savages. Mall rats are still appropriating gangsta rap's romanticized violence, selfishness and sexism (in both directions); while the neo-doo-wop aesthetic finds sexiness galore in solid black-middle-class values: good grooming, hard work, mutual support. Since the black music of today usually becomes the white music of tomorrow, those white hiphop shows of the early 21st century are now more likely to have Boyz II Men cover bands, and today's preteen daughters of Bellevue lawyers may someday go to their first bars awkwardly crammed into En Vogue dresses. *(October 1993)*

Those white authors who've unilaterally declared racism to be "over" aren't living on any planet near mine. Witness David Stennett and Eric Remington, founders of something called the "Euro-American Students Union." They're trying to organize at Tacoma's University of Puget Sound (and are talking about taking their cause to other campuses), under the official guise of cultural awareness and "ethnic pride."

The group's literature and its website are full of barbed-wire imagery and rants against affirmative action, along with euphemistic preachments about a proud, righteous white race persecuted by ashamed-of-their-heritage white liberals and double-standard-bearing minorities. It's all seemingly designed to appeal to the topsy-turvy ideology of hate radio (where some of *academe*'s crudest bullies and bigots regularly turn around and whine about being the pitiful victims of the mean ol' PC thought police).

And Stennett and Remington's own literature is tame compared to some of the "recommended resources" linked from their website — more extreme writings from guys with Idaho P.O. boxes encouraging folks to support "white preservation" by moving to the "New Plymouth Rock" (the Rocky Mountain states, where they've got "the best gun laws").

How do I count the stupidities in all this? First, "white" is a singular population entity only in terms of a heritage of priviliges and in the delusional theories of demagogues. North American caucasians are a beyond-muttness amalgam of dozens of ethnic, tribal, and national

There was this wonderful USA Today story on 10/31 about national ad campaigns that didn't make it. Along with the usual everyday rejections (a Three Stooges fax-machine ad rejected by the Japanese product manager who'd never heard of the Stooges), there was an ad that would've warned against taking an inferior 4 x 4 into remote rugged terrain where it might leave you stranded: "Drive a Landcruiser or drink your own urine." Then there was a magazine ad with a simple before-and-after equation, with a tube of Clearasil photographed on the Before side and a wrapped Trojan on the After side. Wrote the Clearasil managers: "This promise cannot be substantiated." (December 1991)

Dewar's Scotch has a magazine ad with an Alice Cooper/Peter Criss lookalike, complete with boa constrictor as scarf. The headline: "Your tastes in music have changed. Your taste in drinks should too." Yeah, I know just what they're saying: When I was younger, I didn't appreciate acts like that. Now I do. (March 1994)

I've two questions about the current commercial, "Like a robot, I kept using the same tampon." (1) Most humans who use those things don't keep using the same one (unless they use those health-food-store washable sponge thingies). (2) I've never seen a robot that uses such products, have you? (You can imagine to yourself about The Jetsons' *Rosie or the* Heavy Metal *cover droids.)* *(September 1994)*

"It's true!
This local gal
made good
In glamorous,
clamorous Hollywood!
To wine
and dine me
nights, at nine,
The wolves
would line
for miles on Vine.
My footprints at
Grauman's Chinese?
They took
my imprints
to my knees!
They soon
acclaimed me
Miss 3-D:
Delightful,
Dazzling,
De-Lovely!
And what made me
a thing enthralling?
My Formfit outfit.
Really, dah'ling!"
— 1955 magazine ad for Formfit girdles *(September 1994)*

root groups, many of which have fought bitter wars with one another over the past few centuries. (The biggest of those wars were started by jerks like Napoleon and Hitler who foolishly sought to impose a singular nationhood on all Euros.) "White" isn't an ethnicity; it's the absence of ethnicity. You can have whole or partial ancestry from England, France, Germany, Spain, Norway, Latvia, Greece, Italy, and/or a hundred other lands or sub-lands; but there's no Nation of White. What I and other writers have referred to as "whitebread culture" is a complex set of beliefs, styles, fashions, foods, aesthetics, and attitudes rooted in concerted attempts by business and government earlier in this century to forge a common "American" culture from all these diverse ethnic and immigrant groups. That's not really "white culture;" that's mainstream American culture, something adhered to in varying degrees by citizens of varying ethnicities.

(Besides, pure breeding is for primping show dogs, not for healthy work dogs and especially not for humans. Interaction and interbreeding makes us stronger, not weaker.)

Of course, some whites are more privileged than others; class and race were never uniformly synonymous. Demagogues here, in Europe, and in Africa have long exploited racial/national/color "identity" to get the relatively underprivileged to support programs and wars that mainly benefitted the overprivileged of similar ethnicity or skin hue. And it doesn't help that certain help the demagogues by ranting against "White Male Society" as if everyone who was white or male was equally powerful. Most rich people are white, but most white people aren't rich. *(May 8, 1996)*

Opening the American Mind: Multicultural education is NOT a force for intolerance, as a coordinated right-wing push of articles in *Time*, the *New Republic*, the *Atlantic* and elsewhere suggests. Just the opposite: it recognizes the white-Euro "canon" of literature as the philosophy of our country's dominant culture to date, but insists that the cultures of the rest of the world must also be studied, because we must live with those other lands and because America is becoming a "majority of minorities". It's the guys trying to keep non-white lit out of the classroom who are the real "new McCarthyites." *(May 1991)*

Anguish Languish: The whole Ebonics mania is about teaching the ability to communicate. The furor over it shows just how much miscommunication we have to deal with. From hate radio to the op-ed pages, Beemer conservatives and Volvo liberals alike are decrying something Ebonics isn't, something that existed only in oversimplified newspaper descriptions. The Oakland, Calif. schools don't want to "promote" the language spoken in inner cities and the rural south. They want to treat that language as a legitimate idiom, with its own rules and norms — and then to use these notions of rules and norms to teach business English as a second language. Think of it as your *Pygmalion/My Fair Lady* shtick, with school-bureaucrat propriety substituted for Prof. Henry Higgins' classism.

The more rabid critics of Ebonics are using it as an excuse to deride Black English as "gibberish," and those who speak it as "illiterate thugs." This kind of arrogance is part of the whole point of Oakland's Ebonics scheme. It's a scheme to teach kids to speak and write business English without telling 'em they're idiots for not already knowing it. It's a scheme combining California new-age "empowerment" hype with legitimate linguistic studies. Indeed, Black English is a fascinating mix of words and pronounciation patterns from Africa, the U.S. south, and elsewhere. Everybody from beatniks and mall rappers to jazz and art lovers have benefitted from its traditions and continual innovations. The catch is potential employers speak a different idiom.

What might really frustrate both rightists and centrists is where Ebonics departs from the Higgins metaphor. It treats business, or "white," English as a trade idiom (like the old-Northwest "Chinook Jargon" taught by white pioneers to conduct business with different native peoples who spoke different tongues). The idiom of CEOs (and of talk-show hosts and columnists) is treated as just another English variant, not as the language's one and only proper form. *(Jan. 23, 1997)*

The *Times* reported this month that Kenny G's one of the most respected white musicians among black jazz purists. My theory: G represents a stereotype of whiteness corresponding almost perfectly to the stereotypes of blackness profitably portrayed for years by some white people's favorite black acts. *(Feb. 26, 1998)*

The supposed "gang riot" last Saturday at the Fun Forest was, as far as I've been able to determine, really just either an argument or an exhibition of horseplay by a handful of rowdy teens; climaxing either with a few gunshots into the air or (more likely) firecrackers. The ensu-

Which Ad D'ya Read?: Molson Ice beer ad, 1995: "Don't worry. Your tongue won't stick." Rainier Ice ad, 1994: "Warning: Keep tongue off billboard." (Feb. 14, 1995)

Washington Mutual's "Free Checking" billboard shows a checkbook with human female legs jogging at dawn. That's not freedom, that's rigorous discipline (which itself could be a positive metaphor for a bank, but that's a whole other issue). (Sept. 6, 1995)

"Harry Moore — Bringing you the future for more years than we care to remember." — Electronics-store slogan found in The Irish Times *(Dec. 6, 1995)*

Online mission statement from arka.com: "This purpose of this server is to give free-thinking authors a place to put their web pages without fear of content." (Aug. 1, 1996)

Ad Slogan of the Week: "Redhook. *It's not just a beer, it's a companion." Is that meant as a reassurance or as an AA recruiter's threat? (Aug. 28, 1997)*

ing scramble among sweaty, crowded kids set cops scrambling into crisis mode and herding all opposite-race youths off of the grounds.

Live TV reporters got all hussied-up about a Sudden Threat to Public Safety, while the kids passing by just giggled or mugged it up to the cameras — this was a big Dionysian revel that had merely gotten a bit out of hand, not the huge angry mob depicted. More telling was the scene the following late afternoon, in which teams of cops with plastic face masks and billy clubs shooed any and all groups of three or more young African-Americans not just off the Center property but out of the larger vicinity.

It's not just the Mark Sidran gang and the anti-affirmative-action cadre who fear blacks, particularly young blacks. The fear is ingrained in the popular image of a clean, ordered city where everybody's soft-spoken and unassuming. Lots of real African-Americans are just like that, of course; but lots of whites still think (consciously or sub-) that Black + Young = Gangsta.

(White teens can get rowdy too, but tend not to inspire such wholesale crackdowns.) *(July 23, 1998)*

On the night MTV aired the last episode of *The Real World: Seattle,* I was at Pier 70, in an ex-retail space right next to the ex-*Real World* studio, where two campaigns (No on 200 and Yes on Libraries) held election-night parties. You've seen enough TV coverage of such parties to know how they went down. The KCPQ news crew there even had a script prepared for both contingencies: "The crowd here cheered/groaned when the first returns were announced."

As it turned out, just about every progressive stance won, with one extreme exception. The anti-affirmative-action Initiative 200 won big. Why? At the bash, the main explanation handed about was the initiative's clever ballot wording, which, by purporting to oppose racial/gender discrimination in public hiring or education, may have confused anti-racist voters. My old personal nemesis John Carlson, I-200's official leader, is politically sleazy enough to have promoted such confusion, but not clever enough to have thought it up.

For that the blame has to go to the Californians who actually drafted the measure. Hard to believe, but some well-meaning friends still ask why I've never moved to the fool's-golden state. After Nixon, Reagan, Pete Wilson, the "English Only" initiative, the anti-bilingual-education initiative, and the original anti-affirmative-action

The Misc. List

Some still think I'm "just kidding," that beneath the facade of an Angry Young Man there's a carefree, apathetic party boy. There isn't. I'm really like this.

Things that make other people laugh but just make me puke:

*Christian TV, professional wrestling, supermarket tabloids spoof movies, any movie with an ex-*Saturday Night Live *or* SCTV *star (except* Strange Brew*).*

Things that make other people puke but just make me laugh:

The anti-flag-burning amendment nonsense, Nintendo, Milli Vanilli, Channel One, Smurfs.

Things people expect me to adore but I don't:

Science fiction, sword-and-sorcery (especially sword-and-sorcery disguised as science fiction), speed metal.

initiatives now being cloned in assorted states, it's way past time we stopped believing the hype about California as some sort of borderline-pinko progressive paradise.

Adding to the confusion, anti-200 campaign leaders apparently feared racial divisions in Washington state had gotten so bad, white voters wouldn't vote to keep affirmative action unless it was marketed as helping white women. So all you saw in anti-200 ads were white-female potential victims of the measure.

The pro-200 forces (who wanted to restore old white socioeconomic privileges) flew in out-of-state black conservatives to speak for the measure (and even flew in paid out-of-state black signature gatherers), while the anti-200 forces (who wanted to preserve the legal remedies that had jump-started workplace diversity) presented a public face of soccer moms and blonde kindergarten girls. *(Nov. 5, 1998)*

Things people expect me to just loathe but I don't:

Idaho Spud candy bars,
designer sneakers,
working-class people.

(April 1990)

19: WOMEN, MEN, ETC.

or, if you think there's two sexes you're undercounting

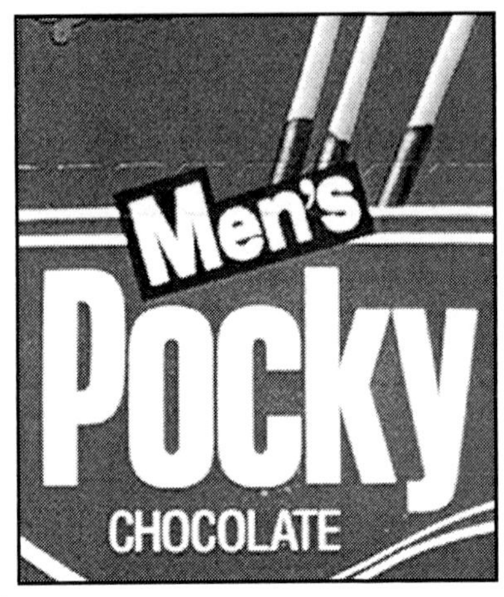

If you think races and generations don't understand one another anymore, wait 'til you get to sexes and sexual preferences and sexual tribes and subtribes. I suspect bestselling authors such as John Gray and Laura Schlesinger are so popular not because they make sense of the natures of women and men (they don't) but because they offer the fantasy that there are two and only two gender-types, instead of our reality of gays and straights and bis and transgenders and dominants and submissives and those who like it rough and those who like it gentle and amateur exhibitionists and professional abstainers and group marriages and serial monogamists and swingers and people who don't know what the hell they are.

The building that until recently housed the Lesbian Resource Center and Seattle Women's Gym is about to become a bridal shop. This trivium is offered merely for the sake of irony, and is not in any way to be considered an encouragement of the new homophobia. *(March 1987)*

I still want to know why certain teen and especially pre-teen boys consider male singers with long hair and high voices to be "real men" but dismiss male singers with predominantly female followings as "faggots" (musical qualities or lack of same being equal). *(October 1990)*

After I saw the Seattle Art Museum's opening-night exhibition, I was just as impressed by the photo show at Benham Studio across the street, including male nudes by female artists. I've since seen two films by R.E.M. videomaker James Herbert that used male bodies as the chief images in hetero-erotic scenes. Finally, there was the life-size male nude sculpture smiling from inside the window at the Donald Young Gallery (a cheesy mannequin to which a California artist had stuck on hyper-realistic, fiberglass genitals).

I concluded that I was attracted to female images that represent people I'd like to be with, and to male images that represent people I'd like to be. In most art and literature by both women and men, the female body is the land where sex lives, while the male body is portrayed as the instrument of work.

Our strongest non-gay male images are of muscular action: athletes, rock stars, socialist working-man art, SAM's *Hammering Man*. It's only since '70s porn that we've had straight male sex objects, viewed with admiration by other straight men. While the porn business treats men as soulless stimulus machines (a view it shares exactly with the anti-porn crusaders), it led to men looking at other men as sexual creatures.

Contemporary artists are going further in demystification, showing that a phallus is an awkward work of biology, not the iron rod or missile invoked by sexists of both genders. These artists are affirming that men are people too. *(March 1992)*

Those Phunny Phoreigners: The University of British Columbia engineering students, who briefly stole the UW Rose Bowl trophy, are known for their pranks. One year, they rigged the lights on Vancouver's Lions Gate Bridge to flash in Morse code: "UBC Engineers Do It Again." UBC's female business students hold an annual Lady Godiva Run, donning bikini bottoms and long wigs to race on horseback through the woods of the university's Endowment Lands. The event's always denounced by male writers on the student paper, who tell the women what's the right and the wrong way to be liberated. *(March 1992)*

My Pleasure vibrators may be the first women's product endorsed by porn queens ("Personally Chosen by the Girls Who Know Them Best"). According to a blurb on the box by one Ginger Lynn, "I like a vibe that's of exceptionally high quality, and with variable speed control. Because I like sexual control. And I am quality." What if sex stars as role models catch on? Would beauty standards come to be based on what men seem to like (instead of what women think men like)? Would women reshape themselves toward plump torsos with fat silicone lips and catatonic eyes? Would they imitate porn "acting" by slurring their words and staring blankly into space? *(July 1992)*

A Riot of Their Own: When you get covered in the *Weekly* and *USA Today* the same week, ya gotta worry about what you're doing wrong. That's the situation faced by the Riot Grrrls, a loose-knit network of punk women with its biggest scenes in Oly and D.C. Neither paper really said that this is hardly a new movement; these 22-year-old women embrace something that goes back to the late '70s with the Slits and Lydia Lunch. I've said before that punk's main difference from most cultural revolutions is that it had women out in front from the start, instead of

Walking the Walk

Here's the final result of our reader poll for a virtual Seattle women's walk of fame, inspired by the parade of shoeprints surrounding the new Nordstrom store but more responsive to the gender which represents, among many other things, Nordstrom's primary clientele.

This listing doesn't include the women who did get on the Nordy's shrine: The late UW Regent Mary Gates (whose contacts may have helped her kid Bill get that IBM contract that put MS-DOS, and hence Microsoft, on top of the cyber-world), KING-TV founder Dorothy Bullitt and her philanthropist daughters, and painter Gwen Knight.

The results of my research and your suggestions, in no particular order:

Thea Foss, *matron of a regional tugboat and shipping dynasty and inspiration for the beloved '30s film heroine Tugboat Annie.*

Princess Angeline, *daughter of Chief Sealth and prominent waterfront figure up to the 1920s.*

Gypsy Rose Lee, *all-time undisputed monarch of burlesque, who combined a great body (and the willingness to show much of it off), a sharp wit, and an instinct for publicity.*

Gracie Hansen, *nice middle-aged lady hired as hostess for the Seattle World's Fair's burlesque show; ahead of her time in announcing through her presence that nice girls enjoyed sex.*

Frances Farmer, *actor and Depression-era socialist sympathizer, who probably would've been blacklisted from the movies in the late '40s even if she hadn't been put away by her equally strong-willed mother.*

Dyan Cannon, *who went from West Seattle to divorcing Cary Grant.*

Pat Suzuki, *Broadway's first Asian-American star.*

Carol Channing, *singer-belter whose performances can not only be heard but seen from the third balcony.*

in an auxiliary or a follow-up (such as the '70s "women's music," a second wave of hippie folk). Also, while some R.G. zines spout the same reverse-sexist slogans as earlier radical feminists, the R.G.'s I've met are open to the support of men who want to help change a society that's hurting all of us. *(September 1992)*

Crimes Against Culture: Nearly two dozen young caucasians were arrested for assorted rowdy behavior at the Guns n' Roses Kingdome show. And yet you never hear any community lobbyists call for a crackdown against white music or the closure of white clubs.

Also, the *P-I*'s Roberta Penn curiously commented that since no female fans took their tops off during the concert, it was a possible sign that "women are refusing to let their bodies be used as entertainment". (Dome officials asked the band not to flash its regular "Show Your Tits" notice on the Diamondvision screen.) If I were her, I wouldn't invoke Axl lovers as representative models of their gender. Besides, a voluntary revelation of natural beauty could arguably be a more wholesome entertainment than that provided by the band. *(November 1992)*

Someone signed only Elvira says she usually likes **Misc.**, but my attitude toward shirt-doffing Guns n' Roses fans "really struck out": "Is the above aimed at women specifically? If so then you are no more 'enlightened' than the band is regarding women! Why would anybody, actually, show a lot of flesh at concerts? Or anywhere else for that matter?"

I can think of a million reasons, starting with: Why not? I can't tell women what to do. And I have no monolithic attitude toward all women. Fifty-two percent of the human race can't be all alike. If some wanna make fools of themselves at dumb corporate-rock shows, I won't go look but I won't condemn 'em either. *(December 1992)*

Where Men Are Men: If Clinton blinked in his first challenge to the sleaze machine on military bigotry, he succeeded in exposing the religious and talk-radio demagogues as naked creeps.

As if the U.S. military that brought you the Tailhook scandal, that turned prostitution into the growth industry of several Asian countries, was a model of gentlemanly behavior.

As if the ban on gay soldiers was some time-honored tradition, instead of a Reagan-era appeasiment to the bigot constituency. He might have floated that issue during his first week as a test, to see just how he might ideologically disarm the right.

The concept of gays in the military also diffuses a major tenet of the gay bohemian left: that gays and lesbians are a species apart. Gays are a lot more like everybody else than gays or straights want to admit. Granted, the military's a declining institution of dubious purpose in an age when our real wars are of the "trade" kind. Still, soldiers are about the most ordinary people you'll meet, having been socialized to be parts of a machine. And ordinary people, people with bad haircuts and clumsy dance moves, can be just as homosexual as any drag queen or lesbian folksinger. *(March 1993)*

***Playboy* had model recruiters** at the UW recently. The *Daily* ran a series of columns and letters reiterating all the 25-year-old complaints about the mag. Most anti-*Playboy* arguments are as trite as the pictures themselves. Here's some fresher criticism:

There's nothing intrinsically bad about the het-male sex drive, or about entertainments that exploit it. But the best erotic art is about passion, about the mysteries and compulsions that drive disparate humans together. Most *Playboy* pix, especially the centerfolds, are bland works of commercial ad-art. The models portray soulless, unlustful characters, overly "dressed" in hyperrealistic lighting and *Charlie's Angels* hair, their flesh digitally retouched to look unlike any real-world biological entity. The models aren't "degraded" in the sense most critics invoke; they're "honored" with the same perverse reverence given to The Brand in magazine ads. These "Playmates" are made to look incapable of having any real fun. I want better. *(May 1993)*

Numbers Racket Dept.: Sorry, I can't believe there are only approximately one million adult gay men in the U.S., as implied in that national sex survey by our Laurelhurst friends at the Battelle Memorial Research Institute. The national gay mags claim more than that many readers (including paid circulation and the industry-standard estimates of "pass-along" copies). I've met guys who claim to have had more than that many guys. If there are that few gay guys, then who's buying all the non-*Nutcracker* ballet tickets and Judy Garland laser disks? *(May 1993)*

Despite what I've said about fashion models, I don't hate them. I've been fascinated by them as an institution.

Diane Schuur, Ernestine Anderson, *and* Marilee Rush, *vocalists-living legends.*

Amy Denio *and* Lori Goldston, *instrumental geniuses who continue to prove "women in music" doesn't just mean singing magazine-cover icons.*

The women in the rock scene: *The assorted members and ex-members of Seven Year Bitch, Kill Sibyl, Maxi Badd, Sleater-Kinney, Bikini Kill, Cadillaca, Mavis Piggott, Cat Food, Whorehouse of Representatives, Violent Green, etc. etc.; and such frontwomen and soloists as Kim Warnick, Laura Love, Anisa Romero, Lisa Orth, Shannon Fuchness, Dara Rosenwasser, etc. etc. They continue to collectively prove "women in music" doesn't just mean out-machoing the men.*

The women behind the rock scene: *Caroline Davenport, Stephanie Dorgan, J.A. Anderson, Lori LeFavor, Kate Becker, Trish Timmers, Kerri Harrop, Susan Silver, Candice Pedersen, Barbara Dollarhide, etc. etc. The level-headed facilitators who keep the chaos possible.*

Mia Zapata, Kristen Pfaff, *and* Stefanie Sargent, *who, if nothing else, proved there's nothing romantic at all about rockers dying too young.*

Jini Dellaccio, *Etiquette Records cover photographer; visualizor of the finely-honed edge of pop and noise behind the Sonics' and Wailers' garage classics.*

Imogen Cunningham, *maker of photographic art at a time when many art-snobs still disdained the idea that such a thing could exist.*

Lori Larsen, *first lady of the Seattle theater circuit and an unsung force in forging the art-as-fun aesthetic still displayed today by others at places like the Annex Theater.*

33 Fainting Steps *and* Pat Graney, *dancer/choreographers helping modern dance find new ways to tell stories and express particular aspects of particular human conditions.*

Anne Gerber, *art collector-patron responsible for helping support and publicize the '50s "Northwest School" painters.*

Supermodels exist because media need female celebrities, but Hollywood won't develop enough star actresses. So editors and ad agencies created a type of celebrity who existed purely to sell products by selling her image. The supermodel presents a persona of leisure, of *yin* being rather than *yang* doing; yet she's is a pivotal cog in the American consumer machine. Nineteenth-century literature was full of pale waifs beautifully "dying of consumption" (TB). Modern magazines are full of pale waifs exhorting you to consume. Old-time femininity was a moral stance that stood above crude and petty things like commerce. Postmodern femininity is an instrument *of* commerce, in the name of that tenuously-defined quality that is beauty. I don't condemn that.

Leftist males often denounce femininity and beauty as counterproductive to the great revolutionary toil. They promote an ideal world in which women would affirm the superiority of masculine behavior by emulating it. I don't. As a suffragette anthem said, "Give us bread but give us roses." We need aesthetic truths as much as political ones (maybe more). Whether the aesthetic of *Elle* is the one we need is another question. *(January 1994)*

Misc. was baffled by a notice on the Internet search site Yahoo! promising a link to a British nudist camp with events for transvestites. How can you be undressed and cross-dressed at the same time? Did the queens just wear wigs and high heels?

But on reading the "Garden of Eden" site, the explanation was simple. By summer it's a normal nonerotic family nudist camp. (The site says, "Our club is widely recognised as being the in place to go for a fun time holiday.") But during the miserable Welsh winter, it holds weekends for fully-cross-dressed closeted queens to express their lifestyles away from the general populace. You have three seconds to fantasize about Robert Morley types or the bluebloods from the movie *Scandal* sharing high tea in frilly lace things. *(Jan. 10, 1996)*

"Seattle loves gay men but not lesbians." That's one of the theories given me by visual-art scenesters to explain the relative unpopularity of the Center on Contemporary Art's first all-lesbian group exhibition, *Gender, Fucked.* (The opening-night party attracted "almost none of the COCA regulars," said a COCA official.)

I wouldn't go that far, but it is true that lesbians are a minority-within-a-minority. (Just look at the proportion of lesbian to gay-male bars on Capitol Hill.) Events like the Pride Parade and all-encompassing monikers like "queer" notwithstanding, the lesbian and gay-male communities aren't as intercommunicative as they perhaps oughta be. (I say it's an aspect of larger forces in a society dividing into ever-smaller, more separate subcultures.)

Additionally (here's where the scenesters' theorizing comes in), lesbian artists have a PR problem. They've been stereotyped as humorless self-righteousness addicts. Gay-male art, the typing goes, is perceived to be outrageous and fantastical and fun even when it's about the direst of topics; while lesbian art's expected to be forever dour, judgemental and hostile to outsiders, even when it's about desire and love. All it takes to disprove this is to look at some of the diverse works being made by lesbian artists in our own region alone, from the hypnotic choreography of Pat Graney to the wonderful cartooning of Ellen Forney to the universal rage and joy in Team Dresch's music. These artists and others (including those at the COCA show) prove lesbians aren't all the same, as the existence of lesbians proves women aren't all the same. *(Aug. 1, 1996)*

Misc., your season-affective column, couldn't help but be cheered up by the January *Playgirl* cover blurb: "Odd Men Are In!" What could be duller than square jaws, pumped pecs, and steely gazes? Conversely, what could be more fun than somebody with a deft wit, a neato wardrobe of mismatched shirts and ties, and a wicked pinball wrist? (At least that's what I've always tried to tell women.) *(Dec. 19, 1996)*

Reader Deborah Shamoon spotted a new fad from Japan: "You have probably heard of that peculiarly Japanese snack food, Pocky (pronounced 'pokie'). It's a thin pretzel stick dipped in chocolate. Well, now there is a Men's Pocky, available at Uwajimaya. It comes in a macho green box, with the word "Men's" in English in stark white letters on a black background. On the back it says in English, "Crispy pretzel dipped in dark chocolate for the intelligent connoisseur who enjoys the finer points in life." It goes on to expound in Japanese about the full cocoa flavor.

"Japanese people generally believe only women and children like sweet food; eating candy is seen as a sign of childishness... I remember my host father announcing scornfully he didn't care for sweets, as he wolfed down box after box of Valentine's chocolate. A semi-sweet chocolate Pocky is the solution to this problem, and by

Guendolen Pletscheff, *fashion collector and advocate of the community-building institution known as high society.*

Nellie Cornish, *founder of Cornish College of the Arts. (So when are they gonna start a football team, the Game Hens?).*

Kay Greathouse, *longtime Frye Musuem empress and defender of visual traditionalism (as jazz teachers know, you need to know the rules before you can properly break 'em).*

Ruby Chow, *restaurateur, politician, and patron of Bruce Lee.*

Mary Pang, *Chow's sister, whose frozen-food mini-empire was the unfortunate target of a son's displaced sympathy.*

Ethel Mars, *co-founder of a family candy dynasty still Snickering along today (and name-inspiration for its Las Vegas-based upscale division, "Ethel M").*

Linda Tenney *and* Sunny Kobe Cook, *frontline soldiers in the battles to preserve locally-owned retail and locally-produced advertising.*

Mary Ann Boyer *("Madame Damnable"), Seattle's first madam; she and her successors kept Seattle going as a weekend destination for outlying lumberjacks while the town's "legitimate" early economy went through massive ups and downs.*

Anna Louise Strong, *organizer-publicist of the 1919 Seattle General Strike.*

Hazel Wolf, *100-esque year old environmental activist and thorn in the side of the likes of...*

Dixy Lee Ray, *Pacific Science Center cofounder and one-term governor; elequently advocated a number of political-economic theories I completely disagreed with.*

adding "Men's" to the name, [manufacturer] Glico clearly hopes to bolster the frail egos of men who have a yearning for a chocolate-coated pretzel snack.

"We have this kind of thing in the U.S., with men's hair dye, hair spray, and (recently, I have heard) nail polish. I think the idea should be expanded: How about "Brawn," the diet cola for men? Oreos for Men? Ben and Jerry's Muscle Man? Clearly there is an untapped market potential."

As for me, I'll patiently wait for the chance to sip a Man's Mai-Tai while adventuresomely perusing a Rrugged Romance by Harlequin For Him. (Hey, it could happen.) *(April 24, 1997)*

We're still trying to make sense of *People* magazine's "Sexy Moms" cover last month. They're surprised moms can have sex appeal? The mag's editors, like many Americans, must not realize that most people who have children have had sex first. And many of them even liked it. *(June 19, 1997)*

We're intrigued by the *New York* magazine headline, "Can Estrogen Make You Smarter?" You can bet superiority-of-women advocates are gloating over faxed photocopies of the article in college faculty lounges across North America. If the claims in the piece get confirmed, it'd make an easier argument for female-domination supporters than rants against testosterone (since the latter hormone exists in all genders).

And I'm sure birth-control pills would mix perfectly into those rave-dance "smart cocktails." I just hope it doesn't inspire phrenologists (those folks who claim they can measure intelligence by measuring the size and shape of someone's skull) to start testing a little lower on the body. *(Aug. 28, 1997)*

A KeyArena crowd cheered when Jane's Addiction singer Perry Farrell shouted, "How many of you here believe God is a woman?" Considering some of the capricious and vengeful behaviors attributed to the Judeo-Christian deity, were these cheering boys were really being all that complimentary to the feminine spirit? *(Dec. 24, 1997)*

Insert Old Holyfield "Ear" Puns Here: If lesbians hear more like men, as a medical study claims, howcum there's not a male-appeal equivalent to Ferron? (Jewel doesn't count.) On a more practical level, imagine if a special tuning fork or whistle could be developed, producing a sound only lesbians (and men) could hear. Single lesbians could find one another in any crowd, avoiding those straight women who think it's hip to pretend to be bi. (And, if affirmed by further research, this could give further credence to something I've long believed — lesbians and straight men have more in common than the more bigoted members of either camp will admit.) *(March 19, 1998)*

The *Times* reprinted a *Washington Post* article claiming increased social stigmas against males, especially boys. It claimed boys were more likely to be ostracized for asocial behavior or "learning disabilities," and more likely to later become perpetrators (and victims) of violence (to themselves or others). *Post* reporter Megan Rosenfeld wrote, "Boys are the universal scapegoats, the clumsy clods with smelly feet... feeling the tightening noose of limited expectations, societal scorn and inadequate role models" amid a lack of positive sex-role imagery (girls can now become most anything, but boys are still expected to be dumb jocks). Other reports, meanwhile, talk of lowered sperm counts and fewer boy babies in the major western nations, even of chemical-therapy estrogen finding its way (via sewage-sludge fertilizer) into the food supply. Whatever happened to the '80s rad-feminist cliché of "testosterone poisoning"? *(April 23, 1998)*

Viagramania: After 10 to 20 years of the magazines and the TV talk shows defining sexual issues almost exclusively from a (demographically upscale) woman's point of view, now *Time* and its ilk are scrambling to out-hype one another on the concept of masculine performance, as a problem now chemically solveable. It comes amid a new wave of skin-free men's magazines like *Maxim*, trying to attract male readers without that pictorial element proven to attract men but to scare off advertisers. So instead, all the sex in these mags is verbal, not visual, and it's often in the how-to format so familiar to women's-mag followers.

Viagra-hoopla might also mean we're finally over the late-'70s orthodox "feminism" in which the erection was depicted as the root of all evil. In the Viagra era, an erection is seen as something all men and 90 percent of women crave and wish would occur promptly, predictably, and on cue.

Another question could be posed from the hype: Is the legal "feel-good" drug industry morally distinguishable from the illegal "feel-good" drug industry? In the past,

Barbara Hedges, *UW athletic director; repeatedly makes bold moves which defy the wishes of the influential football "boosters."*

Patty Murray, *successful soccer-mom icon and less-successful Senator.*

Bertha K. Landes, *America's first female big-city mayor.*

Elizabeth Montgomery (Julesberg), *creator of the* Dick and Jane *books; envisioned a very Seattle quiet-bourgeois fantasy universe.*

Nicola Griffith, *scifi writer (*Slow River*); envisions a different, but still very Seattle, fantasy universe.*

K.K. Beck, J.A. Jance, Ann Rule, *and* Jayne Ann Krentz, *masters of mass-market storytelling.*

Stacey Levine *and* Rebecca Brown, *pioneers of Po-Mo (or is it Neo-Mo or Avant-Pop?) storytelling techniques.*

I've dissed both those who seek all the answers to life thru pharmaceuticals and those who piously seek to punitively condemn such seekers.

Both camps, I wrote, were on ego trips more potentially dangerous than any drug trip. But with ordinary citizens going more or less permanently on chemicals for little more or less than self-confidence, perhaps that dichotomy will transform into something different.
(May 28, 1998)

Lynda Barry, *cartoonist, author, and chronicler of the inner dysfunctional child within most of us.*

J.Z. "Ramtha" Knight, *propagator of a revisionist "ancient warrior" mythology that allowed rich people to feel a little less guilty.*

Mary McCarthy, *author, satirist, and chronicler of the futility of intellectualism.*

Sandy Hill; Good Morning America's *sucked ever since it fired her.*

Ruth "Wunda Wunda" Prins, *early local kids'-TV hostess.*

Mary Kay LeTourneau, *romantic rebel. So what if the rest of the world doesn't understand?*

(Feb. 1, 1999)

Ad of the Week (on the *Stranger* Bulletin Board page): "Lesbian Guitar Teacher." Hmm, an instructor in the heretofore-underappreciated art of the Lesbian Guitar: I could go for the cheap anatomical-reference jokes every guitar student's heard or said at one time, but instead will ponder "Lesbian Guitar" as a specific musical form. Could it be the ever-so-earnest acoustic fret-squeakin' of Holly Near or Ferron? The somewhat more humanistic, yet still stolid, chord-thumpin' of Phranc? The electrified "Torch and Twang" of early k.d. lang?

It's the curse-in-disguise of all these women (and others of their various ilks) that they're known first as statement-makers, second as stage presences, third as singers, and almost not at all as instrument-players.

This neglect of the role of music in female-singer-songwriter-ing is at least partly responsible for the near-total lack of female instrumentalists on both Lilith Fair package tours. It dogged Bikini Kill throughout the band's career; it took that band's co-leader Kathleen Hanna to start a whole new concept with a whole different instrumentation (Julie Ruin) for some critics to even notice that she'd been a darned-good musician all this time. (Lesbian-led bands that have gotten at least partial critical notice for their actual playing, such as Team Dresch, are exceptions that prove the rule.) *(Oct. 22, 1998)*

Icy Dilemma: I've been receiving reports from college towns across the country, via people on my newsletter mailing list. They're talking about what they see as a new social coldness on campuses. Students are shutting themselves off from public displays of affection or courtship. Men and women aren't even looking one another in the eye. Under the new propriety it's OK to have a boyfriend or girlfriend if you publicly treat the relationship nonchalantly, as settled down into blasé platonics; otherwise, you're supposed to be aloof and untroubled by those pesky anti-intellectual hormones. That's not being cool, that's being frozen.

There are plenty of potential causes: a decade-long media campaign to instill a fear of sex (you won't get AIDS by eye contact), ongoing ill-will between macho men and judgmental women, rising heterophobia within the boho/alternative community (reminding me of a line attributed to Robert Anton Wilson or to the book *Principia Discordia* about "what was once compulsory is now forbidden").

It is possible to be a man (or a woman who loves them) and a human being. Don't buy into one-dimensional stereotypes, mainstream or alternative flavors. You don't lose your soul via emotional intimacy, you strengthen it. This neo-puritanism doesn't deter abusive relationships (creeps don't bother with intellectual dogma except when it suits them). It only reinforces the fears of smart but shy young sensitives, the very people who need relationships, who could bring more humanness into the social realm. It's OK to be whatever sex and sex preference you are, even if it's an outré one. It's not what's in your pants that makes you good or evil, it's what's in your heart. *(November 1993)*

If the reason/excuse given for sexual repression nowadays is that we're in the "age of AIDS," howcum gays are still exploring new frontiers of sexual liberation in public and private, while heteros (statistically much less likely to get the virus than gay men) are the ones feeling they have to stay home and settle for porn, phone sex, and/or dildos? Virtually every book, film, performance event, seminar, or public demonstration promising "new, radical expressions of human sexuality" turns out to be by or for gays or lesbians only. Those who enjoy the company of chromosomes other than their own oughta be given the chance to consensually discover their hidden powers and passions too. *(December 1994)*

Workin' It

The Discover U catalog offered a course two weeks ago on the "Secrets for Making Love Work."

For those of you who couldn't attend that day or didn't have the $29 class fee, we hereby offer a few of our own secrets:

Cut off love's phone and cable TV.

Threaten to cancel love's MasterCard and/or bar tab.

Offer love a management-track position with three weeks' vacation, stock options, and full dental.

Show up at love's door in a Ride-Share commuters' minivan. Keep a-honkin' the horn 'til love comes out.

(continued)

20: SEX, LOVE, ETC.

or, can't I be sex-positive too?

Kinks will be kinks, even in this 1962 nightclub ad.

When the column began, the age-ol' girl/boy dance had reached a low point, particularly among the artsy and college-educated crowds; I still believe AIDS had almost nothing to do with it. Prior notions of "sexual revolution" and punk's spirit of self-indulgence had given way to new rigid gender roles, just as repressive as the old roles. In this new propriety, females were instructed to self-righteously refuse all sexual expressions except lesbianism, masturbation, and chaste S/M domination. Males were expected to wallow in universal-gender-guilt, amplified by the depressing zeitgeist of corporate pornography.

In the early '90s a wave of "sex positive" books, zines, and stores had shown up — all for women. In more recent years, our ever-bifurcating scene had spawned newer, often healthier ideals for XX and XY behavior. Girls could admit to liking boys; and in certain spaces, under certain conditions, boys were allowed to like girls.

But for too many, the old-new repressiveness still held sway. In too much of the hipster world, a man could be proudly sexual only if he was gay.

Gay men, meanwhile, had far direr circumstances to face; but many of them got through it by standing together under the gay-pride banner and asserting that safer sex didn't have to mean no sex. All this despite the continuing shrill attacks of the Religious Right's prudes, who in 1998 thought their sex-fear was so popular (as evinced by high news ratings for several notorious sex and sexual-harrassment scandals) they could exploit it to bring down a president and destroy the two-party system.

Brought to You by the Letter "X": Roscoe Orman, the kindly Gordon on *Sesame Street,* celebrated the show's 20th year by settling on child support for a viewer he helped create in Oregon in 1985. Some ex-viewers may gasp at the thought of Orman and his therapist lover singing "Which of These Things Belong Together," but I knew there was another side to him since the time he challenged the "exclusive" terms of his contract by moonlighting as a pimp on *All My Children.* *(January 1989)*

Come On Down Dept.: Darrington-born MC Bob Barker's lately called *The Price Is Right* "the highest-rated game show on network television" — a sly acknowledgment that it's now the only game show on network television. But his triumph as last survivor turned sour when Dian Parkinson, the former "Barker's Beauty" who became a *Playboy* model at 47, slapped him with an $8 million sexual-harrassment suit [later dismissed]. (Barker, now 70, claimed they'd had a voluntary affair in the late '80s, at her instigation.)

Online users love to wean gallows humor from the most serious issues, as in these jokes from America Online: "Would this have happened had he been spayed or neutered?" "The lawyers should have to guess the final settlement amount without going over." "Hope he made sure he didn't get Parkinson's Disease." "Overheard backstage: 'Higher, higher, lower, lower — Plinko!'" And best/worst of all: "I guess he really does like fur." *(July 1994)*

The Mike Lowry Fiasco might not have caused our Governor to reconsider his past actions, but it still offers the rest of us a lesson: There's not a line between excess chumminess and harassment, there's a continuum. A politician, whose success depends on making and keeping friendships, oughta know enough to err on the safe end of that continuum. If Lowry really was the kind of "traditional politician" conservatives denounce him as, he'd have known this. In the end it doesn't matter that Lowry probably wasn't trying to get those staff women into bed when he nudged or slapped them or whatever. But he should know in the world of politics, persuasion is everything. And in the world of persuasion, perception is everything. *(April 12, 1995)*

No Milk, Please: I was amused when a reader sent in six pages clipped from a *Cheri* magazine pictorial about nude waitresses at one "Big Cups Coffeehouse." The story claims the café's been in business in Seattle for four years. It's all fictional, of course (it probably wouldn't even be legal here). *(May 10, 1995)*

The Nth Power: I'd had trouble with the mainstreaming of S/M culture. Then at the Halloween parties I was at along the downtown/Capitol Hill arty circuit, almost half the attendees wore some variation on fetish garb. There were four hetero couples where one partner dragged the other around on a leash (three of the leashees were guys). I finally figured it out. Today's S/M isn't "transgressive." It's sure not "rebellious," save in the minds of those who get off on imagining themselves hated by a stereotyped "Mainstream America."

These days, S/M IS mainstream America, a distillation of the modern American zeitgeist. The newly commodified S/M celebrates power, domination, victimization, ruthlessness — your basic hypercapitalist values. As for politics, I've already written comparisons between "pro-business Democrats" and the consensual bottom position. *(Nov. 8, 1995)*

Workin' It
(continued)

Enroll love in an employees' softball league.

Change the locks on love's room and throw all love's stuff onto the sidewalk.

Get love a really cool metal lunchbox, pre-filled with a pastrami sandwich and a pack of Hostess Sno-Balls.

Enroll love in a community college's career-training program.

(Nov. 20, 1997)

Having a Complex

The change of season often brings a reassessment of one's life situation.

If you're feeling a little too much peace-'n'-quiet in your personal world, here are some handy tips for voluntarily complicating your life:

Start taking heroin.

Start a relationship with someone taking heroin.

Develop a life-dominating crush on someone completely unavailable.

Get a bank card. Max it out on cash advances. Blow the cash on Lotto tickets or "Make Money Fast!" multi-level marketing schemes.

Get, or get someone, pregnant.

Buy a "fixer upper" house, car, or boat.

Become really, really fascinated by liquor, lap dancers, or rare books.

Ordered an evening of Spice Pay-Per-View. Before I did, I believed the only people who ought to suffer through the stifling formulae and monumentally awful production values of hetero hard-porn videos were straight men who needed to see other men's genitalia in action — and that, therefore, the Spice channel (which shows those videos with all the phallic shots edited out) served no earthly (or earthy) purpose.

But after a couple hours of ugly silicone implants, ritualized acrobatics, and laughable "tuff" facial expressions, I caught on to the mood of the thing.

All formula fiction offers "adventure" to its characters and predictability to its audience. Hard-porn is no different. Its strictly-followed rites of banality envelop the viewer in a fantasy universe of cheap surroundings, harsh lighting, crude emotions, unspoken-yet-universally-observed rules of behavior, no thinking, no spirituality, and no love. Sorta like old Cold War-era propaganda stories about life behind the Iron Curtain, but with fancier lingirie. It still turns me off, but I now understand how it could turn on guys who've never gotten over adolescent sex-guilt. *(Jan. 9, 1997)*

High IQ=Low XXX?: The papers were full of smart-folks-get-less-sex headlines the same week IDG Books brought out *Dating for Dummies,* the latest extension of a guidebook series initially aimed at people who needed to run computers at work but didn't like to. Maybe they should've put out *Dating for Smarties* instead.

(On the other hand, a programming-manual format's perhaps an ideal means to show literal-minded people how to survive in such an un-left-brain activity.) (On the third hand, maybe it's all the wrong way; reinforcing thought patterns completely useless for the realm of hormones and emotions.)

Smart ladies at least have Marilyn Vos Savant and the learned lovelies in *Bull Durham* and *La Lectrice* as sexy role models. Who've boys got: The antisocial (alleged) Unabomber? The hygiene-challenged Einstein and Edison? OK, there's the fun-lovin' late scientist Richard Feynman and certain brooding movie master-criminal types, but they're the exceptions.

But the more common image is the drooling fanboy in a three-sizes-too-small Captain Kirk shirt, peering through inch-thick spectacles, looking for love in all the wrong places (like AOL chat rooms), fantasizing about Amazon superwomen but incapable of chatting up a real woman, perhaps still traumatized by high-school crushes who slept with jocks and treated him as a brother. Many hyper-rational people of all genders fear the irrational, and love and sex are about the most irrational behaviors known to humankind.

But becoming more desirable isn't as impossible as it sometimes seems. Practice using a softer, sultrier voice in which to recite post-structuralist literary theory. Memorize love sonnets. Do something to get outside the comfy prison of your own head (yoga, gardening, cycling, pets). Reclaim your place in the physical-biological-emotional realm. To quote a love-struck professor in Hal Hartley's PBS movie *Surviving Desire,* "Knowing is not enough." *(Jan. 29, 1998)*

Get a pet Siberian tiger.

Start your own private zoo.

Settle for nothing less than the latest, most advanced PCs and VCRs.

Decide your life's too full to waste any time on some boring ol' job.

Become a feature filmmaker.

Learn a performance skill worthy of a spot on the next Jim Rose Circus tour.

(Oct. 2, 1997)

The online zine *Salon* ran allegations of sexual harrassment in the offices of *60 Minutes* (following that show's sympathetic treatment of Clinton accuser Kathleen Willey). *Salon's* article was built around eight-year-old allegations by freelance writer Mark Hertsgaard, who'd written a piece for *Rolling Stone* (which published only a watered-down version). He charged the show's bigwigs, including exec-producer Don Hewitt and anchor Mike Wallace, with acts of gender-hostility ranging from lewd jokes to groping and bra-snapping.

It's enough to bring new meaning to my old foolproof formula for "Safer Sex;" Imaginining that the person you're about to have sex with is really Morley Safer oughta stop anything from happening. *(April 2, 1998)*

Putting the 'Sin' Into Insinuation: Misc.'s truth-be-stranger desk notes how the Northwest's biggest recent sex scandals now include one potential soap-stud moniker (Brock) and two potential porn-star names (Packwood and Moorehead). The former two were outspoken pro-feminist politicians who got accused of delivering unwanted gropes to several women. The latter's an outspoken queer-hating preacher who's been accused of molesting several men. It all just goes to show the seductive power of hypocrisy. *(June 4, 1998)*

The Silvery Skin: Didn't see as much of Bumbershoot as in prior years (either the crowds have finally gotten to me or my ongoing diet left me too carbo-depleted to stand in hot lines). But I did find out that the Squirrel Nut Zippers' stadium show really could produce Lindy hopping in the moshpit.

I also saw a few dozen wholesome grownups watch an hour of '30s-'40s stripper movies (projected in an out-

One, Etc., For the Road

Recently, at two different occasions among two different sets of people, the topic arose about whether one could bar-hop in Seattle hitting only places with numbers in their names, in numerical order.

I think I've figured how. Some of these places are far apart so you'll need wheels (as always, be sure to have a designated driver and always drink responsibly):

Van's 105 Tavern *(602 N. 105th St.).*

Either the Two Bells *(2313 4th Ave.),* 2 Dagos From Texas *(2601 1st Ave.), or the* 211 Club *(2304 2nd Ave.).*

Either the 318 Tavern *(318 W. Nickerson), or one of the two unrelated* Triangle Taverns *(553 1st Ave. S. or 3507 Fremont Pl. N.).*

Either the Four Mile Tavern *(15215 Aurora Ave. N.), the* Four B's *(4300 Leary Way NW), the* Four Seas Restaurant *(714 S. King St.), or the lounge at the* Four Seasons Olympic Hotel *(1300 4th Ave.).*

door courtyard) without turning into rampaging degenerates. On a beautiful night, in a beautiful setting (right by the atomic neon art near the North Court meeting rooms), a mixed-gender audience got to witness beautiful B&W footage of beautiful women (including burlesque legend Sally Rand and someone billed on the re-release print as Marilyn Monroe, though I have my doubts) making beautiful moves in beautiful costumes of various small sizes.

After the dance shorts, the projector was stopped while various bigwigs conferred whether to show an encore segment. When they finally gave their OK, the crowd saw 10 minutes of naughty-funny XXX animations from the early '30s (gags involved beastiality, oversized and detachable penises, and copyright-violating renditions of Krazy Kat and Bosko).

As the audience strolled happily into the night, I realized the end-of-porn essay in this paper last month was right when it proclaimed a truly vital city needs a healthy element of public vice. There's nothing like a little good clean sex to help bring people together. These exhibitions like these also help prove the apparently little-known fact that people have been having sex since before you were born. *(Sept. 17, 1998)*

A Disturbing Trend: Recent *Cosmopolitan* and *Playboy* sex surveys claimed collegians aren't doing it as much as their '80s predecessors. Something clearly must be done to reverse this. Maybe part of the problem's in the mags themselves, and the rest of the corporate media. For decades, humans have been commercially urged to sublimate their natural erotic cravings, into the care and feeding of the consumer economy instead of their own and their lovers' bodies.

Men are old that "women leave you" but a Toyota pickup won't; and that "it's a widely held belief" that men who wear a certain brand of shirts "are widely held."

Women are told it's less important to have sex than to merely look sexy, which can only be accomplished via the purchase and use of assorted garments and products. Then there's the postcard ad showing a perfect-preppy couple clutching in their undies with the slogan "Things get fresh when you unwrap it," advertising "the gum that goes squirt."

Maybe instead of using sexuality to sell products, we in the alterna-press, zine, and website communities could re-appropriate the language of advertising to promote more sex:

- "Sex — it's not just for gays and lesbians anymore."
- "Sex-positive attitudes — men can have them too."
- "Don't drink and drive — stay home and have sex."
- "Sex — it does a body good."
- "Eat less, lick more." *(Nov. 12, 1998)*

Men At Work: The old truism that men will pay for sex but women will pay only to "look sexy" may be changing, at least among certain affluent women in remote locations. A loyal reader recently told of her recent trip to Jamaica, where she and her adult daughter were regularly propositioned by male locals on the streets and public beaches. But she says the solicitations weren't expressions of harassment but of commerce. Hetero-male hooking's apparently become such a big tourist draw on the island in recent years, the Jamaica *Rough Guide* travel book even lists the best spots for European and American women to rent what the book gingerly calls "Jamaican steel." Some of the gated seaside resorts are discreetly offering bus tours for the ladies to go partake of a tall, dark toy-boy, then return to the hotel in time for scuba lessons.

This is a different phenomenon from the also-booming business of "swingers' resorts" across the Caribbean and Mexico, where the sex is just as casual but is restricted to one's fellow paying tourists. It's also a phenomenon of potential interest to North America's own remote, economically depressed regions, regions which tend to have ample supplies of rugged if less-than-gentlemanly men.

You'd have to get some anything-for-a-buck politicians to change a few laws, then put the recruited men through some *Full Monty*-esque makeovers and charm lessons; but from there, the only limit would be one's ambition and one's marketing budget. I can easily imagine big layouts in the continental fashion mags, inviting the pampered ladies of Italy and France to really experience the rugged, robust America they've only known through movies and ads, by enjoying a real Akron factory worker or a real Detroit homeboy or even a real Aberdeen lumberjack! *(Nov. 30, 1998)*

Either the 5 Spot *(1502 Queen Anne Ave. N.), the* 5 Point *(415 Cedar St.),* Zak's Fifth Avenue Saloon *(206 5th Ave. N.), or the* Old Fifth Avenue Tavern *(8507 5th Ave. NE).*

Either the Six Arms *(600 E. Pine St.), the Six Eleven (611 2nd Ave.), or the* 6th Avenue Bar & Grill *(2000 6th Ave.).*

Either Cafe Septiéme *(214 Broadway E.), or the* 7th Ave. Tavern *(705 NW 70th St.).*

The Speakeasy Cafe *(2306 2nd Ave.), home of the Web site for Dom Cappello's* Cafe 8Ball *comic.*

Either the Gay 90s *(700 Pike), or the bar formerly known as The Nine (now the* Family Affair, *234 Fairview Ave. N.).*

That's about it sequentially. With the end of Rosellini's Four-10 and Six-10, the closest thing to a "10" joint is the Tenya Japanese Restaurant *(936 3rd Ave.). Then you'd have to skip a couple to get to the* 13 Coins.

[Since this was written, the Gay 90s was demolished and the Speakeasy threatened to close.]

(April 17, 1996)

21: DUDS & THREADS

or, wearing away

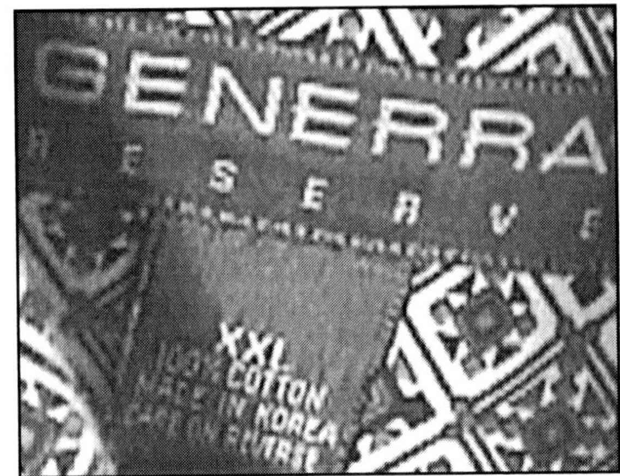

Generra, one of Seattle's former world-fashion leaders.

Despite what author Naomi Wolf or certain Madonna-obsessed college professors will tell you, gender-role is but one of many things expressed by clothing. Seattle had a going little industry in young-hip fashion design during the '80s. But it was driven down into relative unimportance pretty quickly, partly by a supposed "Seattle look" that really came from New York.

Urban "street" imagery is all over this fall's ads for suburban-only clothing chains, from J.C. Penney to Lamonts. If they think inner cities are so cool, why won't they have stores in 'em? *(October 1988)*

No More Fur at Nordstrom: This is how an industry dies, when the first PR-conscious retailer proudly capitulates to public furor (and flat market shares). But fur is more than an inefficient source of outerwear; it's one reason we're here. The trapping of wild fur animals was the first white industry in the Northwest. The Hudson's Bay Co. and others subsidized many of the first non-military settlements in Washington Territory. They were supported by sales to the society ladies of Europe, whose essential financial contribution was totally ignored in last year's books on women in Northwest history. *(December 1990)*

According to the newsletter *Japan Access*, Tokyo's top designers say the 1991 trend in swimwear will be the ecology look: earth-green colors, "designs borrowed from nature, including seashell, fish and flower motifs." The garments themselves are made of non-biodegradable, petroleum-based synthetics. *(February 1991)*

Color Me Bemused: There's a distinct color-scheme generation gap. Yuppies (and yuppie ad agencies trying to appeal to teens) are into bright, gaudy, neony colors. Teens themselves are dressing in black and watching B&W music videos… Also, why is it that the kids who are supposed to be the New Chastity generation strut about in skintight spandex and black bras, while the newly middle-aged who still boast of their wild swinging pasts wear ugly grey sweaters and shapeless faded jeans? *(February 1992)*

Misc. still wears its baseball caps with the brim in front, the way Abner Doubleday intended. Besides, you can tell when a fashion trend has outworn its welcome when they start making custom caps with frat-house letters printed only on the back. *(July 1992)*

Rap Sheet: I've said before that hip-hop is the first black-culture invention that white hipsters haven't been able to convincingly "tribute" (i.e., take over). More proof: the Basic fashion show at Down Under. White guys in baggy candy-color trousers slumped down the butt, a graffiti backdrop, an onstage DJ pretending to spin records and swigging from a quart bottle of malt liquor. Quite silly. *(September 1992)*

Out to Dry: The Squire Shops are in bankruptcy; the remaining 23 outlets are closing. Just as the ugly clothes that made 'em famous are coming back!

Squire sold clothes that young mall-crawlers thought were hip. In its heyday, that meant jeans with cuffs nearly as wide as the waist. Seattle wore bellbottoms years after the rest of the country stopped. Several companies formed here to keep Seattle in clothes the national companies no longer made.

That scene led to the local firms that gave the world loud sweatshirts with goofy slogans and Hypercolors; some of those firms are now on the wrong side of that fad and face money trouble themselves. *(April 1993)*

***P-I* headline on regional fashions:** "It's not just grungy anymore." It never was. How many times do we have to say it: What the media call "grunge fashion" was invented by Marc Jacobs in New York, based mostly on Greenwich Village rich-kid primping. Don't blame anybody here for it...

Or maybe blame *Peanuts* creator Charles Schulz. He's got a new sweatshirt of Pigpen with the simple slogan "Original Grunge." *(November 1993)*

If designer grunge seemed silly enough, just wait for designer riot grrrl. The *N.Y. Times* described designer Nicole Miller's show with "girl gangs" roaming a cinder-block runway, "razor blades dangling from their ears, zippers slashing across the clothes" representing what Miller calls "this whole tough-girl kind of edge going on" as inspired by what she calls "all-girl bands" like Belly, the Breeders and the Juliana Hatfield Three — none of which are, in fact, all-girl. Ever wonder what the boy musicians

Where's the NW In NW Lit?

From a very early age I was instilled with the (probably unintended but unmistakable) message that real art, and by extension real life, were things that only happened in places far away from my rural Washington existence. The stories read to us in class, and later assigned for us to read, all happened in Harlem or Korea or mythical fairylands or mythical Anytowns — until we got to read Beverly Cleary. Her kids had real attitudes. Her grownups had real tics and quirks. And they lived in a real place (Portland) I'd really been to.

Ever since, I've sought out the stories of my own place, the affirmations that, like Dr. Seuss's Whos, "We Are Here."

Eventually, I found some stories that tried to reveal the people and attitudes of the place. And I found other seekers.

Last December, I was involved in an exchange of emails on the topic of Northwest literature. The original question, posed by Raven Chronicles *editor Matt Briggs: "Is there any 'Northwest' in* Northwest Lit*'?"*

Some of the respondents said there wasn't any — that Caucasian-dominant society here's still too new, and too subservient to the national/global society of airports and strip malls and stadiums. I disagreed.

I felt there were indeed distinguishing characteristics in stuff from here, at least the better stuff from here.

Let's define "here" as Washington, Oregon, Idaho, maybe Alaska, and just maybe Montana.

If that's the literary Northwest, then Northwest literature could conceivably include anything set in this place, or written by someone who resides or once resided in this place.

in what clueless grownups call "all-girl bands" think? "Gee, thought I had one last time I looked."
(December 1993)

Barely Understanding: The fad for increasingly graphic female nudity in print ads selling clothes to women continues, from the highest-circulation fashion mags to lowly rags such as this—including ads placed by female-run firms. (That's female #1 (the merchant or maker) showing a picture of female #2 (the model) without clothes, to sell clothes to female #3 (the customer)).

This whole pomo phenomenon of selling clothes by showing people not wearing any is something I've tried hard to understand. Maybe really is a matter of selling "body image," like the feminist analysts claim all fashion ads do. Maybe it's selling the fantasy of not needing the product, like the Infiniti ads that showed perfect natural landscapes bereft of the destructive effects of automobiles. Maybe the ads should say something like, "Don't be ashamed that you have a body; be ashamed it doesn't look like this. Wear our clothes all the time and nobody will know you don't have this body." Or: "The law says you can't go around clothes-free in public, so if you have to wear clothes you might as well wear ours."

Then again, after seeing the stupid designer clothes on VH-1's *Fashion Television Weekend,* I can understand how the industry would want its customers to pretend they were naked. It'd be less embarrassing to be starkers in public than to be seen wearing a lot of that overpriced silliness. *(October 1994)*

Knit Picking: I don't think the discontinued Calvin Klein ads were "kiddie porn" either (more like deliberately antisexual sleaze, using old underground photography as another retro-pop-cult "inspiration"). However, there's now a line of junior-size knit tops (sold at Fred Meyer) called "Betty Blue." Do teenage girls wearing the tops know about the steamy French movie of the same name? Quite possibly. Do moms buying 'em for their daughters know about the movie? Maybe not. *(Oct. 4, 1995)*

Whenever there's a pesky *e.coli* outbreak, vegan activists use the tragedy as a reason to call for an end to meat consumption. Whenever somebody working in porn videos or a strip joint turns out to be facing a troubled or abuse-racked private life, radical feminists 'n' right-wing censors publicly exploit the situation to advocate further suppression of the sex biz. Yet the highly publicized mistreatment of sweatshop textile workers (domestically and across the Pacific) hasn't, to my knowledge, inspired members of the Naturist Society to issue PR blitzes asserting how there'd be fewer mistreated clothes-maikers if fewer people wore clothes. *(Jan. 8, 1998)*

Pinning It Down: Bowling as a source for hip iconography is way on the rise. Bowling shirts (particularly the Hawwaiian variety) have been in for a couple of years now and may have another resurgence this summer (if the collectors haven't stowed away all the good ones by now). New bars from the Breakroom to Shorty's are festooned with balls, pins, and other acoutrements of the sport. It's a way to be fun 'n' retro without the bourgeois trappings of the cigar-bar crowd.

But don't look for any new bowling alleys anywhere around here anytime soon. Banks and landlords think bowling's a sub-optimal use of square footage, compared to other entertainment or retail concepts. When a Green Lake Bowl or Village Lanes or Bellevue Lanes goes away, it doesn't come back. All we can do is support the remaining kegling bastions (including the occasional "rock 'n' bowl" nights at Leilani Lanes in Greenwood). *(April 2, 1998)*

Phases of the Moon: With the warm weather's come an odd masculine fashion statement: dorsal pseudo-cleavage. It involves wearing jeans with a belt, but hanked down to show the tall waistband of designer boxer shorts. I know it originally came from tuff-guy street wear, which in turn was based upon prison garb (oversize trousers with no belts allowed). But in this incarnation, it's like a male version of that "sex-positive" women's book *Exhibitionism for the Shy.* *(May 28, 1998)*

But that could conceivably include everything from Thomas Pynchon's V. *(partly written while he was a Boeing technical writer) to tales where people leave Seattle early on and never return (certain Jack London stories, Douglas Coupland's* Microserfs*).*

So for convenience's sake, let's classify four faces of Northwest lit, and the values and weaknesses of each.

Stuff written here but without "local" content. *John Saul's chillers, Robert Ferrigno's thrillers, and August Wilson's African American survival plays bear little or no relationship to their creators' domiciles. Yet some of these manage to exploit a certain Northwest spirit.*

Stacey Levine's Dra- *and* My Horse *occur in surreal fantasy realms (the former in an all-indoor city); but* Dra-*'s "drab and dreary world of utter dread" and* My Horse*'s "painful psycho-logic" (as described on the cover blurbs) correspond internally to a sense of low-key resignation found in some more "realistic" works from here.*

(continued)

22: STUFF & THINGS

or, semi-obscure objects of desire

Les choses
a story of
the sixties
by Georges Perec
Winner of the
French Prix Renaudot

In the column's early years, there was a fad of trade-paperback novels (largely promoted by a publishing imprint with the contradictory name of "Vintage Contemporaries") in which the main characters were chiefly identified and deliniated by the brand names of the products they owned. French experimental novelist Georges Perec (whom we'll briefly mention in chapter 27) had already ploughed that territory in 1965 with Les Choses *("Things"). The young couple in his novel weren't liberated into full self-expression by their acquisitions, but rather became trapped within the stifling expectations of consumer society.*

While I can appreciate the sentiments of the anti-consumerist advocates, I also believe defining yourself by what you don't buy is just as constraining as defining youself by what you do buy.

Boxing Bout: Buying CDs in jewel boxes, from stores that don't supply those wasteful cardboard longboxes? Think you're saving the Earth? Think again, after you pass the Precision Sound warehouse on Republican Street east of Westlake. On a rainless day you'll see a crew of dudes and dudettes out on the loading dock, tearing off longboxes and tossing them into a Dumpster. Sure they're all recycled, but it's still a waste to make 'em in the first place. Any record company that puts environmental hype in its inserts ought to offer jewel box-only CDs. Besides, longboxes were the last bastion of big cover art; you should have the option of getting 'em. They *will* be collectibles. *(July 1993)*

My Soap Box: When Procter & Gamble's ad agency designed the Tide box in the '50s, it never knew that its concentric patterns would look just like the computer-animated psychedelic visuals of the '90s. The orange box has become an icon of rave graphics.

It's on countless techno-party flyers. Portland's Sweaty Nipples used it on a CD label; a Seattle band was going to use it before the Nipples used it first. I'm told that the brain can perceive the circles as moving in and out at the same time, making the image a "mandala" that can send the mind into another world.

I'm also told that the orange circles look great under blacklight, and that Liquid Tide makes a great medium for making black-light paintings that can't be seen in normal light (the "bleach substitute" ingredient contains a fluorescent dye).

What's next: acid-trip costumes based on the playing-card guy on the ol' White King box? *(March 1994)*

Xmas Xtravaganza: Again this year, the gift industry's outdone itself. Among the wackiest ideas is LifeClock Corp.'s Timisis, a digital clock embedded in a fake-granite desktop pyramid paperweight. Besides offering the current time and "Motivational Messages Every Minute," the top readout line lets you "watch the hours, minutes and seconds counting down until your next vacation, until you must meet your sales quota, until your retirement, OR... the rest of your statistical lifetime!"

Also for the grownups are the Marilyn Monroe Collector's Dolls, with six costumes but no tiny bottles of sleeping pills, and the Scarlett Barbie-Rhett Ken series. Kid stuff's hit a creative lull this year, as violence-genre video games and *Power Rangers* character products grab most of the cash and glory.

One glorious exception: Zolo, a plastic doll-building set sort of like Mr. Potato Head, only with cool modern-art shapes and colors so you can build anything from a Dr. Seuss-like creature to a Calder-like mobile.

Also worth noting are the pocket computer notebooks for kids, including the all-pink girls' model My Diary (at last, something to draw young girls into computing!).

Haven't get gotten around to trying the CNN board game, in which you take the role of your favorite TV correspondent trotting the globe in search of breaking news (I can imagine all the drag-queen-theater people playing it and all of them wanting to be Elsa Klensch).

(January 1995)

Augmentations: Some music CDs are beginning to be released with CD-ROM material stuck in at the end: A low-res version of a music video, say, or an interview with the singer. Imagine the further possibilities: Dylan box sets with extra tracks of "scholars" claiming to have literal interpretations of every lyric. Heck, I'd rent a laserdisc version of a Madonna video collection if it had a Second Audio Program with a round-table of semiotics profs explaining every image. *(July 26, 1995)*

Where's the NW In NW Lit?
(continued)

Locally-set genre novels.
I haven't the space nor the expertise to discuss romances, that last bastion of un-ironic genre fiction (and the only mass-fiction genre predicated on love instead of aggression). But the better whodunit-doers, here and elsewhere, go beyond place names to invoke the spirit of a region in the ways their characters commit or solve crimes. Earl Emerson and K.K. Beck's crime-solvers have a particularly Seattle kind of world-weariness; the crimes they investigate often invoke particularly local versions of ambition and desperation.

Land Lit.
In college I was introduced to a whole "Northwest school" of writers and poets. Only their message, upon initial contact, seemed to be "We Are Not Here."

The poems usually consisted of minutely-detailed nature tableaux, devoid of human life save for the omniscient gaze of their narrators.

The fiction viewed this countryside as verbal Cinemascope settings for noble women and stout-hearted men felling trees and fly fishing and behaving not at all like the all-too-human Norwesters I knew. None of the people in these stories, of course, lived in any city bigger than Port Townsend.

I now understand a little more about the formula's origins. Concurrent with the Asian-inspired "Northwest School" painters and the spiritual-empowerment aspects of the Mountaineers movement, the first generations of nature poets (David Wagoner, Barry Lopez, Lake City kid Gary Snyder) sought to re-connect to nature's cyclical continuum of life. Even the "urban" writings of Richard Hugo are full of references to birds, streams, and native plants.

Body Doubles is a new brand of cosmetics and skin care products, sold via a multi-level marketing scheme. The promise implied in the company's name (but not explicitly given in its ads) is with this stuff, you can look better than movie stars — you can look as good as the models who do the stars' nude scenes for them! *(July 12, 1995)*

Free Enterprise At Its Best: Pee-On-It is a urinal sanitizer-deodorizer by the Ohio-based Anthem Inc., with one of seven pictures: A guy holding an umbrella with the caption "And you thought you were having a rough day," a woman with her mouth open, another woman laughing "What's That, A Joke?", a bull's eye with the caption "If You Don't Have Length Try For Aim," a guy getting a "shower," a guy holding his nose and ranting "You Drank THAT?," and an opened beer can with the caption "Ecology project: Recycle Your Beer Here." *(Aug. 16, 1995)*

Tasty Bits: For a long time, lotsa people thought computer-age aesthetics would be cold-n'-sterile. Then by the mid-'80s, PC-related visual styles (in game software, user-group literature and digital illustration) threatened to drown us in sword-and-sorcery geekdom. Now, I'm happy to report, it's a whole new picture, especially in the homespun covers of CD-ROMs by small developers.

There's something promising about CD-ROMs, even the ones that suck. It's a vital artform that can inspire this kind of generic mediocre content in identical bright-n-bouncy packaging. Just lounging in the CD-ROM section of Future Shop is a thrilling experience. If there's shelf and catalog space for all those discs of generic clip-art, old shareware video games and swimsuit pictures, there's gotta be a market for something really good if and when it ever arrives.

Another thought: Could music CDs be sold in 5- or 10-packs "in promotional packaging" like the grab bags of CD-ROMs? With the *Wall Street Journal* reporting a glut in indie rock releases, maybe low-sellers could be repackaged as *The Five-Foot Pack of Punk,* or *1,001 Straight Edge Rants,* or even *Super Value Bundle of White Kids Who Think They're George Clinton.* *(August 2, 1995)*

Brethren and Cistern: For unknown reasons, the wife of sometime *Stranger* writer Bryan Clark was recently put on the mailing list for *Your Church* magazine ("Helping You with the Business of Ministry"). It's a Protestant *Sharper Image Catalog,* by the publishers of *Christianity Today* but with no theological content. Just blurbs and ads for nifty products: Office-cubicle walls "re-purposed" to house Sunday School groups, vinyl siding, fiberglass baptism pools, choir robes, bulk quantities of communion wafers, candle holders, electronic organs ("the way Sunday should sound"), clear plastic pulpits ("where no visual barriers exist between you and your congregation"), new and used pews, shatterproof fake stained glass windows, kitchen supplies ("Equipping the Saints in a practical way"), computer software to keep track of membership and fundraising, even entire prefab church building sections.

Coolest of all are the electronic music boxes, "digital carillons" (made by a company called Quasimodo Bells) and "digital hymnals" ("Instantly plays thousands of hymns, choruses, praise music, children's songs, wedding music, and gospel favorites").

Our lesson: Even the heirs of Calvinist anti-idolatry can't help but be eternally fascinated by that most basic of human desires, the Quest for Cool Stuff. *(Nov. 22, 1995)*

But the approach had its limitations, especially in the hands of '70s-'80s imitators. What began as a quest for Zen tranquility eventually devolved into cloying sanctimony.

Poet-editor Phoebe Bosche notes, "For a lot of folks/writers who have settled here, 'urban' (a word that needs to be in quotes) has a nasty connotation, versus the perceived ideal sense of how life should be lived. Urban = technology. These are the writers who don't like the sound of a crow, many who are of the Poetry Northwest *[magazine] school."*

Present Tense: After years of wanting to, I finally got in this year to the Seattle Gift Show, a trade show for retailers and wholesalers of less-than-necessary merchandise. It was just as great as I'd imagined — a gigantic bazaar, taking up the whole Convention Center and two Seattle Center buildings to boot; full of booths hawking the widest array of stuff.

There were acres of "country craft" baskets, Husky sweatshirts, "Over The Hill" bras designed to droop, small-penis-joke greeting cards, *Absolutely Fabulous* fridge magnets, cocoa mix from an outfit called Pure Decadence, landmarks-of-hockey-map jigsaw puzzles, Alaska souvenir pennants, men's-restroom plastic miniatures (complete with digitized flushing sounds when you press a button), bonsai mini-fountains, angel statues, Prozac/happy-face T-shirts, Russian dolls, *Men of Africa* calendars, and more. One booth offered the perfect bachelor-pad accessory, the Moon Lamp (a milky-white large plastic globe emanating spots of pastel light). An Issaquah outfit called Loveable Chocolates offered chocolate and white-chocolate novelty gifts in assorted shapes, even as a set of dentures ("We sell a lot to dentists," the woman at the booth claimed).

But the item that might most interest some [of our] readers is Magnetic Jewelry, from the Gravity Free Factory (an N.Y.C. outfit with a Seattle office). It's a line of stud, crystal, and spike-shaped face jewelry giving the appearance of piercing with no holes, thanks to a mag-

Bosche also disagrees with my disparagement of nature writing: "To just dismiss 'nature poetry/writing' is blind to the overriding presence of our surroundings here. There is the presence of nature in all the urban writing being created here. It is different than the open possibilities that infuse writing from southern California, my home. The cynicism here is also different from east-coast or L.A. cynicism. It is rooted in a denser feeling of our relationship with our surroundings, in the character of this city."

The real thing. *The rarest and dearest of Northwest writings are the works that attempt to convey how people here behave, think, and relate. I'm not merely talking about highbrow-appeal, or even what appeals to me. The annoyingly "lite" Tom Robbins certainly expresses the aesthetic of a certain caste of NW residents. But I prefer works expressing the moods Robbins's escapism is escaping from.*

(continued)

netized piece of metal you wear on the other side of your ear, lip, or nostril. (No other applicable body parts were mentioned in the brochure or at the booth.) *(Feb. 6, 1997)*

Kelly, billed by Mattel as "Barbie's Baby Sister," is already showing signs of rebellion against her careerist, acquisition-obsessed sibling. Evidence: the new "Potty Training Kelly" model, shown in Saturday-morning TV ads "tinkling" into her own toddler-size toilet. Besides demystifying the mechanics of female elimination for young male cartoon viewers, the doll allows females just beyond toilet-training age to act out on an inanimate victim any traumas their own moms had imposed on them, potentially preventing deep psychological issues that might surface later in life. *(April 3, 1997)*

Game Theory Revisited: The Seattle Monopoly game, premiered last Friday, is Hasbro's belated answer to Stock Block and CityOpoly, '80s indie games based on the Monopoly concept but with different street and business names for each town they were sold in. There are enough professional game designers in town for somebody to think up a real (not fill-in-the-blanks) Seattle game. Maybe it could be about trying to start a computer-related company that could make it big, but not so big that Microsoft would crush it. Or it could be about coming up with schemes to improve civic life in spite of opposition by big money. *(Oct. 30, 1997)*

iMpressions: The *Stranger* office got a couple of those new iMac computers. They're gorgeous; they're fast; they're fun. The iMac's the first "home" computer designed as a piece of home decor, like old "cathedral" radios (one old radio name, Motorola, makes the CPU chip in the iMac).

Just as importantly, it expresses the Mac OS's visual aesthetic into tangible form. This has the effect of reducing the dissonance, the trance effect a user may have while really concentrating on the "mindspace" of running software. On plain beige-box computers, a user can become almost unaware of his/her physical presence (unless, of course, something goes wrong with the hardware). The iMac's more noticable, yet pleasant, presence might help hardcore gamers and Net-skimmers keep at least partly aware of the tangible world surrounding them. That, in turn, might help relieve or prevent the loneliness and depression cited among computer jockeys by Carnegie Mellon sociologists. *(Sept. 24, 1998)*

Mary Pang's frozen foods; destroyed by her arsonist son.

23: FOODS, DRINKS, & DRUGS

or, styles and substances

After the repeal of Prohibition, hard liquor by the drink could legally be had in Washington only at private clubs. In the '50s the state finally allowed restaurants to open cocktail lounges, usually in back rooms and only if the establishment met a lot of criteria (including a minimal ratio of booze sales to food sales). We got a lot of places trying to sell us a lot of meals, so they could keep selling their more profitable drinks.

At first, these restaurant-lounge combos mostly stuck to classic steakhouse fare, except for some Chinese places. Then came those '70s "cuisine" crazes and all their subsequent permutations — nouvelle, fusion, faux-regionalist, vegan, macrobiotic, gourmet-ized versions of regular American foods, etc. etc.

By the time the state finally relaxed its liquor laws to let more places sell the hard stuff (around the time the "cocktail nation" fad peaked), new "exotic" restaurant concepts were opening (and closing) faster than anybody could taste them — while good ol' meat-and-potatoes places (except a couple expensive ones attached to "cigar bars") were disappearing fast.

From in-flight magazines to the *P-I* to *CBS This Morning,* major attention has been drawn recently to something called "Northwest cuisine." WHAT Northwest cuisine? I'm a fourth-generation Washingtonian and never heard of any of these fancy dishes involving rhubarb, rack of lamb and alternatively-processed fish, let alone of many of their ingredients.

It sounds suspiciously like some of those other western regional cuisines, invented from scratch from ex-L.A. chefs (Santa Fe, Colorado), allowing itinerant suburbanites the fantasy of "place" while the real communities of these places succumb to mall-ism. I am certain that we will see the "discovery" of Montana cuisine, North Dakota cuisine, and even Utah cuisine.

Ya wanna know the true Northwest cuisine (at least among white people)? It's Dick's burgers, barbecued fish with really thin bones, Shake 'n' Bake chicken, canned vegetables, Krusteaz pancakes with Mapeline-flavored syrup, maple bars, strawberry shortcake with Dream Whip, Fisher scones, Red Rose tea, Mountain bars, and Rainier Ale (the now-discontinued weak version). I don't know if Lutefisk counts, since it seems to be perennially given as a gift but never eaten. *(May 1990)*

I remain perplexed by this phony "Northwest cuisine". In the *P-I,* Stouffer Madison Hotel chef Rene Pax insisted that "Seattle food means fresh food and

Where's the NW In NW Lit?
(continued)

Timothy Egan called it "Northwest Noir." Briggs calls it "the slippery sense of place and identity in the Pacific Northwest... a strange dislocation that sometimes expresses itself in deformed characters, like Katherine Dunn's Geek Love; *a reduction of realty into a heavily weighted and controlled narrative, like Raymond Carver's short stories; or in the complete absence of family history and a sort of constant self-invention as in Denis Johnson's* Already Dead, *or stories about isolated and small communities as in Peter Bacho."*

To that roster I'd add Gus Van Sant's philosophical down-and-outers, the Wolff brothers' rambunctious yet worryful teens, Rebecca Brown's obsessively intricate life scenes, Jesse Bernstein's defiant celebrations of despair as a life force, Willie Smith's dark fantasies, and the sublime desolation of Charles D'Ambrosio's The Point.

the best of the fresh produce." If there really is a culinary tradition here, it would have to take into account our short growing season (the freshness obsession comes from L.A.-trained chefs used to year-round growing) and our frontier heritage, particularly of the days before highways or rural electrification.

Truly traditional Northwest foods would be those with brief seasons (cherries), or are made to keep (evaporated milk was invented here). A cuisine that reflects the character of the local populace (as opposed to laid-back fantasies) would stay modest and unpretentious, at least fun. Nothing gaudy or cutesy. An honest smoked salmon, adequate white wine, plain tossed salad, and the quiet elegance of an Almond Roca dessert. *(July 1992)*

Why should you care about junk food (a broad name for things people eat and drink for enjoyment, rather than sustenance)? Because it's the sure sign of a culture.

American junk food represents everything this nation stands for: advanced technology and efficient distribution, under the direction of clever marketing, satisfying people's wants instead of their needs.

Take the new Bubble Beeper, an orange plastic box with a pocket clasp and a metallic front label. Inside the flip-top, the 17 sticks of rather ordinary bubble gum (made by Wrigley's off-brand division) come in wrappers decorated with LCD-style type reading I'LL CALL YOU!, CALL ME, SORRY LINE BUSY, URGENT, or SEE YOU LATER!

It's a "value-added" (costlier than it absolutely has to be) version of what's already an entertainment food product, with no nutritional purpose. But it's an expression of many things — our fascination with personal tech, kids' love of gadgetry and telephony, and corporate America's drive to commodify the accessories of gangsta rap for suburban consumption. *(July 1994)*

Prior to the second *Teenage Mutant Ninja Turtles* movie, there are Turtles Pies ("Fresh from the sewers to you!") and Turtle Eggs. Since there are no female mutant turtles, I don't know where the eggs come from; the pies have "vanilla puddin' power" within the famous Hostess crust and green frosting.

The "vanilla" probably came from a 42-year-old Seattle plant that made over 3 million pounds of vanillin a year, extracted from sulfite-waste liquor from wood pulp, processed with sodium hydroxide and used for important drugs as well as flavoring. It's being replaced by a

Sunbelt plant that will make a synthetic substitute — an imitation imitation. (No grumblings about how unappetizing this sounds. Vanillin is chemically identical to vanilla from a bean. Besides, some food purists drench pancakes with concentrated tree sap.) *(March 1991)*

The official Seattle Seahawks chewing gum is a lot like the team. It seems tough for the first couple of seconds, but very quickly proves just how soft and pliable it really is. *(August 1994)*

I'm still trying to get a jar of Mango Flavor Tang, sold mainly thru Hispanic-oriented groceries in the southern tier states. It presumably tastes as much like mangoes as regular Tang tastes like oranges. I wonder if it was in the spaceship with Bill Dana, the Hungarian-born comedian who made the Mexican-dialect comedy record *The Astronaut.* *(August 1992)*

Mango Tang Update: Ana Hernandez arranged for her cousin to smuggle a case of various Tang and "Frisco" brand 1-liter packets across the Mexican border; I now possess the contraband sugar/citric acid powder.

The mango drink looks more orange than the Orange Tang and tastes vaguely like mangoes, but is too thin and sugar-gritty to make a convincing replica. The guava, melon, lemon and (especially) lime flavors are closer to the mark. *(November 1992)*

Bird Gotta Fry: The Legislature's reclassified flightless birds (ostriches, emus, rheas) as poultry, so they can be raised for food. The AP quotes breeders as saying they "taste just like beef." It's appropriate that Washington starts an industry in birds that run along the ground, since one of the state's top poultry firms is named Acme. *(May 1993)*

Canned Heat: Some folks claim to have found syringes in diet-pop cans. It's really either a hoax or a tampering, but I can't help fantasizing about a company doing it as a stunt to become the Choice of a New Generation, Seattle-style. (Imagine the alternative-rock-star endorsement possibilities!) Note that officials insist any contaminant chemicals would never survive in a Pepsi can (should our kids drink stuff that strong?)

Also note that KIRO-TV handed the commentary spot about the soda scandal to its longtime resident shrink, Dr. Pepper Schwartz (no relation). *(July 1993)*

"There is a common, nervous energy (like overcompensating for the overcast winter) to a lot of the writing that I think strikes me as particularly PNW," Briggs adds. "This spirit I'm talking about is like your weird uncle. Your characters are generally losers. They're not heroic; they're just odd."

Even the humor in NW lit, and there's a lot of it, is off-center (Gary Larson, Ellen Forney, Gregory Hischack's beautiful zine Farm Pulp*), self-deprecating (Spud Goodman's TV skits, Scott McCaughey's song lyrics), or concerned with the dichotomy between crudity and beauty (Jim Woodring, Oregon historian Stewart Holbrook).*

At live readings today, the nature poets have largely been succeeded by slam poets. Younger would-be writers I meet want to be Anais Nin or Charles Bukowski. The economics of publishing virtually dictate that a work with "alternative" appeal reach out to a national or global subculture, while a work with local or regional appeal must hew to a mainstream zeitgeist. And the local mainstream zeitgeist has been thoroughly gentrified.

In such a milieu, hat place is there for the quirky, the depressive, the unparodic noir, in a social landscape dominated by hypercapitalistic monomania?

Marty Kruse, small-press buyer at Powell's City of Books in Portland, says he's "really disappointed with the output from the Pacific Northwest (of late)... There was a great deal more enthusiasm when we all had less to lose."

But if the best NW lit's about people who've left behind, or been left behind by, family and society, then there'll be plenty of material to come about people who've been left behind by the boom.

As Briggs points out, "This has been an industrial town and a seat for the labor movement and there are all of these people who were here before the 1980s (and even those who were there before them, all the way back to the original Salish tribes) milling around, working strange jobs, and who aren't exactly jumping on the Boeing/Microsoft bandwagon, largely because they can't."

(March 27, 1998)

Ralston Purina's new Barbie cereal is the same recipe as its Nintendo cereal; only the shapes and boxes are different. If boys and girls can't be taught to play with the same toys, at least they can eat the same sugar puffs.
(October 1989)

Flaking Out: We may be seeing the end of breakfast cereal as a modern art form. Ralston Purina has stopped its series of limited-run movie and TV tie-in cereals marketed partly to box collectors (Breakfast With Barbie, Nintendo Cereal System, Batman, Urkel-Os, the *Robin Hood* tie-in Prince of Thieves, and the great *Addams Family* cereal). Nabisco has sold its admittedly weak lineup of brands to Post. Recession-weary shoppers are flocking to house brands and Malt-O-Meal's big bags of wheat puffs, which cost less 'cuz they don't support cool commercials, toy surprises or mail-order offers (let alone R&D into new shapes and colors).

Girl Trouble used to toss out cereal at some of its gigs; so did the late Mother Love Bone singer Andy Wood. Cereal is more than the first food of the day, it's pop culture you can eat. Its ever-changing forms and flavors make it the ultimate American hi-tech food. Its modern crass-commercial reputation belies its distant origin in a Michigan health spa, as chronicled in T. Corraghessen Boyle's bestselling novel *The Road to Wellville* (soon to be a major motion picture).

It's time to do your part to keep an essential part of our culture from going soggy. Buy an extra box of Cocoa Puffs today. Future generations will thank you. *(December 1993)*

Trouble On Dextrose Avenue: An even more universal aspect of the youth diet is changing, as Dolly Madison Bakeries wants to buy the much larger Hostess-Wonder empire. As a kid, I knew Hostess goodies as the real thing. Some kids preferred the cup cakes, some the fruit pies. Some kids liked to unroll the Ho-Hos. I myself was a sucker for the Sno-Balls — even at a tender age, there was something mysteriously appealing about two side-by-side pink hemispheres, soft and bouncy to the touch.

Dolly cakes were mysterious things unavailable in this area, known only from commercials on the Charlie Brown TV specials. When the Dollys finally showed up in Washington, they tended to appear at odd convenience stores that for some reason didn't have Hostess. Their sizes, flavors and textures were strange to a Hostess-reared palate; even the sugar-grit of the creme filling was off somehow. Now, the product lines will probably merge, with Dolly's Zingers appearing alongside the Twinkies. Let's just hope the new bosses keep the bright Wonder Bread neon sign in south Seattle (ironically leading you toward our town's least whitebread neighborhood) and the Hostess plant off Aurora, beautiful and oh-so sweet smelling, with its giant exterior intake valves labeled for sugar and corn syrup. *(Jan. 24, 1995)*

Yeah, the tragedy of the four firefighters was a bad thing. But I'll also miss the Mary Pang's foods made in that destroyed plant, which might never resume production. Pang's frozen Chinese dinners, entrees and egg rolls (in their happy '50s-orange boxes) were regular dietary elements for the young and underemployed. Unlike some other slacker staples, Pang's products never wore out their welcome. *(Jan. 24, 1995)*

Two companies are selling candies in containers that look exactly like computer mice. Candy Mouse tarts, made in Mexico by a Wrigley subsidiary, taste like SweeTarts but are shaped like pet-mouse food pellets. Web Fuel mints ("Cool Mints! Cool Sites!"), made in Holland for N.Y.C.-based World Packaging, are triangular faux-Altoids; the paper wrapping inside the aluminum box is printed with addresses of "cool" websites, including that of local kids'-computer-game firm Headbone. The Candy Mouse container looks like a two-button PC mouse and costs less than the Web Fuel box, which looks like a one-button Macintosh mouse and holds a tastier, more powerful product. *(May 21, 1998)*

Booze Nooze: Some legislators think it'd be a good idea to scrap the state liquor stores and let big chain stores sell the stuff. I support any move to dilute the power of the Washington State Liquor Control Board, a truly outmoded institution whose picayune policies helped thwart any real nightlife industry here. However, I'm gonna miss the old liquor stores with their harsh lighting, no-frills shelving, surly clerks, and institutionalistic signage. Every aspect of the experience expressed a Northwest Protestant guilt trip over the evils of John Barleycorn; just like the old state rules for cocktail lounges, which had to be dark windowless dens of shame. *(September 1994)*

Welcome, good buddy, to the high-rollin' 10/4 **Misc.**, in which we attempt to figure out the rationale behind the recent rash of beers with dog names. There's already Red Wolf and Red Dog (one's owned by Coors, the other by

Eat Me

*Following are the results of **Misc.'s** quest for the best grocery stores in Seattle, by weight class.*

These listings leave out organic co-ops and gourmet delis — I wouldn't know how to judge such places. (For the record, Central Co-op got more votes than any other hippie store.)

I also wasn't looking for wine stores with vestigial food departments (sorry, Louie's on the Pike).

Oddly, only one letter recommended anything in the Pike Place Market (DeLaurenti's Italian deli, with its wall of capers).

Convenience Store:

The Hillcrest Deli-Mart *on Capitol Hill. A former pre-supermarket-era Safeway built in the 1920s, it's still got a complete-enough selection of packaged goods, enough fresh stuff to bide you over until your next supermarket run, and either the best or second-best fried chicken in town; all at prices that don't excessively punish you for avoiding supermarket crowds.*

Busch, but I can't remember which is which). Now, Seagram's trying to get into the beer biz with something entering local test markets this week called Coyote. Dunno 'bout you, but as one who grew up in a dog-owning household, the association of yellowish-colored liquids with dogs is not an appetizing one. *(Oct. 4, 1995)*

Welcome to the first 1989 edition of **Misc.,** the column that awaits the end of the 13-year Age of Cocaine. That's about how long American attitudes and behavior have reflected those of coke users (aggressive euphoria, delusions of omnipotence, an insatiable need for more money). In what drug experts call "co-dependency," these traits have spread to non-users, even to many who officially oppose the drug itself. It's clearly shaped the power madness of the Reagan Administration. Reagan himself is a coke-addicted filmmaker's stereotype of a statesman, a "high concept" hero. As violent as today's coke gangs are, the big damage done by the drug is that done to our economy, culture and social fabric by business and government leaders who, often unknowingly, take the coke rush as their model for success. *(January 1989)*

140 Coughs Per Minute: Last year I told you about Rave cigarettes. Now there's a brand that more explicitly targets disco culture. Wheat-pasted posters for Buz cigarettes promise "industrial strength flavor." The packs, cartons and ads have ad-agency re-creations of techno-rave art. Even the Surgeon General's warning is in fake-typewriter type. Remember, dance fans: tobacco is no "smart drug." *(November 1994)*

Without dumb ads in store windows and along highways promoting smoking as a corporate-promoted, mainstream-American habit, how we gonna convince the kids how uncool it is? (The cigarette brands in favor among Broadway's smoking vegans include some of the least heavily advertised, such as that indie brand falsely believed to be made by Native Americans.) Indeed, with all the curtailments on cigarette ads where kids might see 'em, we might be in for even more intense smoking-is-cool pushes inside 21-'n'-over joints. *(July 10, 1997)*

Cylindrical Objects On Parade: I wish the current cigar-mania (stinky, choky, life-threatening, etc.) would stop, but how? It appeals to too many universal temptations (even Freud joked, "Sometimes a cigar is just a cigar"). Besides, in an age where the lowly mass-market ciga-

Small Supermarket:

When supermarkets first appeared as a Depression-era cost-cutting novelty, they were still small enough to fit neighborhood main streets. Every neighborhood should have one, especially if it doesn't have a larger store (Belltown, Cascade, Georgetown, etc.).

The two Ken's (Greenwood and west Queen Anne) win overall. Lori Smith writes about the Greenwood Ken's, "Despite its garish exterior and the number of people there who look they read the Weekly, *it remains the classic example of a good neighborhood store, where they know your name, help you find stuff and don't overcharge."*

Honorable mention goes to the First Hill Shop-Rite *(home of my current-fave generic cereal brand, the imitation Crispix simply called Flavorite Crispy Hexagons!).*

rette's an object of scorn and humiliation, there's nothing like a fat, smelly cigar to make a smoker feel righteously vengeful. As long as there's social pressure to conform to social standards of blasédom, many males and some females will always choose to rebel, albeit often in crude, loud, and ineffectual ways. *(Sept. 18, 1997)*

The Grass-Is-Greener Dept.: The hemp movement revises the pot aesthetic to seem less pathetically complacent, more in tune with the go-for-it dynamism of the '90s. It does this by never mentioning pot smoking (except as a potential pain-killer), even though pot smoking is what it really wants to legalize. Eschewing the popular association of cannabis use with sleepwalking fogheadedness, it markets the drug as an investment commodity, best potential friend capitalism didn't know it had. More sky-high claims are being made for hemp today than were made in the early '60s for the schmoo (a bowling-pin-shaped animal that threatened to solve the world's food problems and thus upset the global economy) in Al Capp's comic strip *Li'l Abner.* *(Dec. 6, 1995)*

For two decades now, the ultimate perjorative for a showy, shallow hippie was "Granolahead." The imagery behind the insult was perfect; granola can be a high-fat, high-calorie sweetened foodstuff that still bears the image of something "good for you." But now, the false image of granola is being stripped away, revealing the chewy oatmeal-honey-brown sugar concoction as just another great American food ingulgence. This reimaging can be partly credited to RJR Nabisco and its new Oreo Granola Bars! They taste better than they sound or look. The oatmeal and glaze blend perfectly with the crumbled-and-solidified cookie crumbs and blotches of "Creme." *(May 24, 1995)*

So That's What's In the Secret Sauce: McDonald's stores now sport Big Mac 30th anniversary posters, featuring pseudo-psychedelic graphics reminiscent of Starbucks' 25th anniversary posters from two years ago. Hippies then and now, of course, have loved to invoke McDonald's as a quintessential symbol of everything they hate about corporate America, suburban lifestyles, and meat consumption.

The mistrust was mutual. The company's dress code frowned on male hirsuteness. More importantly, the whole operation was (and is) built around un-hippie values of conformity, neatness, and efficiency. *The Fifties* (a

Regular Supermarket:

Getting into the realm of the major chains, there's still something to be said for independent spirits like Wallingford's Fabulous Food Giant. *Robert C. Mills calls it "the center of the known universe." Situated in the foot-traffic heart of its area, with most of its parking spaces in a side-street auxiliary lot instead of out front, it combines the meet-'n'-greet ambience of a small neighborhood store with the selection and prices of a big park-'n'-gorge outlet. It's also got a hypnotic neon sign that has a different sector on the fritz every night.*

Superstore:

Larry's has its spots (the wall of cereal, all the imported South American soda pops).

But there's nothing quite like Art's Family Center *on Holman Road. On a site abandoned by Fred Meyer as too small, Art's has built an extremely site-specific collection of perimeter departments around the brightest, boldest food selection anywhere.*

Elsewhere, Ann Allen recommended Stock Market *on Rainier Ave., a "warehouse look" store with a cafe section occupied by just ordinary folk. ("It's not yuppie. It's not bland and sterile. It's what you want a neighborhood store to be.")*

And, of course, nothing can compare to the Costco *experience. It may be where shopping is a baffling ordeal, but it's great for larger households, cheap party catering, and especially for free samples.*

(continued)

Learning Channel series based on David Halberstam's book) featured a memo from McD's top management, calling individualism a dangerous trait and asserting all managers, employees, and franchise owners will be broken into the organization's proper spirit.

McD's arch rival Burger King briefly used the slogan "Sometimes You Gotta Break the Rules;" Outback Steak Houses feature the slogan "No Rules, Just Right." These are so false they're not even preposterous: A restaurant franchise is nothing but rules. Without the standardized products, prices, and premises stipulated in a franchise agreement, there's no reason for the advertising or brand-building techniques that make a chain franchise more valuable to a franchisee than simply starting his or her own restaurant.

(Of course, even that's no guarantee of success, as seen by the bankruptcy of the Boston Market circuit and the resulting closure of its Northwest outlets.) *(Oct. 15, 1998)*

The day after Stroh Brewing (current owners of Seattle's Rainier and Portland's Blitz-Weinhard) announced it was selling off its brewing plants and brands separately, the sandwich sign at Second Avenue Pizza read: "Keep Rainier in Seattle." The loss of the Rainier Brewery (Seattle's oldest manufacturing enterprise) would mean more than some 200 lost jobs. It would mean the end of one of our proudest institutions, even if beer continues to be sold under the Rainier name.

In the days before microbrews and Bud Light dogs, most of the beer drunk in the Northwest came from five places: Rainier in Seattle, Carling-Heidelberg in Tacoma, Olympia in Tumwater, General-Lucky in Vancouver, and Blitz-Weinhard in Portland. Rainier owned the Seattle market; Blitz-Weinhard (and its later flagship brand, Henry's) likewise in Portland. But Oly was the biggest of the quintet, once America's #6 beer vendor. But sales stagnations and the onward pushes of Bud, Miller and Coors saw these favorites tumble. The Lucky and Heidelberg plants closed; the other three changed owners several times. Now, perhaps only the Oly plant will be left, making what's left of all five plants' old lines.

A Rainier not brewed in Seattle, or a Weinhard's not brewed in Portland, would not carry a fraction of the goodwill built into their names. For Stroh to sell the brands without the plants will only doom them to tertiary status, like Olympia itself. *(Feb. 15, 1999)*

24: CORPORATE AMERICA

or, giving America the business

Rules matter in fast-food chains, as in all of corporate America (and, come to think of it, isn't "corporate America" a redundancy?), and so does public image. When the economy's doing well (at least for some sectors), the image has to be maintained that the rising tide will, one of these years, lift all boats. When even the speculator caste isn't doing too hot, the image has to be maintained that this simple period of "correction" will soon resolve itself and we can get back to again making the rich richer. And enterprises on the wrong end of economic, technological, or environmental trends often find themselves imagining that all they have is an image problem; that the right PR blitz will make the dirty seem clean, the discriminatory seem egalitarian, the selfish seem practical.

Gone Fission: With the potential collapse of the nuclear-weapons business, the electricity side of the atom biz tries to restore past momentum with a hilariously ironic PR push — that nukes somehow are the most environmentally benign energy source. It started with "Every day is Earth Day with nuclear energy" newspaper ads, followed by a hype-laden article in *Forbes* that claimed, "It is hypocritical to claim to be in favor of clean air and water but against nuclear power." Nuclear power uses radioactive materials (strip-mined and expensively processed) to boil water to turn turbines. The only "clean" aspect of nuclear power is that its waste products aren't pumped out of smokestacks; they're stored for future burial someplace where, it's hoped, the radiation won't leak out for the next few centuries. There are much better ways to spin some turbines around, including the wind. *(July 1990)*

A sense of realistic despair fell over the country rather swiftly, after years of strained overconfidence and hip nihilism. America's high-tech/service sector future was replaced by visions of a nation of glorified temp workers with no pensions, no insurance, no futures, no ability to buy the luxury goods and services that our economy was restructured around. What little investment was made in this country was made in the expectation of an affluent professional class that the rest of us would serve. That class is now shrinking, and nobody's making anything for any other class.

We're reaping the fruits of the cynical '70s-'80s, from non-voting liberals to conservatives who'll sell themselves (and the country) to anybody. From spec-

Eat Me
(continued)

Ethnic:

Uwajimaya *is the name to beat in Asian foodstuffs, but some prefer the recently-grown cluster of Vietnamese stores at 12th and Jackson. One store there,* Hop Thanh, *has an in-store butcher presiding over the biggest all-pork meat dept. you ever saw.*

In more assimilated immigrant delights, smart consumers like Leanne Beach know the discount Italian goodies at Big John's Pacific Food Importers, *open daytime hours only on 6th Ave. S. near the INS office. Beach also likes how "They write out your bill by hand, just like an old-fashioned market!"*

[Since this was written, both Food Giant and Art's Family Center were taken over by the QFC chain, which was bought by Fred Meyer, which was bought by the Ohio-based Kroger company. Consolidation marches on...]

(Sept. 27, 1995)

ulators who buy companies to loot their assets, to CEOs who annihilate their workforces (decimating the consumer wealth needed to support their own companies' products). *(February 1992)*

Sam Walton, 1918-1992: The king of discount wasn't known here. Even in the states Wal-Mart's in, it's not big in the metro areas where media people live. Thus the press was shocked in the '80s to see it become the #1 retailer. Its stores were so big, in towns so small, that they destroyed thousands of Main Street merchants across the southern-tier states. Walton aided the '80s consolidation of wealth from the many to the few, and naturally became a favorite Reagan-Bush insider.

But just as shoppers are re-learning the value of selection and service, so are they getting upset at our Wal-Mart government (with its Neiman-Marcus military). Postmodern America is the discount society: A land of slipshod engineering, lousy quality, few real choices, and service that's not "efficient" as much as nonexistent. The tax-cutters are wrong to think that discount taxes will ever bring prosperity. We've already got the lowest overall tax rates in the industrial world; it shows in our inadequate civilian services (education, health, arts, infrastructure). Countries that still respect the value of public investment are whipping us in the world marketplace (or are at least doing less poorly). *(May 1992)*

Their Money: Let's set the story straight about that ubiquitous right-wing bogeyperson, the infamous "added costs" that prevent businesses from pricing products and services at the cheapest price. Anything beyond the cheapest possible cost of making and shipping a product is "added cost." Yes, that includes the standard old talk-radio nemeses of taxes and environmental regulations, plus the new talk-radio nemeses of employee health insurance; but it also includes mob payoffs, excessive executive salaries and perks, advertising, lawyers, bank fees, lobbying, donations to the symphony, losses on bad real-estate investments, etc. Any Gucci-clad executive who whines that health care for his workers would be an excessive "added cost" oughta be willing to give up half his salary. *(June 1994)*

Misc. says goodbye this week to one of its favorite conglomerates, American Home Products, maybe the biggest company you never heard of. It's being broken up, with divisions sold off, so management can focus on its drug operations (Anacin, Advil, Dristan, and many lucrative prescription patents).

Unlike the late Beatrice, AHP kept its corporate profile low while promoting its brands (Chef Boy-Ar-Dee, Pam, Brach's candy, Ecko kitchenware, Easy-Off, Aerowax, Black Flag) with near-monomaniacal aggression. It was said if you didn't have a headache before you saw an Anacin commercial, you had one after. When Procter & Gamble's '50s soap operas offered up Presbyterian homilies of hope and family alongside the tears and turmoil, AHP's soaps (*Love of Life, The Secret Storm*) relished in unabashed melodrama, the harsher the better.

While AHP was never a household name, its contributions won't be forgotten by anyone who ever dined on Beefaroni while listening to a Black Flag LP. *(May 22, 1996)*

A Burning Issue: It's hard right now to think about heating equipment, unless it's everybody's favorite gas-powered industrial space heater. I speak, of course, of the mighty Reznor.

When a rock singer using that surname showed up, some fans wondered whether he was related to the brand name bearing down from near the ceilings of stores, warehouses, artists' studios, garages, nightclubs, etc.

Turns out ol' Trent is indeed a descendent of the company's founder, George Reznor (who entered the furnace trade in 1888, in the same central-Pennsylvania town where Trent grew up). But the Reznor family's had little to do in decades with the company, which has changed owners several times.

Current owners gave 120 or so employees an "offer" last year: Take pay cuts of up to 28 percent, or else. The workers stood their ground. The owners shipped the jobs off to Mexico. Northeast politicians are now invoking the ex-Reznor workers as poster children for the injustices of NAFTA and the Global Economy.

So next time you hear Trent's moans about frustration and helplessness amid a decaying industrial landscape, look up. If you see a Reznor heater above you, it's a Labor Day-week reminder that, for some, such feelings aren't just an act. *(Aug. 27, 1998)*

Work (Out) Music

These go out to all those working at home these days, whether by choice or otherwise. If your home office sometimes gets as nonsensical as Letterman's, maybe it's time to get a good set of headphones beside your workstation and heed some of the Muzak company's old research into music's role in aiding worker productivity. Herewith, suggested accompaniment for personal deskbound accomplishment.

SAM SPENCE/JOHN FACENDA
The Power and the Glory: Original Music and Voices of NFL Films
(Tommy Boy) ****
There are days when you need this: Monday mornings, deadline days, times when you must do something really scary (say, a job interview) or otherwise head into battle. The glorious symphonic anthems of classic 16mm pro-football documentaries will stir you into action like, well hopefully not like recent Seahawk seasons.

(continued)

25: CORPORATE CULTURE

or, the culture trust and its discontents

Burlesque, vaudeville's evil twin (or was it the good one?).

Entertainment is far from America's biggest industry, but it just may be America's most important product. Vaudeville, tabloid newspapers, comic strips, magazines, dime novels, movies, and radio imposed a single mass culture on what had been a vast geographic space populated by folks who came, or whose forebearers came, from all over.

In so doing, the Broadway/Madison Avenue/Hollywood nexus found the formula to become everything to everybody, to smother the whole world under Gable & Lombard, Lucy & Ricky, Mickey & Donald, and Simon & Garfunkel; all persuading us to cheerfully buy all the stuff adorned with their images or advertised alongside their messages.

Once you see entertainment as the lubricant of the late-industrial economy, it's easy to understand why certain anti-establishment folks would sequester themselves in college-town coffeehouses or in rural cabins, proclaiming themselves to be pure and unsullied by all the economically-motivated crassness out there.

But it's a bigger challenge to remain in the world, to actively question the corporate mass culture (or, now, the corporate specialty cultures) and demand better. It's an even bigger challenge still to sort through what the big boys have wrought and to critically discern which of its products are worthy of keeping around as influences toward a hopefully better, more decentralized cultural realm.

Happiness Is a Bigger Space: *Peanuts* has suddenly switched from four small panels a day to three larger ones. It's the first major structural change ever to Charles Schulz's comic. Four square panels every day, six days a week, was a perfect metaphor for the chilling purgatory of characters stuck at the same presexual age for 38 years.

(To see Schulz on adolescence, look for his rare '60s paperback *"Teen-Ager" Is Not A Disease.* All the kitsch of *Peanuts,* none of the charm.) *(April 1988)*

Stripped: The worst comic strip in the daily papers in recent memory was *Mallard Fillmore,* billed in a *P-I* blurb as "a conservative *Doonesbury.*" But *Doonesbury* sets its liberalism in solid character gags. Old-time conservative strips (*Li'l Abner, Little Orphan Annie, Steve Canyon*) anchored their politics in a set of traditional cultural values, including the values of solid storytelling and fine draftsmanship. *Mallard* simply has an unattractively-designed, boorish duck character spout snide personal insults about the Clintons. *Mallard* doesn't know it's not funny... *(September 1994)*

Drawing the Line: Earlier this year, the *P-I* ran what it called a week-long test run of eight new comic strips. This month, the paper added all eight newcomers. It made room by shrinking some Coffee Break features and dropping others — including Bill Griffith's up-from-the-underground classic *Zippy the Pinhead.* None of the new strips so far show any wit or style or reason for being (other than demographic target-marketing) Some of the new batch are almost amazingly amateurishly drawn.

Zippy, however, is a masterpiece of exquisite draftsmanship, precision dialogue, and multi-layered humor. It treats its readers not as statistics but as intelligent fun-lovers. And it loves to eat a great corn dog. *Zippy* is in the domain of the *P-I*'s fellow Hearst subsidiary King Features Syndicate, as are four of the paper's new comics. Back in the day, William Randolph Hearst made his papers run George Harriman's now-acknowledged classic *Krazy Kat* even though it scored low in popularity polls, because Harriman's surrealistic shenanigans added that little touch of quality Hearst's papers sorely needed. The folks running today's *P-I* (Hearst's second-largest remaining daily paper) ought to do what the old man would've done and bring the Pinhead back. [The paper did just that a week later.] *(Aug. 28, 1997)*

There's one piece of electronics I do despise: Compact discs. They don't give you big cover art or colorful labels. You can't make a scratch mix with them. They sound sterile, flat, too clean for any of the music that made this country great: Hot jazz, swing, bebop, bluegrass, gospel, folk, blues, R&B, country, and their mongrel child rock 'n' roll. What's worse is that the record biz is realigning itself to favor the high-priced spread. Already Motown has dropped 82 oldies albums, which henceforth will be sold only on CD. Those records, like most good non-classical music made since 1950, owe their original existence to the low cost and mass market created by cheap vinyl discs. *(November 1986)*

Now it can be told: Before Muzak moved its HQ to Seattle in 1987, three-quarters of its 4,000-selection library had been recorded by a Czechoslovakian state radio orches-

Work (Out) Music
(continued)

VARIOUS ARTISTS
Organs in Orbit
(Capitol Ultra-Lounge)
***

WALTER WANDERLAY
Rain Forest *(Verve)*
****

In the long hours before lunch (if you even take a scheduled lunch break at home), you need something light 'n' lively that'll keep you at a steady pace. The friendly tones of the lustrous Hammond fit this task with a smile. Let your worries go, let your work-output flow.

NINO TEMPO & APRIL STEVENS
Sweet and Lovely: The Best of Nino Tempo & April Stevens
(Varese Sarabande)
****

Muzak never used vocal cuts on its "Stimulus Progression" channel, believing voices attracted too much listener attention. But at certain points in the workday, a little mental diversion can help. For calm-down moments after the stress moments, nothing could be finer than this brother-sister team from 1962-67 and their friendly, upbeat, jazzy-pop renditions of Broadway and Brill Building song standards.

Also included: Stevens' torch solo, "Teach Me Tiger"—recorded in '59 and still too steamy for mainstream airplay, due both to the words (wherein Stevens pleads to her boy to initiate her into sexual knowledge, then turns around and offers to initiate him instead) and to the heavy-breathing growls between the lines.

tra. The old owners liked its price and tolerated its admittedly odd musical flavor. It's being replaced by new tunes recorded mostly by synthesizers and "electronically enhanced" quartets. You have to wonder, though: what if Commies were hiding secret subliminal messages that got into offices and factories across America, messages like "Lower your productivity" or "Let America become a second-rate industrial power"? *(July 1991)*

Open Memo to CURSE ["Censorship Undermines Radio Station Ethics," a group of DJs at, and fans of, college radio station KCMU, who protested station management's moves toward more mainstream programming]: You've successfully exposed the hypocritical machinations behind KCMU-Lite and its instigators. But to restore the station as a community resource, you've gotta deal with the UW Board of Regents, who control the license.

The current managers were turning the station into nothing but a self-serving fundraising machine, something the Regents can identify with. Tell them you don't want to restore all of the station's rough-hewn past. You want to build on its heritage, to more strongly serve students, alternative-music communities, and others now unserved by local radio.

Even after that, you'll have to deal with KUOW management down the hall, people who've asserted excessive control over KCMU and who honestly don't get what's wrong with institutionalized "public" radio. People who only seek the most upscale listeners. People who mistake blandness for a virtue. The announcers on NPR stations all sound like HAL 9000, for chrissakes! They oughta sound more like the booming, colorful voice who used to announce the Metropolitan Opera broadcasts. They oughta reflect the glorious pomposity of orchestral and opera music, the twee affectations of chamber music, the life-affirming spirit of real jazz, instead of a yup variation on BBC English. *(April 1993)*

Copy Wrongs: Actually found myself agreeing with something Newt the Coot said, when he championed the Internet and other "new media" for "many-to-many" communication rather than "few-to-many" corporate entertainment.

Gingrich saw the rise of right-wing talk radio, religious TV, and magazines become a counterforce to the "objective" corporate media, and thinks the new telecommunications could further strengthen his favorite voices. (Let's not tell him his favorite media's just the same few-to-many syndrome without the old-school bureaucratic propriety Newt mistakenly calls "liberal." Real many-to-many communication would encourage real empowerment, not passive-aggressive submission to the rich and to their PACs.)

Anyhow, another reason Newt wants to keep the new media (the Internet, umpteen-channel cable, video dial-tone, et al.) out of the claws of the established media industry's 'cuz the latter has been in bed with the Clinton/Gore crowd. Of course, the media biz also loved Reagan, and any politician who supports the industry's expansionist agenda.

One example: the way Reagan, Bush and Clinton-era FCC officials kept rewriting the broadcast rules to favor ever bigger radio-TV station ownership groups, to the point where broadcast properties are increasingly held by out-of-town financiers bent less toward serving the stations' communities than toward speculation and empire-building.

Another example: the Clinton administration's proposed copyright law rewrite. Clinton's National Information Infrastructure Task Force has drafted legislation to drastically limit what folks can do with information. Among other nasty provisions, it'd trash the "First Sale Right" that lets an info buyer do whatever she wishes with the copy she bought — the right that allows the video-rental industry to exist.

In addition, the "fair use" provision (allowing authors to use brief relevant quotes from copyrighted works) would be greatly restricted; devices that could undermine electronic anti-copying systems would be outlawed; and "browsing" a copyrighted work, in a store or online, would be technically illegal.

The punk/DIY decentralization aesthetic isn't just a cute idea. It's vital if the "info age" isn't going to be a globally-centralized thought empire. Newt, despite his rhetoric of "empowerment," wants a thought empire controlled by the Limbaughs and Robertsons; Clinton wants one controlled by the Viacoms and Time Warners. It's up to us to demand None Of The Above. *(January 1995)*

Beaming: Viacom boss Sumner Redstone has spoken of one of his new acquisitions, *Star Trek,* as a "global branded identity."

Several analysts over the years have seen the United Federation of Planets as a metaphor for an cold-war-era American self-image, an image of the benevolent colo-

VARIOUS ARTISTS
Music for TV Dinners
(Scamp/Caroline) ***
VARIOUS ARTISTS
Music for TV Dinners, Vol. 2: The '60s
(Scamp/Caroline) ***
A quick early-afternoon pick-me-up, these two are as close to Muzak's old-time "stimulus progression" sound as you can get on commercially-available CDs. Old tracks from a British company that sold (and still sells) royalty-free stock music for use in any and all occasions (commercials, B movies, game shows, cartoons). Hear the full, original versions of songs you've heard in cut-up form on Ren & Stimpy, *CBS Sports, Russ Meyer movies, Vaseline Intensive Care ads, and more.*

VARIOUS ARTISTS
Easy Tempo Vol. 6: A Cinematic Jazz Experience
(Easy Tempo/Right Tempo import) ****
Back to the light-'n'-lively, but with a more assertive tone for the afternoon when the outside world's temptations must be drowned out for just a short while longer. Soundtracks from European commercial-entertainment movies of the '70s are so darned cool because they had to be. The films they were made for needed such clever touches to keep up, even in their domestic markets, against Hollywood's big-budget product.

Any of Easy Tempo's releases will envelope you in a dreamscape of fast Euro-cars, hot Euro-sex, and suave Euro-spies. This volume's a particularly spectacular starting point.

Purists might call these 18 tracks commercial affectations of '50s-'60s U.S. jazz greats, but don't you mind.

nial force bringing order and commerce while allowing at least on-paper autonomy to its "partners."

A case could now be made for the Federation reflecting Hollywood's self-image of a culture empire enveloping the universe, either smothering local arts and customs or using them to its ends. Redstone wants to have everybody on at least this planet viewing, reading and listening to the same things. This is the polar opposite of what many of the acts now on [the then Viacom-owned] KNDD believe or originally believed.

As further example, note the *Week in Rock* segment on MTV (another Viacom property) about indie labels — it gave most of its camera time to those "indies" that have alliances with or are part of the Big Six record giants; it talked about the likes of Sub Pop not as patrons of marginal voices but as generators of future major-label stars; and it was peppered with ex-indie singers who unanimously assured viewers that an act could get screwed by an indie just like by a major.

Mind you, there's plenty that Big Entertainment has given us (I've been heard to compare modern American politics to the *ST* episode with the Evil Kirk vs. the Ineffectual Kirk). But it's time to put a new concept to work. Instead of global identities, we need to promote and empower the whole motley world at home and abroad. Make it so. *(Feb. 14, 1995)*

Good news: Centralized globalist culture may have peaked! An *N.Y. Times* story, "Local Programming Cuts Into MTV," notes with thinly-disguised alarm how broadcast and cable producers in assorted European and Asian countries are capturing viewers by offering local videos, in local languages — something MTV's continent-wide satellite feeds just can't offer.

Since some global MTV acts in recent years have emanated from Seattle, some of you might see this as another sign of the long-hoped-for end of Seattle's musical influence. I don't.

Most of our best bands and promoters weren't trying to become global superstars; they were trying to smash the concept of global superstars. They were trying to promote a different attitude toward making and listening to "pop" music, as a creative force speaking directly to audiences rather than a brand-name entity to be manufactured and marketed. The more people there are around the world who make their own sounds, the more the Seattle scene's real message to the world will have taken hold. *(April 10, 1996)*

I know I'm not the only one disturbed by the new Blockbuster Video slogan, "One World, One Word." It harkens back to a line used in the '80s by its now sister company MTV, "One World, One Music, One Channel." Both phrases envision a singular corporate deity commanding the entire Earth's population with a single brand of formula entertainment. It's not just monopolistic, it's monotheistic. And it's not what either music or video ought to be. Rather, millennial pop culture is (or is becoming) a pantheon of sources, ideas, aesthetics, genres, sounds, and looks; something as vast and chaotic as the world itself. *(Jan. 23, 1997)*

More, More, More!: A recent *Business Week* cover story calls it "The Entertainment Glut." I call it a desperate attempt by Big Media to keep control of a cultural landscape dividing and blossoming to a greater extent than I'd ever hoped. *BW* sez the giants (Disney, Murdoch, Time Warner, Viacom, et al.) are trying to maintain market share by invading one another's genre turfs and cranking out more would-be blockbusters and bestsellers than ever before, to the point that none of them can expect anything like past profit margins. (Indeed, many of these "synergistic" media combos are losing wads of dough, losses even creative accounting can no longer hide.) It gets worse: Instead of adapting to the new realities of a million subcultures, the giants are redoubling their push after an increasingly-elusive mass audience.

Murdoch's HarperCollins book company scrapped over 100 planned "mid-list" titles to make up for losses on costly big-celeb books. *BW* claims the giants' movie divisions are similarly "spending lavishly" on intended Next *Titanic*s and trying "to stop producing modestly budgeted fare." Their record divisions are dropping acts after one album, while ardently pushing the retro rockstar-ism of Britpop. The longer the giants try to keep their untenable business plans going, the better the opportunities for true indies in all formats — if the indies can survive the giants' ongoing efforts to crowd 'em out of the marketplace. *(Feb. 26, 1998)*

Two For the Show: At least one secret to understanding the eternal conflict of American culture can be found in the decades-old conflict of burlesque vs. vaudeville. Burlesque wasn't just raw as in naked (or rather as naked as the law allowed or could be bribed into allowing). It was raucous; its dancers and skits and comic monologues celebrated the boistrous passions of turn-of-the-

VARIOUS ARTISTS
Samba Brasil
(Verve) ****
"World music" that's not curated by or for Volvo-drivin' post-graduates. Easy-going and lively at the same time. Perfect for passing the early-P.M. hours in mindless data entry. Your hands and eyes are at the computer; your mind is in the Rio Sambadrome.

EDD KALEHOFF
Music from
The Price Is Right
(released only online)
***
You've probably heard these music cues several times (America's last surviving network game show has been on since the Nixon administration), but never in their full-length, announcer-free form. They turn out to be bouncy, breezy, HI-NRG synth-and-horn anthems; perfect for that last-hour push toward completing the day's tasks.

(Available as RealAudio files from www.webhangers.com/~tvthemes/gameshows/tpir/tpir.html.)

ROYAL PHILHARMONIC ORCHESTRA
F.A.B.: Music From the TV Shows
by Barry Gray
(Silva Screen import)
***
Workday's done, tasks completed, deadlines met, documents e-mailed or FedExed away. Time to give yourself a thundering brass-band salute, with a blast of re-created themes from the Gerry Anderson "Supermarionation" puppet adventure shows. Thunderbirds Are Go!

STAR SYSTEM:
***** = Executive suite*
**** = Corner office*
*** = Cubicle*
** = Temp pool*

(Nov. 18, 1998)

century urban immigrants. It also regularly barbed politicians, judges, bosses, and other authority figures. Vaudeville (as shown in a KCTS documentary late last year which still haunts my memory) was squeaky clean, celebrated "wholesome family entertainment," and promoted a monocultural America of thorough white-middlebrow dominance (with just a few ethnic touches inserted for the mildest of spiciness).

Vaudeville led to the everywhere/nowhere America of Hollywood movies (several of the big studios trace their corporate history from vaudeville-theater chains), Lawrence Welk, Mickey Mouse, *Reader's Digest,* Miss America, soft rock, light beer, weak coffee, and eventually to what *The Nation* and *The Baffler* call today's global "culture trust."

Burlesque, conversely, led to Milton Berle, Betty Boop, the prewar version of *Esquire,* drag-queen shows, the comedy-relief segments in early porn films, and (eventually and indirectly) to punk rock, S/M showmanship, and zine culture.

Despite its handful of often fondly-remembered burlesque "box house" theaters, and its status as home to burlesque star Gypsy Rose Lee (born into a vaudeville family), Seattle was a vaudeville town through and through. Seattle's first corporate inroad on the national entertainment biz was the locally-founded Pantages vaudeville circuit.

The battle continues. Across the country, governments are trying to banish strip clubs and adult video shops (slicker yet raunchier descendents of burlesque), making downtowns safe for Planet Hollywood and The Disney Store (dining and shopping as toned-down descendents of vaudeville).

At its best, the spirit of vaudeville represents precision, energy, showmanship, and a pleasant good time. But at its worst, it represents cloying paternalism and sentimental "family entertainment" that bores kids and insults grownups' intelligence. Burlesque's descendents have their own downsides; particularly the recursive traps of parody and ironic detachment seen in so much pseudo-hip art, music, and advertising.

But we need more of burlesque's assertive populism, its healthy skepticism about authority and its healthy affirmation of the life force. Somewhere between post-vaudeville's mandatory naiveté and post-burlesque's relentless cynicism lies the naked truth. *(Dec. 7, 1998)*

This former Seattle clothing label capitalized on romantic, exotic connotations associated with the news media.

26: CORPORATE NEWS

or, infotainment at its most infotaining

As a student and sometime employee of the journalism industry, I've gotten to see the process of how facts and ideas are turned into print space-fillers and broadcast time-fillers. As a one-time rural child, I've also gotten to see the process of how cattle are slaughtered and cut up, and the latter process has a lot in common with the former one.

Info Attainment: Pledge of Resistance, a local pro-Sandinista group, visited hundreds of newspaper boxes throughout Seattle in the wee hours of Nov. 14, wrapping its own two-page *Seattle Past-Intelligencer: Special Citizens' Edition* around copies of the real *Post-Intelligencer.* The result would make for a semotician's field day: All the normal local crime stories and human-interest fluff inside, while the front page spoke exclusively of Contra and El Salvador Army atrocities (with an "Editors' Apology" for not having reported them sooner). The desktop-published type made the new cover an obvious phony, but the split-second illusion of a local paper with a backbone inspired a hope that more political advocates will make active, accessible attempts to truly communicate with the populace. *(December 1989)*

Tattle Tales: Mark Goodson and his late partner Bill Todman are famous for producing TV game shows. But, says a profile in *Forbes,* they made the bulk of their fortune owning a string of suburban newspapers in the Northeast. I don't know if the reporters ever vowed to tell the truth, or whether they were stopped by the sound of a bell after asking a few questions (or if they had to stop if they got a no answer). *(April 1990)*

Flaherty Newspapers, R.I.P.: For 30 hellish months, I worked for sub-survival wages with past-death-rate typesetting equipment in Flaherty headquarters, a crumbling shack in the Rainier Valley with weeds rising from cracks in the concrete floor. There, I typed up the alleged "news" sections of seven neighborhood weeklies — smarmy hype stories for advertising merchants, cutesy notices for Catholic schools, a gardening column by an elderly lady who occasionally inserted anti-sex-education sermons, and, always and above all, unquestioned enthusiasm for the Seattle Police. I typed up too many of the squalid police-blotter columns (low-grade tragedy turned into morbid sensationalism), and to this day I lash back at anyone who refers to them as a source of camp humor. The papers were distributed by an ever-changing crew of pre-teens who had to deliver them to every house in a territory and hope some of the recipients would pay the small voluntary fee. Now, the little chain has been bought by an out-of-state takeover artist and will soon be merged with its onetime arch-rival Murray Publishing. *(October 1990)*

The Sabot Times is an occasional four-page newsletter by some disgruntled *Seattle Times* reporters, vowing to sabotage the corrupt newspaper biz from within. Topics include how and when to fabricate quotes, a defense of "checkbook journalism" (the paying of interviewees and sources), and the shenanigans of creepy bosses. While the *Times* is the apparent topic of many items, issue #3 also discusses the Gannett chain's papers, "where all of the stories (but none of the men) are eight inches long." *(September 1992)*

The Noam-Mobile: Congrats to all of you for making *Manufacturing Consent: Noam Chomsky and the Media* one of the biggest documentary hits in a long time, even though I don't agree with much of it. Chomsky treats the mass media as one monolithic, unstoppable force exercising mind control over all America (except for himself and his East Coast intellectual pals). He can't, or won't, notice how tentative that hold really is. People who consume lots of media are very cynical about what they're consuming.

Compare the faux-ironic, "air quotes" speech patterns of MTV viewers with the blind-faith naiveté of tube-loathing neohippies. A typical TV viewer takes nothing by faith, treats everything with (excess?) skepticism. A typical nonviewer is ready to believe almost anything, as long as it's told in the proper "alternative" lingo by recognizably "alternative" faces. The Robertson right, the Perot moderate-right, and the Chomsky left all hate the commercial mass media. Everybody's a "rebel" these days, and the press is one of the few universally recognized symbols of what everybody's rebelling against. Newspaper circulation is flat, and ad revenues have plummeted. (Ratings and ad revenues for TV news are also down.)

Most people are already aware that their local newspaper is beholden to its town's business and political bigshots. It doesn't take listening to three hours of Chomsky to figure out that national and Eastern-regional media might be similarly beholden to the N.Y./D.C.

If The World Should Stop Revolving...

Like Hewlett-Packard, '70s easy-listening singer David Gates (no relation to Bill), and some public-domain poet whose name I forget right now, ***Misc.*** *never stops asking, and sometimes even gets around to answering, that simple yet profound question,* ***IF:***

IF *I were Jack in the Box, I'd think twice before I tied all my fourth-quarter ad budget in with a movie (*Star Trek Generations*) that promises the death of one of its two main characters.*

IF *I were a conspiracy theorist, I'd wonder whether the fashion industry deliberately made clothes as ugly as possible so customers could be convinced the next year of how foolish they'd been. Ponder, for instance, the new slogan of Tower Records' clothing racks: "Tower Clothing, Because Some People Look Better With Their Clothes On." (Indeed, many folks do look better in their own clothing than in Tower's snowboarding jackets, gimme caps and mall-rat "hiphop" shirts.)*

bigwigs. Just as leftist economists talk as if the world's economy was still based on heavy industry, so do media critics like Chomsky still "analyze" an American media comprised only of three networks, two wire services, two weekly news magazines, five opinion magazines, and two or three big Eastern newspapers. Can Noam adapt to a media, and a nation, that are becoming more decentralized and diffuse (but perhaps no more "progressive")? Stay tuned. *(August 1993)*

Dillard's Dullards: During a post-speech Q&A at a Michigan writers' conference some six months ago, Connecticut essayist/poet Annie Dillard was asked if she missed living in the Northwest (she was holed up in Bellingham and the San Juans in the late '70s). She said no, claiming "it's no place for an intellectual woman" and offering a brusque retort imaging Northwest females as breast-feeding, fruit-canning, chainsaw-wielding mutes.

Dillard's remark eventually caught the attention of editors at the *Seattle Times,* who don't have a particular interest in intellectualism but do have a lot invested in the image of Seattleites as at least a pseudo-sophisticated sort. A Scene section front page was assembled around Dillard's brief quotation, headlined "Women intellectuals: A Northwest oxymoron?" To fill the rest of the space, the paper added interview quotes from local citizens and defensive editorial commentary ("OK, Northwest women, dab that drool off your chin, put down your chainsaw and listen up"), treating readers as if they were as dumb as Dillard claimed they were. The *Times,* which would rather cultivate readers who can grapple with complex wines than ones who can grapple with complex ideas, treated Dillard's throwaway remark as a call to defend, not the Northwest Mind, but the Northwest Lifestyle. The notion that there could be some bright earth mamas out there, or some well-dressed urbane ditzes, hasn't seemed to occur to the paper.

Incidentally, here's a perhaps-fortuitous slice of Dillard's only novel to date, *The Living* (set in 1890s Bellingham): "...But *the times* had gotten inside them in some ways as they aged, and made them both ordinary... No child on earth was ever meant to be ordinary, and you can see it in them, and they know it, too, but then *the times* get to them, and they wear out their brains learning what folks expect, and spend their strength trying to rise over those same folks." [Italics added.] *(Oct. 10, 1996)*

IF *you're really into those two great tastes that taste great together, you'll eat Reese's Peanut Butter Puffs cereal with Butterfinger flavored milk (recommended only for the brave).*

IF *I ran the city, I'd change the name of Dexter Avevenue to "Dextrose Avenue," after one of that street's most prominent and aromatic sights, the Hostess bakery.*

IF *I were a betting man (and I'm not), I'd start a pool to wager on the day, week and month Newt Gingrich is forced to resign from the House speakership for saying something just too dumb or outré. Speaking of which...*

IF Pogo *cartoonist Walt Kelly were still with us, he'd have a field day satirizing ol' Newt. Imagine, a right-wing politician with the same name as a salamander!*

(continued)

27: THE VERBAL ARTS

or, it's only words

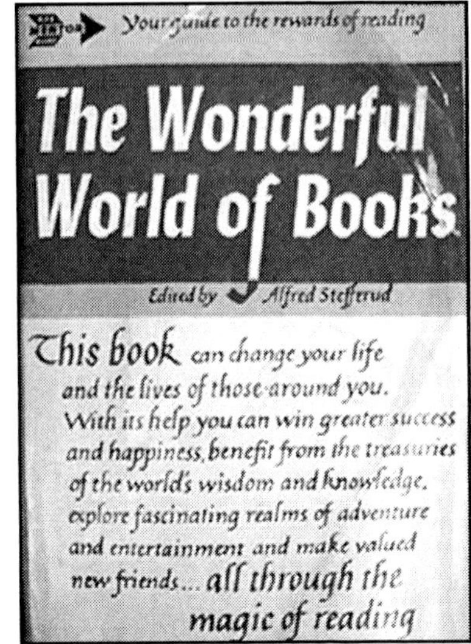

Your guide to the rewards of reading
The Wonderful World of Books
Edited by Alfred Stefferud
This book can change your life and the lives of those around you. With its help you can win greater success and happiness, benefit from the treasuries of the world's wisdom and knowledge, explore fascinating realms of adventure and entertainment and make valued new friends... all through the magic of reading

At least the aforementioned Annie Dillard debacle proved literary authors can indeed make an impact, even if it isn't necessarily the type of impact they intend. I don't believe those sourpuss prudes who forever whine about the Death of The Word. The Word's not dead; though in my more frustrated writing moments I've wished I could kill it.

I believe in the power of the written word, though I have a healthy respect for its limitations. I don't believe in "serious literature," nor in the lifestyle and belief system "serious" writers are expected to conform to. Writers are some of the most aesthetically reactionary folks around, so pathetically conservative about everything in life except politics. If only modern novels had one percent of the vitality found in the best modern music, dance, and visual art.
(Nov. 18, 1991)

Writes & Wrongs: In my day job at *The Comics Journal*, I was phoned by a University of Chicago intellectual writing an article on "the declining role of words in American society." He pumped me for any info that would support his presupposition that we (or our younger peers) have become non-reading, non-writing, non-talking image addicts.

I replied that we're really more inundated with words than ever: In little publications like this, piles of documents in schools and offices, computers and fax machines, hundreds of specialty magazines, thousands of paperback novels. Talk radio, phone sex, rap, and virtually all TV (except commercials and music videos) depend on the spoken word. My caller refused to consider my arguments. He sounded like one of those non-thinking highbrows who blissfully assume that "those kids" have all gone to hell since his generation was in young-adulthood (whether his generation is that of 1945 or of 1968 doesn't matter; the syndrome's the same). So-called "serious" writers can be the most reactionary people in the cultural world, so pathetically conservative about everything in life except politics. *(December 1991)*

There's a common assumption, based on unsupported charges in Neil Postman and Jerry Mander books, that you kids today aren't reading anything, and that the younger kids in back of you won't even learn to read. In truth, according to the book industry's own figures, bookstore sales boomed in the '80s and are holding better in the '90s recession than many other retail sectors. The big bookstore chains are granted prime mall space precisely because they do such good business. Books for children and young adults showed the most spectacular rise of all. (Total book sales might be down, if you include school and library purchases affected by government budget cuts.)

The thousands of zines produced across the country, and the hundreds of spoken-word and "poetry slam" events in hip bars, prove that this is a generation more, not less, devoted to the word. Not since the '50s beats (a much smaller minority of their era) has a generation worked so hard at documenting itself in print, with so little encouragement from its elders. Instead, the Volvo-drivin', Joni Mitchell-listenin' English profs eagerly swap horror stories in the faculty lounge about how stupid you are because you wear different clothes than they do or because you didn't come to college already knowing all about their favorite '60s heroes. *(Oct. 19, 1992)*

Nite Lit: Insomniacs such as myself have found a great companion and aid toward tiredness in the USA cable network's *Up All Night,* which takes old drive-in sex movies and cuts out the sex, making them even duller. Book lovers deserve their turn, so I propose a new book club. "Boring Books Inc." would issue special editions of the classics, condensed to skim over the exciting parts and leave in all the tedium. (They'll also help you write book reports when you've only seen the movie versions.)

Just imagine the possibilities! The BBI *Moby Dick*: Just the documentary accounts of the whaling business. The BBI *Lady Chatterly's Lover*: Just the passages about the decline of England's agrarian society. The BBI *Razor's Edge*: Just the gossip about Somerset Maugham's rich friends. The BBI *Fear of Flying*: Just the parts about being a lonely affluent American in Germany, waiting for her weekly dose of *The New Yorker*. The BBI Thomas Hardy: Everything he ever wrote. *(February 1993)*

'Other' Wise: Where did this now-ubiquitous term "The Other" come from anyway, and why do all these white het male art critics use it to complain about white het

If the World Should Stop Revolving...
(continued)

***IF** I were a real conspiracy theorist, I'd wonder whether the fashion, music and media industries invented and promptly denounced all that phony "Seattle scene" hype as a way to dissuade young people from catching the real message behind what's been going on here, the message that you don't have to remain a passive consumer of media-invented trends. In this theory, the corporate elite deliberately tried to redefine a rebellion against shallow fads as a shallow fad. But that would require big business to be smarter than it probably is.*

IF Brian Basset was really laid off because the Times *couldn't afford an editorial cartoonist anymore, howcum the lower-circulation P-I still has two? The Newspaper Guild claims* Times *editors tried to fire Basset over personal disputes, but his union contract wouldn't allow it, so they eliminated his position instead. The Guild's suing the paper to get Basset hired back. Both sides insist content censorship's not an issue here; Basset's cartoons have drifted rightward along with the paper's editorial stances. (The* Times *still runs Basset's syndicated strip* Adam.*)*

males? I know there was an N.Y. underground rag long ago called *The East Village Other,* but they presumably got the term from somebody else. The critics invoking it imply that there are only two classes in American society: the class of all the people they don't like (called either The Patriarchy or The New World Order) and the class of all the people they like (The Other); the critics analyze all artworks accordingly. Shoehorning art into oversimplistic ideology is just silly, and sheds no insight onto either art or politics. In the '70s, academic leftists claimed that Everything Is Political. I'm starting to believe Everything Is Aesthetic. Besides, anybody who thinks there are only two cultures in the U.S. isn't looking very hard. *(July 1993)*

'Other' Wise: Two readers have suggested that the source of "The Other" was Simone de Beauvior's classic essay *The Second Sex.* She apparently used it to describe how people divide the world of their own minds and bodies ("The Self") from everything else in the universe ("The Other"). Most of the folks using the term today intend to denounce other people's bigotries, but inadvertently reveal their own. We need alternatives to bigotry, not just alternate forms of bigotry. *(September 1993)*

A *Wired* article traces the currently-popular notion of "The Other" to French postmodern philosopher Julia Kristeva. She's apparently the one who first thought of collapsing sociopolitical class analysis into an oversimplified two-tier model of The Dominant Order and The Other, a model that so narrowly defines society's insiders that it allows many affluent white English majors to classify themselves as outsiders. *(July 1994)*

Literama: Clever people across the country are discovering a real use for the Apple Newton Messagepad, that overpriced electronic Rolodex that's supposed to read your handwriting but usually can't. It may not be able to make an exact digital version of what you write on it, but it can turn it into computer-assisted cut-up poetry! Yes, you can make your own faux-Burroughs without having to shoot anybody or get addicted to anything.

In my own experimental-fiction days, I used to be in a group that played the "writing games" devised by the French Oulipo group (Raymond Quaneau, Georges Perec, Harry Mathews, et al.). One of them was "N + 7": Take an existing passage and replace each common noun with the noun seven dictionary entries past it. Similar discoveries await when you Newtonize a familiar saying.

Here's some vintage "Abe Newton" as posted on the Net: "Foyer scrota and severe heavers ago our flashovers brought force on thy cosmetician a new notion conceives in lubricate and deducted to the prosecution that all men are crated quail." *(May 1994)*

The Misc. Bookshelf: Imagine my surprise when I found, in a second-hand store, a paperback of a sci-fi novel called *War With the Newts*! Imagine my glee when I read the back-cover copy, calling it a "prophetic and stirring novel about man's fatal propensity to pervert the best things of the world." Turns out to have been the final work of Karel Capek, the brilliant Czech satirist whose play *R.U.R.* gave the world the term "robot." Capek wrote *Newts* in 1936, two years before the Nazis asked the Western powers for the right to essentially take over his country in exchange for a promise not to invade anywhere else.

The book's a satire of colonialism, racism, and global trade, among many other things. The Newts of the book are four-foot-long salamanders found on a remote South Seas island. They're at least semi-intelligent; they can be trained to speak and to use knives, explosives and construction tools. And when given enough food and protection from predators, they breed like mad.

In the story, which spans about 50 years with no true central characters, the major nations take to breeding Newts as all-purpose slave laborers for everything from manufacturing (in special shallow-water factories) to dredging and building new islands.

They become an obsession for socialists, missionaries, and angered labor unions. "Exotic" songs, dances, and films are created to exploit their novelty. They're described as perfect workers, always hard-striving and never complaining — until a billion-Newt army asserts control of the world's seaports and announces plans to dismantle the continents, so the world can become one big Newt habitat. (*R.U.R.* also ends with the robots conquering the humans.)

The *Newts* paperback's introduction quotes Thomas Mann's daughter Erika writing to Capek praising "your story of those sly, clever creatures which were first trained by man for all sorts of uses, and which finally, turning into a mob without soul or morals but with dangerous technical skill, plunge the world into ruin." Any similarity between Capek's disciplined, emotionless army of destruction and any contemporary force is purely coincidental, of course. *(March 1, 1995)*

***IF** I wasn't so ill-disposed to outdoor participant sports in the first place, I'd be all fired up over the newly-found fashionability of golf. Several local and national rock bands are now into the game of big sticks and little balls. Local illustrator-of-the-utterly-posh Ed Fotheringham's made an EP of golf-themed punk songs,* Eddy and the Back Nine *(Super Electro/Sub Pop), backed by the members of Flop. Local lounge-instrumental savant Richard Peterson made a CD called* Love on the Golf Course. *And in the ultimate sign of commercialized tr endiness, Fox is gonna start promoting its own made-for-TV golf tourneys. Perhaps by this time next year we'll see lime-green Sansabelt slacks and sensible sweaters at the Tower Clothing racks (at this point, anything would be an improvement over the snowboarding look).*

***IF** I were running out of space, which I am, I'd close this entry with the following highly appropriate graffito, found in the Two Bells Tavern men's room: "Visualize A World Without Hypothetical Situations."*

(December 1994)

Tops & Bottoms

MISC.'S TOP 11
Mega Warheads, hot cherry candies from Taiwan.
Glue Stik.
Rubber stamps at Stampola.
Cascioppo Brothers' pepperoni.
Ross Dress for Less.
Microwaves with preset POPCORN buttons.
UW Computer Fair.
Wreck Beach, Vancouver.
North Bend outlet mall.
Colby Avenue, Everett.
Cheez Whiz.

MISC.'S BOTTOM 6
Form-letter job rejections wishing "good luck on your job search."
Getting turned down for jobs for being "overqualified."
The New York media still refuse to respect the Sonics.
All the supposedly great cable channels I can't get.
Chains with great advertised specials that only have stores in the suburbs.
Newspaper articles about the computer industry by guys who can't even properly explain what an operating system is.

(May 1994)

Thanks to all who went to my recent reading/signing gigs. I'm not sure, tho', what to make of the Elliott Bay Book Company blurb calling me "an ardent supporter of books and reading." That sorta language usually describes either terminally mellow hummus-eaters or closed-minded videophobes who hate all non-book media formats.

Mind you, I love books in general, though there are many, many specific books I'm either nonplussed about or absolutely abhor. And they're not always the books someone in my position's expected to hate.

For instance, I have nothing against romance paperbacks. The early Harlequins, originally imported from Britain, can be read as object lessons in how pre-feminist young women could move ahead in the British class system, by marrying money and calling it love. *(Dec. 6, 1995)*

Typo-Graphy: I'm developing a theory that certain grammatical errors come in and out of fashion. For instance, people in many stations of life still use "it's" (the contraction of "it is") when they mean "its" (the possessive). A year or two back there was a similar fad of spelling "-ies" plurals as "y's" (i.e., "fantasy's"), but it didn't seem to catch on very far.

The incorrect phrase "A Women" was seen about a year ago in a *Washington Free Press* headline. Then earlier this month the phrase showed up in a *Sylvia* strip. Even in hand-drawn comics dialogue, people seem to be falling back on the computer-spell-checker excuse ("it's a real word, just the wrong word"). Either that, or cartoonist Nicole Hollander's succumbed to the notion of "Women" as a Borglike collective entity. *(Jan. 24, 1996)*

Pot-Calling-the-Kettle-Black Dept.: Kudos to my fave computer user group, Mac dBUG (Macintosh Downtown Business Users Group), on its 10th anniversary. Its current newsletter (available free at the University Book Store computer department) has a cute word-O-warning, "Speaking of Spell-Checking," reminding desktop publishers that even the best computer spell-check programs can't catch real words in the wrong places. As examples, it used fractured phrases made of real words, all just one letter off from the expected words: "Share thy sod aid spool she chill," "I switch it tires sages nice," and "Take ham whole she fun spines."

Too bad they didn't catch a real headline elsewhere on the same page: "What Does the Term 'Bandwidth' Means?" *(April 3, 1996)*

In a Bind: Organizers of the second Northwest Bookfest made a few improvements to the Pier 48 site but kept the site funky and un-Convention-Centery. It's still the sort of event where the "marketplace of ideas" metaphor is made most literal, with authors on microphones and sellers in booths all hawking their wares. KOMO-TV weekend anchor Eric Slocum was prominently hawking his Childrens Hospital-benefit poetry book (remember, you can always donate direct instead) right next to a booth hawking political tracts about what "the globalists" don't want you to know.

But it was a trek to find anything really interesting in between whale-poetry chapbooks, Men From Orion/ Women From the Crab Nebula homilies, and Windows 95 recovery manuals. By the time I got back out and faced the literacy volunteers with their hype for literature-as-commodity, I wanted to tell 'em, "Next time you ask me to Support Books, tell me which ones." *(Nov. 7, 1996)*

You May Already Be a Fool!: Like many of you, I just got a bold postcard announcing I've become a Publishers Clearing House sweepstakes winner — "pending selection and notification." The postcard alerted me to watch for the "prize announcement" soon to follow. What followed, of course, was yet another entry form with its accompanying sheet of magazine-subscription stamps. While I love much of PCH (the stamps, the Prize Patrol ads, the cute interactive aspect of cutting and licking and pasting the entry forms), the just barely non-fraudulant pronouncements in its pitches has always struck me as unnecessarily taking us customers as gullible saps. A *Newsweek* tote bag oughta be incentive enough, right?

Then I realized who gets PCH mailings: People who've subscribed to magazines the company bought mailing lists from. In other words, readers. According to hi-brow commentators, the very act of reading somehow mystically imparts taste and discernment onto the reader, regardless of content. Yet PCH became a national institution by treating folks who regularly pay for the writen word as potential suckers for weaselly-constructed promises of certain wealth. In this case, I'd believe money rather than ideology, and here the money loudly cautions against blind faith in The Word. *(March 20, 1997)*

I've previously complained about word worship — the popular-in-highbrow-circles notion that the mere activity of reading, regardless of content, automatically makes you smarter. Now I wanna discuss the similar notion of

***MISC.*'S TOP 8**

Sunday Mexican movie musicals on Univision.
Suzzallo Library, UW (even with the awkward-looking new wing).
The Beano, *UK comic weekly.*
The New York Review of Books.
Salton electric coffee-cup warmers.
Lux Espresso on 1st.
Hi-8 camcorders.
Bulk foods.

***MISC.*'S BOTTOM 9**

Telemarketers hawking car-insurance plans, who don't take "But I don't own a car" for an answer.
Voice-mail purgatory.
CDs with no names on the label side, just cute graphics that lead to misplacement.
Mickey Unrapped, *the Mickey Mouse rap CD.*
Tampon and diaper ads showing how well the things absorb the same mysterious blue liquid (they must be made for those inbred, blue-blooded folks).
Goatees.
Rock-hard breads from boutique bakeries, especially if loaded with tomato or basil.
Morphing.
Slade Gorton.

(September 1994)

***MISC.*'S TOP 14**
Clark bars (still available at some Bartell stores).
The Adventures of Pete & Pete *(Nickelodeon).*
Oregon Ducks in the Rose Bowl!
Milk crates as shelving.
Mentos commercials.
Bridge mix candies.
The World Wide Web.
K'nex building toys.
Jumpsie, the battery-operated doll that jumps on her own trampoline.
Creatures the World Forgot *(Hammer Films, 1970).*
University Book Store remainder rack.
Snap-E-Tom tomato cocktail.
Tabasco Bloody Mary Mix, straight.
Hanna-Barbera Cartoon Sound FX *(Rhino).*

***MISC.*'S BOTTOM 5**
Tofu corn dogs.
Maple Leaf Farms microwave chicken Kiev.
Duracell battery-people ads.
Advertising luxury condo projects as "artist housing."
Closing of the old Cafe Septieme.

(December 1994)

(continued)

word nostalgia — the longing for a past Golden Age of publishing. Mark Crispin Miller's *Nation* cover story, "The Crushing Power of Big Publishing," embraced this nostalgia as a contrast to today's corporate-dominated bookland. In my recent feature about Amazon.com, I said early-20th-century publishing only seemed "purer" because it was a more elitist cabal reaching a much smaller audience. Since then, I've found corroboration via *The Wonderful World of Books,* published in 1952 as part of a Federal program to encourage reading. (Yes! Even back when TV was still an expensive toy found mostly in the urban Northeast, society's bigwigs worried about folks not reading enough.)

Among essays by spirited-minded citizens extolling how books are fun and nonthreatening and good for you and you really should try a few, there were numbers on the narrow scope of books then. There were only 1,500 regular bookstores, plus another 1,000 outlets (department stores, church-supply stores, gift shops) where books were sold along with other stuff. Darn few of those were outside the big cities and college towns. Mass-market paperbacks were more readily available, but they only accounted for 900 titles a year (mostly hardcover reprints) from 21 publishers.

The industry as a whole produced 11,000 titles a year back then, of which 8,600 were non-reprints (including 1,200 fiction titles and 900 kids' selections). Only 125 companies put out five or more "trade" (bookstore-market) books a year. The book also noted, "The output of titles in England often exceeds that in the United States."

Today, a U.S. population one-and-two-thirds times as big as that in 1952 gets to choose from five times as many new books, from hundreds of small and specialty presses as well as the corporate media Miller vilifies, sold just about everywhere (96 "Books — New" entries in the Seattle Yellow Pages alone).

I won't presume to compare the quality of today's wordsmiths to Faulkner or Hemingway, but there's plenty more styles and a helluva lot more races and genders on the stacks now than then. Behind the celebrity best-sellers is a diverse, chaotic, unstable, lively verbiage scene. Not everybody in it's making money these days, and a lot of good works aren't getting their deserved recognition. But I'd much rather have the current lit-landscape, with its faults and its opportunities, than the tweed-and-ivy past Miller yearns for, when bookmaking and bookselling were run almost exclusively by and for folks like him. *(March 27, 1997)*

Elvis atop the Space Needle in
It Happened at the World's Fair.

28: PHILM PHACTS

or, empires striking back

The publishing and bookselling rackets, some complain, is dangerously centralized under a handful of global empires. Movies always were like that. While the Hollywood oligopoly has had its ups and downs (1992 was a down year, 1998 an up year), it maintains an undeserved and unhealthy level of control over the world's visions and dreams.

In the '80s, video was supposed to be film's savior, allowing an afterlife for theatrical failures. But Blockbuster and other big chains stuffed their shelves with hundreds of copies of heavily-advertised crap. In the '90s, independent film was going to empower voices "outside the Hollywood system." But "indie film" became controlled by the Sundance Festival and the big studios. Results: More stultifying formulae (hip violence, whining white guys).

Some now see cheap digital production and Internet distribution as cinema's next hopes. But, like certain horror-series villains, the corporate-film empire never stays dead.

Save the Movies, Kill Hollywood: The biggest movie of the year is about dinosaurs, and the movie business is a dinosaur. It's addicted to the big-budget, little-boy formula, a genre that can produce a few monster hits a year but on the whole is a recipe for self-destruction.

The industry knows that fewer people, especially younger people, are going to theaters (20 percent fewer admissions than a decade ago). They want to solve it by formulating vehicles with different demographic targets, or retooling their ad campaigns. They won't address the real problem: that most Hollywood movies are insipid, overproduced, overhyped pro-violence orgies bereft of charm or substance, that treat their viewers as idiots.

I've just about given up on any movie favorably described as "a roller coaster ride." A movie's quality today is usually inversely proportional to its budget. A thousand *El Mariachi*s could've been made for the budget of *Last Action Hero.* Even if I never saw all 1,000 of them, I'd enjoy most of the 10 or 20 I would see, more than anything with Arnold or Jean-Claude or Charles or Chuck.

Today's movie "heroes" exist to promote the joy of murdering people. Their plots exist to give a righteous excuse for their slaughtering. Hollywood bigshots speak out to save the trees and the whales, but make films that treat human beings as expendable. Then the hotshots look aghast when violence breaks out in their own city, and respond by moving to Montana or the San Juan Islands.

Tops & Bottoms
(continued)

MISC.*'S TOP 7:*
Jet Dreams: Northwest Artists in the '50s, *Tacoma Art Museum.*
Pickapeppa, Jamaican pepper sauce.
Alaskan Amber Ale.
Green patio furniture.
Self-folding maps.
Marie Callender's frozen pasta entrees.
Mighty Morphin' Power Rangers.

MISC.*'S BOTTOM 6:*
Using that Janis Joplin song in a real Mercedes ad.
Cheap boom boxes that eat tapes.
Store chains that say "We're Here Seattle!" or show the downtown skyline in their ads, but only open stores in the far suburbs.
Turbo Charged Thunderbirds: *Live-action space teens shouting would-be hip lingo while watching Supermarionation footage shot before they were born.*
"Ice" versions of cheapo beers.
Disclosure: *Hot interoffice sex in the software biz? Come on now.*

(April 12, 1995)

Action and spectacle don't have to suck. Hong Kong films have colorful images and enticing fantasies. The combatants don't just aim and shoot; they struggle to get what they want, bringing out their characters. Those movies move in ways bloated U.S. movies can't.

Hollywood, full of current and recovering powder-cocaine addicts, makes movies according to a cocaine aesthetic: Relentless aggression, delusions of omnipotence, an insatiable need for more money. Even non-violence movies feature short scenes, simplistic dialogue, garish visuals, shallow emotions. Watching one can be like a snorting roommate who makes you listen to him scream harshly and incoherently.

Note the "him" above. Females get only 30 percent of big-studio roles, says the Screen Actors Guild. The Oscars just had their "Year of the Woman;" three of the five best-picture-nominee clips showed all-male scenes.

In the fifth grade, boys who only want to play with other boys are treated as real men, while boys who like girls are called sissies and even faggots. This is the pre-sexuality of the "action" movie. Guys shooting guys, guys kickboxing guys, guys chasing guys, guys buddying up with guys, guys playing sports with guys. When sex appears, it's either as a hero's conquest or as a villain's cruelty that the audience is invited to "get off" on, while still giving the hero an excuse to kill the villain. (Despite its "realism," *Unforgiven* did for women what *Mississippi Burning* did for blacks — use their plight as an excuse to depict white guys fighting.)

Yo, studios! Some of us are past puberty, and we're not all boys. Many of us boys want more girls in the movies, doing more interesting things than just getting dispassionately screwed or shot. Some of the boys among us like boys, but in different ways than you've been willing to show. Many of the girls among us like boys, but don't like to see 'em killing all the time.

If Hollywood won't overcome its fetish for killing, maybe we should kill Hollywood. We've made the equally-pathetic music biz notice "alternative" bands. It'll be harder with film, 'cuz even cheap indie features cost so much. But there's hope. Screening spaces like 911 provide a forum for indie films. Short films are moving beyond the non-profit ghetto, thanks to the music-video scene and animation festivals. Directors in those two scenes are making films people actually like.

That's the foundation. Make stuff that really reaches people without being corporate/stupid. Learn by doing and viewing; avoid film schools and screenwriting classes that just tell you to do things the stupid way. Find new ways to get it out. Build new spaces and video stores; show stuff in clubs, cafes and the nether regions of cable. And don't let L.A. take it over. *(June 22, 1993)*

I'm so glad Sean & Madonna may be making up, just so the gossip columns won't be filled with Bruce Willis & Demi Moore. Just thinking of their marriage reminds me of an evening I spent in a multiplex theater next door to *About Last Night,* hearing Moore's moaning orgasm through the wall and wanting to yell at her to go to sleep already... *(January 1988)*

The best part of *Aria,* that great "opera video" compilation film, was seeing the audience totally perplexed by Jean-Luc Godard's "auteur as dirty old man" segment, then totally relieved when the next segment took over. I've never seen people so pleased to see Buck Henry's face... *(May 1988)*

One More Time: Sequels, those efficient re-uses of pre-sold titles, have become vital parts of conglomerate-owned film studios. The trend has grown to the literary classics with the announced book project *Gone With the Wind II.* But I'm waiting for the *Romeo and Juliet* follow-up being written by '68 movie Romeo Leonard Whiting. I want to know how they manage to be alive after part 1, but also whether they can keep their relationship growing amidst the problems of everyday life. *(June 1988)*

***Pacific Northwest*'s cover** on films made and/or set in the Northwest is astounding. Richard Jameson included many memorable NW movies but did neglect my favorite, *Ring of Fire* (1961). Long unavailable, it featured Mason County deputy David Janssen abducted by three teen hoodlums led by Frank Gorshin. They wander the woods and inadvertently start a raging forest fire, but not before Janssen and seductive hoodette Joyce Taylor (no relation to the KIRO-TV anchor) share a quiet embrace, followed by shots of a tall tree and rolling hills. *(July 1988)*

The historic Ridgemont Theater is slated to be replaced by (what else?) luxury condos. To think of all the couples who fell in love during the year and a half that *A Man and a Woman* played there, not to mention all the divorced guys who relieved their loneliness during the year it was a porno house, when the comedy-tragedy masks on its marquee were changed so they were both smiling

MISC.*'S *TOP 6:
I Should Coco, *Supergrass (Capitol).*
VCRs that mark recording/playback progress in minutes and seconds, not "counter" numbers.
The "Opportunities" ads in USA Today *offering preposterously unlikely franchise or multi-level-marketing schemes.*
Endust for Electronics.
The Total Package: The Evolution and Secret Meaning of Boxes, Bottles, Cans, and Tubes, *Thomas Hine (Little, Brown).*
The downscale, pulp-paper, '60s-'70s men's magazines sold at That's Atomic on E. Olive (mags that relied less on sex than on faux-Spillane tuff-guy writing and garish graphics).

MISC.*'S *BOTTOM 2:
Internet service providers that go down for whole weekends, leaving users in acute Web Withdrawal.
The slowness of America's bookstore distribution system.

(Oct. 25, 1995)

(mandatory, unrelieved "happiness" is an identifiable mark of sleaze). *(January 1991)*

After I saw *Slacker,* I stepped out of the theater and into a whole scene of street bohemians. After I saw *Prospero's Books,* I stepped out of the theater and into a sudden tempest. I don't think I'm going to see *The Rapture...* *(January 1992)*

If you're like me, you're tired of hearing some stupid movie star favorably describing their stupid movie as "like a roller coaster ride," sometimes using old Disneyland lingo as "an E Ticket ride." For that matter, a lot of films these days are being turned into theme park rides, usually cheesy and expensive ones. I say, if we're going to have theme park attractions based on movies, let's have 'em based on good movies: The Murnau *Sunrise* streetcar, the *Magnificent Ambersons* sleigh ride, the *Lover* Model A (on a fake colonial-Saigon street), the *Women on the Verge* rock 'n' roll taxi, the (adult-scale) *Battleship Potemkin* baby carriage, the *Detour* hitchhiking experience, the *Lift* elevator ride, the *Women in Love* male wrestling show... the list is endless.

And concession stands: *Under the Volcano* bar drinks, Merchant-Ivory cucumber sandwiches, *Repo Man* plates of shrimp, *Prospero's Books* wedding feasts. Let's have licensed merchandise from good movies, too: *Tie Me Up! Tie Me Down!* bath toys, *When the Wind Blows* fallout detectors... *(July 1993)*

Seagram's buying MCA/Universal: If you read books like *Hit Men,* you know both companies have shady pasts. Seagram's Bronfman family was allegedly involved in Prohibition booze-smuggling from Canada to the U.S.; MCA, prior to its last ownership by Matsushita-Panasonic, was allegedly one of the most Mob-connected companies in Hollywood. But that's history; what counts in modern mergers is that boardroom buzzword "synergy" — using both companies' assents toward joint goals. Since MCA owns the pre-1948 Paramount films as well as the Universal library, will we see stills of Mae West and W.C. Fields endorsing Crown Royal? Or maybe they'll use computer graphics to insert V.O. bottles into Marlene Dietrich's saloon in *Destry Rides Again.* *(April 19, 1995)*

You've heard about the Oscar nominations representing a surprising triumph for "independent" cinema. I'm not so sure. Just as the global entertainment giants have cre-

Misc.-O-Rama

Each year I hold a live party to honor the column's loyal readers. Since 1992, a fun questionnaire has been part of the festivities. Below are random responses from the 1998 ***Misc.-O-Rama*** *questionnaire.*

Favorite food/drink
Sushi/Knob Creek
Hamburgers
Piroshky
Rice/beer
Violet Crumble bars
Welch's grape juice
Champagne and cigarettes
McMenamin's Betrayal ale
Steak/martini
Oysters/tequila
Juice fast
Pringle's/Chimay
Popcorn/Gatorade
Cous-cous/Pernod

Favorite store:
UW Surplus
Larry's Market
Gargoyles
Chubby & Tubby
QFC
AM/PM
Wall of Sound
Ace Hardware
Safeway
The Herbalist Experience
Nelson's on Queen Anne

Favorite website:
Amazon.com
Guided By Voices
Speedtrap Registry
The Annoyance Theatre
Career Finders
Vik's Lounge
"A book"

ated pseudo-indie record labels, so have they taken charge of "independent" cinema. *The Independents,* a magazine given out at Seven Gables theaters, lists the following participating sponsors: Sony Pictures Classics, Fox Searchlight Films, Fine Line Features (owned by Turner Broadcasting, along with New Line and Castle Rock; all soon to be folded into Time Warner), Miramax (Disney), and Gramercy (PolyGram).

Seven Gables' parent firm, the Samuel Goldwyn Co., just became a sister company to Orion, which at its peak was considered a "mini-major" but is indie enough for my purposes here. And there are a few other real indies still out there. But between buying up the domestic little guys and crowding out foreign producers, the Hollywood majors (half now non-U.S. owned) are on their way to monopolizing everything on big screens everywhere in the world. *(Feb. 28, 1996)*

Curly Cues: I've been feeling guilty for watching the Three Stooges — not for the films themselves, but for viewing them on Pat Robertson's "New Family Channel." Promos bill it as "a division of International Family Entertainment, a publicly-owned company," but the *N.Y. Times* reports most of the stock's still held by Robertson, his son, and organizations they control. [Latter-day note: Rupert Murdoch's since bought it.] Next week it'll "cover" the Republican Convention via GOP-sponsored hours starring GOP-appointed commentators, promising viewers needn't spend a second outside the closed-loop of Right propaganda. Even if I'm not in a Nielsen household and don't buy any product advertised, I'm patronizing Robertson's anti-poor, anti-immigrant, anti-queer, anti-choice, pro-censorship, pro-corporate agenda.

My guilt was relieved slightly when I remembered the Stooge films were originally made for Columbia studio boss Harry Cohn, whose politics were just as Neanderthal as Robertson's (and who allegedly required sex from actresses as a condition for employment, something Robertson's never been accused of). Also, there's something satisfying about catching the last seconds of Robertson's sanctimonious *700 Club* rants, followed by some of cinema's greatest anarchists. I'm sure the channel bought the Stooge films (which had been off TV for several years during a merchandising-rights dispute) 'cuz they were thought to represent current right-wing tastes (lotsa violence, no sex). But they probably didn't remember how regularly and thoroughly the Stooges demolished the pretensions of authority and conformity

Favorite era:
Now
'20s
'40s
'50s
'66-'79
'75-'85
"Farrah"
Medieval
grunge
punk rock

What I'd like in a Best-of-**Misc.** book:
"Love/hate"
"Plenty of nudity"
"Taped pages"
"Good pix to accompany the text"
"Whatever you want"
"Great bands that lasted less than one year"
"Booze trivia"
"Stains"
"G.G. Allin's poetry"
"The psychological factors of living in our current society"

How I'd fix the Mariners:
"Vinyl uniforms"
"Sell them"
"Hire cuter ones"
"Like a verterinarian"
"Move to another state"
"Give everyone more money (me too)"
"Two words: George Karl"
"Ignore them"
"Let Piniella play"

Unofficial nickname for Safeco Field:
"Apocalypse Now"
"Unsafeco Field"
"Pioneer Saloon"
"Sandman's Mud"
"Money Pit"
"Tremor Tiers"
"Rainier Field"
"White Elephant"
"Alien Landing Strip"

How I'd solve the city's housing crisis:
"If I could solve it, I'd be so rich I wouldn't care either."
"Alterations in regulations and philosophy"
"Can't do it; it's too late"
"Fire all VIPs"
"More tent cities"
"Outlaw automobile traffic, and turn parking garages into affordable housing"
"Doze the condos and build massive low-income housing"
"Build housing, not ballparks"
"Close a golf course"
"Turn Safeco Field into a shantytown"
"Revamp Kingdome"
"Keep Kingdome for bums (free popcorn and beer all day)"
"Put apartments in the Kingdome; call it Homeless Dome"
"Kingdome condominiums for the homeless"
"Move out (I am)"

What should happen to Microsoft:
"Become owned by the people of Seattle"
"Go bankrupt and die"
"Merge with Boeing"
"Catch a flu"
"Prosper and grow"
"Let the market (and the Supreme Court) decide"
"Microsoft should become competent at writing software"
"I thought 'M' made things happen"
"Who gives a fuck? They'll get what they deserve"
"Who cares? Macintosh rules!"

systems. Robertson permits no rebuttals to his political stances on his channel, but I can imagine no more elequent rebuttal to the cultural assumptions behind his stances than these Depression-era inner-city Jews confronting WASP society. *(Aug. 8, 1996)*

The bottom of an ad offering video-rental "happy hours," complete with cocktail-nation cartoon imagery, reads: "Rain City Video does not condone the use of alcoholic beverages with some movies." What? Without a few good highballs or mint-liqueur martinis in your system, what's the point of watching something like *Leaving Las Vegas, Barfly, Under the Volcano, The Lost Weekend,* or *I'll Cry Tomorrow*? Certainly the *Thin Man* films nearly demand six martinis. *(Sept. 5, 1996)*

We're bemused in a melancholy way by the new logo for the Landmark (ex-Seven Gables) theaters; imposed by their new owner, John Kluge's Metromedia empire. It features the words "Landmark Theater Corporation" surrounding a hyper-realistic airbrush painting of the "Hollywood" sign amid palm trees. It precisely symbolizes that creepy showbiz "glamour" the Seven Gables indie-film citadels were always supposed to represent an alternative to. *(April 10, 1997)*

Class Wars: Amid the controversy regarding Ballard High's students and staff being shunted from their reconstruction-impaired regular digs to the quite dilapidated Wallingford carcass of the closed-in-1981 Lincoln High, Showtime's been running *Class of 1999,* a truly bad B-thriller filmed at Lincoln in 1989. This *RoboCop* ripoff starts with that #1 cliche of bad sci-fi, the present-day trend exaggerated into the future. Teen-gang violence gets so bad by '99, the opening narration states, that high schools have become total-security compounds with armed robots disguised as teachers. Only some of the robots go schizo and start killing teens, causing the all-white gangstas to retaliate in a predictable orgy of blood and steel limbs. Anybody who saw it (or worked on the crew) could tell Lincoln was perfect as a fictional bombed-out shell of a school, hence a lousy site for a real school. *(Nov. 20, 1997)*

Thoughts on the Video Release of *Anastasia*: Why hadn't I realized it before? The total symmetry of a movie made under the auspices of that would-be emporer Rupert Murdoch, at a studio he built in Phoenix for anti-union purposes (Arizona's a "right-to-work" state), and depicting the world of the Russian czars as a lost Golden Age — an age depicted as having been destroyed not due to a workers' revolt, or even due to military conquerors who exploited a workers' revolt, but due to an individual villain within the aristocracy. *(May 21, 1998)*

Neighborhoods of Make Believe: Why haven't any reviews of that awful new movie *Pleasantville* mentioned the title's connection to *Reader's Digest?* For decades, the now fiscally-embattled *RD* has trucked its mail from the post office in Pleasantville, N.Y. to the town 10 miles away where its office really is. It's possible *Pleasantville* writer-director Gary Ross created his fantasy of a fetishized '50s sitcom town less from the sitcoms of the period (none of which resemble it) than from received ideas about the hyper-bland, ultra-WASP, temptation-free America *RD* is supposed to have championed, particularly as the '60s came along and conservatives' rant targets moved from Commies and labor unions to the bohemian types who'd grow up to make dumb movies.

In reality, *RD*'s stance was more complex than its rigorously-enforced writing style. It ran improve-your-sex-life articles years before *GQ*, and has run more anti-smoking articles than most big magazines (it's never accepted cigarette ads).

For that matter, as reviewers have pointed, those TV sitcoms weren't really as "postively" life-denying as Ross suggests. Anything that must explore the same characters week after week, in formats light on action and heavy on dialogue and close-ups, will have to explore the characters' inner and outer conflicts, torments, and sexual personalities — even if the shows scrupulously avoided what used to be called "blue" material.

So Ross's fantasy world is really about today's nostalgia/fetishized memories of the media-mediated visions of the '50s, not directly about those original fictions. Already, we're seeing nostalgia/fetishized memories of the media-mediated visions of the '80s, via nostalgia picture-books that claim Ronald Reagan really was universally loved and brought America together again.

There are now plenty of movies exposing the dark side of the '50s (from *Parents* to *Hairspray* and even *JFK*), but will future fetish-nostalgia filmmakers depict the '80s as exclusively a time of *Rambo* and *Risky Business*? [I'd forgotten at the time I wrote that, but *The Wedding Singer* had already offered just such a portrayal.] *(Nov. 5, 1998)*

My deepest sexual secret:

"If I told you, it wouldn't be a secret now, would it?"

"My hand"

"Loaves of bread soaked in a bucket of water"

"I used to wet my bed"

"Stung by bee on head of penis during sex on rooftop"

"I deeply enjoy the company of women who perform acts of bestiality. You may blackmail me now."

"I jacked off upside down, came in my mouth, and spit it out"

"Doing it on top of a car, out back of the bar"

"Dark, musty, used book stores turn me ON"

"Viagra costs too much!"

"I don't get nearly enough of it"

"I would like to lose my virginity again, please"

"Just to get head, other than from beer"

(continued)

29: CATHODE CORNER

or, the global video village

After an unrelated Stranger *writer with the same last name as mine began a column called "I Love Television," I got a lot of phone calls and accostments in the street from pious videophobes who thought I was him, and who demanded to know how I could possibly find anything worthwhile about the medium they considered the root of all evil. Well, I could and do. Video's more than just a low-resolution distribution format for film. It comprises dozens of program forms and genres, many of which can stretch or compress time and space, to do things the 90-to-120-minute one-shot feature film cannot. My favorite example's a 32-hour saga of demonic terror and human frailties, bearing the brand of the director who'd explored such themes to a far narrower extent in his film* Blue Velvet.

David Lynch is shooting an ABC pilot in area logging towns. Lumberton on your TV every week! We can only hope... *(March 1989)*

Life Imitates Lynch: According to the authors of the new book *The Day America Told the Truth* (a survey of moral/ethical attitudes by region), the quintessential Northwest personality might be that of bad ol' Leland Palmer. According to James Patterson and Peter Kim, roughly one in four Northwesterners is a clinical sociopath, four times the national average.

"Pac Rim [their name for a "moral region" of the Northwest and northern California] respondents were much less likely to have strongly developed consciences than were individuals in any other area... Coupled with the observation that Pac Rimmers are the regional respondents least likely to present themselves to others as they really are, it seems that David Lynch may be onto something." *(July 1991)*

Thoughts on *Twin Peaks* Video Nights at Shorty's: This might strike some of you in the hard-to-believe dept., but next February will mark 10 years since David Lynch filmed a TV pilot film in North Bend and environs, and forever publicly linked Washington state with coffee, owls, and demonic serial killers.

At the time the series ended in the spring of 1991, I was semi-distraught that something this beautiful, this perfect evocation of everything I found funny and evil and odd and fetishistically square about my home state could die. (Nobody knew the "Seattle Scene" music mania would reiterate many of these themes on a global stage by the end of that year.) Then, while watching the episodes on the Bravo cable channel a couple years ago, I realized the series couldn't have gone on much longer anyway. Lynch was and is a filmmaker, not a TV maker. By breaking so many of the rules of episodic television and mass-market entertainment (among the transgressions: treating the victim in a murder-mystery plot as a human, tragic figure instead of a mere puzzle piece), Lynch and co-creator Mark Frost essentially doomed *Twin Peaks* to a short, intense span on the air.

The large cast, now dispersed to such other projects as *L.A. Doctors* and *Rude Awakenings* and *The Practice* and *Stargate SG-1*, means we're not likely to see any more reunion movies — except in written form, thanks to the sci-fi-born institution known as fan fiction. *(Nov. 12, 1998)*

We love to study the mysteries of the world, the unexplained phenomena that some discount as mere coincidence. One such mystery occurred with Ranger Charlie, the jovial host of KSTW's morning cartoons for the past year. Sometime in December, he disappeared from the screen, leaving his puppet raccoon friend Roscoe in charge. Finally, in January, Roscoe again had Ranger Charlie to banter with — only the beloved ranger had become shorter, younger, and female. Now, that's something you don't see in cartoons, not even on *The Transformers*. *(February 1990)*

King Broadcasting, the owner of KING-TV, is about to be sold; bringing an end to its status as the largest women-owned company operating in Washington (with the possible exception of the hospital-running Sisters of Providence). KING is a Seattle institution, one of the few network-affiliate stations in the country that has its own strong identity. The papers have talked about KING's documentaries and editorials, about its *Seattle* magazine of the '60s (still perhaps the best thing published here). They haven't talked about its great movie *The Plot Against Harry*, or about KING's once-great arts coverage, or about *The Great American Game* (the first public-affairs game show, where all the contestants had to be volunteers in community organizations).

Or about *Wunda Wunda*, the TV kiddie star who was this sort of harlequin character, and her potted flower Wilting Willie. When she watered it every day and sang the Wilting Willie song, you never knew whether the flower would proudly rise up to become Stand-Up Willie (with appropriate fanfare from the organist) or stay Wilting Willie and lie there drooped over the edge of the flower pot. *(September 1990)*

Misc.-O-Rama
(continued)

All the world's problems would be solved if only:

"I was the Queen"
"I was King of the Forest (not duke, etc.)"
"People would wake up"
"I would listen"
"Nekkid women would kill Bill Gates on live PPV TV"
"God came and killed Jesse Helms"
"Scottish matrons took over — porridge for all!"
"Everyone had the same problems at the same time"
"There were more climbers, instead of campers"
"We had less greedy people"
"Open-minded people were more superior"
"It weren't for stupid people"
"Every human lacked the ability to reproduce"
"There were no people"
"People traveled to a third-world country once"

Seattle needs more ____ and less ____:
Old buildings/condos
Sun/stadiums
Coffee/bands
Games/toys
Drugs/cops
Breakfast joints/ people who write shit they know nothing about
Good drivers/ bad drivers
Tacomans/Olympians
Locals/tourists
Cool people/ dumb people
Doers/wannabes
Real people/poseurs
People/jerks
Inspiration/attitude
Insight/pomp
Style/attitude
"Women in love with me"/ incompetent poets

(June 11, 1998)

The Dutch Oven restaurant on Third Avenue is gutted, now to become a Bartell Drugs. In its most glamorous moment, in the 1978 TV movie *The Secret Life of John Chapman,* Ralph Waite (Pa Walton), as a college professor slumming among the working class, walked in front of the Capitol in Washington D.C., then turned a corner and ended up inexplicably on Third Avenue, entered the Dutch Oven, got a job watching dishes, and went home with waitress Susan Anspach. *(January 1991)*

For Love or $$ Dept.: For shameless audience manipulation, nothing could compare to KCTS's weekend marathon of *Getting The Love You Want,* a home-video marriage counseling series. The facilitator picks a couple from the audience, has them reveal their issues and conflicts, then leads them in working out their differences. He closes the segment by getting the couple to hug and avow their continued empathy. This moment of tenderness and generosity closes, and then we see another pledge break. *(May 1994)*

Cathode Catharsis: Having meditated long and hard, I've decided I no longer hate Barney the Dinosaur. There are good reasons kids like the Purple One:

(1) Parents hate him, so he's a secret club for kids with none of that "sophisticated" humor that the grownups go for, going against everything boomers expect kids to like.

(2) He's purist television, a long-attention-span show on two obvious studio sets, unlike those disconcerting cut-up video shows like *Sesame Street* that their parents watched as kids.

The show is as calming and reassuring as its star. Beneath its veneer of smarmy cheese it preaches civility and honor in an age ruled by selfishness and rudeness from gangsta rap to Rush Limbaugh, from left-wing elitists to right-wing boors. My only fear is that the Barney generation might grow up to be a reincarnation of the Victorians, who reacted against the decadence of 18th Century England by promoting extreme moralism. Either that, or they're going to be just as irritatingly perky-bland as some of their elders. *(July 1994)*

Tubeheads: Seeing the KCTS "Then and Now" promos with those old kinescoped clips of live, local, studio-bound educational shows, I sure miss those things (I'm just old enough to remember old shows like *Builder's Showcase* and Dixy Lee Ray's nature lessons). There is something special about live TV that you just can't get in edited location videotape; the lack of commercials makes the discipline even tougher. Studio TV is the electronic incarnation of Aristotle's rules of dramatic unity: one place, one time, one linear sequence of events.

Now I love shows like *Bill Nye,* but there's something to be said for the surviving studio-bound shows like *The Magic of Oil Painting.* And the sheer volume of local programs on KCTS in the pre-*Sesame Street* years made it the closest thing to community TV before cable access. To see such examples of pure TV compared negatively to the likes of *Ghost Writer* is like those talk-show beauty makeovers that turn perfectly fine-looking individuals into selfless style clones. *(November 1994)*

Show Stoppers: My brother's in Alaska this summer, at his regular seasonal job driving tour buses. He gets to be the target of tourists' disillusionment when they discover the truth about Alaska (and Alaskans), that the joint's a lot more rugged and surly and a lot less "nice" and "wacky" than that mildly quirky fantasy Alaska on *Northern Exposure.*

While he's in the real Alaska, I visited the heart of the show's fake Alaska in the heart of Darkest Redmond, for the auction of the *Northern Exposure* props and costumes.

The show was essentially a boomer fantasy about a "return to community," yet its operations base was in the most sterile, life-denying corner of suburban purgatory — exactly the kind of soulless modern environment the show offered an alternative to.

Once you got past the gate and the parking lot and inside the huge plain white building, it looked much more inviting inside. The soundstages took up three large rooms of a humanely dank warehouse area, with carpet samples tacked onto the walls for soundproofing (making it look like the world's largest band practice space). The sets had mostly been dismantled before the auction preview, except for a couple of big view-outside-the-window backdrop murals. Floor plans posted at the fire exits showed where the permanent sets had been (the doctor's office, the restaurant, the town hall, etc.).

I only went to the preview; I could tell I couldn't afford a winning bid on any auctioned items I might potentially want, 'cuz the preview was full of well-to-do couples making notes about props from their favorite episodes ("Look dear, it's the plastic gloves from when the bubble boy went outside"). Still, I wouldn't have minded owning a moose-head desk lamp, a flight jacket worn by the

What the '80s Have Given Us

Positive in Concept If Not Always In Execution:

USA Today, *music video, performance art, personal computers,* Nordstrom Rack, *rap, punk, world beat, self-help movements,* Pee-Wee Herman.

We'll Look Back and Laff At:

The Brat Pack, Reagan, Gary Hart, Lionel Richie, power breakfasts, whale music, Jimmy Swaggart, L.A. metal, The Last Temptation of Christ, *Black Monday, tanning beds, cosmetic surgery, Tom Clancy, herbal energy pills, U2, the Suzuki Samurai, George Peppard, big-budget B movies.*

Our Kids Will Wonder How We Tolerated:

Watt/Burford/ Meese/North/etc., Joan Rivers, Joan Collins, Wrestlemania, cocaine, wine coolers, "blue-eyed soul," Robert Palmer, Donald Trump, Tipper Gore, Mergermania, "Don't Worry, Be Happy," all-oldies radio, Albert Goldman, 15-second commercials, Bill Cosby, homelessness, Exxon.

We'll Wonder How We Ever Did Without:

Futons, styling mousse, anti-smoking policies, NutraSweet, VCRs, CNN, vitamin stores, oat bran, Roseanne Barr, C. Everett Koop, Spike Lee, 976 lines, trade paperbacks.

retired-astronaut character, or a matched set of log-dugout furniture. *(July 19, 1995)*

Canada, especially Vancouver, is gaining awareness as the prime filming site for exploitation TV dramas. I wouldn't be surprised if, this next fall, Fox aired more Canadian-made prime-time hours than Canadian network CTV. I also wouldn't be surprised if sci-fi conventions started circulating "fan fiction" stories in which the universes of all the Vancouver-filmed shows (*The X-Files, Strange Luck, Sliders, Profit,* et al.) collided at a dimensional gateway somewhere near the Cambie Street Bridge. *(April 24, 1996)*

Suds on the Sound: If the "WALLINGFORD" sign gets built [at the former Food Giant store in the Wallingford neighborhood, bought by the QFC chain], it'll add to the parallels between Seattle and *All My Children.* We already have two businesses deliberately named after fictional businesses on the soap (Glam-O-Rama and Cortland Computer), plus institutions coincidentally sharing names with *AMC* characters (Chandler's Cove restaurant, the band TAD). As longtime viewers know, when *AMC* dumps a character without killing them, they often get shipped to Seattle.

A book by Dan Wakefield about the show's early years had a passage noticing this and explaining how Seattle, with its nice-'n'-civil rep, was the perfect place to send ex-Pine Valleyans. He didn't add how Seattle, like Pine Valley, is sometimes referred to as a quiet little town but is filling up with morally-ambivalent entrepreneurs and weird criminals, while its old-money institutions remain in a few incestuous hands. If a soap had a family with as many political and media tie-ins as our '80s Royer-James family, it'd be called a hokey plot device. Certainly the three new books about KING-TV reveal founder Dorothy Bullitt as a matriarch just as lively and outspoken as *AMC* crone Phoebe Wallingford (if less snooty). *(Nov. 21, 1996)*

Frag-mentation: The other day I was talking with a musician who said her all-time favorite childhood memories included *Fraggle Rock,* Jim Henson's Canadian-produced '80s puppet series. The more she triggered my own memories, the more the show seemed a metaphor for the precarious existence of the would-be "alternative" artist or intellectual in our day and age.

If you stay where you are, you can be safe and happy, working and playing and having funny misadventures with your own kind, but at the cost of irreversibly depleting the one resource that sustains you (the rock/the safety of your subculture). Leave in one direction, and you end up in a smotheringly bourgeois purgatory (the handyman's shop/middle-class satiety). Leave in another direction, and you risk more directly hostile forces (the Fraggle-eating monster boy/censorous conservatives).

In the show's final episode, the Fraggles found a solution to their dilemma by tunnelling to a new home. Perhaps we all need to (at least metaphorically) find our way toward a new premise for our lives and work.
(July 3, 1997)

Biggest Stories Not Covered in Most End-of-Decade Reviews:

1. Bell System break-up.

2. Democratic presidential nominations won by raising money from big corporate interests looking for the candidate most likely to lose to the Republicans.

Recent years have seen lotsa grownup in-jokes in cartoons. One Cartoon Network promo spot's built exclusively around material kids aren't supposed to know about. It features the Tex Avery dog Droopy and *Scooby Doo*'s Shaggy in a convertible, talking about how the Time Warner-owned cable channel's now seen worldwide, when Shaggy asks, "Do you know what they call *Pound Puppies* in France?" Explaining how there's no such thing as "pounds" in the metric system, Shaggy then asks, "What do they call *Smurfs* in Spain?" His answer: "*Los Smurfs.*"

To quote the Cartoon Network show *2 Stupid Dogs*, "Well isn't that cute — but it's *wrong!*" As anyone who went to the Smurf theme park in France knows, the late Belgian cartoonist Peyo's critters have a different cutesy name in each major Euro language (*Stroumphs, Schlumphs,* et al.). In Spain, *"Los Pitufos."* *(Oct. 9, 1997)*

Dishing It Out: I hear from more and more people these days who're getting, or wish they could get, a satellite dish. There's even one guy who works on a public access program who told me he wants to replace his cable TV connection with a dish, even though he'd no longer receive his own show at home. The cable companies, meanwhile, are still feeling the PR fallout from prior censorship drives and are shying away from promoting the access channel as an asset you can only get with cable.

The cable people promise to combat the dishes with digital transmission and dozens more channels — one of these years. If that doesn't stem cable's loss of market share, how will access producers make their works available to ex-cable households? Maybe via streaming-video web sites, particularly if promised higher-speed modems and more powerful home computers make that more feasible. But that won't be free to producers, unless

Sources of Hope:

1. Cmmunications technologies available to individuals, from the computer programs that make this document possible to the fax machines that helped give the world the real news from Beijing.

2. The end of economies of scale favoring big business over independent business, as merged corporations make consumers and employees pay for the misadventures of the speculation parasites.

3. The whole Eastern Europe thing.

4. A progressive, aware populace that doesn't know how big it is compared to any era except '67-'70.

5. A slowly-growing realization that the sins of the Nixon-Reagan era shouldn't be mistaken for virtues.

(continued)

somebody donates server space at an Internet service provider. I could imagine that happening for shows allied to established political or religious groups.

But what of the more personal statements? Who'll support the streaming of *Goddess Kring* or *Tea Talk with Leroy Chin*? An arts group or producers' co-op could do it, but even those outfits would probably have somebody deciding who could or couldn't use their services. The freewheeling, no-gatekeepers thang that is today's access channel might be something we'd better enjoy while still in its prime. *(Feb. 12, 1998)*

Borders Books held an *Ally McBeal* fan party and trivia competition on Aug. 20. Seeing this tribute to gushily pathetic "vulnerability" next to the diet and fashion books brought me a revelation: *Ally* isn't a sex-object fantasy, it's a target-marketing fantasy. An attempt at female-oriented counterprogramming opposite the male-targeted *Monday Night Football* and cable pro-wrestling shows, built around the most exploitive stereotypes from modern women's-magazine articles. Of course, that's just as antithetical to feminist precepts as any sex-object fantasy would be. *(Sept. 3, 1998)*

As you might expect, the last week of KSTW's local news (mandated by the station's current owner, Viacom) played out as both personal desparation (clips of old cute-dog stories strung together by a staff obviously intent on assembling demo reels for its resumes) and light pathos (co-anchorman Don Porter holding up a "Will Anchor For Food" sign). The headline graphic for the top story on the final newscast (a story about a newly-found cache of dynamite in Puyallup): "TNT Destroyed." KSTW's original call letters, several owners ago, were KTNT (from its original owner, the *Tacoma News Tribune*).

Also throughout the final broadcast, the station ran the logo from its old ownership by Gaylord Broadcasting — not the ugly "UPN 11" symbol Viacom management had imposed. The cancellation means 62 newsroom and studio layoffs, and turns what had been one of the strongest non-big-three-network stations in the country into just another mere outlet for reruns and forgettable semi-network shows (can you even name any UPN original production other than *Star Trek Voyager*?). *(Dec. 7, 1998)*

An ex-Soviet republic exploited the fifth anniversary of Cobain's death to sell stamps to foreign collectors.

30: 'GRUNGE'

or, the other dreaded G-word

Our local officials used to spend a lot of money trying to lure Hollywood producers to use Seattle and Washington state as location-filming sites (something far different than, and ultimately less economically rewarding than, indigenous cultural production). In more recent years, taxpayer millions have helped build a fancy art museum, a fancy symphony hall, and several fancy playhouses.

But Seattle's biggest contribution to the world's cultural landscape was not only realized without handouts, but with the active opposition of many officials, who tried to crack down against street posters, homeless-teen panhandlers, and all-ages concerts (while the town's established nightclub circuit almost completely shut out creative rock bands in favor of boomer "blues" formulas).

Some of these same politicians later said they couldn't understand what there could possibly be for young rebels to rebel against in this supposed best of all possible regions.

That tireless champion of the Bellevueization of Seattle, city attorney Doug Jewett, is out to eliminate a major contributor to public ugliness — no, not megadevelopers like Martin Selig or Harbor Properties, but struggling local musicians and theater groups who put up street posters.

Art Chantry's book *Instant Litter* proved that poster art, by bringing new ideas by "outsider" artists to the public, can raise the visual literacy of a city. This has helped lead Seattle to national leadership in graphic design. Local designers are working for corporate clients throughout the world; the success of our teen-fashion companies is firmly based in their bold "street" graphics. A vibrant cacophony of posters helps bring a truly cosmopolitan air to a city, something the makers of sterile towers hate almost as much as they hate housing advocates. *(January 1988)*

We're prouder than heck that *Rolling Stone* declared Seattle the "New Liverpool". This must mean we're a decaying western seaport, far from its country's power centers, inhabited by roughhousing gay sailors with an incomprehensible accent. Or, to quote UK statesman Benjamin Disraeli, "I am deeply sorry for the unkind things I said about Liverpool. I had not seen Leeds at the time." *(May 1992)*

What the '80s Have Given Us
(continued)

Top Local Stories:

1. Few noticed in 1980 when tiny Seattle Software sold a computer operating system to a slightly bigger company, Microsoft. MS-DOS made King County the world leader in making computers work for people. It was this leadership that led an obscure Japanese toy company to put its U.S. HQ here, leading to the Nintendo video games now sharpening the hand-eye coordination of so many pre-adolescents.

OK OK OK, Misc. is now ready to admit that the "Seattle Sound" is dead. The evidence: not *Singles,* but the Sept. 13 travel page of the Sunday newspaper insert *USA Weekend* (stuffed into the Bellevue *Journal-American* and dozens of other papers around the country), right after the Haband ad for mail order men's slacks. The headline: "Get Set for the Seattle Sound: Next weekend's rockin' movie *Singles* puts the limelight on this musical metropolis."

As Jim Kelton writes, "Just as Memphis has the blues, Chicago and New Orleans have Jazz, and Nashville owns country, Seattle now has its own hard-driving sound, dubbed 'grunge rock,' giving travelers another reason to visit the city... Visitors will find entertaining and fiercely outspoken music in nearly every corner of this sprawling city. But first-timers should note that the best spots to hear its sounds aren't always upscale. You can take in the sights during the day, then fill the nights with the fresh Seattle sound."

The page gave prospective grunge-tourists listings of five clubs, two costly hotels (including the Meany Tower, inaccurately described as being close to many important grunge venues), the youth hostel, and two eateries: 13 Coins and the Dog House ("the 'in' place for musicians and music fans").

Now let's get this straight: The article encourages tourists to come here to see live gigs by the very bands that got into making records in the mid-'80s because they couldn't get live gigs. The music that was rejected by so many clubs for so many years might now become a boon to the state's hospitality industry.

Maybe we should just replace Seattle Center with a Grungeland theme park!

Flannel-shirted costume characters could sneeringly blow Export A smoke into the eager eyes of affluent American families, on their way to enjoy hourly indoor and outdoor performances in between stops at a Jimmy the Geek house of thrills, senior citizen moshing lessons, an all-vegan food circus, bumper cars that look like beat-up Datsuns, wandering Iggy impersonators, beer-can crushing competitions, a detox clinic fantasy ride, (for the gents) a contest to become L7's chaste bondage slaves, and (for the ladies) an all-scrawny, all-longhair male strip show. *(October 1992)*

That "Seattle fashion" craze invented in New York has reached Europe, according to articles in the London *Sunday Times* and the Italian edition of *Glamour.* The

Sunday Times piece called Seattle "almost Canadian in its boringness." *(February 1993)*

Moshpit Tourism Update: I told you before of a dorky *Boston Globe* story about the spread of "grunge culture" to that city. The paper's since run a two-page Sunday travel piece about "the Seattle mindset," which writer Pamela Reynolds calls "a vague cynicism paired ironically with progressive idealism." She calls Seattle home to "funky organic restaurants, odorous boulangeries, and inviting juice gardens." She lauds North 45th Street as a bastion of "dining, Seattle Style. That is to say, if you have a taste for hamburgers, hot dogs, steaks, or French fries, this is not the place to be" (must not have been to Dick's).

If there is a "Seattle mindset," it's one that throws up at sentimental touristy pap like this. Think about it: If we're now world famous for our angry young men and women, maybe there's something here that they're justifiably angry about. *(March 1993)*

In Bloom: When I told people I wanted to write a book about the local music scene, most said "you'd better get it out right away. Nobody will care about Seattle next month." I don't know if the "Seattle sound" is really the flash in the pan that so many local wags think (hoping they can go back to their familiar nihilism?). People here are so used to obscurity, when the spotlight shines they squint and wait for it to stop.

But like I've written before, this could just be the flash that lights a lasting fire. Sub Pop record entrepreneurs Jonathan Poneman and Bruce Pavitt shrewdly took a subgenre that's been developing for 10 years, put a slogan on it, made it the Next Big Thing and made us its capital. But the sound they built isn't one of those short-half-life sounds like power pop. It's an identifiable sound, imitable yet sufficiently diverse to allow infinite variations. The dozens of "generic grunge" bands now playing opening sets at the Off Ramp could form the tourist bedrock of a permanent scene, like the "generic country" bands in small Nashville bars, bringing in the bucks and attention to support more advanced work. If we play our cards right, Seattle could become the Nashville of rock.

But not if the forces of repression have their way, as led by our city's "progressive" political machine. Most mayors like to kiss up to their town's fastest growing industry, but not ours. From feminist/prohibitionists to the tepid *No Nukes* concert film, some of the most adamant political liberals were cultural conservatives. Norm Rice wrote

2. In 1982, I was among those who scorned the new official nickname "Emerald City." It was totally inappropriate to the Seattle I knew and loved. In the eight years since, large portions of the city and its suburbs have been rebuilt to fit the name. The bus tunnel, the Bagley Wright Theater, Westlake Center, 10- and 11-cornered office towers, "luxury townhomes," candy-colored Archie Bunker houses in the north end and the fake chateaus on the eastside, the planned gussying-up of Seattle Center — all these reflect the dangerous idea that this is some fantasy paradise where all will be mindless nirvana. This is a real place, with real people and real problems. The sooner we all realize this, the sooner we can start working on real solutions.

(January 1990)

the Teen Dance Ordinance as a City Council member; as mayor, he's apparently behind the actions to shut down all-ages concerts and raves and the effort to seize part ownership of RKCNDY. Rice comes from the disciplinarian side of the black middle class, where adults want young people to strive hard at all times and avoid idle temptations like pop music. Rice doesn't get that the rock scene is a hard-working, industrious bunch of people empowering themselves. He calls himself a "supporter of the arts" while clamping down against Seattle's first indigenous artform since the '50s Northwest School painters. He promotes Seattle as a "KidsPlace" while trying to shut young people up. *(April 1993)*

Dept. of Amplification: The city should support punk culture, instead of continuing to harass it. Seattle's government and mainstream media still believe in the sentiments uttered by KIRO-TV commentator Lou Guzzo back in 1986, supporting the infamous Teen Dance Ordinance. In one of the most reactionary utterances ever made on local airwaves, Guzzo essentially called punks worthless losers; if teenagers were bored, he said they should take up hiking or skiing — consumer leisure pursuits that wouldn't lead to questioning the established sociopolitical order.

Punks believe in living in big cities. They believe in creativity. They believe in making their own world, in making up their own minds. Punks believe in downtown shopping, public transportation, and public gathering places. Punks seem like nihilists to many outsiders, but really believe in actively working for a better world. In the developing information age, they're pioneers in info-entrepreneurism. They make their own records, they book their own gigs, they paint their own posters, they publish their own zines — a collection of skills that seem like marginal pursuits to most people over 40, but which will be vital to the key industries of the 21st century.

Punks aren't hopeless dropout ne'er-do-wells. They've created one of the Seattle area's four or five top export industries. They've helped make us a world-class arts center, with a reputation as a focal point for aspiring enthusiastic creative types from all over. *(April 1994)*

Punk rock had developed in New York as an arty affectation. England took it seriously as a voice of youthful anger. The local new wave scenes across the U.S. took the DIY aesthetic of punk even more seriously, eventually questioning the very need for New York/London

Name That Tune

A couple weeks back, ***Misc.*** *asked you to name formerly-popular North American musical genres that haven't been subjected to "hip" revival attempts in recent years.*

I wanted to see what, if any, pieces of America's musical heritage could still be enjoyed as honest expressions of art or showmanship, without PoMo irony smoothing out their creases.

Some of your recommendations, with some of my comments:

Accordions. *Nominated by someone who'd likely never heard of the Black Cat Orchestra, Those Darn Accordions, the various "punk polka" sub-fads, or even Weird Al. Face it: Accordions are hip, and have been for some time.*

tastemakers. Kurt Cobain emerged amidst this indie-rock movement, among guys who'd chosen not to listen when the industry said punk was dead.

Cobain and Krist Novoselic started playing together when they were 19. By the time Cobain turned 21 in 1988, Nirvana was becoming a big fish in the still-small pond that was the Seattle club scene. By the next year they had an album and were part of TAD's European tour; by all accounts it was a miserable experience, with Cobain having a nervous breakdown onstage at the last show.

While tagged by out-of-town media as the Leader of the Grunge Rock Revolution, he hadn't been a central member of the hard-partying, extroverted schmoozers who had developed the punk-metal crossover sounds in Seattle.

He was an inwardly-directed soul who, during Nirvana's club years, holed up in an Olympia apartment and lived on corn dogs and cough syrup. While he kept his private life private, he put his personal torments into his work with a rare purity and clarity. It was his curse/blessing to be the best songwriter of his generation, and to be ripe for the picking just as "alternative rock" was becoming a big business.

But it was his decision to go to Geffen Records; if *Nevermind* had come out on Sub Pop, as was first planned, it might have sold a few thousand copies, the label would have continued its slide into bankruptcy, and the Seattle rock hype would have died down leaving Soundgarden as national stars but few others.

We'll probably never really know what finally led him to quit the world. Perhaps it was the slip back into drugs after the highly-publicized hell he went through to get off heroin. Or perhaps the hype and the pressure finally got to him. *(May 1994)*

Gathering of the Vultures: The vehemence with which conservative and old-hippie commentators alike treated Cobain and his fans is unprecedented in my lifetime, unless you count the bio-sleaze books of Albert Goldman (who thankfully died before he could write a Kurt exploitation book) or the Arizona politicians who wanted to prevent a Martin Luther King holiday by red-baiting King 20 years after his death.

Rush Limbaugh called Kurt "a piece of human debris" and treated Nirvana listeners with equal disrespect; thus proving for all time the essential cruelty behind his worldview. If Limbaugh deliberately gloated over the demise of an opposition spokesperson, Andy Rooney

Political folk (pre-'60s), *such as IWW rally songs. Joe Kiethly (a.k.a. Joey Shithead of Vancouver punk pioneers DOA) included some of these in his Bumbershoot solo-acoustic set. They fit perfectly with his own kill-the-yuppies ballads, showing how a punk can grow old, stay angry, and stake his place in an older protestt radition.*

Gospel. *One of Paul Simon's earliest homage victims back in the '70s, its influence can be at least indirectly felt in some of those R&B love-song harmony groups so big on KUBE these past couple of years.*

Ragtime. *If the Squirrel Nut Zippers can bring back the jitterbug, somebody can bring back the rag, last revived a quarter-century ago in the aftermath of* The Sting *soundtrack (Randy Newman's score for the 1981 film* Ragtime *doesn't count).*

Pan flute.
One of the few foreign-exotica musics not yet assimilated by the Luaka Bop/World Beat homogenizers. I like it that way.

Muzak.
The real thing, not merely easy-listening instrumentals like 101 Strings. The Grunge Lite CD *(made in 1994 by Sara DeBell) came close, but lacked the essential ingredient of real Muzak: "Stimulus Progression," the Muzak company's trademark for a 15-minute set of tunes that starts slow-'n'-soft and ends up slightly less slow-n'-soft toenhance workers' spirits and productivity. God knows plenty of bands could use this principle in planning their sets.*

Lawrence Welk.
(And, presumably, other conserva-core ensembles like the King Family, Mitch Miller, and Guy Lombardo.) This would be darn near the ultimate challenge: Making something hip out of something whose utter and complete squareness was its entire raison d'etre. It'd be even tougher if it were attempted on a non-parody level.

was merely clueless in his denunciation of Cobain, and by extension anyone who loved him, as a "loser" not worthy of respect, only condescending pity.

Locally, that pious hypocrite John Carlson echoed the Limbaugh party line in claiming the "sad and pathetic" Cobain should have quit music and found religion (as if Carlson has ever represented sincere Christian charity).

P-I cartoonist David Horsey was at least more sympathetic when he suggested that Kurt could've found solace if he'd done more hiking in the woods; Kurt grew up near the woods, and from all accounts was more in touch with the terror of timber country than with its majesty.

Then there's *Times* columnist Eric Lacitis, whose profound and utter incomprehension of Cobain, his music, his depression and his audience was matched only by his intransigence. First, he wrote a snide "joke" about Cobain's March coma for a Sunday feature section that was printed before his death but distributed after it. Then, he wrote a "serious" column questioning what somebody with all that money could possibly have to worry about. Then, when many readers rightfully objected, Lacitis wrote a succession of shallow arguments attempting to defend his earlier bluster.

This is more than just the case of some oldsters who don't get that new music (even though Cobain worked in a nearly 20-year-old genre). It's the case of people who are paid to communicate, yet who lack a basic understanding of their topic, and in some cases have been defensive and even proud of their own ignorance. If the media business really wants to know why today's young adults are consuming more books but far fewer newspapers and TV newscasts, it need only look to its own industry-wide "just call me another old white guy who doesn't get it" attitude. Not "getting it" is not a positive quality, and neither is inhumanity. *(May 1994)*

Reminder to the Media: When Bob Hardwick, Seattle's leading middle-of-the-road radio personality for some 30 years, tragically shot himself a year or two ago, you didn't see any dorky commentators claiming the suicide proved that all middle-aged Sinatra fans were pathetic losers. *(June 1994)*

Fade Away Not: In the first weeks after the Cobain tragedy, I heard several locals privately refer to it as the closing chapter in the "Seattle scene" mania. Does it really mean "the party's over" locally? Ever since Mudhoney first appeared on the cover of *Melody Maker* almost six years ago, some people here have expected (and even hoped) that the bigtime music-biz would quickly tire of Seattle and everyone could go back to playing just for one another. It hasn't happened yet, despite the concerted efforts of the media to shoehorn all Seattle bands into one stereotyped fad, and then to declare that fad over.

Face it: The corporate entertainment establishment's scared of people outside N.Y./L.A. making their own culture, refusing to be good passive consumers. Seattle rock isn't one singular sound, but it does represent an attitude of DIY production and distribution, of creating things you really like that communicate directly with audiences because they really like it. Just how well this formula worked was proved by the immensity with which Cobain's death shocked and saddened people.

The tragic loss of a singular artist and the end of Seattle's premier band threw everybody for a big harsh wallop and made everything seem a whole hell of a lot less fun, but it doesn't change the fact that the Northwest has two dozen other major-label bands at last count. There are as many as 50 other world-class indie acts in Washington and Oregon, playing a wide variety of sounds, plus hundreds of fascinating/fun/dull/bombastic club acts.

I've found that California people used to like Seattle when it was thought of as little more than a good market for California-made culture product (L.A. films and fashions, S.F. bands and authors), a friendly rival to the L.A. aerospace-defense industry, and a middle-aged-hippie retirement home with good pot and lotsa magic mushrooms ripe for the pickin'.

But somewhere along the line, us Nordic hicks started getting uppity; some of us thought we could create some of our own culture for a change. Maybe it was these Seattle rock bands and theater troupes that got the southwesterners to notice our new attitude; maybe it was when the pivot point of the PC biz moved from Palo Alto to Redmond. In any event, I've seen a lot of attempts by California writers and commentators to put us northern yahoos back in our place.

The corporate culture industry of L.A. and the bohemian culture industry of S.F. both have a vested stake in preventing the DIY empowerment Seattle represents. All the rock-journalism hype about "Looking for the Next Seattle" was based on trying to promote the image that Seattle had just been a place where a few good bands were ready to be absorbed into the media machine, and that any other town might have similarly-exploitable tal-

Marching tunes. *Now we're getting somewhere. As local-radio vet Norm Gregory writes, "I don't think Dr. Dre has sampled march music yet... but I might be wrong." It's a form not heard on the pop charts since "Tusk" in 1979 (perhaps Fleetwood Mac's greatest moment). A decade before that, the Monty Python folks took their theme from ol' J.P. Sousa's "Liberty Bell March," finding the spirit of old English music-hall bombast in this most American of composers. There was an "Anti-Fascist Marching Band" in town in the late '80s and early '90s, but if it's still around it's kept a mighty low profile lately. Slightly-skewed marches are a big part of the Doo Dah Parade, mounted by Pasadena, Calif. locals every November as a Rose Parade alternative.*

Sousa's compositions helped launch the recording industry 120 years ago — they were short, loud, and brassy; perfect for Edison's unelectrified horn mics and cylinder phonographs. They're still loud, short, and brassy, and they involve instruments taught at almost every high school. All they need is a different context, so kids stop thinking of them as something militaristic (or worse, as something teachers and parents force upon kids).

Calypso. *Jesse Walker writes, "I hereby predict that by the end of 1998 we will have been treated to a spate of headlines that announce, 'Generation X Is Discovering Harry Belafonte!'" Actually, Belafonte was rediscovered almost a decade ago, with the* Beetlejuice *soundtrack. Calypso tuneage (particularly the bizarre Robert Mitchum LP* Calypso Is Like So...*) gets heavy play at neo-cocktail venues.*

ent. They're not willing to admit that Seattle and the other local scenes represent a threat to corporate rock's very existence. *(June 1994)*

Stock It To Me: Stock-music production companies are now coming out with "alternative rock" production music for use in commercials, TV shows, low-budget films, industrial films, video games, porn, etc. The Minnesota-based HyperClips company offers "Alterna," a package of 40 "alternative rock and dance tracks. Give your project an edge with these grungy and atmospheric pieces. With all the moodiness and aggression that the Alternative styles have to offer, with everything from mellow acoustic grooves to hardcore distorted jams." The Fresh Music Library, meanwhile, claims its "Alternative Rock" CD features "production values heard on today's college and alternative rock radio stations... These themes evoke U2, Nirvana, R.E.M., the Smithereens and others. Exactly the disc for youthful energy." *(May 29, 1996)*

The major record companies, MTV, and commercial radio have succeeded at killing "alternative" music by ignoring or mishandling today's more original artists in favor of promoting the most formulaic, derivative bands. (How can anything called "Blur" be distinctive? How can anything called "Garbage" be really good?) That, and the maturing of the late-'80s music scenesters beyond prime moshing age, has left a distinct malaise over the local scene. Many of the more promising 1993-94 bands have broken up. Others are wallowing in the purgatory of record-label nonsupport. The three top local clubs get their biggest draws from touring acts. Everybody from the *N.Y. Times* to *Time* has noted how the latest Pearl Jam, Soundgarden, and Presidents discs are vastly underselling their predecessors.

But they're underplaying the fact that overall record sales are holding steady, despite the drop in superstar sales. This means more listeners are listening to a wider variety of stuff, not just the same few hyped celebrities. For everyone except the major labels and the celeb-obsessed media, this is good news. It's good for musicians, for indie labels, for the stores that bother to stock indie labels, for clubs, for fans who prefer non-arena venues, for publications like this that tell you who the heck all these touring indie bands are, and especially for my oft-stated ideal of a decentralized culture, where smaller groups of people are into things they really like instead of following the dictates of mass marketing. This is, at least on one level, what the Seattle music scene had been all about — not providing material for the rock star machine, but building an alternative to the rock star machine. To quote one of Sub Pop founder Bruce Pavitt's early zines, "A decentralized cultural network is obviously cool. Way cool."

When the dust settles from this industry-wide reorganization, I fully expect Seattle's bands, managers, and labels to be better equipped than most for a post-superstar world. (And don't worry about the Soundgarden guys; they can always sell more of their band-photo phone cards thru their fan club.) *(Jan. 2, 1997)*

After the Gold Rush: Spent three hours the other day being interviewed by an Amsterdam magazine writer. She wanted to know how much everybody here loved the "Seattle Scene" hype of a few years back, how grateful everybody was that it had ended, whether everything had now "returned to normal," whether it all could've ended up differently, and what'll happen here next. My replies:

(1) Actually, different people here had different takes on the mania. Nearly everyone wanted a music scene that'd be bigger than it'd been in 1989, with just a couple of tiny clubs and near-nonexistent opportunities for recording or touring. But a lot of folks were (and some still are) adamant about the indie-rock ideology and did not like the forces of Corporate Rock barging in, strip-mining the better bands, and abandoning the remaining refuse.

(2) Many musicians who didn't get signed by the majors in 1991-93 were disappointed the A&R reps stopped showing up in droves. But others were grateful for the perceived chance to promote their work outside the media glare — like all those bands who'd spent so much effort explaining how they weren't "grunge," they didn't get around to letting people know what they were.

(3) Thankfully, things aren't all back to the sorry state they'd been in. The mania left us with an infrastructure of clubs, labels, studios, producers, promoters, and (perhaps more important) the idea that you can indeed make your own music and art and it can be good and it doesn't have to conform to outside dictates. (I wish this lesson could be learned by the local dance-music community, which has gotten more progressive than it had been but is still too content to follow styles dictated from elsewhere, too afraid to attempt its own things.)

(4) The interviewer thought we'd have had more of a legacy had bands here been more willing participants in

Indian ragas. *Thanks to India being an ex-UK colony, the lushly over-the-top sounds of Indian movie musicals are common in London immigrant neighborhoods these days. These tunes are starting to infiltrate London's white-hipster DJ clubs. There've already been raga nights at Seattle dance clubs like the Vogue; they're bigger in Vancouver, with its bigger Subcontinent immigrant community.*

Truck drivin' songs. *The roots-country revival chronicled in* No Depression *magazine seems to have passed by such gems as C.W. McCall's "Convoy" and Red Sovine's "Teddy Bear." 'Tis a pity.*

Bluegrass. Reader James Freudiger, describing himself as "an old fart of a beatnik, and in my fifties," says he remembers "nothing more in the spirit of D.I.Y. than sitting around someone's living room… shamelessly attempting falsetto harmonies while two or three friends plucked away at banjo, mandolin, etc. Even if you didn't play an instrument there was always the jug, spoons, and inverted pots." Sounds almost like a typical early-week night at the Tractor Tavern.

(Sept. 11 and 25, 1997)

the music-industry game. She seemed to think if Eddie Vedder had been more willing to make videos and tour with TicketMaster, the industry wouldn't have bothered with the likes of Blur or Stone Temple Pilots. I'm not sure.

By insisting on doing things their way (Sir Mix-A-Lot not going "gangsta;" Mudhoney staying out of big record-company debt; Bikini Kill staying out of big record companies altogether), the bands might or might not have had a bigger hit or two, but they stayed truer to their own visions, which'll probably prove best for their art and their careers.

(5) Five years ago, the world saw Seattle as a teeming pool of youthful angst against restricted economic opportunities and stifling social conservatism. Today, the world sees Seattle as a fortress of imperial capitalists out to smother the world under cookie-cutter coffee shops and mediocre software. Neither vision's very accurate, but that's beside the point. Seattle is, however, a generally more prosprous place today, at least for the white middle-class segments most music people come from. With relative prosperity comes a different angst, the feeling that everything "real" is threatened by upscale-bland yuckiness. That will create a different notion of rebellion. Maybe we'll see some artistic results of that notion next year. *(Dec. 18, 1997)*

Closing Time?: An *N.Y.Times* story on Oct. 15 discussed the precipitous decline of commercial rock as a music-biz force, noting sales charts now dominated by rap and rap/R&B hybrid acts. One quoted industry expert said "the Seattle bands" had been rock's last best hope, but Nirvana ended and Pearl Jam got lost in its politics and the whole Rock Reformation got sidetracked.

I'd put the blame on the suckiness of chain-run rock radio and MTV, which have bled the patient (themselves) to near-death with their repitition, selection of awful bland-rock acts, and stupidity. Of course, the suckiness of corporate rock radio (and of corporate rock promotion in general) is one of the things the Seattle bands had been trying to rebel against. *(Oct. 22, 1998)*

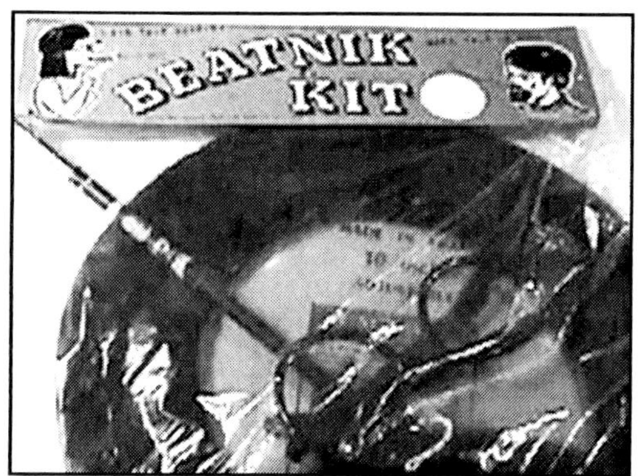

31: 'ALTERNATIVE' CULTURE

or, it's square to be hip

The Baffler's 1993 essay "Alternative to What?" proposed that "rock 'n' roll is the health of the state," that "rebellious" attitudes and styles are necessary in a consumer culture built on target marketing and planned obsolescence.

I'd go a little further — "rebellious" attitudes and styles, as practiced according to U.S. hipster traditions dating at least back to the 1920s, only reinforce the tired old values of the so-called "mainstream America" the bohemians claim to be rebelling against.

If I'm right about this being a new era, we're gonna need a new aesthetic to go with it. It's not just that the Clintons and Gores don't like harsh lyrics and other shock art, but that they don't like the divisive concept behind them.

The visions of Karen Finley and Henry Rollins are clumsily reversed clones of the GOP's politics of hate. The Young Republicans long ago co-opted the image of the self-made rebel sneering at the petty concerns of the little people; there's no point in alternative artists acting like that anymore. There's still a helluva lot to be angry about, but it needs to be answered by a more inclusive kind of anger, something that goes beyond the mere vilification of enemies. Now that 62 percent of the voters have rejected the organized Right, it may be time for the art world to reconsider its hostility against the so-called "sap masses" and to start communicating with people about the real problems. Leftist art used to be about promoting solidarity with the working classes; it can be about that again.

The post-Bush era also means there's less value in enduring bad art just so you can smugly know that you've consumed something the Right would hate. What counts now is whether you like it. *(December 1992)*

I don't just want you to question the assumptions of mainstream culture. I want you to question the assumptions of *your* culture. The hip-vs.-square concept is the alternative culture's unexamined legacy from the beats' misinterpretation of jazz lingo. In the N.Y. jazz scene, "hepcats" (derived, sez local author/filmmaker Zola Mumford, from the Senegalese word *hipicat,* "one who is very aware of their surroundings") were those who played and/or listened to advanced black music (instead of the watered down Paul Whiteman versions) and who'd mastered the complex codes of social gamesmanship in Manhattan. It was a concept for a specific time/place that no longer exists.

Futures Trading

This li'l corner-O-newsprint ain't my sole ambition in life. There's plenty of other things I've always wanted:

My own restaurant. *Under the big neon sign that just says EAT, the Merry* **Misc.** *Cafe would serve honest grub at honest prices. On the menu: Burgers, cheese steaks, whole-cut fries, meat loaf, fruit-cocktail salad. In the lounge: Old fashioneds, Brew 66, naughty-joke cartoon napkins. On the walls: framed drawings by alternative cartoonists, a Silent Radio LED displaying post-post-modern aphorisms, a TV displaying old-time car commercials or women's bowling coverage.*

My own cereal. *Frosted Miscberry Crunch would have the taste, and the crunch, that wakes a person up after a long night of arguing in bars about macroeconomic trends. Each box comes with a mini-Mensa exam on the back and a "Great Postpunk Singer-Songwriters" trading card inside.*

Square people these days are a lot hipper than a lot of self-proclaimed hipsters. Squares enjoy drag queens on *Geraldo* and buy male pinup posters. Squares buy Soundgarden CDs and watch *The Simpsons*. Squares grow and haul the food we eat. Squares make our cars. Squares support education and world-relief drives. As Wes "Scoop" Nisker writes in his book *Crazy Wisdom*, "the illusion that we are separate and special is the root of our suffering." There is no superior race (not even yours). There is no superior gender or gender-role (not even yours). There is no superior culture (not even yours). *(April 1993)*

Over-the-Counterculture: You sometimes hear about old radical groups that got infiltrated by FBI informers. In some accounts, the plants prodded the groups into illegal acts or spurring internal dissentions. But I wonder if they ever got subliminal messages into those old light shows, implanting time-release instructions to the freaks: "By 1971 you will get hooked on pot, move to the country, and care only about yourselves."

When I was in college in the early '80s, some of the most personally complacent and artistically reactionary people were the ones who also wouldn't stop bragging about how open-minded they were in The Sixties. When I was on KCMU I closed my DJ shift with the tagline, "Rock on — never mellow out." I didn't want my listeners to turn into self-obsessed fogeys intolerant of anything that didn't conform to their increasingly narrow worldview.

Now, hardly a week goes by that I don't meet somebody 10 years younger than me emulating everything that frustrated me about the people 10 years older than me. Here in the *Geraldo* era I meet young adults who still find something "rebellious" about Hunter Thompson, that professional self-aggrandizer who presaged today's reporter-as-celebrity hype. I've read Terence McKenna essays that criticize "linear Western Civilization" as if it still existed. And it's not just 40-year-olds anymore who mistake "What a long strange trip it's been" for a profound statement.

I'm even getting young people treating me with the same stereotypes old people used on me — like the stereotype that anybody who doesn't adhere to a "leftist lifestyle" must be a political conservative. I've heard food co-op purists condemn all supermarket shoppers or all TV viewers as fascist rednecks; the argument reminds me of the Fundamentalists of my hometown who avowed that the Mormons would go to Hell because of their incorrect doctrine.

That's a perfect attitude for moralistic posturing, but a lousy way to build a progressive political movement. To see why, let's examine some unexamined presumptions going back to the Beat Generation.

The button-down conformity of the '50s was not the way society had always been. Some WWII-generation intellectuals saw '50s culture being created, and rebelled against it. Their central premise, as watered down and reinterpreted over the years, was that all of America could be neatly divided into two groups: Hipsters (enlightened intellectuals and artists, plus those whom the intellectuals and artists chose to romanticize) and Squares (everybody else).

The hippies took this premise to its logical extreme, and in doing so tore the American left apart from the working class it once claimed to champion. By stereotyping all non-hippies as fascists and rednecks, they wrote off the potential support base for any real populist uprising. They sometimes claimed to be the voice of The People, but their definition of The People got narrower every year. Spiro Agnew got away with calling leftists "effete snobs" because leftists allowed themselves to be perceived as a self-serving elite.

By the early '70s, black activists started charging that the counterculture didn't even care about minorities anymore, only about white middle-class women and white middle-class gays.

More recently, minority leaders have questioned the environmental movement's priorities, asserting that toxic waste sites in ethnic neighborhoods are at least as important an issue as hiking trails.

Today, BMW drivers call themselves "rebels" and beer commercials promise to make you "Different From The Rest." There is no "mass culture" to rebel against anymore. Society's been fragmented into demographic and subcultural mini-states, influenced by specialty advertising concepts and demographic target marketing.

The "counterculture" is now just another market niche; organic foods in this store, ethnic foods in the next. If you tout yourself as somehow "apart" from Big Bad America on the basis of what you eat or what you wear or what age group you are, you're still letting the segmented-consumer metaphor define you.

To be truly "political" would be to forge alliances with people beyond your own subculture, to reach out across our fragmented society, to build coalitions and exert

My own hydroplane. *Watch the valiant Miss* **Misc.** *roar in the time trials, with rock-band bumper stickers strewn over its sponsons! Shudder as it flips on a harsh turn in Heat 2A! Cheer as the underfunded, underequipped pit crew uses duct tape and extra stickers to fix it in time for a come-from-behind victory in the Consolation Heat!*

My own travel agency. *Misctour would arrange charter bus, train, and journeys to all the truly great vacation spots — Tacoma! Ritzville! Bend! Wisconsin Dells! Akron! Tulsa! Moose Jaw! Dollywood! Wall Drug! And the finest traveling amenities — clothing-optional planes; scat-singing tour guides; the Game Show Network in every motel room; complementary copies of DeLillo's* Underworld; *emocore karaoke parties; free ice.*

My own (commercial) TV show. *I've actually tried to make this happen, rounding up crews and shooting test footage on three occasions in the past two years.*

But it's proven a tough nut to get an independently-produced series onto a regular broadcast station (not cable access).

I've heard from producers with much more experience than I, who've all told the same stories of stations afraid to take a chance.

Still, I believe broadcasters will eventually realize local programming (of all sorts, not just sports or mayhem-centric news) is their best competitive weapon against the growing horde of cable, satellite, and (soon) Net-based video feeds.

(June 11, 1998)

influence to help make a better world. We don't need to tear the fabric of society apart; big business already did it. We need to figure how to sew it back together. *(April 1994)*

The local boomer-generation litzine *Point No Point* just came out with an Allen Ginsberg tribute by Stephen Thomas, who claimed "every left-of-center social movement since the '50s is traceable back through Ginsberg's poetic vision." For good or ill, Thomas might be right.

In the months since his demise, I only found one obit (in *The Nation*) that emphasized his writing instead of just how kewl a dood he was. This may be how he'd want to be remembered. He exemplified many annoying hipster trends: the incessant self-promotion, the championing of celebrity above artistry, the simplistic Hip vs. Square dichotomy, the concept of culture as something created exclusively in N.Y./L.A./S.F. and merely consumed elsewhere. No wonder the folks at MTV loved him. He had the same business plan! *(June 5, 1997)*

En 'Garde': A kindly reader spotted the following graffito on a recent trip to Montreal: "Artists are the shock troops of gentrification." Actually, it's not as cynical a notion as it might first sound.

Remember, the term "avant-garde" originally meant the the vanguard of an advancing army (i.e., the shock troops). The notion, which goes counter to the more currently fashionable image of the permanently underground art world, was that the cutting-edge artists led where the rest of us followed.

So it'd only be natural to extend that metaphor into formerly industrial urban neighborhoods as well as urbane aesthetic styles. *(May 7, 1998)*

GO FLY A KITE...
And choose one from our large selection.
UWAJIMAYA
JAPANESE IMPORTS
9:00-6:00 DAILY

32: SUB GOES THE CULTURE

or, civil wars and 'civil society'

One of orthodox bohemianism's problems is its self-proclamation to be the one and only possible way to think or behave besides the way of dumb ol' Wonder-Bread America. As mentioned in the preface, Jack Kerouac tried his damndest to turn people on to the incredible life and energy that is America at its best.

Of course, America, like any individual within it, doesn't always behave at its best. But even in cruelty it's a place of vigor and passion, of all sorts of people from all sorts of places, saying and doing an increasingly varied amount of things.

Some people are afraid of this cacophany. They want to promote something they call "civil society," a concept based on the fantasy that the late-'50s political stability had been based on mass consensus instead of a few interest groups hogging all the power for themselves.

The Artists for a Hate-Free America show at the Seattle Center Arena was great, and its cause is greater: combating hate crimes, anti-gay initiatives and all-around bigotry. But its PR packet is wrong when it recounts examples of hate at work and then asserts, "This Is Not America." Alas, it is. America was and is, to a great extent, a country run on fear and greed, on conquest and demonization. But some of us like to think it doesn't have to stay that way.
(October 1994)

Freaks R Us: Don't have my annual Snohomish County suburbanization rant 'cuz I stayed home this Christmas. Went back for Thanksgiving, tho, and decided then that there's one thing you can say about going home for the holidays. It reveals that all of us are connected by fewer than six degrees of separation to at least one potential *Montel Williams* or *Jenny Jones* guest. Indeed, tabloid TV serves a vital purpose in remaking our social myths.

In the past, people were intimidated into thinking they, or the people they were close to, were just about the only people around with nasty secrets That may have been especially true in places like the Northwest, where a fetishized vision of bland "normality" is virtually a state religion. Weirdness isn't something that happens only to strangely-dressed people who live in "abnormal" parts of town. And no matter what people do to escape weirdness (like building ever-blander suburbs ever-further-out), it'll always be there with 'em.

"Normal" is simply a wishful fantasy. Understanding this could become one step towards the left-wing populism I've advocted. We Outré Artsy Types aren't the only people who transgress against whitebread-Christian behavior. Everybody (almost) is doing or has done it. Need more proof? Just go to any 12-step meeting in a middlebrow neighborhood. The confessions there are enough to make the people on talk shows seem positively blasé.

Artsy folks like us aren't really rebelling against square people, only against their delusions. We're only exhorting folks to stop hiding their weirdness and start celebrating it. As Boojie Boy said nearly two decades ago, "We're All Devo." *(January 1995)*

The militia and posse cults, such as those being blamed for the Oklahoma City bombing, are the carriers/victims of a classic American ideology, ultimate individualilsm. Individualism is why "socialism" never got far in this country. It's the root of much of what's wrong with this country, and also of much of what other countries admire about us. But the flavor of extreme individualism expressed by the militia cults is something different. It's a case of people foolishly really believing an ideology meant to be taken cynically.

The government-bashing associated with the militias and their less extreme counterparts in religious right is a tool used by the political sleazemeisters to buy votes and to promote a culture of fear and greed. But it may be a tool of something else as well.

The way I read my Bible prophecy, the "Antichrist" isn't one individual corporeal being. It's a spirit, a compulsion for doing the devil's work in the lord's name. It's been around throughout the history of Christendom.

The religious right, which for at least three decades has been out looking for 666 under every governmental rock, is now among this spirit's victims. It bought into conspiracy theories that a single Antichrist dictator would emerge to form something called The One World Government. The real "world government" in the post-USSR era is global business, the real patrons of the politicians vying for Fundamentalist votes. The Trilateral Commission? That was an above-ground club of think-tankers who wanted to make individual governments more responsive to big business (just like that Global Business Network the *Whole Earth Catalog* and *Wired* magazine people belong to). Conservatives used to claim that Communists promised freedom but delivered tyran-

Misc. Moments

Scripts for a proposed series of miniature commentaries for the local TV show Bombshelter Videos *(some were taped; none aired).*

Memo to Dan Quayle: We're not laughing at traditional family values. We're laughing at you.

Seattle's big and clumsy, but thinks it's still little and cute. In cartoon terms, we're the Baby Huey of cities.

If John McCaw's so proud to be one of the new Mariner owners, why won't he show his picture in the paper? Has he got really bad pimples or what?

Folks tell me they won't vote for Clinton 'cuz of his slick personality. Look: If you vote for a guy 'cuz he's got a winning charisma, you end up with Ronald Reagan.

ny; modern conservatives promise individualism but deliver globalism.

And the Four Horsemen of the Apocalypse? They could easily be seen as representing the kind of environmental destruction now advocated by "pro growth" politicians and "property rights" lobbyists.

Similarly, many commentators have contrasted Jesus's disses against rich people to the right's demonization of the poor and deification of money and property. This contradictory appeal of anything-goes for polluters and developers with fiscal S&M for the rest of us not only contradicts the Big Book, it harkens back to the days of decadent *Madness of King George*-era England, the England our forefathers had good reasons to secede from. The people most loudly invoking the imagery of the American Revolution are being increasingly corrupted by some of the values this country was founded against. I'm not saying evangelicals or business executives (or even Republicans) are soldiers of a personalized devil. I'm saying they're components in a self-perpetuating system that's accelerating the rich/poor gap, the depletion of the earth's resources, and other trends that contradict any reasonable definition of "personal liberty," "Christian stewardship," or "family values."

What we're seeing is a cultural feedback loop. The "programmers" of this loop are the folks who built an economic system that generates byproducts of alienation, greed and fear, but have cleverly found a way to channel that greed and fear back into the system.

Yet where else is there for the disempowered to go? Release the clutch of corporate interests from the right and you end up with the world of the militia cults. If there are Republicans who haven't succumbed to the sleaze, they're keeping low. The middle-of-the-road Democrats have been trying to sell the idea of a Right Lite for over a decade, and may now have lost that crusade for good. The American Left was never much able to sell the value of socialism in a nation of individualists; in most of my lifetime, it hasn't even bothered to offer a coherent vision of an idealized society, let alone try to sell that vision to people who don't live in college towns. But that's a topic for another week. *(May 3, 1995)*

The free *Seattle Weekly* appropriately debuted with the cover headline, "Status Quo Under Siege." The paper that's always identified itself as the voice of the Inner Circle finds both that circle and itself under attack. The issue's main essay was poignantly nostalgic in its defense

How come every vegetarian I know smokes the highest-tar cigarettes you can get? Do they think they're getting extra protein?

If you don't vote, you're doing exactly what the right wing wants you to do.

Somebody told me a racist joke, then tried to say it was just a parody of a racist joke. I asked him if he'd like a parody of a punch in the face.

If we published fewer poems about trees, we'd have more trees.

The government doesn't want us to have abortion rights or affordable health care. What do they want, lots of babies who all die off quickly?

(June 1992)

of the notion that "progressive" politics means leaving everything in the hands of professional "leaders." It's a relic of the old upper-Midwest "progressives," who identified liberal pieties with "nice" WASP culture — partly to rally WASP farmers and laborers against decadent N.Y.C. financiers, but also to keep German Catholics and other immigrants out of local power. (One of the original tools used in the Upper Midwest to keep those-who-know-better in charge was at-large city council elections, which the *Weekly* piece exhorted Seattle voters to keep.)

The Progressives' spiritual descendants are trapped in a contradiction between advocating "multiculturalism" and preseving its own hyper-bland monoculture. The Right cheerfully exploits this contradiction, while promoting its own contradiction between "We the People" talk and PAC-ass-kissing action. *(Nov. 15, 1995)*

Something called the Council on Civil Society put out a treatise claiming "Americans must find a way to agree on public moral philosophy if democracy is going to survive." Its report (*Why Democracy Needs Moral Truths*) claims, "If independent moral truth does not exist, all that is left is power." An Associated Press story about the group cited Madonna choosing single momhood as evidence of such social decay. At best, it sounds like Dr. Laura's radio rants demanding a return to impossibly rigid social and sexual conformities. At worst, it's like the hypocritical pieties of "Family" demagogues who've been degenerating moral and religious discussion into a naked power game, selling churchgoers' votes to politicians who really only care about Sacred Business.

Yet any successful demagougery has an appeal to honest desires (for stability, assurance, identity, etc.) at its heart. It's a complicated, complex populace. Cultures and subcultures will continue to branch off and blossom. Attempts to impose one official religion, diet, dress code, sex-orientation, etc. are dangerous follies at best.

So what would my idea of a standard of conduct be? Maybe something like this: There's more to life than just "lifestyles." There's more to well-being than just money. There's more to healthy communities than just commerce. There's more to spirituality than just obedience (whether it's evangelical obedience or neopagan obedience). We've gotta respect our land, ourselves, and one another — even those others who eat different food or wear different clothes than ourselves. We're all the same species, but in ever-bifurcating varieties. Live with it. *(June 18, 1998)*

Post-Easter Special

A few weeks ago, we asked your responses to the premise, "What if Jesus were alive today, in his teens, preparing to return to public life at the dawn of the new millennium?" Excerpts follow.

Jilliann Sims and Leigh Dunham: *"Jesus would be one of the fine, upstanding citizens we lovingly call 'Ave Rats.' He would hand impressionable, young students fliers proclaiming, 'Love thy neighbor (but not too much, and safely please)'."*

Brenda Martin: *"The Catholic churches would hunt him down and have him killed for security reasons."*

Mustafa Patwa: *"Jesus is indeed alive and well. He is currently preparing for public life in the early 21st century by playing Doogie Howser, America's favorite teenage doctor, on the show of the same name."*

(continued)

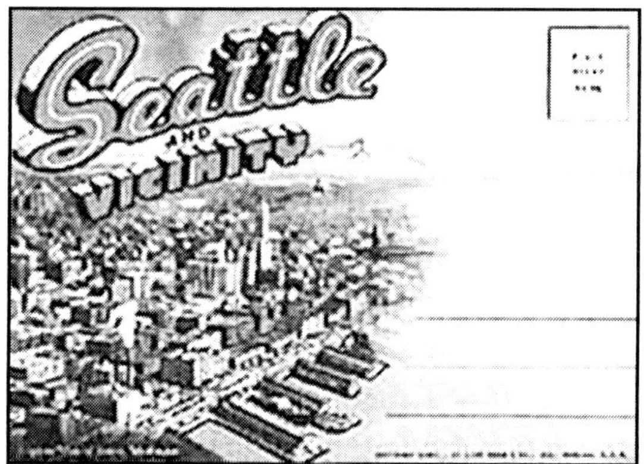

33: YESTERDAYS

or, nostalgia just isn't the same anymore

"The past," William Faulkner is said to have said, "isn't dead. It isn't even past." It keeps coming back in endlessly re-morphing forms (compare the '70s version of '50s nostalgia to the '80s version). Competing nostalgias can bring out competing visions of both the past and the present. That's because no vision of the past can fully re-enact it (memory, like fresh fruit, is traditionally "preserved" by sweetening it up and pulping it down).

So some people look back at a time they did or didn't live in for its strides of progress, while others can only remember what people were trying then to progress from.

Recently viewed tape: *Urgh! A Music War,* 1981 concert footage of some 35 bands gathered under the awkward, inaccurate label "new wave." Only one of them was big at the time (the Police, who helped finance the film). Others became stars (the Go-Go's, UB40, Devo), had solid cult followings (Magazine, Steel Pulse, XTC), or met deserved obscurity (Athletico Spizz 80, Splodgenessabounds).

I found myself viewing the proceedings as nostalgia for my own generation, and seeing how, even while many of the best bands never had a major hit, the attitudes they represented have become quite pervasive in American society — in butchered form, of course. A lot of the worst aspects of punk/new wave (shallow imagery, aggressive hype, destructiveness to self and others as romanticism, bigotry as nostalgia, lousy manners, celebrations of stupidity) have become everyday aspects of business, government and lifestyles. Even our agriculture has gone punk: It's dependent on drugs and panhandling, lives fast, dies young, and leaves a good-looking corpse. *(September 1986)*

The Summer of '67 commemorations turned out to be largely duds. That's OK, really; it's good to see folks being respectfully apathetic towards the hippie dregs' shrieks about their own importance. I mean, everybody back in the late '60s can't have been as hip 'n' progressive as the ex-rads now claim everyone was — somebody voted for Nixon. *(October 1987)*

Deja Vu All Over Again: The *Wall Street Journal* says an '80s nostalgia theme nightclub is about to open in N.Y.C. It's a hopeful sign that the more wretched aspects of recent history might be past us. The question is, now that the Age of Sleaze might finally end, how will it be remembered? I fear that the '80s could

Post-Easter Special
(continued)

Bruce Long:
"The whereabouts of the adolescent Jesus: Someplace blessed with a bumper crop of second chances."

Sid Miller:
"Jesus is probably a sophomore at a high school east of Lake Washington. Real trendy haircut with shaved sides and a pigtail/rattail down the back. Wants his own TV show or his own band. Doesn't have the gumption to practice his guitar — too busy with skateboard. Hopes grungy skateboard buddies will piss-off Mary, who is preoccupied with telling all who will listen that Joseph has 'run off'. She recently blurted out, 'He's not really your father.'

Jesus has been talking with his buddies about how 'cool' it would be to set a wino on fire. Bought gun for $25 from acquaintance and brings it to parties. Wants a car so he can go cruising. Mother of his child will turn 16 three weeks before baby is due."

end up fetishized like the '50s, whose most preposterous images are mistakenly perceived as the truth of American life then (or even as it had always been).

For anyone reading this in the future, Reagan was not as universally popular as he claimed (or as opponents were too willing to believe); his economic "miracle" was a trick engineered by funny-money; the Religious Right was no mass movement (Pat Robertson's viewership is half that of feel-good preacher Robert Schuller); lots of people opposed the wasteful arms buildup and gulf war; and violent action movies coincided with a decline in the moviegoing audience (the Stallone/Schwarzenegger killfests depended on a few addicts coming repeatedly for their adrenaline fix). *(November 1992)*

Turn Off, Tune Out, Drop Dead: Yeah, Woodstock '94 is a big crass commercial operation — but so was the original. It hastened the consolidation of "underground" music into the corporate rock that by 1972 would smother most true creativity in the pop/rock field. If there was a generation defined by the event, it was one of affluent college kids who sowed their wild oats, called it a political act, then went into the professions for which they'd been studying. The Demographically Correct, the people advertisers and ad-supported media crave to the point of ignoring all others. By telling these kids they were Rebels by consuming sex, drugs and rock 'n' roll, the media dissuaded many hippie-wannabes from forming any real movement for social change, which might have broken down the class, racial, and other divisions that boomer-centric "Classic Rock" serves to maintain. *(September 1994)*

On the Make: Was reminded this month of the good ol' days of American business, the days when this country was interested in making things instead of just marketing them. The first was the *Times* obit for Weyerhaeuser exec Norton Clapp. The article's lead labeled Clapp with the now-quaint rubric of "industrialist." The second was *Our World,* the monthly *USA Today* ad supplement touting things like new concrete-fabrication plants in ex-Soviet republics. The third was when I got to play with a friend's CD-ROM drive. Among his discs was *The Time Almanac,* with texts and pix from old *Time* magazines through the decades. But it didn't have the real joy of collecting *old* Time issues — the ads. Old *Time* ads from the '40s and '50s are wonderful evocations of a time when the Opinion Makers of most towns outside N.Y.C. were bourbon-swillin', tweed-wearin' managers of small and mid-size manufacturing plants. The ads sold roller bearings, conveyor belts, commercial air conditioning systems, semi rigs, axle greases, grinding wheels, and all that other cool stuff you never see around the house. I'd much rather see more ads of that type than the ads you see in today's *Time* for import luxury cars and prescription hair-growth tonic. *(May 10, 1995)*

Other Worlds, Other Sounds: *Esquire* magazine's been so pathetic in recent years, it's amazing its lounge-culture cover story turned out not-half-bad. Pity it didn't more thoroughly explore one curious quotation from critic Milo Miles at the *Salon* website, complaining that the retro-cats were championing a worldview the Beats and hippies had desired to destroy. That's true, but that's also one of the movement's positive points.

At its broadest definition, lounge culture is the culture of the first Age of Integration. It's Sammy Davis refusing to perform at hotels that made him eat in the kitchen. It's Sinatra demanding to tour with an integrated band. It's Juan Garcia Esquivel, Antonio Carlos Jobim, Eartha Kitt, Yma Sumac, Perez Prado, Sergio Mendes, Nat "King" Cole, Desi Arnaz, Vikki Carr, Harry Belafonte, and Quincy Jones. (In comparison, can you name more then four stars of color in the past quarter-century of "progressive rock"?)

It's the sounds and sights of other lands, curated and juxtaposed to jostle the audience's expectations (as opposed to the smiling-peasant complacency underton-ing much of today's "world beat" industry.) It reflects an aesthetic of respect for oneself and others, and also a postwar philosophy that personal and social progress were not only necessary but possible.

Sure, there's a lot of posing and play-acting among today's cocktail kids. But within the most "shallow" pose, as gay-camp afficianados know, lies a truth, or at least a desire for a truth. In the lounge revival, it's a desire for seemingly long-lost ideals of beauty, adventure, community, mutual respect (the only source of true cultural diversity), economic advancement, and fun. *(April 10, 1997)*

End the Beguine Already!: One good thing about this column no longer appearing in *The Stranger* is I can now comment on things in it, such as Juliette Guilbert's 7,000-word diatribe against retro-swing mania. The Swing Era was not the nadir of race relations Guilbert makes it out to be, but rather a first, halting step out from that abyss (at least for African Americans — Japanese Americans

Bob Armstrong:
"He'd be an illegal immigrant in east L.A. who got turned onto computers by a white nerd at his high school, and will soon make a raid on the interlocking banking computer network, shifting funds around to more appropriate accounts. He's Catholic, but hasn't been seen around the church in some time."

Oran Walker:
"Jesus would be the son of a working-class family; the father a professional craftsman, possibly union. The mother would be a secretary in a Catholic church. He had his pick of schools and ended up at a small college not far from New York City, where he spends his holidays and weekends, to the chagrin of his mother.

She knows he doesn't attend church and hangs out on the Lower East Side with God knows what socially marginal types, most likely Hispanics and Queers. She doesn't know that he has been fucking around with his friends, both boys and girls, since he passed the age of accountability five or six years ago. 'Safer sex' has been more than a catch phrase with Jesus, since he realized early that sexual contact is such a complicating factor in the lives of both participants...

He is making above-average grades, especially in ecology policy courses. He has written two essays on the need for global awareness and human charity among the earth's peoples and probably will expand his ideas into his master's thesis, but it's early yet. He has been assured that he'll live to a grand old age — unless he gets those messianic ideas again."

(May 1992)

faced problems of their own at the time). I've written about the previously-nostalgized Lounge Era as the dawn of the Age of Integration. The seeds of this progress were sown when white sidemen first played under black bandleaders, when Josephine Baker calmly demanded to be served at the Stork Club, when Jackie Robinson donned a Brooklyn Dodgers uniform, when thousands of black families migrated from the rural south to northeast cities (and to Seattle), etc.

Sure, there aren't many African Americans in today's swing revival. Traditionally, black audiences rush to the Star-Off Machine to abandon black music forms once they've gone "mainstream" (white), which with retro-swing happened sometime after Kid Creole and the Coconuts. (When Hollywood promoters marketed gangsta rap at white mall kids' stereotypes of black men as sexy savages, black audiences rushed to support acts I might consider sappy love-song singers, but they saw as well-dressed, well-mannered, prosocial alternatives.)

Similar statements could be made gender-wise about the swing years, especially when thousands of women took over civilian jobs during the war. It was at swing's end when gender roles temporarily went backward. The *Pleasantville* movie connection here is Ozzie and Harriet. Ozzie Nelson was a swing bandleader, Harriet Hilliard (who used her own last name when their show started on radio) an RKO contract actress who'd become Ozzie's singer-wife. When they saw the market for swing bands collapse after V-J Day, they invented new, desexualized, images for themselves on their radio show. It was the end of the Swing Era that coincided with (or presaged) the movement to get women back in the kitchen.

It all goes to show you. If a lot of young people do something (anything), some grownup's gonna whine about it. Having lived through at least three or four attempted swing revivals (remember Buster Poindexter? Joe Jackson's *Jumpin' Jive* LP? The Broadway revues *Five Guys Named Moe* and *Ain't Misbehavin*? The movies *Swing Kids* and *Newsies*?), it amused me at first to see a new generation actually pull it off.

Of course, as with anything involving large masses of young adults, it tended to become something taken way, way too seriously. Guilbert also takes it very seriously, perhaps more seriously than the kids themselves. My Rx for her: A good stiff drink and a couple spins of an Ella Fitzgerald compilation. *(Nov. 23, 1998)*

34: TOMORROWS

or, futurism just isn't the same anymore

Which brings us back to one of our introductory topics, how wonderful the Seattle World's Fair said our world would become, and the world we got instead. Science-fiction writers love to toy with the gimmick of "alternate futures." They're all really out there, at least in our imaginations. My imagination fears the vegans' utopia as much as it fears the militias' utopia.

Past Futures (from *Uncensored* magazine, April 1970): "A fascinating new book, *The Country of the Young,* paints a gloomy picture of what life will be in 1990 — when the generation war is all over and the drop-outs, pot-heads and sandaled freaks have become Old Hippies. The author, John W. Aldridge, says that the failure of the young today to develop their human resources, to cultivate discipline and skills, is going to backfire on them. If the hippies have their way and become catatonics, with all their needs supplied, 'They will simply stare at walls for weeks on end, looking fascinated at such things as the copulation of insects. Having been relieved of the struggle of becoming, they would simply exist to be.'" *(May 1990)*

God Help Us in the Future: My used-bookstore wanderings have landed *Criswell Predicts,* a 1968 paperback by the late syndicated prognosticator who narrated the cult film *Plan 9 From Outer Space.*

Here, he predicts a Soviet leader whose five-year rule will transform the USSR toward free enterprise "with only a few symbols of communism remaining;" the death of another socialist leader and the breakup of his country in a civil war (only he thought it was gonna be Mao); a series of "homosexual cities" ("small, compact, carefully planned areas... complete with stores, churches, bars and restaurants"); bald women on the streets of a major city (he blames it on pollution); contraceptives in the water supply (industrial contaminants might make us sterile, so it could happen); the evacuation of New York City due to floods; and the end of the world in 1999, just like Nostradamus, Prince, and certain evangelists. [His specific date: Aug. 19.]

He also makes predictions for each state. "I predict that the state of Washington will become the art center of America, for it is in that state that a Federal Arts Center will be built. Persons showing aptitude in any of the arts — painting, music, dance, writing, acting, etc. — will be allowed to go to this Federal Arts Center and live at government expense to pursue their talents.

From this arts center will come road companies of performing artists who will tour the nation." Hey, Kurt & Courtney: You're just fulfilling a destiny. *(September 1992)*

Active Cultures: A few months ago, I called for the death of Hollywood. Now, the decentralization of American culture looks unstoppable. New means of production and distribution are bypassing (or influencing) media monarchies. With Hi-8 camcorders people can make pro video for less than the annual cost of many prescriptions. The music video format has freed a generation of moving-image makers from the tyrannies of linear narrative and feature length. With desktop publishing and quick-printing, the last financial barrier to self-publishing is the cost of binding to bookstore specs.

The revolution is here, it is being televised (at least on odd cable channels), and it's gonna be rough. You'll see a lot of unlistenable indie records, unwatchable direct-to-video movies, unreadable desktop-published books, and unbearable fringe-theater plays. It's the natural stumblings of people learning painfully to make their own culture, instead of merely choosing which prepackaged worldview to adopt. *(October 1993)*

Inter-Activity: The promised big cable TV/phone/computer hookups could profoundly improve the world — if our "leaders" don't ruin it. Every new media technology has had political implications. Phones and telegraph developed under corrupt administrations that, fat with railroad payoffs, looked the other way on monopolies.

Radio and talkies arose in the Coolidge-Hoover era, friendly to consolidation of power into four commercial networks, seven studios and five big theater chains. Truman tried to maintain the media status quo by holding up new TV stations; once Ike came in, big-sponsor-controlled TV was allowed to essentially run free. (Until 1953, there was only one station in Seattle and none in Portland.)

The Nixon crew developed PBS precisely to be a bureaucratic farce, in submission to corporate money. The Reaganites revoked commercial TV's few remaining requirements for public service and journalistic fairness.

Meanwhile, two by-products of Cold War military investment, the microprocessor and the Internet, helped create a new aesthetic of direct communicating, without the compromises or corruption of Hollywood and Madison Avenue. The 500-channel future could give just lots of pay-per-view blockbuster violence movies. Or we

God As I Understand Him

GOD IS:

Lonely.

Wet and Wild.

Sorry to have made mosquitos, but too proud to say so.

Not one to tell good cholesterol from bad cholesterol.

Uncomfortable with being called "he" until more human languages have a personal neuter pronoun.

About to lose the mineral deposits on Pluto in a bet.

A much better dancer than you might think.

Confused by all the furor over nude beaches, since "he" can always see everything anyway.

About to perfect a truly superlative cheesecake recipe.

Still buying vinyl records.

Intense, really intense, but only when necessary.

Not very excited about the new millenium.

Capable of sex, but usually occupied with greater tasks.

could have universal two-way access, where anyone can transmit anything to anyone. This wouldn't mean the end of pop culture but its fullest blossoming. Just as the best "pop" music of the past decade has been outside the Top 40, the best "pop" video of the next decade will be made by small troupes who love their work.

The "information superhighway" is currently more hype than policy; the danger is that it'll become a policy of profit above empowerment. Let the powers that be know you want "common carrier video," or something that can be upgraded to it. *(January 1994)*

Fair Game: If you get the chance, get to Uptown Espresso to view John Rozich's utterly beautiful chalk paintings on the menu boards, commemorating next week's 35th anniversary of the Seattle World's Fair (a.k.a. the Century 21 Exposition). Rozich's exquisite works, modeled after original Space Needle ad art, engender a nostalgia for something once called the future. A mythical state, located in real space and unreal time, where most everything would be better.

I've been watching videotapes of KING-TV's 25th-fair-anniversary telecasts from 1987, based on kinescope films of live fair coverage. The tapes show KING's first news anchor, Charles Herring, hawking the fair as "a futuristic look into the future... How man will live and work and play in the year 2000."

In other moments, olden-throated announcers present incredible inventions-to-be: Sun power. A 200-mph pneumatic passenger train. An automated highway. Gas-turbine cars. Microwave ovens. Picturephones.

One scene takes viewers to the "World of Century 21" exhibit in the old Coliseum. As the camera views scale models of domed cities connected by monorails, an unseen narrator booms, "We think and plan differently now. Science and technology are the twin architects of tomorrow's homes... Our energy sources: solar or atomic. Climate control is automatic. Built-in vacuum systems keep our home spotless. The home communication center brings the world's news, culture and entertainment to our homes in color and perhaps three dimensions... It's not just any day. It's tomorrow. The fine day you and millions like you plan and build. And it can be both beautiful and practical. City Century 21. The highest concentration of civilization. The ultimate expression of man's collective endeavors... Home and work are closer to each other, and near to nature. Our transit-ring monorail provides commuters rapid and enjoyable mass transit.

Showing Einstein's scientific errors to him, only to get counter-arguments back.

Still unwilling to take sides in Northern Ireland.

Wondering how they get the creme filling in a Ho-Ho.

Still hoping Garbo will make another picture.

Bored.

Unwilling to tell the total value of pi*, even to friends.*

Trying to recall a way to have made the Earth without putting any uranium in it.

Disappointed in what the Beatles did after Revolver*.*

Fully aware of the contradictions in most religions, but that's just how these things go.

A Honeymooners *fan, especially of the adoption episode.*

Refereeing a wrestling match between Zeus and Apollo.

Able to leap in seconds across the Gemini constellation (which, from beneath, looks more like THREE people).

Just THIS tall in "his" most compressed form.

Available in all styles and colors.

Collecting every Basie record ever made.

Commissioning a Shakespeare play about the Marcoses.

The last romantic.

A true night person.

Still mourning the destruction of the library of Alexandria.

Not at all responsible for George Michael.

Only slightly responsible for Zsa Zsa Gabor.

As vast and beautiful as America itself.

Trying to show humans the vital medicines that can be made from horse pancreatic fluid.

In stereo where available.

Free to be you and me.

Unconstrained by the restrictions of time, space, or jobs.

Done for now with the empty thrill of creating life.

Real gone.

Dismayed at Barbara Cartland's errors on human nature.

Electronic streets serve as safe, pleasurable secondary highways... Our city is a place men want to live in, not have to."

But the mood of the fair was more important than any specific predictions. As John Keister noted on one of KING's retrospective shows, "It was a time of optimism, knowledge, and beauty. And I loved it."

Within five years, the fair's vision became popularly denounced as an empty promise, derived from a pro-industry, anti-environmental agenda. But it really represented something more complex: Postwar liberalism, the world of the original Pro-Business Democrats.

Senators Magnuson and Jackson, who helped bring the fair here, sincerely felt America could and would be led forward into a Golden Age by Big Business, Big Government, and Big Labor working hand-in-hand-in-hand to ensure mass prosperity (without socialism), strengthen science, popularize education, advance minority rights, and promote artistic excellence.

There have, of course, been several futures since then. Various religious and military cults' utopias fantasize vicious, vengeful doom for all guilty of not belonging to the right cliques. Ernest Callenbach's *Ecotopia* sees Washington and Oregon becoming colonies of a San Francisco city-state, wihch in turn would be run by a plutocracy of the environmentally-enlightened. William Gibson and other cyberpunk authors dream of a dark, violent external world overshadowed by an internal world enhanced by virtual-reality software.

Today's most intensely promoted future is that of cyber-futurists like George Gilder and Alvin Toffler. But instead of gleaming cities in the sky, these guys look forward to a day when the top-income-bracket folks will never need to leave their gated exurban compounds.

Indeed, most currently-promoted futures are anti-city, if not anti-social. White-flighters, black separatists, eco-communalists, Bainbridge nature poets, right-wing mountain men: Most everyone seems to want to be around only their own sort.

Perhaps not since the fair did professional visionaries forsee diverse peoples wanting to live among one another. Even the concepts of "urban villages" and "civil society," at least as intrepreted by Seattle's top political brass, invoke a definition of "the people" extending no further than Nordstrom's target demographic.

Still, the Space Needle beckons as its promised century draws closer. Don't just look on it as a relic of yesterday's industrial optimism but as a call forward, encouraging us to imagine better, more inclusive tomorrows than the tomorrows we've been imagining. *(April 17, 1997)*

Wasn't Tomorrow Wonderful?: Two weeks or so ago, I asked for your ideas as to which late-'90s popcult trends would be the likeliest nostalgia fodder in future decades. Reader Ian Morgan expressed doubts on the whole idea: "This entire decade has been a flaccid rerun of the seventies! A second Woodstock, Sex Pistols reunion, platform shoes, bellbottoms, etc. Don't forget grunge. Sorry, the punkers did nihilism better the first time around. If history is merciful we'll all forget the '90s. Everyone here wishes they were sometime else."

Kim Adams was more hopeful, sorta: "Future generations, inundated with a gazillion sources and sites for information and babies whose first words will be ISDN or TMI (too much information), will long for a return to the simpler times of single-phone-line households and mere 33.6k modems."

As for me, a few passing fancies are evident. DVDs will make today's CD-ROM games seem quaintly primitive (such small video windows; such choppy animations). When digital video lets anybody become a moviemaker, today's big-budget action films will become popularly disdained as bloated dinosaurs, then later inspire subsequent generations as mementos of a second Hollywood Golden Age.

And 21st-century genetic engineering might make both tattoos and breast implants seem positively retro-chic. Of course, all this depends on what the future generates, then finds missing. Maybe there'll be a huge hammer-dulcimer mania in the 2010s, causing kids in the 2020s to yearn for the good old days of techno. *(Dec. 4, 1997)*

Revolution One-Of-These-Days Maybe: I've talked to four people in recent weeks, who've mentioned either their desire or fears of a new American revolution. I have a hard time imagining a violent overthrow of the U.S. of A., especially in times of relative prosperity for many.

The topic's becoming popular; to the point that it's now a selling tool.

Taco Bell and Dos Equis invoke bizarre takes on Poncho Villa to sell consumer consumables. A golf ball called the Maxfli Revolution advertises it'll help you "Seize Power and Take Control." Closer to home, the highly institutional-looking ARO.Space nightclub says its initials stand for "Art and Revolution Organization." (Its ads even say, "Viva le Revolution!")

Aware of ten women who could have been pretty good U.S. presidents, in the 19th century alone.

So tedious when talking about the structure of flaxseed.

Marrying Confucius to a late Caracas hotel barmaid.

Fully cognizant of your prayers for world peace, but asking your patience until the right configuration of societies can be reached.

Not ready for prime time.

Very easy to shop for.

Looking very relaxed.

Terminally eternal.

Able to see the past, present and future simultaneously, hence forbidden a seat on the Stock Exchange.

Largely non-malignant.

Obsequious to Aphrodite.

Fast, compact and virtually noiseless.

Totally naked without a dinner jacket.

Not at all sorry about crabgrass; it serves a vital function in nature, if humans could only learn to appreciate it.

Fabulously freaky.

A Jet all the way.

Just a bit curious about how an evil thought might feel.

Gnarly.

About to live in the form of a west African ranch worker.

An untranslatable pun.

Quality, performance and dependability at a low price.

On time, and under budget.

Fairly sure "he" exists, but not too sure about you.

Simply stunning in pink chiffon.

Definitely NOT Elvis, and certainly not Eric Clapton.

Faster and safer than a microwave.

Planning to reincarnate Cantinflas in Hungary.

Aware of many other planets with stupid TV, too.

Resistant to heat, rain, oil, salt water, most chemicals.

Ready to take your order on our toll-free lines 24 hours.

So what would a revolution be? (I mean a real sociopolitical revolution, not some advertised "fitness revolution" or "style revolution.") Here's some ideas:

The revolution will be televised. It just won't be made possible by a grant from Archer Daniels Midland.

It probably wouldn't be led by the English-department radicals. As *Achieving Our Country* author Richard Rorty notes, the tenured left's too obsessed with poststructuralist theory to actively care about economic injustice; too focused on folks a few rungs beneath the top of America's caste ladder (such as professional-class women and gays) to seriously bother with those closer to the bottom.

It also wouldn't be led by today's Religious Right, though it wishes it could. The "reconstructionist" dream of some right-wingers, of a palace coup that'd smash constitutional democracy but leave corporate power intact, won't sell to enough would-be troops in a time when the real threats to mass well-being come from the consolidation of wealth and power by the business elite the Christian Coalition gang really serves.

The militia cults might have a part in it, but only if they give up their romanticism of conquest and their ethno-religious exclusivity. They'd have to join efforts with all those facing diminished opportunities, whether from the ghettos, the barrios, the abandoned factory towns, or the depleted mining lands.

To succeed, it wouldn't be about The Good People vs. The Bad People (as defined by such inaccurate criteria as race, gender, language, sex-preference, religion, diet, etc.). It'd be about changing an unjust system, while recognizing such a system has innocent beneficiaries as well as innocent victims.

It wouldn't promise an instant Golden Age. Most folks are too cynicized from decades of misleading advertising to believe anything as abstract as a new governmental organization could bring eternal peace and prosperity. What it could claim would be to build a healthier, more just society. One where all our races and subcultures don't just learn to get along but to work together. One where money and power counted a little less and wisdom and love a little more. *(July 2 and Aug. 27, 1998)*

Millennium Buggy: The Year 2000 Computer Problem hysteria hasn't spawned a new survivalist cult, as some commentators and periodicals have claimed; but it has breathed new life into existing cults. The "head for the hills with canned goods and guns and gold" folks, having missed out on predicted apocalypses involving nukes, race riots, U.N. "black helicopters," oil shortages, etc. etc., now get to invoke a simple yet oft-misunderstood software-upgrade failure as their new premise to solicit converts and customers — a premise conveniently scheduled on a date steeped in religious mysteries and referenced by prophets from Nostradamus to Criswell.

Many "Y2K" scenarios promoted by survivalists read less like knowledgeable tech writing and more like excuses to shoehorn in pre-existing survivalist dogma. Like the parts about inner cities turning into instant war zones while the rural inland west remains serene and posse-protected. Not only does this line ignore that over half the country now lives in suburbs, it ignores that major metro areas are usually the first to get upgraded civic electronics, while the countryside's still stuck with some of the most antiquated phone and power-delivery systems — the ones most likely to not get fixed so their databases understand years that don't start with "19."

What the alarmists get right is how nearly everything in the modern world (air-traffic control, oil refineries, long-distance lines, Social Security, medical equipment, stock markets) is intertwined in mainframe-computer networks, the real "world wide web." But the Y2K problem won't crash everything at once. It just means companies and governments that let these unprofitable but necessary system upgrades slide now have to implement them at once.

At the least it'll mean a hit on most everybody's financial bottom lines for the next two years; draining cash-flows and spurring various degrees of layoffs. At worst, some of the various software/hardware fixes around the world might not be ready (or adequately tested) in time, so some databases might have to be put off-line for a few weeks and some utility and industrial-control systems might have to be switched to planned backup mechanisms. In an absolute-worst plausibility, some fixes that were thought to work won't, causing scattered system crashes. And some stand-alone industrial machines with pre-programmed computer chips inside might hiccup; but even most of those failures should be predictable and worked around.

So don't give in to the fear-profiteers in the canned-food and gun industries. If you want to believe in a Biblical-style apocalypse, remember the verse about how mankind "knoweth not the day nor the hour."

(Sept. 10, 1998)

Just impossible to talk to about politics or religion.

User-definable.

Ready to love you the way you want to be loved. The former baritone in one of the fake Ink Spots groups.

Designed for the modern business user.

Colossal, stupendous, and even mediocre.

Wondering just how to create a truly unisex mammal.

Out of context.

Never undersold.

Pure chewing satisfaction.

An effective decay-preventing dentifrice when used in a conscientiously applied program of oral hygiene and regular professional care.

Realizing the final result of centuries of intense genetic research: A toilet-trained dog.

Disgusted with all the communications satellites obstructing "his" view of the South Pacific islands.

Mass rad.

(continued)

35: MY LIFE

or, retro-introspection

The biggest thing in Tacoma during my grandmother's time there, the fall of the old Narrows Bridge.

I make it a policy to rarely write about my private life in the column, believing writers are among the least worthy-of-being-written-about folks around. Here are two of the most prominent exceptions to this policy.

City of Destiny: I went to my first graveside funeral last month, for my grandmother, Nelyphthia ("Nellie") Clark Humphrey, 92. ("Nelyphthia" came from a fictional ancient-Greek character in a novel grandma's mother had read.)

The bus to Tacoma is called the "Seattle Express." It swiftly jaunted down I-5 to the downtown Tacoma transit mall. Inside the Pierce Transit info center, I overheard a clerk advise two foreign visitors to take the Seattle Express ("There's nothing in Tacoma to see. Everything's in Seattle").

Back outside, I paid silent respects at the former UPS Law School building — previously the Rhodes Bros. department store, where my grandmother worked for decades in the employees' cafeteria. Grandma ranted a lot about how the Tacoma Mall had killed downtown. She was feisty and argumentative when she wanted to be, which was often. Sometimes I'd wished she wasn't, like when she spouted common-for-her-generation tirades against blacks and Mexicans. I know you're not supposed to talk about people's bad parts when they've just gone, but she wasn't strict about the social graces so in a way I think she'd understand.

Anyhow, two buses later I was at Captain Nemo's restaurant on Bridgeport Way, to rendezvous with several relatives including my cousin who looks just like Marie Osmond (she'd probably appreciate the comparison, even though her religion differs from Osmond's Mormonism). Got the typical "Todd, you've gained a few" remark from an aunt pretending to mistake me for my younger brother. The conversation I'd interrupted was about the differences between the moods at evangelical vs. Baptist church services.

These relations on my father's side are real Tacoma people, Caucasian non-military subtype. Theirs is a world defined by church, angel books, QVC products, RVs, movie-star gossip, and all-American food. If you really are what you eat, I come from a long line of apple pie with Cool Whip, cottage cheese, canned string beans, Tater Tots, and margarine.

A short caravan brought us to the New Tacoma Cemetery. Grandma had been declining for several years, so when I served as a pallbearer there wasn't much to lift. I'd always seen her as old and scrawny; I was surprised to see on display a photo of her young, as full-cheeked as I, without the frown of Edwardian disapproval I'd always seen on her.

Thirty-three people gathered for the brief service, conducted by grandma's chapter of the Eastern Star, a women's Masonic order. Five elderly women took turns describing how grandma's life represented each of the points on Eastern Star's five-colored logo, each representing the virtues of a different Old Testament woman.

Afterwards, I was taken aside by two who looked far younger than their real ages and who exuded way too much life energy to be related to me. Turns out they were the daughters of my late grandfather's sister and her husband, whom I'd known as a kid as Uncle Joe. They told me how, as kids, they'd known my parents before they were married and how much in love they seemed to be.

They also talked about their dad. Uncle Joe ran a Shell station at Third and Lenora, razed circa 1972 for Belltown's first condo tower. We visited his beautiful house in the hills above Carkeek Park every Christmas when I was little. The last time, I still remember entering into a spirited conversation with him about just what was "Platformate," the mystery gas ingredient Shell was plugging that year. (He knew what it was, or at least gave a convincing lie.) He seemed to enjoy the chat, but afterward my dad scolded me for my untoward behavior. The cousins assured me Joe undoubtedly did enjoy the talk.

In my head, I'd always resisted the heredity-as-destiny theory. But deep down, I'd quietly feared I was fated to end up just like grandma, all bitter and grumbling about one thing or another, with little room for life's joys. I'd make some curt remark to a waiter and then wonder if it was a sign of impending grouchhood. Then the memory of outgoing, boistrous Uncle Joe entered my life and gave me hope — until I remembered I was only related to him by marriage. *(Aug. 15, 1996)*

Now 20% Off!: Turns out it was easy to lose 41 pounds (one-fifth of my old weight) in 21 weeks, after years of vowing to get around to it.

Just my usual intake cut to an average of 1500 calories a day, plus a daily half-gallon of water and regular conditioning workouts. No Jenny's Cuisine, no macrobiotics, no fat-gram counting, no simple vs. complex carbos.

God As I Understand Him
(continued)

In love with Rita Hayworth and always will be.

Quiet,
almost too quiet.

Ready to strike at
a moment's notice.

In touch with
"his" feelings.

Fresh, hot and GOOD.

Here today,
tomorrow,
next week.

Tough without
needing to prove it.

Pro-social, with
an original sound
and look.

An everyday
part of life
like sex, weather,
and stale bread.

A cheery, colorful
addition to every
home

Your gold,
your precious silver,
your power tools.

On the line with
us now from our
Washington studio.

Really very.

(December 1989)

Designs For Living

A bookseller of my acquaintance recently tipped me off to one of the nonsexual passages (yes, there are several) in the Kama Sutra: *a list of "the sixty-four arts and sciences to be studied" by a learned man or woman. They include some universals ("singing," "dancing," "tattooing"), some obscure-around-these-parts cultural practices ("binding of turbans and chaplets"), and some practical matters of life in ancient India ("storing and accumulating water in aqueducts, cisterns, and reservoirs").*

Anyhow, it's inspired me to compile some arts and disciplines (from the practical to the spiritual to the just plain fun) a modern person should know, in no particular order:

Appreciating different aromas, textures, and tastes. Discerning the difference between Ritz and Hi-Hos.

Rudimentary knowledge of a foreign language.

Intelligent discourse with persons of other subcultures.

Hosting a successful party.

Dancing (Lindy hop, Virginia reel, tap, lap).

Because I'm big on prepackaged foods, it was easy to read calories on the "Nutrition Facts" label listings. For dining out, I carried a *Brand Name Calorie Counter* book. I used Sweet Success diet shakes at first, but realized I could have cereal or soup or toast for the same calories.

Some parts of the regimen were odd. Most diet books are written for women, and don't mention the masculine predicament of awakening at 4 a.m., needing to expel a lot of that drinking water yet turgidly unable to do so.

I used nonprescription appetite-suppressant pills the first few months. They made me want and not want to eat at the same time. I also found myself losing interest in other favorite stimuli, like movies and concerts. I worried I'd become one of those bland boomers I've always ranted against.

I pondered why those turn-of-the-century railroad moguls were so fat — maybe they had a hunger to grow, to acquire. I also pondered the words of an ex-anorexic acquaintance; she'd been reared to fear sex, to the point where she literally couldn't stand to have anything enter her body.

By the end, I'd lost fat faster than my skin shrank, leaving billowy folds of empty flesh containers. I felt like that *Dick Tracy* villain who smuggled guns in the folds of his multiple chins.

One reason I did this was to look more desirable here in an "alternative" subculture where the single straight male is a decidedly surplus commodity.

In his recent book *Eat Fat,* Richard Klein claims fat feminizes men. He notes how Shakespeare's *Antony and Cleopatra* refers to Cleo's lovers getting fat in her presence as a symbol for ceding their manhood to the Egyptian seductress.

Lesbians have zines like *Fat Girl;* gay men have the "bears" clique. Men who love fat women, however, are often stereotyped as manipulative "chubby chasers," out to control low-self-esteem women. And women who love fat men? Unheard of, except in places like the North American Association for Fat Acceptance.

"You Must Not Be Fat," warns Jim Deane in *The Fine Art of Picking Up Girls* (1974). Deane claims there's no such thing as a sexy fat man. I tried to think of some but only got to Brando, the later Elvis, Pavarotti, Babe Ruth, Barry White, and rapper Heavy D. More prevalant were images of near asexuality (Buddah, the later Orson Welles), arrested childhood (Curly Howard, John Belushi, John Candy), or inhumane lords of expanse (Jabba the Hutt, Henry VIII, Louis XIV, those railroad barons).

Klein's book notes an archaic definition of "corporation" as a bodily protruberance, such as a gut: "...Like their anatomical counterparts, these great abdomens seem to aim only at expanding, greedily incorporating and consolidating in view of increasing their volume."

Yet Klein also claims fat's associated today with low-income, low-self-esteem people, while thinness is the visage for the rich and glamorous. The image of financial success these days is not the personal chef but the personal trainer; while today's companies seem as insistant as Oprah to showcase their "downsizing" into new "lean and mean" forms. Klein quotes essayist Hillel Schwartz as calling yo-yo dieting "the constant frustration of desire," a necessary mental state for Late Capitalism to function properly in selling unneeded goods (both excess food and diet schemes).

I still support International No-Diet Days and the Fat Pride movement. What I did was for me, and is not intended as a go-thou-and-do-likewise lesson. Different people have different bodies. Others may need or want to do something else, or nothing.

As for me, now comes phase two, best described by a zombie-bite victim's deathbed promise in *Dawn of the Dead:* "I'll try not to come back." *(March 6, 1997)*

Holding your liquor; preventing or relieving hangovers.

Personal health and hygeine; including brushing and flossing.

Contraception and STD prevention.

Chemistry; including different pharmaceuticals' good/bad effects.

Tanning without burning.

Posture and bearing; preventing carpal-tunnel syndrome.

At least one athletic or semi-athletic activity (downhill skiing, swimming, yoga, step aerobics, bowling, bicycling, Buns of Steel).

One or more social games (poker, Scrabble, Twister, pinball, foosball, Quake, street hockey, et al.).

Knowledge of the major pro sports (other than wrestling).

Food preparation and storage; knowing how long to microwave a leftover pizza slice.

Dining for pleasure, not merely for sustenance.

Creating unusual food combinations (peanut butter on mashed potatoes).

(continued)

36: WORDS TO LIVE BY

or, lovely parting gifts

Every so often I like to close with some well-intended words of advice. Like now.

Misc. Rules For Life:

• Don't trust anybody who *nevvuh* watches *teh-levision.*

• Don't trust anybody who calls a car "an investment."

• Don't trust anybody who only talks about how "hot" a movie or a band is, not about how good it is.

• Don't buy diet pills from an infomercial with the fine print "No Orders Accepted From Iowa."

• Don't buy anything advertised by white guys in Dockers dancing to James Brown's "I Feel Good."

• And don't move into a former slaughterhouse or brothel that's been "restored to its original elegance." *(March 1994)*

All I Really, REALLY Needed to Know I Learned on the Playground:

• Knowledge, by itself, means very little on the asphalt.

• If a boy starts to like girls too soon, other boys will call him a faggot.

• Having rich parents doesn't stop a kid from stealing; it does stop him from being punished.

• Leaky balls don't bounce high or hard, but they're much more fun.

• The best candy bars don't have the most TV commercials.

• If you wear good clothes well, you can get away with anything.

• Authority figures will tell you that ignoring the bullies will make them stop; when you've already learned that it just makes them hit you worse.

• Last year's cool toy is this year's dull zone.

• Unlike evil cartoon characters, evil people don't say, "I'm evil." They say, "I'm so good, I can do evil things and it's OK."

• As soon as you're old enough to do what the older kids are doing, they stop doing it and start saying it was stupid.

• The most precious toy WILL break the day you bring it to school.

• Nobody likes you very much if you're too popular.

• Black people aren't really like what white people think they're like.

• Bullies don't appreciate logical arguments.

• Girls like to look at stolen porno mags too.

• There are reasons to eat or drink something besides whether it tastes good.

• "Fuck" and "fucking" really are the most versatile words in the English language.

• Things supposed to make you feel good can really make you feel worse.

• You can tell yourself that a good dessert is better than bad friends, but it doesn't really work. *(February 1990)*

Clark@40: My adoration of Jack Benny notwithstanding, I decided years ago I wouldn't rue or deny the inevitable entry into the forties.

I wouldn't be like those pathetic boomers, forever striving to retain ever-fading remnants of youthful bodies and identities. (My recent diet-exercise regimen had nothing to do with staying young; I was as out-of-shape at 17 as I was last year.)

No, I plan to age disgracefully into a crochety old geezer. Having bosses younger than me, at a paper targeted at readers younger than me, has offered plenty of practice. "Back in my day Sonny, we had real music. Einsturzende Neubauten! Skinny Puppy! That crap they listen to these days: Why, it's just noise!"

I also plan to enjoy the collected experience of my years on Earth. A few years ago I wrote something called "Everything I Ever Really, Really Needed to Know I Learned on the Playground." Since then I've learned a few more things, including the following:

• If you're not part of the solution, you're part of the concentrate.

• Everything retro is neo again.

• Women aren't just different from men. They're different from other women.

• Hipsters can be just as prejudiced as anybody. They just have a different set of targets.

• People whose lifestyles are different from yours are not necessarily fascists.

• People who let downtown Manhattan tell them how to think are no more "empowered" than people who let midtown Manhattan tell them how to think.

• *The New York Times* really is the Cadillac of American newspapers. It's bigger, and it's weighted down with more luxury features, but it's still built on the same Chevy drive train.

• In an average week, America generates 1,000 books (including 300 new and reprinted fiction volumes), 500

Designs For Living
(continued)

Discernment of fine yet reasonably-priced liquors and beers.

Knowledge of agriculture, food technology, and the dangers of fad diets.

Architecture and civic planning.

Home building and repair.

Interior design and Feng Shui.

Gardening; mulching and composting.

Acquaintance with U.S. and world literature, art, comics, film, theater, TV, and periodicals.

Knowledge of the world's assorted cultures, philosophies, and religions.

Music theory and history; awareness of at least one country singer other than Patsy Cline.

Awareness of the natural environment of your home and the larger world.

Awareness of the history, politics and economics of your home and the larger world.

Grammar and spelling.

Political action and organizing.

Dealing with business/government bureaucracies.

Judging people not by the color of their skin, but by the color of their lip gloss.

Inquisitive skepticism toward public, political, and commercial speech.

Holding your own amid hostile situations (i.e. workplaces, playgrounds). When to engage in verbal self-defense; when to keep your big flap shut.

Value shopping; bargaining and haggling.

Cordial relations with neighbors, relatives, and postal workers.

Politely yet firmly declining the entreaties of proselytizers and telemarketers.

Being nice to young children without letting them walk all over you.

Caring for and feeding pets (biological or virtual).

Getting along with housemates, lovers, cubicle mates, or bandmates without killing one another or even wanting to.

Social negotiation and consensus-building (deciding which film to see or which pitcher to get at happy hour).

CDs, 150 porn videos, 55 soap-opera episodes, 152 TV talk shows, about 10,000 issues of daily newspapers, 115 prime-time TV shows (in season), a couple hundred magazines, 20 direct-to-video movies, and three theatrical films. Decentralized culture isn't pretty. Live with it.

• Hedonism makes a lousy premise for a revolution, but a great premise for advertising one.

• I used to laugh at people stuck in the '60s, until I met people stuck in the '80s.

• Other things happened in the '60s besides affluent college kids getting stoned and/or laid. In fact, that's probably the least important thing that happened then.

• You're not personally guilty of anything that happened before you were born.

• If you're born into relative privilege, use it to help make a better world. There are enough real victims around, negating any need for victim wannabes.

• Feeling good about yourself isn't enough. Feeling bad about yourself isn't enough either.

• Protesting isn't enough either. You've gotta be for something.

• There's more than one way to think about everything. There's even more than two ways.

• Natural born hustlers don't have a clue about what it's like to not be a natural born hustler.

• There's nothing inherently truthful about The Word or corruptive about The Image. Images merely deceive; words lie.

• People who suck up to the real centers of money and power are not "rebels," no matter how loud their custom-painted Harleys are.

• Punk's older now than hippie was when punk started.

• There is no master race. There is also no master gender, no master sexual orientation, no master bioregion, and no master dietary regimen.

• White women, white gays, and white leftists are still white.

• Grammatical rules are made to be broken, with one exception: Never put an apostrophe in the possessive version of "its."

• If you like to view images of women's physiques, it doesn't necessarily mean you hate women. It probably means you like them.

• Everybody's ignorant about something.

• A dictatorship of the proletariat would still be a dictatorship.

• Love is more important than self-righteousness.

• Even among misfits you're misfits. *(June 12, 1997)*

Stay: Misc. hereby calls for a 12-month moratorium on Seattle artists (in all genres) from moving to New York or California. If you must get out of town, go somewhere where you can learn more about life or where you can help build another decentralist scene.

I know things look relatively bleak for indie arts round here; many photographers, actors, writers, playwrights, and artisans are again becoming tempted by the old belief that their careers would immediately take off if they only got the hell outta Seattle.

But this is one of those times when the needs of the larger society outweigh the individual career goal. And what the larger society needs, I still believe, is the building of decentralized production and distribution infrastructures for painting, photography, literature, drama, performance, music, even film and TV.

At this point, it might not matter how "rebellious" a song or an image is — if it's sold through the same old culture machine (even the "alternative" departments of the machine), it's still enforcing a top-down, producer-consumer mindset.

At one time, I thought the Seattle music scene would provide the fulcrum for breaking the machine. I underestimated the machine's self-defense. By using its hype mechanisms to redefine the Seattle threat into a single "sound" and "look" to be promoted to death then discarded, the machine was able to resume selling safe, manufactured "rebels" to demographically specified markets. Despite this, more indie bands are selling records now; but more still needs to be done, in music and other fields.

You might be thinking…

"But what can little old me do without an established market?"

You can help build such a market. This region now has the population base and the income base. It has artists. It has art buyers (anybody who reads or watches or listens to or looks at or wears anything). It has pieces of a sales infrastructure, at least in some fields (galleries, boutiques, record labels). It needs a little more of that last connecting piece, that hard-to-describe level of identity consciousness that binds a community together instead of leaving isolated individuals to absorb prepackaged identities from outside.

"Dammit Jim! I'm an artist, not a marketer."

Yes, you're an artist. A communicator of ideas. Bringing those ideas to life involves a set of skills. Getting cash out of the products of those ideas involves a different, only

Falling in love hard; falling out of love soft.

Developing a healthy self-esteem, not an unhealthy egomania.

Reinventing oneself every few years, a la Madonna or George Carlin.

Personal discipline (getting to the center of a Tootsie Pop without biting).

An area of knowledge associated with a different ethnicity or gender (for a man, Barbara Cartland novels; for an African American, butoh).

Fashion design, selection, color-coordination, accessorizing, and repair.

Sorting laundry. Programming a VCR and remote (not that hard, really!).

Personal law (wills, contracts, income tax, warranties, et al.)

Improving or repairing your credit.

Packing a carry-on suitcase.

Traversing your city via public transportation; reading a timetable.

Solving crossword and jigsaw puzzles.

Ability on a musical instrument (including the voice).

At least one of the visual arts (painting, drawing, calligraphy, photography, cinematography, videography, Photoshop).

Rudimentary computer usage.

Desiging a website with no annoying "construction signs" or bad MIDI synth-music files.

"Netiquette:" Writing e-mails to the point, but not too pointedly.

Short-term weather forecasting.

Composing effective thank-you notes, resumes and cover letters, yearbook salutations, personal ads, and responses to threatened legal actions.

Dressing and grooming for various occasions (seductions, funerals, job interviews, Halloween).

Magic tricks and parlor games.

A healthy sense of humor; jokes and anecdotes for all occasions.

A repertoire of film, music, and TV trivia.

How to tell different types of trees from a far distance. Number one — the larch....

(July 23 and Aug. 13, 1998)

partly-overlapping, set of skills. These skills can be learned; or they can be hired or bartered for.

"But I'm killing my dreams if I don't go for the Big Time."

No, you're killling them if you make them subservient to the industry's machinations.

"But everything here just plain SUCKS."

Then start working to make things suck a little less. It'll be hard, but for most of you it won't be harder than trying to survive among the thousands of identically "transgressive" art-hipster wannabes in Frisco and SoHo.

I'm not merely wishing for a bigger Northwest role in the corporate culture biz. (Certainly Nike and Microsoft are Northwest-born outfits playing the mainstream marketing game as heavily as anybody.)

No, I'm calling for nothing less than the realignment of how Americans think and dream. I want an American theater that treats the nation as the nation, not as raw-material sources for Manhattan. I want more movies made here, not just location-shot. I want more (and more work for) local costumers and video artists and curators and set builders and comedians, all of whom would build their careers by drawing audience bucks away from the tentacles of Global Entertainment. (There's a lot of big-entertainment products I like, but I still want strong competition to them.)

And, yes, I have my selfish reasons as well. I want a great urban, contempo thang to thrive right here in City Light. It's not that an indigenous regional culture isn't developing here. It is, and I don't like it. We've still got so much potential. I don't want to settle for a Seattle whose artistic ambitions don't go beyond glass bowls and latte jokes. *(July 24, 1997)*

Coming in October 1999:

LOSER

THE REAL SEATTLE MUSIC STORY

by Clark Humphrey

(updated second edition)

Read about the interconnected origins and spectacular rise of

Nirvana • Pearl Jam • Hole
Soundgarden • Alice in Chains
Gas Huffer • Seven Year Bitch • Flop
The Supersuckers • Sir Mix-A-Lot • TAD
Built to Spill • Bikini Kill • Sky Cries Mary
Screaming Trees • Mudhoney • The Posies
The Young Fresh Fellows • Beat Happening
The Presidents of the United States of America

and all the other stars of the early-'90s Seattle Music Scene.

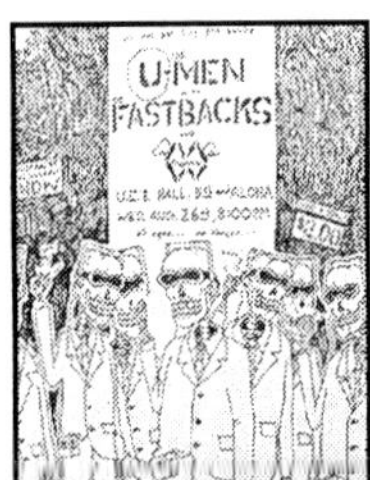

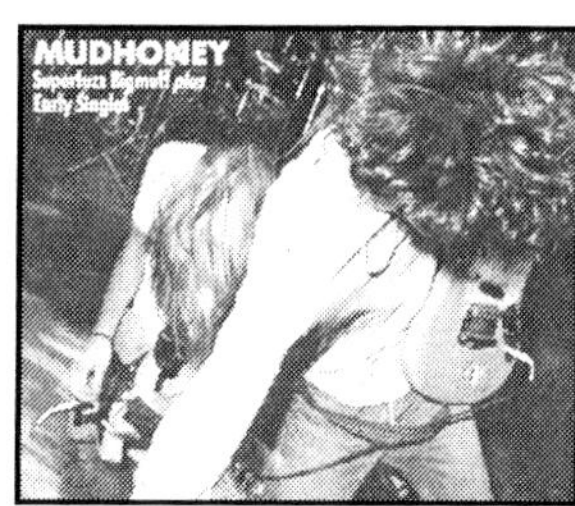

Learn how a subculture of self-proclaimed "losers" wrote their own songs, started their own bands, and became the darlings of the record industry, only to get tossed aside like an old grungy shirt once the industry was through with them.

The newly updated second edition has even more pictures and stories, an updated discography, and many "whatever became of…" listings. It's the most lavishly illustrated, achingly detailed account of a phenomenon that rocked the world.

256 Big Pages • Over 800 Illustrations

To pre-order your copy, send $18
plus $3 shipping and handling
(and $1.68 sales tax for Washington state residents)
by check or money order to:

MISC.media

2608 2nd Ave., P.M.B. #217
Seattle, WA 98121-1276 USA
or log onto **www.miscmedia.com**.

order form

Tear out or photocopy and mail to:

MISC.media
2608 2nd Ave., P.M.B. #217
Seattle, WA 98121-1276 USA

( ) Copies of **The Big Book of MISC.** at $16 ____________

( ) Copies of **Loser: The Real Seattle Music Story** at $18 ________

Total Cost of Books ____________

Shipping/Handling ($3 for one book, $2 each additional) ________

Washington state residents add 7.9% sales tax ____________

Total Amount Enclosed ____________

Name ____________

Address ____________

City ____________ State _____ ZIP Code ________

Phone # ____________ E-mail ____________

Send check or money order in U.S. funds, payable to MISC. MEDIA.
Allow 2 to 4 weeks for delivery.
(**Loser: The Real Seattle Music Story** ships in October 1999.)
Add $1 for Canadian shipping; $2 for other international shipping.
There's a 30 percent discount for orders of 10 or more total copies.
Your satisfaction is guaranteed or your money back.
We won't sell your name to any lists.
No C.O.D.s, please.
For credit card payment, please order online at **www.miscmedia.com**.